"The authors meticulously examine each justification used in America's unyielding reliance on sentences of life without the possibility of parole. Readers will come away from this book convinced that such extreme sentences are both inhumane and unnecessary on public safety grounds."

—**Ashley Nellis**, Senior Research Analyst,
The Sentencing Project

"Life Without Parole offers readers a comprehensive account of the role and impact of LWOP in the US. The book relies on various sources and methods, including the powerful voices of individuals who are serving life without the possibility of parole to illustrate the human and societal costs of this form of punishment. I recommend this book to those who study criminal justice sanctions, as well as those seeking to reduce inequality in the justice system."

—**Professor Nancy Rodriguez**, Department of Criminology,
Law and Society, University of California, Irvine

"Life Without Parole by Ross Kleinstuber, Jeremiah Coldsmith, Margaret Leigey and Sandra Joy makes a clear and compelling case that LWOP—life without parole—is a death penalty in its own right that should be abolished. This sanction, we learn from compelling interviews with affected inmates, is no more humane than capital punishment and may indeed create more suffering and injustice than the traditional death penalty. Real reform requires sentences that offer hope of release from prison, however tenuous that hope might be in individual cases."

—**Professor Rob Johnson**, Justice,
Law, & Criminology, American University

Life Without Parole

This book is an in-depth critical examination of all pertinent aspects of life without parole (LWOP). Empirically assessing key arguments that advance LWOP, including as an alternative to the death penalty, it reveals that not only is the punishment cruel while not providing any societal benefits, it is actually detrimental to society.

Over the last 30 years, LWOP has exploded in the United States. While the use of capital punishment over that same time period has declined, it must be recognized that LWOP is, in fact, a hidden death sentence. It is, however, implemented in a way that allows society to largely ignore this truth. While capital punishment has rightfully been subject to intense debate and scholarship, LWOP has mostly escaped such scrutiny. In fact, LWOP has been touted by both death penalty abolitionists and tough-on-crime conservatives, which has allowed it to flourish under the radar. Specifically, abolitionists have advanced LWOP as a palatable alternative to capital punishment, which they perceive as inhumane, error-prone, costly, and racially biased. Conservatives, meanwhile, advocate for LWOP as an effective means of fighting crime, a just form of retribution, and necessary tool for managing incorrigible offenders. This book seeks to tap into and help inform this growing debate by subjecting these key arguments to empirical scrutiny. The results of those analyses fail to produce any evidence in support of any of those various justifications and therefore suggest that LWOP should be abolished and replaced with life sentences that come with parole eligibility after a maximum of 25 years.

The book will be of great interest to students and scholars of criminology and criminal justice and will also have crossover appeal into the fields of law, political science, and sociology. It will also appeal to criminal justice professionals, lawmakers, activists, and attorneys, as well as death penalty abolitionists, opponents of mass incarceration, advocates for sentencing reform, and supporters of prisoners' rights.

Ross Kleinstuber is an Associate Professor of Justice Administration & Criminology at the University of Pittsburgh at Johnstown. His research focuses on the intersection of law and society, capital punishment, life without parole, mass incarceration, racial inequality in the justice system, and human rights abuses.

Jeremiah Coldsmith holds a PhD in sociology. His individual research focuses on the intersection of identity and stratification, and as a methodologist and statistician, he has an active research, in collaboration with Dr. Kleinstuber, that focuses on quantifying LWOP's effects on violent crime rates.

Margaret E. Leigey is a Professor and Chair of Criminology at The College of New Jersey. Her research explores the experiences of those serving life without parole, in particular aging individuals, those who were sentenced as juveniles, and women.

Sandra Joy is a Professor of Sociology at Rowan University, licensed clinical social worker, mental health clinician, and activist in the movement to abolish capital punishment and LWOP. Her research explores the grief and loss issues confronting the families of those on death row, life without parole, and coalition politics in the anti-death penalty movement.

Routledge Frontiers of Criminal Justice

Collaboration and Innovation in Criminal Justice
An Activity Theory Alternative to Offender Rehabilitation
Paulo Rocha

Genetic Surveillance and Crime Control
Social, Cultural and Political Perspectives
Helen Machado & Rafaela Granja

Impending Challenges to Penal Moderation in Germany and France
A Strained Restraint
Edited by Kirstin Drenkhahn, Fabien Jobard and Tobias Singelnstein

Policing and Boundaries in a Violent Society
A South African Case Study
Guy Lamb

Consent, Stealthing and Desire-Based Contracting in the Criminal Law
Brianna Chesser & David Nader and April Zahra

The Impact of Covid-19 on Prison Conditions and Penal Policy
Edited by Frieder Dünkel, Stefan Harrendorf and Dirk van Zyl Smit

The Virtual Reality of Imprisonment in Russia
"Preparing myself for Prison" in a Contested Human Rights Landscape
Laura Piacentini and Elena Katz

Life Without Parole
Worse than Death?
Ross Kleinstuber, Jeremiah Coldsmith, Margaret E. Leigey and Sandra Joy

Penal Responses to Serious Offending by Children
Principles, Practice and Global Perspectives
Nessa Lynch, Yannick van den Brink and Louise Forde

For more information about this series, please visit: www.routledge.com/Routledge-Frontiers-of-Criminal-Justice/book-series/RFCJ

Life Without Parole

Worse than Death?

Ross Kleinstuber, Jeremiah Coldsmith, Margaret E. Leigey, and Sandra Joy

Routledge
Taylor & Francis Group
LONDON AND NEW YORK

Cover image: © Annmarie Young Photography/Getty Images

First published 2022
by Routledge
4 Park Square, Milton Park, Abingdon, Oxon OX14 4RN

and by Routledge
605 Third Avenue, New York, NY 10158

Routledge is an imprint of the Taylor & Francis Group, an informa business

British Library Cataloguing-in-Publication Data
A catalogue record for this book is available from the British Library

Library of Congress Cataloging-in-Publication Data
A catalog record has been requested for this book

ISBN: 978-0-367-75271-2 (hbk)
ISBN: 978-0-367-75269-9 (pbk)
ISBN: 978-1-003-16178-3 (ebk)

DOI: 10.4324/9781003161783

Typeset in Bembo
by KnowledgeWorks Global Ltd.

Dedication

To those serving life without parole and all those fighting to end death by incarceration

CONTENTS

Figures

Tables

Acknowledgements

We would like to thank Ashley Nellis and the staff of The Sentencing Project for collecting and publishing the data on the number of people serving life and LWOP sentences in each state. We would not have been able to complete this project without access to those data. Furthermore, we are grateful to Dr. Nellis for graciously sharing much of her unpublished raw data on LWOP sentences with us. Without those additional data, the analyses in Chapters 4 and 5 would have been impossible.

In addition, we wish to acknowledge the individuals, some of whom cannot be identified by name because of institutional review board protections, who agreed to participate in our studies, for sharing their experiences serving sentences of death, life without parole, or both. We are grateful for the opportunity to share your stories and hope that by doing so, we are able to ease some of your suffering. We are further indebted to Gary Tyler, Mark Clements, Shryl Lamar, Kempis "Ghani" Songster, Robert "Saleem" Holbrook, and Gladys Scott, who graciously shared their phenomenal stories of redemption with us, including their experiences behind bars after being sentenced to life without parole and their lives on the outside after being given a second chance. We hope that your stories help to provide more people with a second chance.

We would also like to thank Riley Osterlind for her assistance with designing the cover image.

Lastly, we offer a heartfelt thank you to our families, who supported us throughout this project.

Introduction

Meet the New Death Penalty: Life Without Parole

The obituary of the death penalty in the United States (US) is being written. In it, the staggering decline in the American death penalty over the last quarter-century is described. In the mid-1990s, the US was issuing more than 300 death sentences per year. By 2021, that number had plummeted to 18 (Death Penalty Information Center, 2021a). Executions, meanwhile, fell from a high of 98 in 1999 down to just 11 in 2021 (Death Penalty Information Center, 2021a). Since 2007, eleven states have abolished capital punishment (Death Penalty Information Center, 2021b), and as of 2021, 36 states had either abolished the death penalty, imposed a moratorium, or had not executed anyone in over a decade (Death Penalty Information Center, 2021a). Public support for capital punishment has also fallen precipitously since the mid-1990s. According to Pew, support for capital punishment peaked at 80% in 1994 before falling to a modern era low of 49% in 2016 and then creeping back up to 60% in 2021 (Oliphant, 2016; Pew Research Center, 2021). Similarly, Gallup also reported death penalty support reaching an apex of 80% in 1994 and then declining to a modern era low of 54% in 2021 (Jones, 2021), and when given the option in the 2019 survey, a wide majority of Americans preferred life in prison over capital punishment for the first time (60% versus 36%) (Jones, 2019).

These facts have led some journalists to suggest that "the era of capital punishment is ending" (Von Drehle, 2015), but this progress is illusory. The death penalty in America is not, in fact, declining or fading out; it has insidiously changed forms and even expanded dramatically. Its proliferation has largely gone unnoticed and uncontested. The 300-a-year death sentences of the mid-1990s have been replaced by thousands of "semantically disguised sentences of death" (Villaume, 2005, p. 266) per year or what some refer to as "death by incarceration" (Johnson & McGunigall-Smith, 2008): life without parole (LWOP). LWOP is typically treated as less severe than capital punishment, which has

DOI: 10.4324/9781003161783-1

allowed it to escape the scrutiny that has accompanied the death penalty, but upon closer examination, it is not clear that the two punishments are meaningfully distinct from each other. After all, both sentences result in the extinguishment of the most basic existential features of life that make it worth living and then, ultimately, the defendant's physical death in prison (Miao, 2020). The only difference is the manner of death. Therefore, in both instances, the defendant is cast aside, permanently removed from the community, denied the experience of freedom for the rest of his or her days, and declared to be incapable of being rehabilitated and therefore "unworthy of ever re-entering society" (Leigey, 2015, p. x). This murky distinction between the death penalty and LWOP explains why Kenneth Hartman, a co-founder of the group the Other Death Penalty Project who is serving LWOP in California, described LWOP as an "execution in the form of a long, deliberate stoning that goes on for as long as I draw breath" (Gottschalk, 2012, p. 264). This has led to a sort of Pyrrhic victory for the abolitionist movement in which capital punishment is being replaced by "a law that holds twenty-five men in prison until their natural deaths in order to spare one man the death penalty" (*Harvard Law Review*, 2006, p. 1854).

Prior to the 1970s, LWOP was virtually unheard of in the US (*Harvard Law Review*, 2006; Miao, 2020). Before the Supreme Court temporarily halted the death penalty in 1972 by declaring then-existing capital sentencing statutes unconstitutional in *Furman v. Georgia* (1972), only seven states even authorized the use of LWOP, and within them, it was rarely used and typically came with the realistic possibility of commutation within a decade or two (Garrett, Seale-Carlisle, Modjadidi, & Renberg, 2021; Gottschalk, 2012; Nellis, 2013). That is, until the 1970s, a life sentence rarely meant that the sentenced individual would actually die in prison. As an oft-cited example, a 1913 law made those serving life sentences in the federal system eligible for parole after 15 years (Gottschalk, 2012; *Harvard Law Review*, 2006; Nellis, 2013). Even in some of the nation's most punitive states, parole review for life sentences occurred relatively quickly until the 1970s. For example, in Louisiana, which today has the second-highest incarceration rate in the nation (and thus the world) (Carson, 2021), a 1926 law allowed most lifers to be released after serving ten years and six months if they had good behavior and the support of the warden (Gottschalk, 2012), and in Florida, which today boasts the nation's largest LWOP population (10,438 or 18.7% of the nationwide total) (Nellis, 2021), the typical lifer admitted from 1957 to 1972 served less than ten years (Seeds, 2018).

The story of LWOP in the US began to change in the 1970s as states started passing LWOP statutes, and by the 1990s, its use was expanding exponentially—and at a far faster rate than the formal death penalty was declining (Henry, 2012; Nellis, 2013). LWOP was not just being used for capital offenses or solely for those convicted of murder. Rather, it was being used against habitual offenders and even first-time nonviolent drug felons (*Harmelin v. Michigan*, 1991; Henry, 2012). The reasons for this growth are complex and varied, differing by state. For example, in response to the Supreme Court's decision in *Furman*, Alabama,

Louisiana, and Illinois passed LWOP statutes so they could detain those convicted of certain offenses for life in the event that their new capital statutes also failed to pass the Court's muster (Garrett, Seale-Carlisle, Modjadidi, & Renberg, 2021; *Harvard Law Review*, 2006; Miao, 2020). In other places, like Florida, LWOP developed incrementally and in a piecemeal fashion over the course of decades rather than being deliberately planned (Seeds, 2018). In still other states, LWOP developed as part of the "tough on crime" political environment that was emerging in the 1970s and 1980s due to efforts by conservative politicians to win over disaffected white southerners with "law and order" rhetoric in the wake of the Civil Rights Movement (Alexander, 2012; Beckett & Sasson, 2004; Garrett, Seale-Carlisle, Modjadidi, & Renberg, 2021; Gottschalk, 2012). Due to the rising crime rates of the period, this messaging began to gain increasing salience nationwide, which helped to fuel LWOP adoption even in northern states (Garrett, 2017). For example, as part of his "get tough" approach, in 1984, President Reagan signed into law the Comprehensive Crime Control Act, which eliminated parole and thus transformed all life sentences in the federal system into LWOP sentences (*Harvard Law Review*, 2006). Many states enacted similar "truth-in-sentencing" legislation, which required individuals to serve 85% of their sentence before becoming eligible for parole, and six states eliminated parole altogether (*Harvard Law Review*, 2006; Nellis, 2013).

Conservatives were also able to capitalize on high-profile crimes committed by formerly incarcerated people to paint liberals as "soft on crime," win elections, and drum up support for ever harsher sentencing policies. One of the widest reaching examples of this occurred in Pennsylvania. Although Pennsylvania has had a LWOP statute on the books since 1941, until the 1980s, governors routinely used their clemency power to commute life sentences after around 20 years (Mauer, King, & Young, 2004). For example, from 1971 to 1978, 251 life sentences were commuted in Pennsylvania (Pennsylvania Board of Pardons, 2021). This practice changed when, in 1994, Reginald McFadden went on a crime spree in which he committed at least two rapes and two murders shortly after being released from a life sentence that he had received at the age of 16 (Berger, 1995). In Pennsylvania, the lieutenant governor also serves as the chair of the Board of Pardons, and in 1994, then-Lieutenant Governor Mark Singel was running for governor. He was ahead in the polls at the time of McFadden's spree, but his challenger, Republican Tom Ridge, used the incident to paint Singel as soft on crime and as a threat to law-abiding citizens, which torpedoed Singel's chances of winning the governor's race (Broun & Allison, 2016). Shortly after Ridge was sworn in, the state legislature convened a special session on crime that made it substantially more difficult for lifers to have their sentences commuted, and the results were dramatic (Broun & Allison, 2016). During Ridge's nearly seven years as governor (1995–2001), only 15 life sentence commutation applications were even heard by the Board of Pardons, and Ridge granted *none* of them (Pennsylvania Board of Pardons, 2021). In the quarter-century since the new law was passed, only 44 lifers in Pennsylvania have had their sentences commuted—38 of them by the current governor, Tom Wolf, whose current lieutenant governor, John Fetterman, is an advocate for ending LWOP (Melamed, 2019; Pennsylvania Board of Pardons, 2021)—and Pennsylvania now boasts the nation's second-largest LWOP population behind only Florida (Nellis, 2021).

So, by the 1990s, it was becoming clear that the Republicans' "tough on crime" messaging was extraordinarily effective at winning elections, which caused Democrats like Bill Clinton to capitulate on the issue of crime and to begin positioning themselves as equally hard on criminals (Alexander, 2012; Beckett & Sasson, 2004). This opened the floodgates for sentencing punitiveness, and what had been a wave became a tsunami. "By the mid-1990s, states increasingly rejected parole entirely for many or all types of sentences, driving LWOP adoption" (Garrett, Seale-Carlisle, Modjadidi, & Renberg, 2021, p. 289). At the same time, once the Supreme Court re-authorized capital punishment in *Gregg v. Georgia* (1976), death penalty abolitionists began to support LWOP in the hope that it might sway public opinion away from capital punishment and reduce the number of executions (*Harvard Law Review*, 2006; Miao, 2020). Therefore, "Starting in the late 1970s and picking up pace through the '80s and '90s, the life-without-parole movement became a de facto part of the death penalty abolition movement" (*Harvard Law Review*, 2006, p. 1841). This propelled many death penalty abolitionists into a marriage of convenience in which they joined forces with proponents of more punitive sentencing policies "to push life-without-parole statutes through state legislatures" (*Harvard Law Review*, 2006, pp. 1838–1839). Although it seems that these efforts probably had little actual impact on the number of executions, they were crucial in helping LWOP gain both legitimacy and bipartisan support (Gottschalk, 2012; *Harvard Law Review*, 2006; Miao, 2020). By pitching LWOP as an alternative to the death penalty, abolitionists helped to normalize the sanction, which contributed to its increasing use around the nation (Garrett, Seale-Carlisle, Modjadidi, & Renberg, 2021; Gottschalk, 2012; Miao, 2020; van Zyl Smit & Appleton, 2019).

These factors have all contributed to a nationwide explosion in the use of LWOP. What was once a virtually nonexistent penalty is now a commonplace feature of the American penal landscape. Currently, 49 states, the District of Columbia, and the federal system all authorize LWOP. As of 2020, there were 55,945 persons serving a LWOP sentence in the US (Nellis, 2021), which is more than the entire rest of the world combined (van Zyl Smit & Appleton, 2019). This figure represents a 350% increase from 1992 (Maguire, Pastore, & Flanagan, 1993), far outpacing the overall growth in the size of the US prison population. Whereas those serving LWOP represented just one out of every 68 sentenced prisoners in 1992, by the start of 2020, they accounted for more than one in every 25 sentenced prisoners! Despite being pitched as a humane alternative to the death penalty, LWOP's growth has primarily come at the expense of individuals who were never at risk of an execution or even eligible for one. From 1973 to the end of 2020—the so-called "modern era" of capital punishment—there were 8,752 different individuals sentenced to death (Death Penalty Information Center, n.d.a) and 1,529 executions in the US (Death Penalty Information Center, n.d.b; Snell, 2021). At year-end 2020, there were 2,469 individuals on death row (Snell, 2021), and the highest-ever reported death row population according to the Bureau of Justice Statistics (BJS) was 3,593 at year-end 2000 (Snell, 2001).[1] This means that the number of people *currently serving* a LWOP sentence (which is less than the total number of people who have received such a sentence in the last 50 years) is more than *six times* greater than the number of people who have been sentenced to death and nearly *37 times* greater than the number of people who have been executed in the modern era of capital punishment. It is also more than *15 times* greater than the size of death row at its peak, which means there are now more people sentenced to die in prison in the US than there were at the height of capital punishment and that tens of thousands of individuals who were never at risk of a death sentence will now die by incarceration.

There have been numerous justifications put forward in support of this growth—from both the left and the right. Viewing LWOP as more humane, more amendable in the event of an error, less expensive, and less racially biased than capital punishment, many on the left have uncritically accepted and legitimated LWOP as a palatable and thus viable alternative to the death penalty. On the other side of the political spectrum, tough-on-crime conservatives have championed LWOP as an effective tool in the fight against crime, as a just form of retribution, or as a regrettable but necessary means of warehousing incorrigible offenders. Since both sides support LWOP (albeit for different reasons), these views typically get presented uncritically and without any real consideration as to whether LWOP is truly superior in any of these facets than its alternatives. Whereas capital punishment has been the subject of intense—and often emotional—debate, LWOP has been able to grow under the radar, with little public awareness or debate. Even courts, which are supposed to be the bulwark of the rule of law, have been reluctant to scrutinize LWOP. Since the 1970s, the Supreme Court has extensively regulated the death penalty and imposed limits on eligibility for a death sentence, but with the exception of some limits on when juveniles can be sentenced to LWOP, the Court has essentially given states carte-blanche to sentence any adults they like to LWOP. While the Court has prohibited mandatory death sentences (*Woodson v. North Carolina*, 1976), it has permitted mandatory LWOP sentences except for juveniles (*Miller v. Alabama*, 2012). The Court has also declared that the death penalty can only be used against adults who have been convicted of an aggravated murder and only after a separate sentencing hearing where a jury is able to consider both aggravating and mitigating circumstances and then determines death is the appropriate penalty (*Gardner v. Florida*, 1977; *Gregg v. Georgia*, 1976; *Lockett v. Ohio*, 1978; *Ring v. Arizona*, 2002; *Roper v. Simmons*, 2005). Meanwhile, LWOP can be imposed on nonviolent offenders, first-time drug offenders, low-level habitual offenders, and even children (*Harmelin v. Michigan*, 1991; Henry, 2012; *Jones v. Mississippi*, 2021; Nellis, 2010; Nellis, 2021; Robinson, 2012; Rovner, 2021). The Court does not even require a separate sentencing hearing or any consideration of extenuating circumstances in order to impose LWOP.

A penalty this severe, which shares many features in common with capital punishment while ensnaring tens of thousands more individuals, deserves to be subjected to intense critical analysis to see if its use can be justified. Therefore, it is our objective to perform this overdue analysis of LWOP by subjecting, to the extent possible, each of the potential justifications for LWOP to empirical scrutiny. That is, is LWOP really more humane than the death penalty? Does it actually save money or better protect the wrongly convicted? Is it really less racially biased than capital punishment? On the other hand, is LWOP truly superior to lesser penalties at preventing crime, does its current application align with the basic tenets of retribution or fundamental fairness at the heart of the justice system, and are those being sentenced to LWOP truly incorrigible—or can some of them be reformed and redeemed? It is these research questions that animate this book, and in the chapters that follow, we will explore each of these questions in greater detail by using currently available quantitative and qualitative data to determine the answer to each question as informed by the best available evidence.

This book will be divided into two parts. In Part I, we will empirically assess the claims made by death penalty opponents who support LWOP as an improvement over capital punishment. In Part II, we turn our attention to the "tough on crime" arguments in favor of LWOP. As we briefly summarize next, in both sections, our findings suggest that the claims made by proponents of LWOP—both liberal and conservative—are dubious at best and that there are some profound issues with LWOP as a sentencing policy. As such, we conclude by offering some suggestions for reform, chiefly, the abolition of LWOP.

Is LWOP More Humane than Death?

The argument that LWOP, as harsh as it is, is more humane than the death penalty is often presented uncritically by abolitionists, as if this is a given. But since both sentences have the same outcome—the individual spending the rest of his or her life in prison and dying there—it is not quantifiably obvious that death is a harsher sentence than LWOP the way a 20-year sentence is demonstrably harsher than a ten-year sentence. In fact, since the time spent serving a LWOP sentence typically lasts longer than a death sentence, it may actually allow for *greater* suffering than the death penalty (Berry, 2010). It is hard to imagine abolitionists arguing that death by hanging as a means of execution is more humane than a firing squad because a hanging lasts longer. Similarly, it is not obvious that "death by incarceration" is inherently more humane than death by execution. Therefore, we utilize interviews with individuals serving LWOP, those under a death sentence, and people who have been re-sentenced to LWOP following a death sentence to get their perspective on the humaneness of each sentence and whether they agree with the claim that LWOP is more humane than death. From these interviews, it will be revealed that most people who have actually lived under these sentences do not, in fact, view LWOP as less severe or more humane than a death sentence, and many of them would rather be executed than spend the rest of their lives in prison. To supplement this analysis, we will also look at how other nations and several international bodies view LWOP to illustrate that the view from abroad comports with the idea that rather than being a humane alternative to the death penalty, LWOP is a brutal, degrading, and inhumane sanction.

Is LWOP Better for the Innocent?

One of the most compelling arguments against the use of capital punishment is the risk of executing the innocent. Humans are fallible, after all, and therefore legal mistakes are inevitable. A number of high-profile death row exonerations, not to mention several questionable executions, such as those of Troy Davis and Cameron Todd Willingham, have thrown this inherent flaw in the death sentencing regime into stark relief. As of this writing, 186 individuals sentenced to death have been formally exonerated (Death Penalty Information Center, n.d.c), and there are several others who were probably innocent and have been released from death row despite not meeting the formal requirements for exoneration. Since 1973, a shocking one out of every 49 persons sentenced to death has been exonerated—many after having served *decades on death row*.[2] Even more disconcerting, a recent statistical analysis suggested that this is less than *half* of the factually innocent individuals sent to death row, estimating that more than one out of every 25 individuals sentenced to death was wrongly convicted (Gross, O'Brien, Hu, & Kennedy, 2014).

These disturbing estimates have been the impetus for many of the recent death penalty repeals (Warden, 2012; Wozniak, 2012), but what this opposition often overlooks is that the reversal rate for death sentences is so high because "far more attention and resources are devoted to death penalty cases than to other criminal prosecutions, before and after conviction" (Gross, O'Brien, Hu, & Kennedy, 2014, p. 7230). In other words, the only reason we even know about many of these wrongful convictions and were able to reverse them is because the defendants were sentenced to death. Most other wrongly convicted defendants do not have that ability because "no one makes any effort to reconsider" their guilt and because these defendants do not enjoy the same access to the courts as those sentenced to death do (Gross, O'Brien, Hu, & Kennedy, 2014, p. 7230). Therefore, for the wrongly convicted, a death sentence may actually be a legally advantageous predicament. Those serving LWOP are, in essence, sentenced to die in prison in obscurity, with very little chance to have anyone reconsider their guilt. So, to explore whether the wrongly convicted are likely to benefit by receiving a LWOP sentence instead of a death sentence, we analyzed nationwide exoneration rates, and in that analysis, we discovered that those sentenced to death are the ones most likely to be exonerated. As such, unless the same super due process protections that are currently afforded to those on death row are extended to those serving life sentences, by making it harder to clear their names, LWOP is likely to condemn *more*, rather than fewer, innocent people to die in prison.

Does LWOP Save Money?

On the surface, this seems like a question that has been asked and answered. Numerous studies have been conducted, and they all reach the same conclusion: a death sentence costs substantially more than a life sentence (Dieter, 2014). However, this fact is misleading for two reasons. First, many of the costs associated with the death penalty are related to the fact that capital defendants and those on death row are afforded substantially greater legal protections and access to the courts than other defendants are. If we are truly concerned with the wrongly convicted, as abolitionists claim to be, then these super due process protections need to be extended to all defendants—or at least to all those facing the possibility of a life term—not eliminated. Yet, calls to abolish the death penalty for the purpose of saving money implicitly call for the elimination of these extra protections because extending them to other defendants would substantially increase the cost of the criminal justice system and thus offset the cost savings achieved by death penalty abolition. Second, the cost comparisons that have been done compare the cost of executing a single person or sentencing one person to death to the cost of sentencing a single person to life in prison. However, the use of LWOP has been expanding at a far faster rate than the death penalty has been declining, and it is now being used for crimes that were never death-eligible, including nonviolent offenses. In fact, there are now nearly *twenty-three times* more people serving LWOP in the US than there are on death row (Nellis, 2021; Snell, 2021). Therefore, we factored in this greater scope in calculating the cost of both sentences and found that the overall cost of the LWOP sentencing regime is almost certainly greater than the cost of the death sentencing regime, even without extending super due process rights to people who are not on death row. Therefore, LWOP as it is currently practiced is not an effective means of saving the state money, and if we are truly concerned about uncovering miscarriages of justice, the cost of LWOP needs to be increased.

Is LWOP Less Racially Biased than Capital Punishment?

The racial biases that pervade capital punishment in the US—from charging decisions to sentencing decisions—have been extensively documented in the empirical literature (Grosso, O'Brien, Taylor, & Woodworth, 2014), leading many scholars to conclude that the death penalty exists not as a tool for crime control but as a tool for racial control (Banner, 2002; Kleinstuber, 2016; Marquart, Ekland-Olson, & Sorensen, 1994; McFeely, 1997). These racial biases have been a crucial part of the argument against capital punishment in recent decades and have been referenced by commissions set up to inform legislative debate over death penalty abolition (Maryland Commission on Capital Punishment, 2008; New Jersey Death Penalty Study Commission, 2007). However, no evidence suggests that LWOP operates in a more racially just manner. In fact, as LWOP is really just a hidden form of the death penalty that can be imposed for more crimes and with less oversight, then it stands to reason that LWOP is likely to suffer from the same racial biases as capital punishment and therefore to serve the same function of racial control.

A brief look at the racial distribution of the LWOP population supports this view, and even suggests that LWOP may be *more* racially skewed than capital punishment. The most recent data indicate that 14% of the US is Black or African American (US Census Bureau, 2021) but that 33% of sentenced prisoners (Carson, 2021) and 41% of those on death row are Black (Snell, 2021). Yet, the Sentencing Project reports that 55% of those serving LWOP (Nellis, 2021, p. 18) and 62% of those serving LWOP for crimes that took place when they were children are Black or African American (Rovner, 2021). These disparities increase when looking just at those serving LWOP for nonviolent crimes. According to the American Civil Liberties Union (2014), nationwide, 65.4% of this group are Black and 82.2% are people of color, and in Louisiana, a whopping 91% of those serving LWOP for nonviolent crimes are Black (American Civil Liberties Union of Louisiana, 2013). These numbers alone are disturbing, and clearly indicate a disparity, but they do not prove discrimination. Therefore, we will show that the offenses eligible for LWOP target minorities. For example, LWOP is typically reserved for street crimes, but it is never utilized for white-collar crimes, even when those white-collar crimes are part of a pattern of law-breaking, lead to multiple deaths, or do more damage to society. Similarly, "three strikes laws," which are often the vehicle by which people are sentenced to LWOP, target three-time street felons, not three-time corporate criminals (Reiman & Leighton, 2017). Additionally, while there are only a few studies specifically examining whether there are racial biases in the imposition of LWOP sentences, those that do exist indicate that, like with capital punishment (and all sentences for that matter), LWOP is more likely to be used when the defendant is Black and the victim is white (Chen, 2008; Garrett, Seale-Carlisle, Modjadidi, & Renberg, 2021; Gross, Possley, & Stephens, 2017; Johnson, Spohn, & Kimchi, 2021; Mills, Dorn, & Hritz, 2016).

Moreover, although the Supreme Court has prohibited the use of the death penalty for non-homicides (*Kennedy v. Louisiana*, 2008), which is one of the primary mechanisms by which the death penalty was able to exert racial control in previous generations (Banner, 2002; Kleinstuber, 2016), LWOP can still be imposed for nonviolent offenses. Therefore, LWOP is, in many ways, fulfilling the same function that the death penalty used to. The use of LWOP for nonviolent offenses cannot be justified using any sentencing rationale, but when considering the well-documented biases in policing practices, especially for nonviolent offenses, traffic stops, stop-and-frisk practices, and "quality of life" policing where police have a lot more discretion (Alexander, 2012; Harris, 2002), this practice is essentially guaranteed to impact minorities more than whites and thus to serve as a form of racial control that helps to keep people of color "in their place." Although these laws are facially race-neutral, the uneven nature of policing practices in America and the greater likelihood of police stopping and searching minorities is essentially criminalizing blackness and brownness in our society and using the threat of LWOP as a means of controlling a "threatening" urban, minority population and monitoring where they can and cannot go.

Lastly, it is important to note that the use of LWOP against juveniles also reeks of racial bias. Nearly two-thirds of those serving LWOP for crimes they committed as children are Black, and Black children arrested for murder are almost two times as likely to be sentenced to die in prison as white children arrested for murder (Mills, Dorn, & Hritz, 2016; Rovner, 2021). This disparity increases in inter-racial homicides, reflecting the biases we see in capital punishment (Rovner, 2021). Some have even suggested that the racial disparities in juvenile LWOP are greater than they are in *any other* part of the American criminal justice system (Mills, Dorn, & Hritz, 2016). Whether or not these disparities can be attributed to different levels of involvement in crime is irrelevant because LWOP is an unjust sentence when imposed on *any juvenile*. Because of their cognitive development, adolescents have less problem-solving ability and capacity for rational thought, are more likely to engage in risk-taking behavior, and are more susceptible to peer pressure than adults, which led the Supreme Court to abolish the use of the death penalty for juveniles in 2005 (*Roper v. Simmons*, 2005). The same logic should apply to "death by incarceration." Granted, the Supreme Court has since limited the ability of states to sentence juveniles to LWOP (*Graham v. Florida*, 2010; *Miller v. Alabama*, 2012), but it has not eliminated it, and in fact, the Court recently made it easier to sentence juveniles to LWOP (*Jones v. Mississippi*, 2021). The US remains the only nation in the world that sentences children to die in prison (Garrett, 2020), a violation of the United Nations Convention on the Rights of the Child. In summary, LWOP has no public safety benefit and disproportionately affects minority youth, which indicates that the sentence serves as a form of racial—rather than crime—control. As such, it is not an improvement over capital punishment.

Does LWOP Reduce Crime?

As discussed earlier, in addition to being touted by abolitionists, LWOP has also been championed as part of a broader "tough on crime" campaign (Gottschalk, 2012). Many politicians pushed for natural life sentences as a way of fighting crime (Gottschalk, 2014; *Harvard Law Review*, 2006; Robinson, 2012; Spohn, 2014; Steiker & Steiker, 2016; Tonry, 2016; van Zyl Smit & Appleton, 2019). In essence, the logic goes that by increasing the severity of sentences, crime should go down because dangerous offenders will be incapacitated, and potential offenders will be deterred. LWOP, therefore, should produce large reductions in crime because it makes incapacitation permanent for the most dangerous offenders, and no rational person would be willing to risk the rest of their life in prison. However, the deterrence literature is nearly universal in indicating that the certainty of punishment is more important than its severity and that increasing the severity of already severe sentences does not produce any additional deterrent impact (Nagin, 2013; Travis, Western, & Redburn, 2014). Furthermore, it is a truism among criminologists that criminal offending typically peaks in late adolescence or early adulthood and then declines rapidly thereafter (Hirschi & Gottfredson, 1983; Snyder, Cooper, & Mulako-Wangota, 2017; Sweeten, Piquero, & Steinberg, 2013), which suggests that once individuals have been incarcerated beyond this crime-prone age range, additional years of imprisonment are unlikely to prevent any crimes.

Therefore, LWOP may not be as effective at reducing crime as many conservative proponents would suggest, so we subject LWOP to several statistical analyses in an effort to quantify what, if any, effect LWOP has on violent crime rates. These tests reveal that implementing a LWOP statute does not have a consistent relationship with future violent crime rates, suggesting that merely enacting a LWOP statute is insufficient to produce lower violent crime rates. Our analyses further reveal that *using* LWOP more often, relative to life *with* parole, also does not result in measurably lower violent crime rates. In other words, denying lifers eligibility for parole does not appear to produce any public safety benefit. Taken together, these results indicate that LWOP probably cannot be justified as a means of reducing crime.

Is LWOP a Just Form of Retribution?

The effectiveness (or lack thereof) of LWOP notwithstanding, many proponents of the punishment argue that LWOP is a justified form of retribution—that its goal is not to reduce crime but to provide a fair and deserved punishment for serious offenses and that it would be unfair to society and to victims to treat them any more leniently. Although the legitimacy of retribution as a punishment goal cannot be empirically measured since it rests on value judgments, the degree to which a specific sanction aligns with the core tenets of this sentencing philosophy can be assessed, and so we perform this assessment. Based on our evaluation of LWOP's current usage in the US, LWOP appears to violate the proportionality balance required for retributive or "just deserts" models of punishment and fails to serve victims. As noted earlier, LWOP is being used far more expansively and for a wider range of offenses than the death penalty ever was. In fact, LWOP is an available sentencing option for a whole range of offenses, including nonviolent crimes. Since LWOP punishes the person for the remainder of their life, its use for any non-homicide offense is disproportionately harsh. Even when being used for homicide offenses, the current use of LWOP ignores important differences in culpability and moral blameworthiness, which is a crucial consideration for a "just deserts" model of punishment (Robinson, 2012). Currently LWOP sentencing practices typically punish all parties to a crime the same regardless of their role in the crime (Robinson, 2012), and, unlike the death penalty, LWOP is often a mandatory sentence that does not allow for the consideration of relevant mitigating circumstances (Nellis, 2017). The Supreme Court barred the use of mandatory death sentences (*Woodson v. North Carolina*, 1976) and required sentencers in capital cases to consider mitigating circumstances (*Gregg v. Georgia*, 1976; *Lockett v. Ohio*, 1978) because these circumstances are relevant for determining what a just sentence is (Haney, 2014). However, it has not restricted "death by incarceration" in similar fashions. Furthermore, as noted earlier, due to their cognitive immaturity, adolescents are less culpable than adults and thus LWOP is disproportionately harsh when imposed on any child. Yet, despite recognizing that executing juvenile offenders is "cruel and unusual," the Court has not prohibited the use of juvenile LWOP. Thus, the American use of LWOP is at odds with the proportionality and justice tenets of retribution.

Furthermore, although retribution is often touted as "justice for victims," there is little evidence that victims or their survivors benefit from punitive sanctions. On the contrary, the current adversarial system that is focused on punishment typically cuts victims out of the process, and by focusing on vengeance, it can even be harmful to victims. The existing research indicates that victims are better served by being offered a chance for reconciliation and forgiveness (Dreisinger, 2016; Exline, Worthington, Hill, & McCullough, 2003; Umbreit, 2001; Witvliet et al., 2008). As such, LWOP has the potential to be detrimental to victims and their recovery. Therefore, LWOP does not benefit the offenders, society, or victims.

Can Those Sentenced to LWOP Be Redeemed?

A final rationale for LWOP is that "the truly 'incorrigible' should not be treated but simply detained for the rest of their lives with no prospect of release" (van Zyl Smit & Appleton, 2019, p. 9). The idea here is that those who are sentenced to LWOP are inherently and irredeemably bad, that they cannot be rehabilitated, and that they have no redeeming value. It follows, then, that even if LWOP does not reduce crime, there is no alternative way—short of an execution—to manage these individuals and that society is better off with their permanent removal. But is this true? Are those being sentenced to LWOP really beyond redemption? Are they unable to make a positive contribution to society? Through interviews with people who have received a LWOP sentence, we intend to show that this presumption is inaccurate. There are people who, despite having been sentenced to LWOP, are making positive contributions that tangibly benefit society. Thus, they were neither incorrigible nor irredeemable, and continuing to incarcerate them not only fails to produce any public safety benefit, it may even *harm* society.

This is not to suggest that everyone sentenced to LWOP or even life with parole is able to make a positive contribution to society, but it does show that not everyone sentenced to LWOP is irredeemable. We cannot know at the time of sentencing who will be reformed or who will be able to make a positive impact on society; therefore, LWOP does not make sense as a sentencing option. Why deprive someone the chance to be released if we do not yet know if they will continue to pose a threat or if they will change for the better? Instead, all incarcerated people should be given a credible opportunity to be released if they are able to demonstrate that they have indeed matured and been reformed, do not pose a continued threat to society, or are likely to make a positive contribution to society. This is the benefit of life with parole sentences relative to LWOP sentences. They make it possible to make real-time evaluations of whether and when people can be released rather than making this determination at the time of sentencing without knowing what the future holds, but they do not guarantee that anyone will be released. There may be some people who can never be safely released, and parole boards can ensure that they remain incarcerated without needing to imprison, and over-punish, those who have been reformed.

What Policy Changes Should Be Enacted?

After having reviewed the evidence on LWOP and its societal effects, we find no evidence that LWOP produces any of the benefits touted by its supporters. We also find evidence that it produces some clear harm—to offenders, victims, and society. Therefore, the continued use of LWOP cannot be justified and should be abolished, but in repeating a question that is commonly asked when discussing abolition of a sanction, what should replace it? To bring the US into alignment with current international norms, we propose that life sentences be reserved for adults convicted of first-degree murder and that all life sentences be eligible for parole within 25 years. Those convicted of lesser sanctions should be ineligible for a life sentence or for any term of years that exceeds their likely life expectancy and should all become eligible for parole after a *maximum* of 20 years. This reform should be retroactive so that anyone currently facing a life sentence has the opportunity to be re-sentenced within these parameters. We recognize that there may be a few people who can never be safely released, but we cannot know who those people will be at the time of sentencing. As such, it is necessary to have a body of experts who can make continuous evaluations of when or if someone is able to re-enter society.

We are aware of the current problems with the parole system for lifers. If LWOP were to be abolished, then individuals serving life with parole need to have a realistic chance of release. Otherwise, a life with parole sentence would be a hidden death by incarceration sentence in the way that LWOP is currently a hidden death sentence. As Henry (2012) has noted, "the actual granting of parole to individuals serving a life sentence is increasingly rare" (p. 69). The reason for this is that parole boards are typically politically appointed and thus have become highly politicized (Henry, 2012). Therefore, parole boards also need to be redesigned. These parole boards should be apolitical, staffed with career experts who are not appointed by politicians, who are independent of political considerations, and who enjoy civil service protections (Nellis, 2021). These parole boards should also provide lifers with a legitimate chance for release if they can demonstrate evidence of rehabilitation and a lack of continuing threat. In fact, we propose that release should be the presumptive outcome of these parole hearings and that applicants for parole should only be denied release upon a showing that their release will likely endanger public safety. We believe these changes will help push the US justice system toward achieving greater justice and allow it to save money by dramatically reducing the number of life-sentenced individuals without risking an increase in crime.

Notes

1 The BJS only reports the death row population on December 31, so it is possible that at some point throughout the year the population of death row was slightly higher than the count provided, but it would not have been substantially higher. There certainly have never been more than 4,000 people on death row at any one time in the US (Garrett, Seale-Carlisle, Modjadidi, & Renberg, 2021).

2 As of this writing, 180 out of the 8,770 death sentences imposed since 1973 (2.05%) have resulted in an exoneration (Death Penalty Information Center, n.d.c).

References

Alexander, M. (2012). *The new Jim Crow: Mass incarceration in the age of colorblindness* (Revised ed.). New York: New Press.

American Civil Liberties Union. (2014, October 27). *Written submission of the American Civil Liberties Union on racial disparity in sentencing.* Retrieved from American Civil Liberties Union: www.aclu.org/sites/default/files/assets/141027_iachr_racial_disparities_aclu_submission_0.pdf

American Civil Liberties Union of Louisiana. (2013, November). *A living death: Life without parole for nonviolent offenses.* Retrieved June 26, 2020, from American Civil Liberties Union of Louisiana: https://www.laaclu.org/sites/default/files/field_documents/2013_Report_Life_Without_Parole_Louisiana_1.pdf

Banner, S. (2002). *The death penalty: An American history.* Cambridge, MA: Harvard University Press.

Beckett, K., & Sasson, T. (2004). *The politics of injustice: Crime and punishment in America* (2nd ed.). Thousand Oaks, CA: Sage.

Berger, J. (1995, April 4). *Accused serial killer and 92 days of freedom.* Retrieved July 22, 2021, from New York Times: https://www.nytimes.com/1995/04/04/nyregion/accused-serial-killer-and-92-days-of-freedom.html

Berry, III, W. W. (2010). More different than life, less different than death: The argument for according life without parole its own category of heightened review under the Eight Amendment after *Graham v. Florida*. *Ohio State Law Journal, 71*, 1109–1147.

Broun, S., & Allison, J. (2016, March 1). *A life sentence: Victims, offenders, justice, and my mother.* Retrieved from Transom: https://transom.org/2016/a-life-sentence-victims-offenders-justice-and-my-mother/.

Carson, E. A. (2021, December). *Prisoners in 2020—Statistical tables.* Retrieved December 21, 2021, from Bureau of Justice Statistics: https://bjs.ojp.gov/content/pub/pdf/p20st.pdf

Chen, E. Y. (2008). The liberation hypothesis and racial and ethnic disparities in the application of California's three strikes law. *Journal of Ethnicity in Criminal Justice, 6*, 83–102.

Death Penalty Information Center. (2021a, December 16). *The death penalty in 2021: Year end report*. Retrieved December 20, 2021, from Death Penalty Information Center: https://reports.deathpenaltyinfo.org/year-end/YearEndReport2021.pdf

Death Penalty Information Center. (2021b). *State by state*. Retrieved March 30, 2021, from Death Penalty Information Center: https://deathpenaltyinfo.org/state-and-federal-info/state-by-state

Death Penalty Information Center. (n.d.a). *Death sentences in the United States since 1977*. Retrieved January 13, 2021, from Death Penalty Information Center: https://deathpenaltyinfo.org/facts-and-research/sentencing-data/death-sentences-in-the-united-states-from-1977-by-state-and-by-year

Death Penalty Information Center. (n.d.b). *Execution database*. Retrieved January 12, 2021, from Death Penalty Information Center: https://deathpenaltyinfo.org/executions/execution-database

Death Penalty Information Center. (n.d.c). *Innocence database*. Retrieved October 1, 2021, from Death Penalty Information Center: https://deathpenaltyinfo.org/policy-issues/innocence-database

Dieter, R. C. (2014). The issue of costs in the death penalty debate. In J. R. Acker, R. M. Bohm, & C. S. Lanier (Eds.), *America's experiment with capital punishment: Reflections on the past, present, and future of the ultimate penal sanction* (3rd ed., pp. 595–609). Durham, NC: Carolina Academic.

Dreisinger, B. (2016). *Incarceration nations: A journey toward justice in prisons around the world*. New York: Other Press.

Exline, J. J., Worthington, E. L., Hill, P., & McCullough, M. E. (2003). Forgiveness and justice: A research agenda for social and personality psychology. *Personality and Social Psychology Review*, 7, 337–348.

Furman v. Georgia, 408 U.S. 238 (US Supreme Court 1972).

Gardner v. Florida, 430 U.S. 349 (US Supreme Court 1977).

Garrett, B. L. (2017). *End of its rope: How killing the death penalty can revive criminal justice*. Cambridge, MA: Harvard University Press.

Garrett, B. L. (2020, October 19). *Life without parole for kids Is cruelty with no benefit*. Retrieved February 22, 2021, from The Atlantic: https://www.theatlantic.com/ideas/archive/2020/10/life-without-parole-kids-cruelty-no-benefit/616757/

Garrett, B. L., Seale-Carlisle, T. M., Modjadidi, K., & Renberg, K. M. (2021). Life without parole sentencing in North Carolina. *North Carolina Law Review*, 279–332.

Gottschalk, M. (2012). No way out? Life sentences and the politics of penal reform. In C. Ogletree, & A. Sarat (Eds.), *Life without parole: America's new death penalty?* (pp. 227–281). New York: NYU Press.

Gottschalk, M. (2014). *Caught: The prison state and the lockdown of American politics*. Princeton, NJ: Princeton University Press.

Graham v. Florida, 560 U.S. 48 (US Supreme Court 2010).

Gregg v. Georgia, 428 U.S. 153 (US Supreme Court 1976).

Gross, S. R., O'Brien, B., Hu, C., & Kennedy, E. H. (2014). Rate of false conviction of criminal defendants who are sentenced to death. *Proceedings of the National Academy of Sciences of the United States of America, 111*, 7230–7235.

Gross, S. R., Possley, M., & Stephens, K. (2017, March 7). *Race and wrongful convictions in the United States*. Retrieved May 7, 2021, from National Registry of Exonerations: https://www.law.umich.edu/special/exoneration/Documents/Race_and_Wrongful_Convictions.pdf

Grosso, C. M., O'Brien, B., Taylor, A., & Woodworth, G. (2014). Race discrimination and the death penalty: An empirical and legal overview. In J. R. Acker, & C. S. Lanier, *America's experiment with capital punishment: Reflections on the past, present, and future of the ultimate penal sanction* (3rd ed., pp. 525–576). Durham, NC: Carolina Academic Press.

Haney, C. (2014). Mitigation and the study of lives: On the roots of violent criminality and the nature of capital justice. In J. R. Acker, R. M. Bohm, & C. S. Lanier (Eds.), *America's experiment with capital punishment: Reflection on the past, present, and future of the ultimate penal sanction* (3rd ed., pp. 497–524). Durham, NC: Carolina Academic Press.

Harmelin v. Michigan, 501 U.S. 957 (US Supreme Court 1991).

Harris, D. A. (2002). *Profiles in injustice: Why racial profiling cannot work*. New York: New Press.

Harvard Law Review. (2006). A matter of life and death: The effect of life-without-parole statutes on capital punishment. *Harvard Law Review, 119*, 1838–1854.

Henry, J. S. (2012). Death-in-prison sentences: Overutilized and underscrutinized. In C. J. Ogletree, & A. Sarat (Eds.), *Life without parole: America's new death penalty?* (pp. 66–95). New York: NYU Press.

Hirschi, T., & Gottfredson, M. (1983). Age and the explanation of crime. *American Journal of Sociology, 89*, 552–584.

Johnson, B. D., Spohn, C., & Kimchi, A. (2021). Life lessons: Examining sources of racial and ethnic disparity in federal life without parole sentences. *Criminology, 59*, 704–737.

Johnson, R., & McGunigall-Smith, S. (2008). Life without parole, America's other death penalty: Notes on life under sentence of death by incarceration. *The Prison Journal, 88*, 328–346.

Jones v. Mississippi, 593 U.S. (US Supreme Court 2021).

Jones, J. M. (2019, November 25). *Americans now support life in prison over death penalty*. Retrieved June 30, 2020, from Gallup: https://news.gallup.com/poll/268514/americans-support-life-prison-death-penalty.aspx

Jones, J. M. (2021, November 18). *Death penalty support holding at five-decade low*. Retrieved December 20, 2021, from Gallup: https://news.gallup.com/poll/357440/death-penalty-support-holding-five-decade-low.aspx

Kennedy v. Louisiana, 554 U.S. 407 (US Supreme Court 2008).

Kleinstuber, R. (2016). Discrimination and the death penalty. In I. Šimonović (Ed.), *Death penalty and the victims* (pp. 111–127). New York: United Nations Office of the High Commissioner for Human Rights.

Leigey, M. E. (2015). *The forgotten men: Serving a life without parole sentence*. New Brunswick, NJ: Rutgers University Press.

Lockett v. Ohio, 438 U.S. 586 (US Supreme Court 1978).

Maguire, K., Pastore, A. L., & Flanagan, T. J. (Eds.). (1993). *Bureau of Justice Statistics sourcebook of criminal justice statistics – 1992*. Washington, DC: US Government Printing Office.

Marquart, J. W., Ekland-Olson, S., & Sorensen, J. R. (1994). *The rope, the chair, and the needle: Capital punishment in Texas, 1923–1990*. Austin, TX: University of Texas Press.

Maryland Commission on Capital Punishment. (2008, December 12). *Maryland Commission on Capital Punishment: Final report to the General Assembly*. Retrieved January 13, 2021, from Maryland State Archives: https://msa.maryland.gov/megafile/msa/speccol/sc5300/sc5339/000113/012000/012331/unrestricted/20100208e.pdf

Mauer, M., King, R. S., & Young, M. C. (2004, May 1). *The meaning of "life": Long prison sentences in context*. Retrieved from Sentencing Project: https://www.sentencingproject.org/publications/the-meaning-of-life-long-prison-sentences-in-context/

McFeely, W. S. (1997, November). *A legacy of slavery and lynching: The death penalty as a tool of social control*. Retrieved from The Champion: http://www.nacdl.org/CHAMPION/ARTICLES/97nov03.htm

Melamed, S. (2019, October 16). *Convincing Pennsylvania prison lifers to apply for clemency is Lt. Gov. John Fetterman's toughest campaign yet*. Retrieved June 1, 2021, from Philadelphia

Inquirer: https://www.inquirer.com/news/pennsylvania-lieutenant-governor-john-fetterman-commutation-board-pardons-life-without-parole-prison-20191016.html
Miao, M. (2020). Replacing death with life? The rise of LWOP in the context of abolitionist campaigns in the United States. *Northwestern Journal of Law & Public Policy, 15*, 173–223.
Miller v. Alabama, 567 U.S. 460 (US Supreme Court 2012).
Mills, J. R., Dorn, A. M., & Hritz, A. C. (2016). Juvenile life without parole in law and practice: Chronicling the rapid change underway. *American University Law Review, 65*, 535–605.
Nagin, D. S. (2013). Deterrence in the twenty-first century. *Crime & Justice, 42*, 199–263.
Nellis, A. (2010). Throwing away the key: The expansion of life without parole sentences in the United States. *Federal Sentencing Reporter, 23*, 27–32.
Nellis, A. (2013). *Life goes on: The historic rise in life sentences in America*. Washington, DC: The Sentencing Project.
Nellis, A. (2017). *Still life: America's increasing use of life and long-term sentences*. Washington, DC: The Sentencing Project.
Nellis, A. (2021, February 17). *No end in sight: America's enduring reliance on life imprisonment*. Retrieved May 6, 2021, from Sentencing Project: https://www.sentencingproject.org/publications/no-end-in-sight-americas-enduring-reliance-on-life-imprisonment/
New Jersey Death Penalty Study Commission. (2007, January). *New Jersey Death Penalty Study Commission Report*. Retrieved January 13, 2021, from New Jersey Legislature: https://www.njleg.state.nj.us/committees/dpsc_final.pdf
Oliphant, J. B. (2016, September 29). *Support for death penalty lowest in more than four decades*. Retrieved June 3, 2021, from Pew Research Center: https://www.pewresearch.org/fact-tank/2016/09/29/support-for-death-penalty-lowest-in-more-than-four-decades/
Pennsylvania Board of Pardons. (2021, August 2). *Commutation of life sentences (1971–present)*. Retrieved September 17, 2021, from Pennsylvania Board of Pardons: https://www.bop.pa.gov/Statistics/Pages/Commutation-of-Life-Sentences.aspx
Pew Research Center. (2021, June 2). *Most Americans favor the death penalty despite concerns about its administration*. Retrieved June 3, 2021, from Pew Research Center: https://www.pewresearch.org/politics/2021/06/02/most-americans-favor-the-death-penalty-despite-concerns-about-its-administration/
Reiman, J., & Leighton, P. (2017). *The rich get richer and the poor get prison: Ideology, class, and criminal justice* (11th ed.). New York: Routledge.
Ring v. Arizona, 536 U.S. 584 (US Supreme Court 2002).
Robinson, P. H. (2012). Life without parole under modern theories of punishment. In C. J. Ogletree Jr., & A. Sarat (Eds.), *Life without parole: America's new death penalty?* (pp. 138–166). New York: NYU Press.
Roper v. Simmons, 543 U.S. 551 (US Supreme Court 2005).
Rovner, J. (2021, May 24). *Juvenile life without parole: An overview*. Retrieved September 3, 2021, from Sentencing Project: https://www.sentencingproject.org/publications/juvenile-life-without-parole/
Seeds, C. (2018). Disaggregating LWOP: Life without parole, capital punishment, and mass incarceration in Florida, 1972–1995. *Law & Society Review, 52*, 172–205.
Snell, T. L. (2001, December). *Capital punishment 2000*. Retrieved January 2, 2021, from Bureau of Justice Statistics: https://www.bjs.gov/content/pub/pdf/cp00.pdf
Snell, T. L. (2021, December). *Capital punishment, 2020–statistical tables*. Retrieved December 21, 2021, from Bureau of Justice Statistics: https:// bjs.ojp.gov/content/pub/pdf/cp20st.pdf
Snyder, H. N., Cooper, A. D., & Mulako-Wangota, J. (2017, August). *Arrest rates by age for violent crime index offenses*. Retrieved May 17, 2021, from Bureau of Justice Statistics: https://www.bjs.gov/index.cfm?ty=datool&surl=/arrests/index.cfm#

Spohn, C. (2014). Twentieth-century sentencing reform movement: Looking backward, moving forward. *Criminology & Public Policy, 13*, 535–545.

Steiker, C. S., & Steiker, J. M. (2016). *Courting death: The Supreme Court and capital punishment.* Cambridge, MA: Harvard University Press.

Sweeten, G., Piquero, A. R., & Steinberg, L. (2013). Age and the explanation of crime, revisited. *Journal of Youth and Adolescence, 42*, 921–938.

Tonry, M. (2016). *Sentencing fragments: Penal reform in America, 1975–2025.* New York: Oxford University Press.

Travis, J., Western, B., & Redburn, S. (2014). *The growth of incarceration in the United States: Exploring causes and consequences.* Washington, DC: National Academies Press.

Umbreit, M. S. (2001). *The handbook of victim offender mediation: An essential guide to practice and research.* San Francisco, CA: Jossey-Bass.

US Census Bureau. (2021, August 12). *Race and ethnicity in the United States: 2010 census and 2020 census.* Retrieved August 18, 2021, from US Census Bureau: https://www.census.gov/library/visualizations/interactive/race-and-ethnicity-in-the-united-state-2010-and-2020-census.html

van Zyl Smit, D., & Appleton, C. (2019). *Life imprisonment: A global human rights analysis.* Cambridge, MA: Harvard University Press.

Villaume, A. C. (2005). "Life without parole" and "virtual life sentences": Death sentences by any other name. *Contemporary Justice Review, 8*, 265–277.

Von Drehle, D. (2015, June 8). *The death of the death penalty: Why the era of capital punishment is ending.* Retrieved June 2, 2021, from Time: https://time.com/deathpenalty/

Warden, R. (2012). How and why Illinois abolished the death penalty. *Law and Inequality, 30*, 245–286.

Witvliet, C.V., Worthington, E. L., Root, L. M., Sato, A. F., Ludwig, T. E., & Exline, J. J. (2008). Retributive justice, restorative justice, and forgiveness: An experimental psychophysiology analysis. *Journal of Experimental Social Psychology, 44*, 10–25.

Woodson v. North Carolina, 428 US 280 (US Supreme Court 1976).

Wozniak, K. H. (2012). Legislative abolition of the death penalty: A qualitative analysis. *Studies in Law, Politics, and Society, 57*, 31–70.

Part I

Examining the Abolitionist Case for LWOP

1

Is LWOP Inhumane? The View from Death Row

Once a capital defendant is found guilty, the case moves to the sentencing phase. In most states, the two potential outcomes of this sentencing hearing are either a death sentence or the sentence of life without the possibility of parole (LWOP). Considering the two options, it comes as no surprise that the sentence containing the word "life" is generally preferred by many of those affiliated with the defendant. The defense team implores the jury to choose LWOP over the death penalty for their client, and family members of the defendant often take the stand to beg for the life of their loved one to be spared. When the judge condemns the convicted defendant to death, then most people—including most death penalty abolitionists—assume that the worst possible outcome for the defendant has occurred. Yet, what do those who have been condemned think about their new fate? Are they just as devastated to receive a death sentence, or do they consider this outcome preferable to a LWOP sentence? To answer this question, in this chapter, we will consider the words of individuals who have actually experienced this outcome, including those who "volunteered" to be executed, those living on death row, and those with the unique experience of having initially been sentenced to death before having their sentences altered to LWOP. The answers provided by these individuals challenge the commonsense notion that LWOP is a better fate than death. Instead, their stories point to the counterintuitive and surprising possibility that LWOP may be a fate worse than death.

The Phenomenon of Death Row "Volunteers"

One phenomenon that seriously challenges the idea that LWOP is preferable to a death sentence is the existence of so-called death penalty "volunteers." These are individuals who have dropped their appeals in an effort to hasten their own executions (Blume, 2005). According to data collected by the Death Penalty

DOI: 10.4324/9781003161783-3

Information Center (DPIC), between 1976 and 2019, there were at least 149 of these so-called volunteers (Death Penalty Information Center, 2019), or about 10% of all executions over this time period. But why would anyone willingly forfeit their attempt to overturn their death sentence and, in essence, reduce the amount of time until their own death? While previous research has found that the harsh and inhumane conditions of death row itself often produce severe depression, anxiety, and suicidality—a condition referred to as "death row syndrome"—which contributes to the decision of some to "volunteer" for an execution (Smith, 2008), the data gathered by the DPIC indicate that for a significant number of "volunteers," their decision was driven by a desire to avoid the dreaded alternative of a long, agonizing life sentence without the possibility of parole, which is all that many death row inhabitants ever expect to "win" from their death penalty appeals (Death Penalty Information Center, 2019).

The DPIC's data include all details that could be found from media sources about the reasons why "volunteers" made the decision to turn down their appeals and volunteer for their own execution, so it is possible to hear from these individuals in their own words. While most "volunteers" did not provide a reason for their decision, among those who did, nearly half (46%) indicated that their decisions were driven by a desire to avoid the only alternative that they were able to see to their death sentence: being made to live out the rest of their natural life in prison. For instance, in 2006, Alabama death row inmate Mario Centobie opposed his attorney's attempts to block his execution, saying that he was "sane, but preferred death over life in prison" (Death Penalty Information Center, 2019). In 2004, Nevada volunteer Terry Dennis was more specific with his opposition, having said at a hearing that he refused to appeal his death sentence because "Death is preferable to another 15–20 years in prison" (Death Penalty Information Center, 2019). After sitting on Florida's death row for eight years, Newton Slawson similarly ended his appeals process, telling a judge "there simply comes a time when death is a release, not a punishment" (Death Penalty Information Center, 2019). In the most blatant statement listed among the volunteers noted on the DPIC website about the humanity of the death penalty versus that of LWOP, Indiana death row inmate Kevin Conner told Governor Mitch Daniels that "killing a person is far more honest and humane than imposed repression under the guise of justice in the penal system" (Death Penalty Information Center, 2019).

Numerous other volunteers are quoted on the DPIC website, having made similar statements of their motivation for refusing to pursue their appeals. Over and over again, statements of volunteers read that they simply did not want to spend the rest of their lives in prison. Several of them added that they were "tired of prison life," thus had come to see their execution as offering them a release from the horrors of death row, as well as a way to prevent them from experiencing the horror that they were able to imagine awaited them if they were to "win" a life sentence behind bars. Still others decided to speed up the process even further by taking their own lives. The suicide rate on death row is typically many times greater than the suicide rate in free society—even though the suicide rate in state prisons is almost always *lower* than the suicide rate in free society (Tartaro & Lester, 2016). While we cannot know for certain the reason these individuals chose to take their own lives, it is a reasonable assumption that for many of them, death was preferable to living in prison for the rest of their lives.

The Perspective of the Non-Volunteers

Of course, since most of those sentenced to death do not volunteer to be executed, the perspective of "volunteers" may not be representative of everyone sentenced to death. Otherwise, we might expect even more volunteers. Therefore, to get a fuller understanding of how those facing a death sentence perceive their own fates, as part of an earlier study, one of the authors interviewed 14 of the 16 men (88%) who were on Delaware's death row at the time (the other two men declined to participate) (Joy, 2014). All of these men revealed that they were fighting their death sentence in hopes of being released, either because they maintained their innocence and hoped to be exonerated or because they were hopeful that they may be commuted to a lesser sentence that would eventually allow them to be released from prison. When asked about their stance on LWOP as an alternative to the death penalty, *all 14* of these men indicated that they do *not* view LWOP as an acceptable alternative. These men stated that they are fighting their cases in the courts in hopes of being released back into society, and nearly all of them indicated that if they knew that their legal battles would end with a LWOP sentence, they would *not* continue their fight. In such a case, they would resign themselves to their death sentence and many of them stated that they would even expedite the process by turning down their appeals and volunteering for their own execution. As one Delaware death row inhabitant shared at that time, approximately one decade ago, "I would not fight for a life sentence in this prison EVER! And if I knew that LWOP was my only option, no I would never fight." To highlight this point, another condemned man stated, "I would consider suicide if my sentence was reduced to LWOP. I don't wish to spend the rest of my days on earth in this place." Another man who sat on Delaware's death row at the same time echoed this sentiment, stating, "I would rather die than spend the rest of my life in prison because LWOP *is* a death sentence. It's just a long and slow death that will eat at your soul and your mind until you die. Think of it like a Band-Aid. You would much rather pull it off quickly, with one pull. Sure it hurts, but not as long as it will if you try to pull it off slowly." This man further indicated that he would go as a volunteer to avoid LWOP, stating "I would stop all my appeals that were still in court to make sure that I didn't end up with a LWOP sentence."

Shortly after gathering data from the 14 men on Delaware's death row who agreed to participate in the study, another individual on Delaware's death row, Shannon Johnson, "won" his battle with the courts to be executed. Ever since he was convicted of capital murder in 2008, he told every judge, jury, and lawyer that he saw that he wanted to be executed. Just four years later, Mr. Johnson finally won his fight to reject his appeals and became the fifth volunteer in Delaware to be executed during the contemporary death penalty era (out of a total of 16 executions in Delaware that had occurred since the state resumed executions two decades earlier in 1992). Johnson's last words before he was executed were "Death before dishonor." While he was not explicit with his meaning of these words, it can be argued that he considered life in prison as dishonoring him and thus felt compelled to choose death instead.

This perspective is not unique to Delaware. A 1991 study in Tennessee revealed that *half* of the state's death row inhabitants who were surveyed preferred death to LWOP (Wright, 1991). Two decades later, the Campaign to End the Death Penalty surveyed California's death row about their views on Proposition 34, a 2012 voter referendum that attempted to repeal capital punishment in the state and replace it with LWOP. Of the 50 who responded to the survey, 47 (94%) opposed the repeal effort (Egelko, 2014). In an op-ed for the *Socialist Worker* in 2012, Darrell Lomax, a California death row inhabitant who maintains his innocence, explained his rationale for opposing the repeal, writing that "it is wrong to advocate for a sentence of life without parole (LWOP)—which is a death sentence simply being called by another name." He went on to refer to the state's proposed death penalty repeal referendum as "a slow death for all those currently incarcerated on California's death row—still death just by a different name" (Lomax, 2012).

The Experience of Being Resentenced from Death to LWOP

Skeptics could easily question the resolve of individuals on death row who adamantly state they would rather choose death over LWOP when LWOP is merely a hypothetical possibility. Would they so easily prefer the death penalty over a sentence of LWOP if the latter became a reality? Unbeknownst to the men who sat on Delaware's death row a decade ago, they would soon be able to answer this question, as LWOP did become a reality for them in 2016 when the Delaware Supreme Court deemed the state's capital sentencing statute unconstitutional (*Rauf v. Delaware*, 2016), thereby resentencing the 13 men who remained on death row at that time to LWOP. Nine of these 13 men who were resentenced to LWOP were members of Joy's (2014) original sample of 14 death row inmates who had been interviewed a decade ago.[1] In 2021, eight of those nine men agreed to be re-interviewed for the present study, and another two men who had been added to death row shortly after Joy's (2014) earlier study also agreed to be interviewed. This new sample of ten men for the present study all share the unique experience of having sat on death row before suddenly finding themselves resentenced to LWOP.

At the time of their interviews, five years had passed since the Delaware Supreme Court had ruled that the death penalty was unconstitutional, and the ten men in the new sample had served anywhere from seven to 20 years on death row before being resentenced to LWOP. The majority of them (eight) had served at least 15 years on death row. The two more recent additions to death row had served seven and ten years on death row before being commuted to LWOP. For the present study, each of these ten men was asked to compare their experiences on death row with their experiences over the last five years as lifers without parole. To allow these men, many of whom still have appeals pending with the courts, to feel safe enough to express themselves, their identities will be protected through the use of pseudonyms. The differences these men noted between death row and LWOP included legal representation and access to the courts, daily life challenges, getting to see what awaits them as they grow old in prison, healthcare concerns, and changes in their support systems. While not all of the changes these men experienced as they moved from death row to the general population were negative, the common thread throughout each of the interviews with these men is the *overall* view that LWOP is worse than death.

Legal Representation and Court Access

Moving from death row to the general population of the prison as a lifer immediately changes one's legal possibilities. Those who are sentenced to death row are provided with a public defender appointed by the state, as well as a series of automatic appeals that can span many years before they are exhausted. Capital cases are "reviewed with a high degree of scrutiny because of the irrevocable nature of executions" (Nellis, 2013, p. 448). LWOP cases, on the other hand, are not guaranteed appeals and "the mandatory nature of LWOP sentences allows important features of a case or defendant to be overlooked" (Nellis, 2013, p. 448). Clearly, the level of protection offered to those facing death sentences and risking state execution is not provided to those facing LWOP.

When the men in this sample moved from death row to the general prison population to begin serving their LWOP sentence, they were initially unsure as to whether they would be entitled to keep the remainder of the automatic state-funded appeals that they were afforded when they were given a death sentence. Fortunately, most of them found that they were able to take their unused appeals and the required legal representation with them from death row to pursue appellate review. Many of them have been fortunate enough to receive *pro bono* services from attorneys associated with the Defenders Association of Philadelphia. However, if it were not for their initial death sentences, these men who are currently serving LWOP in Delaware would not necessarily have these legal avenues available to them. Those defendants who are initially sentenced to LWOP generally have fewer opportunities to pursue legal action in the courts if they aim to appeal their LWOP sentence. Some of the men who were interviewed are able to relate at least to some extent to the legal challenges confronting those sentenced to LWOP. As Gary shared, "I've been waiting thirty-two months on a decision. The only difference is time. On death row, the decisions come faster. On LWOP, they know you aren't going anywhere so there is no hurry on decisions." One of the other men, Kenneth, shared that he was not as lucky as most of the other former death row inmates, as his attorney sent him a letter after he was resentenced to LWOP, saying that he would no longer be able to represent him. This has been extremely frustrating for Kenneth because he has always maintained his innocence, yet is finding himself struggling to find legal representation:

> It is discouraging, to say the least, because I don't have the money nor does my family have the money to go out and hire an attorney to represent me in the next stage of my appeals process. I haven't used all of my appeals so I have filed a motion to get representation so I can get help. Sitting here as an innocent man knowing that you did not do what they convicted you of yet you don't have anyone to help fight for you? It's hard!

Clearly, a significant challenge that comes with living under a LWOP sentence is the difficulty that these lifers have seeking and securing legal assistance. The cost of legal representation for those with the sentence of LWOP typically falls on the defendants, leaving them far less fortunate than those sentenced to death, for whom this financial burden falls on the state. Adding the factor of innocence to this financial burden that LWOPers must bear, as described in the earlier quote by Kenneth, further complicates this process. These complications are not readily recognized by most people and may even seem to be counterintuitive. The results of a 2010 national public opinion poll reveal that the vast majority of the public believes that the excessive amount of time spent behind bars that accompanies a sentence of LWOP affords those with new evidence of their innocence ample opportunity to pursue the legal action required to allow their cases to be reopened (Death Penalty Information Center, 2010). As we will discuss in greater detail in Chapter 4, however, this is an erroneous belief since the opportunities available for the incarcerated to pursue post-conviction appeals have declined drastically in recent decades (Gill, 2010). Time limits that are mandated for such post-conviction appeals can range from periods as short as 21 days to 3 years in most states (Nellis, 2013). Even if an innocent person serving LWOP manages to raise the necessary legal funds or finds a *pro-bono* attorney willing to represent them, these time limits often go unmet due to the frequent view of supporters, attorneys, and judges that there is less urgency with LWOP cases in comparison to those under a death sentence. This point is upheld by Gary, who stated in the earlier quote that he believes that he has been waiting for a court decision for nearly three years because the court knows that he "isn't going anywhere."

Daily Life Challenges

It is quite obvious that the legal challenges confronting those serving LWOP are an ongoing reality ever looming in the minds of those who either already have appeals pending with the courts or have hopes to bring their cases back into the courts. In the meantime, the day-to-day struggles of prison life are competing for their immediate attention. This is the one area where, at first glance, it appears that moving from death row to a LWOP sentence benefitted these men, but the interviews also reveal that their moves to general population were not universally beneficial. When Delaware ruled the death penalty unconstitutional in 2016 and began moving the 13 men who remained on death row out of the secure housing unit (SHU) to live among prisoners within the general population, these men were not necessarily surprised by the living conditions they found. Before they were sentenced to death row, they had spent time in general population at least during their pre-trial period, if not also during periods of incarceration for prior convictions earlier in their lives. However, the differences they noted between the two living arrangements were profound.

The first difference they were immediately reminded of between death row and the general population is the degree of structure, consistency, and routine they encountered in their daily lives. While they were "on the row," the men were in single cells, living in conditions typically found in solitary confinement, with only an hour out of their cells every other day for showers or recreation time in a small pen, limited contact with loved ones, minimal interaction with each other, and daily contact with the same set of correctional officers day in and day out. Once death row was shut down and they were released from the SHU and out among the general population, they found much less structure and were permitted significantly more movement about the prison. In order to make any movement in SHU, they were handcuffed and shackled, but in the general population they are able to walk around the building unrestrained for the most part. Some of them have managed to be assigned to the typically coveted single cell, though most of them are doubled up with cellmates. They can be out of their cells during most of the day, with vastly more recreation time and even working jobs in various areas throughout the prison, which includes places such as the kitchen, out cutting the grass around the prison grounds, engaging in trades such as carpentry or upholstery, or in the barbershop.

Of all the changes these men encountered in the structure of their new daily lives, the most exciting ones by far provided increased opportunities to interact with their loved ones. On death row, they were only permitted two, ten-minute phone calls per week with their loved ones. Since being commuted to LWOP, they have been able to make daily phone calls, even several calls a day if they wish. The quality of their visits with family significantly changed as well. When these men were on death row, they had to be handcuffed and shackled while visiting with their loved ones. The visits were held behind glass, prohibiting any contact between the men on death row and their families. After they were moved to the general population within the prison, these men were permitted contact during their visits. Some of the men shared that they had not realized just how much their visits from behind the glass over so many years on death row had impacted upon the quality of their relationship with their loved ones until they were suddenly able to have contact visits with them. Anthony described the impact of the heavy weight of the stigma on his visits with family during his death row years with the following words:

> I never got used to being shackled and handcuffed. It *just burned* physically and mentally. Actually, it was *more mental.* They handcuffed and shackled you to diminish you and you know this, but it's still kind of hard to fight against it. And when the family comes in, it's that *feeling of shame* for them to see you shackled there. You can see through the glass barrier, but it's distorting. You *just don't feel normal.*

Anthony continues with a description of the much more desirable visitation arrangements afforded to him and the other LWOPers now that they are housed in general population. As he spoke about the greatly improved conditions of contact visits, his despondent tone lifted and he smiled for the first time since the interview began.

> Here you can actually have contact visits and you can *actually hug* your family and have them actually *touch you* and have that connection. Here your mom can see that you're eating and she'll say let me touch your hands and look at your fingernails so that I can see everything is okay and that you're well. You can actually move your hands and move your body a little bit. The security is better and the scrutiny is less, so that gives you more *breathing room* as well, both physically and emotionally.

Many of the men shared that soon after their transfer to general population, they were thrilled to receive another privilege that would have never been available to them during their time on death row. Even better than the opportunity for a contact visit is the annual "honor visit" that the Delaware DOC instituted several years ago. For two summers in a row, men in general population who had not received any infractions during the year were permitted one two-hour-long visit on the prison grounds at a picnic table alongside five of their loved ones. Most importantly, family members who attend these honor visits are permitted to bring outside food to share with their incarcerated loved one. For the men in this study who were fortunate enough to have an honor visit, it became the first time that they were able to eat a home-cooked meal (or food from the restaurant of their choice if they prefer) with their family in nearly two decades.

Thus, at first glance, it appears that the men interviewed for this study found the daily life on death row to be worse than the living conditions they now experience in the general population. Upon closer examination, however, there are other aspects to daily life in general population that the men consider *worse* than the conditions they endured when they were on death row. When stacked up against these additional conditions, the positive aspects of life in general population lose much of their overall appeal. The lack of structure and consistency, as well as the frequent number of people, both guards and incarcerated people, encountered by the men serving LWOP in general population can be stressful in ways that outsiders may not expect. For example, when comparing the daily existence of death row to his current existence serving LWOP, Anthony stated:

> The difference is you're less isolated out on the compound. On the row you're isolated to a couple of tiers and there's only a certain number of personalities that you have to deal with on an everyday basis. With LWOP you have a wider peer group, so you have more people to deal with, but that has its nightmares. I mean, it's obviously less stressful because you don't have a sword hanging over your head, but you still in prison and you still have COs telling you asinine things that you have to deal with. Like a few days ago, we went through an x-ray machine and what was the purpose of that x-ray machine? I mean, why send us through an x-ray machine? But that's par for the course here. So, you deal with a lot of everyday frustrations and a lot of those you didn't have when you were on the row.

Samuel goes even further with his views of the frustrations that come with living in general population, making it perfectly clear that, in spite of all the extra privileges that come with the sentence of LWOP, he easily prefers the environment that he dealt with on death row.

> There is *no comparison* from death to LWOP. I take death over this bullshit *any day* of the week. And I work, I can go to school (and have) take up groups (and have), yet I would *trade all that* to be back on death row. The officers around here can be trying in so many ways. This prison has *no structure whatsoever* for no one, not for the guards, the administration, or the inmates! It's sad. I have to live in a *world of chaos* and for what? I feel my mental state has taken a big jolt just putting up with the bullshit in this place on the regular. On death row, I had a structure that was in place every day no matter what. I did not live in chaos like I do now. I don't know how to explain it.

Derrick is another former death row inmate who spoke about the differences he has found between death row and life "on the compound," while serving a sentence of LWOP. For him, a major difference rests on the degree of community that he has found between the two environments. Anthony would certainly agree with Derrick's view of the community found on death row, having closed his remarks about the closeness he felt with the men there with the comment, "It's a club that nobody wants to be in, but it's a club nonetheless." Derrick adds to his comparison of death row and general population with the view that he much prefers the way that the men on death row related to one another than the way he has found that his fellow prisoners relate to each other in the general population.

> This is going to sound crazy, but it was better on death row. When we were on death row we were like a dysfunctional family, but family. And nobody on death row ever went hungry. When I came off death row somebody was trying to sell me some coffee and I said, "What?!" Because we didn't do that on the row because if someone needed coffee, we gave it to them. Out here on the compound the way that they think is completely different. Even the way the COs treated you on the row was different. It was like they were saying, they got the penalty, so let's just leave them alone. Out here? They try to do every little thing to keep you back. Not all of them, just certain ones. Like we have one that works here five times a week and he always wants to start our rec late and wants to end our rec early and we will say we still have 15 minutes and then he will say, "Either cuff up or I will call a code!"

Gary echoes Derrick's sentiments and goes on to add further insight into why those on the row may be more predisposed to nurture a community among themselves than the incarcerated men in general population. Death row contained a smaller number of people and they were all facing the same horrific sentence. General population, on the other hand, is more densely populated and the men there are much more transient, as most of them will be leaving the prison (and sadly all too often returning) after much shorter-term sentences than those serving LWOP, which adds a degree of mental anguish to those serving LWOP. In 1958, Gresham Sykes described five "pains of imprisonment" that "captives," as he called them, must endure. One of those pains is the deprivation of liberty (Sykes, 1958). While all those who are incarcerated experience this pain, as Gary explains, in general population he experiences this deprivation much more acutely than he did on death row:

> The difference is that Delaware made a Death Row unit. We were all housed in single cells on the same tier. We were out of our cells three hours a week, including showers. All of our visits were through plexiglass. It was an easier existence. Every day was the same. I think it's more of a feeling of resignation than hope. It was what it was. It's actually easier to push away from people because you don't know what you're missing. I think we were left alone by the guards for the most part. LWOP is worse because it's a slower death. You also realize more of what you won't and don't have. You see the same people leave and come back. You make more friends and most of them are going home at some point. It's a more insidious mental sentence. Some days you just don't feel like dealing with people.

In other words, LWOP is more challenging for these men than death row because in general population, they get to watch other men get released from prison, which is a privilege they know they will never get to experience. Gary is not the only LWOP prisoner who is challenged by this transient nature of general population. Many of the men who spoke about the stressors they encounter from the daily life of their LWOP sentence also noted that it is difficult for them to see so many people whom they had come to know leave the prison. This is stressful for a variety of reasons. The LWOP prisoner may have developed meaningful friendships with some of their peers, making it extremely hard to lose daily contact with these friends when they are released from the prison or moved to another building on the grounds. Anthony reminds us outsiders that the support system of those who are incarcerated is not only drawn from family and friends in society, but also from within the prison. As the years behind bars pass, one's support system often dwindles, yet Anthony notes the challenges this brings to daily life within the prison when people in your support system "leave."

> Not only do you have a support system on the street that leaves, but you have a support system in the prison that leaves and when you have LWOP, they move and they forget about you or maybe they don't forget about you, but you are not a priority because they're trying to survive.

Surprisingly, even when LWOP prisoners see men with whom they did not get along leave the prison, it is no less stressful for them, but for very different reasons. This may seem counterintuitive because many people might expect those prisoners who remain behind bars to be relieved to watch the despised inmates who have been troublesome walk out of the prison doors. However, several of the LWOPers stated that they find it extremely frustrating to see the "hard-headed," often much younger inmates leave the prison, only for most of them to return in an extremely short period of time. For instance, Ernest grumbled in disgust about the young prisoners, "When they leave, I know I will see them again because they are too stupid then to just stay the fuck out there. I know I will see them again in three weeks!"

When this happens time and time again, the cycling of the same men in and out of the prison, the men who are sentenced to LWOP often feel incredibly discouraged. It is tough for them to watch these (typically young) men squander the second chance they have been given (even third, fourth, or greater chances are given), only to be charged with another crime and return to prison. The discouragement found among men serving LWOP sentences is due to the fact that while they are not even being given a second chance, they are also forced to watch others who have been given another chance take that opportunity for granted. Kenneth's words ring true to the sentiments of most of his fellow death row turned LWOP peers when he exclaims "*I know* that I would *never come back* here if I could just get the same second chance that these knuckleheads get over and over and over again!"

The second reason that some of the LWOP men expressed discouragement upon watching the other, younger men cycle in and out of prison is related to their efforts to serve as mentors to these men. Since their move to general population, a few of them indicated that they have sought to find some meaning behind their LWOP sentence by serving as mentors to these younger inmates. When they were on death row, similarly situated with men who faced the same horrifying, gruesome end to their sentence, any mentoring that the longer-term death row inmates were able to offer the newer additions to the row was very limited. They certainly could, and frequently did, offer advice to the younger inmates as to how they could best "do their time on the row," yet mentoring takes on a whole new meaning "on the compound." There they have the potential to help the younger inmates learn from their mistakes as they advise them on how to change their lives in a way that will help them stay out of prison after they return to the streets.

Upon reuniting with the former death row-turned-LWOP inhabitants the first time in a decade or more to conduct interviews for this study, several of them chuckled as they shared their relatively new status of "old head." Gary smiled as he pointed to the gray in his hair during a prison video visit and exclaimed "Look! I'm an old head now!" Having been sent to death row in his early 20s, Gary is closely approaching 50 years old. The status of "old head" has been conferred upon those inmates for whom age and prison knowledge intersect (Kreager et al., 2017). Anthony expressed both the pros and the cons that come with the status of old head, at least insofar as he has been able to experience it thus far with the sentence of LWOP:

> Not everybody has the same sentence as you, so that can make it difficult. But it's a plus and a minus because sometimes you may know someone who has eighteen months and you can plant a seed and you can see the growth and that's helpful because you can say to yourself, "I did something there to put something in that fellow's head." When you can see somebody and give them a little bit of advice that is helpful, to see somebody go through something that you went through when you were their age, "Let me tell you something I learned so you don't make the same mistake that I did."

The benefits that Anthony and other LWOP prisoners stand to receive from their mentorship role include the sense of meaning and purpose that comes from feeling as though they have made a difference in the lives of young men who may turn their lives around as a result of their influence as the wise old heads they have become. For the men in this sample who identify as old heads, this is a fairly new status, given that they only transferred to the general population approximately five years ago. As a result, they have not yet been able to see many fruits from the labor of their mentorship. On the other hand, Kenneth shares his discouragement, saying that all too often,

> I try to talk to a lot of these guys, but it goes in one ear and out the other because actions speak louder than words. They act like they are listening and being receptive to what you are saying, but their actions speak otherwise because they go off and do the opposite of what you are telling them, so it just goes in one ear and out the other.

A Window to the Future and Fears of What's to Come

While many of the men in this study shared such frustrations around seeing the *younger* prisoners leave the prison, either because they will miss their new friends or because they are distressed by the virtual revolving door that much too frequently brings them back, the anguish that they voiced more often centered on the *aging* lifers whom they have encountered over the last five years since they were transferred to general population. Having survived anywhere from one to two decades on death row and five years in general population, some of the men in this study have certainly achieved "old head status," as noted earlier. At the same time, they are still relatively young in comparison to the elders in the prison. Most of the men interviewed for this project were initially incarcerated as relatively young men and now all ten of them are in their 40s and 50s. The lifers who they find disturbing are much older than them, in their 70s, 80s, and even older. As Kenneth explained, most of the men view the existence that elderly lifers must endure as horrifying:

> When it comes to the elders doing life without parole and their aging, you can see that their faculties are not as sharp as they used to be. It's kind of like they're withering away. It's difficult if you don't have a support system because you have nobody to lean on, you only have yourself. And in here it is hard to really have genuine relationships because everybody in here has a different mentality. And a lot of guys are selfish and only think about themselves so it is hard to build genuine relationships in here because you can't really trust nobody. So, I look at that and I think I don't want to be like that person. I don't want to get a place to where mentally this place has just sucked me up and taken my mental stability away from me and you're medicated, walking around looking like a zombie. You're really not here, you're really not knowing what's going on.

Derrick adds a racial component to his fears about his future as an elderly lifer, should he lose his current appeal in the courts. Watching aging *white men* deteriorate in the lifers building especially alarms him because it tells him that a criminal justice system that does not honor the privileged treatment white men would typically receive in our racially stratified society certainly is not set up to care about *him, as a Black man.*

> If I wait for natural causes to kill me that could be another 20 or 30 years. I don't want to be here just to deteriorate. I'd rather them just kill me. I'm over in S1 and that is the lifers building and you have guys who have been there for more than 30 or 40 years. This is what scares me, if the administration is going to do this to *some white guy*, what will they do *to me*?! There's this one white guy over there who's almost 80 and they want him to push a cart, but he can't do it. He is no longer a threat to society. And you have the taxpayers paying for this! He's already rehabilitated so you might as well just let him go!

Samuel shares similar unsettling observations that he has drawn from some of the elders he encounters daily, which has formed the basis of his greatest fear:

> I used to have the biggest fear in jail about dying alone. That's no longer my fear. My fear now is watching these individuals suffer the way they are. There's one guy who I serve with his chow because he can't even open up his food. He has to wait for someone to open his food. I'm not here to judge you.

Just as Samuel takes it upon himself to help feed a disabled aging peer during meals, Anthony offers his time to some of the elders who appear particularly lonely. As his comments below make clear, Anthony's kindness is driven, at least in part, by his desire to help take care of his aging peers in the way that he hopes younger inmates will help to care for him in the future, should he find himself in a similar position as an aging LWOPer.

> Seeing the old guys is a reminder why they're grumpy old men and they get on people's nerves. You get it because I'm looking at it from their point of view. People say, "Anthony you have a lot of patience there!" and I say, "Man, that could be me if my appeals don't go the way that I want them to." I would hope somebody younger would be understanding of me, so I'll stop and have a 10-minute conversation with them just about nothing to give them a little bit of human contact with somebody. I'll just sit there and talk about Otis Redding and sing a couple of verses that keeps them going. I would hope if I were in that situation, they would do the same thing for me because I can see myself there. Some days it's sad and you try not to focus on it, but some days it weighs on you.

Prison Healthcare

The fear of being left alone, due to a dwindling, if not totally vanished support system is certainly a worry that drives the anxiety that many of the men shared when they consider the bleak outcome of their LWOP sentence. While the length of time they could potentially remain behind bars is distressing, it is the *quality of life*, more so than the quantity, that fuels their fear. While it can certainly be argued that everyone desires to have a high quality of life, whether they are incarcerated or not, the intense fear that these LWOPers have about their future quality of life reflects a widespread view of the extremely poor healthcare offered by the prison.

Samuel is in his late 40s, yet he has already suffered numerous medical issues for quite some time and says that he is in constant pain. He is currently battling with the prison because the authorities are not willing to pay for the treatment or even the medical supplies required by his rare condition, nor are they willing to give him pain medication. His current medical condition is already unsatisfactory, yet as he imagines it worsening as he ages, he only needs to look around him to see what his future health condition may look like.

> I saw a man in the infirmary who's had brain cancer for 12 years, in the final stages, and I still haven't seen nothing happen for him. And I saw another man with cancer of the brain, and he doesn't even know who he is. He is just curled up in the corner all day. You see, that deters me even more because I don't want to be that person balled up in the corner, or that person who wakes up and doesn't even realize he's in jail. These are the things that I get to see first-hand. This is the main reason I am against LWOP, and would rather face the death penalty, because of the poor healthcare.

These men are not alone with the poor review that they gave the healthcare services provided at the Delaware prison that houses them. The quality of the healthcare system across the entire Delaware Department of Corrections has been in question for many years. The concerns had elevated to such an extent that over the summer of 2019, Delaware Department of Corrections Commissioner Claire DeMatteis ordered a review of the healthcare services provided at seven DOC facilities across the state. By the time the review was conducted, seven different vendors had provided healthcare services to those incarcerated in the Delaware institutions within the previous 34-year period. When the report generated by the review was released in December 2019, the findings were quite critical on many levels. The review found the health care system in all facilities of the Delaware DOC to be "plagued by poor communications, little accountability, and a lack of data collection and analysis" (Chase, 2019).

The details of the report confirm much of the critique that these men shared about the prison healthcare services. For instance, Samuel complained that he has had to pay out of his own pocket for the medical supplies required for him to address his medical condition since the prison health system has refused to order the supplies that he needs. Among the findings within the report was an acknowledgement of the scarcity of supplies at the prison. This point was emphasized in the report when it noted, "It was not unusual to hear that when a box of supplies arrives on site, it is like 'opening presents on Christmas'" (Eichmann, 2019). The news source containing the report goes on to provide some of the details about lawsuits that have arisen.

Connections Community Support Programs, serving as Corrections Department's medical contractor, has faced a multitude of lawsuits. One such lawsuit alleges that Connections ordered their employees to forge documents incorrectly claiming that mental health services were provided to prisoners. Another one of the lawsuits that is mentioned refers to a suit brought by the family of a prisoner who died suddenly in 2018 after various prison staff members ignored his pleas for medical assistance (Eichmann, 2019). Coincidentally, if this prisoner had received proper medical care in 2018, enabling him to survive, he would have qualified to be in the sample for the present study. He was a death row inmate who was among the other men in this sample who were commuted to LWOP just two years before his death, and he had been interviewed approximately one decade earlier for Joy's (2014) prior research study focused on death row inmates and their families. Among the comments that he shared about the challenges he encountered during his time on death row in that earlier study, he stated these eerily prophetic words: "If you need to see a doctor you have to wait forever to see him and most times by the time you get to see the doctor, you don't need him anymore and you still get charged." Sadly, it is too late for this man to be spared from the horrors brought by the LWOP sentence he was serving at the time of his death. His comments quoted earlier, however, can be considered evidence of the long-term nature of the medical neglect that the men in this study are still able to relate to today.

Declining Support Systems

Just months after the report focused on the problems found with the medical services at the Delaware DOC was released at the close of 2019, COVID-19 brought a worldwide pandemic, causing prisons around the world to shut their doors to visitors. The urgency for adequate medical and mental healthcare across our prisons has heightened, just as contact with family has been drastically reduced. This combination of a serious healthcare crisis with the elimination of family visits has added a new layer to the suffering experienced by the LWOP prisoners in this study, as well as those in prisons around the nation. During the quarantine mandated by the pandemic, prisoners have been impacted in ways not typically appreciated by outsiders. Movement around the prison had to be reduced significantly to reduce the risk of COVID transmission, which meant a reduction in the usual escapes from the daily stresses of prison life. The men in this study shared their frustrations with the more intensified isolation brought by the quarantine, such as the mandate to eat all of their meals in their cells and the suspension of their jobs, family visits, and the programs they would normally attend.

In 2020, as the world scrambled to adjust to the pandemic, most people began to wonder if this was our "new normal." What the men in this sample of former death row inmates had just come to view as "normal" prison life in general population was suddenly changing drastically, before they could complete their adjustment to life as LWOP prisoners. After the pandemic began, they were soon given access to "tablets" that allowed them to purchase access to movies, music, and most importantly, email access to maintain daily contact with their loved ones through the Global Tel Link Corporation. They have also been given increasingly more access to video visits, though even that privilege fluctuates depending upon the number of COVID cases in the prison, given the challenges presented by the need to move the inmates to another part of the prison where the kiosks are located in order for the video visits to occur.

When the men shared their anxieties about the future, it was common to hear concerns about how the pandemic threatens to permanently change their daily life in ways that only stand to make it more difficult. The concerns that the men have about permanent changes brought by the pandemic are echoed around the world, as evidenced by research that has started to accumulate. One such research study, led by the Institute for Crime & Justice Policy Research, based at Birkbeck (University of London), conducted a widescale analysis of the impact of the pandemic on incarcerated people housed in prisons across ten different nations, including the US (Heard, 2020). This study concludes with the following words, which certainly corroborate the fears of the LWOP men in Delaware.

> It is likely that some of the technology introduced during the pandemic to make up for lost in-person visits will be placed on a permanent footing, either to provide extra connectivity for prisoners and better linkage with the outside world, or as a cheaper, easier substitute for face-to-face visits and real-life interactions with people from outside the prison. While remote contact would help increase the frequency of contact with family, in-person contact plays a key role and its facilitation should remain a priority even after technological connectivity has been enhanced. The "new normal" as we move out of the pandemic should therefore mean that prison systems provide and promote in-person visits and real-life activities to the widest extent possible, *and* make wider use of remote technology-enabled communication and learning.
>
> *(Heard, 2020, p. 859)*

If the "new normal" leads our prisons to eliminate, or even diminish physical contact between the incarcerated and their loved ones, the men in this study stand to lose the major benefit they gained when they were moved off of death row and onto the compound. Visits with family when held through a computer screen are not much different from the "no-contact" visits that are held on death row, behind glass. Even with the contact visits that they have acquired since they were moved to the general population, the former death row, new LWOPers who were interviewed for this project consistently indicated that the prospect of living out the rest of their lives is so overwhelmingly bleak that it outweighs the momentary light that a contact visit with their loved ones brings into their lives.

Other than some degree of hope that they may win one of their final appeals, the primary motivator that keeps most of them going day in and day out is the obligation to their families. The only member of this sample who admitted to having attempted suicide shared that he has been "abandoned" by his family, thus has no family support. Several of the other men admitted that they have also had thoughts of suicide but have not acted upon them. While their faith is part of what keeps them from acting on these thoughts, more importantly, it is their family that keeps them from acting on them. In fact, it was often stated that family is what gets them through their days and sustains their will to get up each day and avoid doing anything that will get them into any trouble. John expressed this position well with the following words:

> I have children and it means a lot to me when I have feedback from them, that they are in some way proud of me, and I don't want to disappoint them. I don't want to hurt my mother any more than I already have. With those things in mind, I am more open or receptive to things. I have always been aware of and in tune with how people perceive me.

Overall LWOP Is Still Worse than Death

While the love that these men have for their families is enough to keep them out of trouble and the daily living conditions of LWOP are, in some ways, better than they were on death row, neither of these realities is enough to change the overall feeling that most of the men have that a LWOP sentence is worse than a death sentence. Nearly all of them are early enough in their sentence that they are still holding on to a glimmer of hope that they may win one of their final appeals that is pending in the courts. At the same time, they repeatedly indicated that if they lose all of their appeals and/or their mother or other close family dies, they are likely to "give up." They didn't always articulate what "giving up" looks like and one of the men said that he cannot answer the question about whether he is suicidal because he does not want anyone to know if or when he is ready to "take myself out of here." When Charles was asked if he is suicidal, he indicated that he has about three years until his appeal is decided upon, so he indirectly answered by saying, "Get back to me in three years with that question," suggesting that he would indeed consider suicide if he loses his appeal. Richard's words were common when he stated, "There can be relief in death. A life sentence and a death sentence both end the same way. The only difference is, with a life sentence you languish in prison before you die."

Conclusion

For most people, the idea that a "life" sentence—even a life sentence without the possibility of parole—is more humane than a "death" sentence is taken as an obvious truism that requires no additional proof or justification. In this chapter, we decided to put this assumption to the test by using the words of individuals who have been sentenced to death to see if they agree with this idea. While we recognize our data may not be representative (constructing such a sample would be impossible due to the restrictions most of those living on death row experience), the overall picture that emerges is one that challenges the idea that LWOP is more humane than a death sentence. First, the mere existence of so-called death penalty "volunteers" in and of itself suggests that for many people sentenced to death, death is preferable to life in prison, and reading the statements of those individuals who chose to end their appeals and to expedite their own executions confirms that it is the reason many of them chose to do just that. Second, turning our attention to those on death row who have not given up their appeals reveals that even though they are not (yet) trying to hasten their own deaths, they do not necessarily perceive LWOP as a preferable alternative. Rather the men in Delaware discussed in this chapter indicated that the reason they were still fighting is because they still had hope that they might be released one day. If they knew that their efforts would result in a LWOP sentence, most of them indicated they would drop their appeals and try to speed up their own executions. These views are corroborated by surveys of those on death row in other states who also indicate that for them, the movement to replace death with LWOP is not seen as a positive step.

Lastly, the ten men interviewed here who had initially been sentenced to death and then had their sentences converted to LWOP when Delaware abolished capital punishment in 2016 maintained their view that, on the whole, LWOP was still worse than death. While it is true that they did identify some benefits of LWOP relative to death, in particular improved living conditions and more contact with loved ones, this was not enough to overcome the myriad of drawbacks associated with LWOP that created *increased* suffering for these men. These drawbacks included a decline in legal representation and access to the courts, a lack of structure and consistency in the general population, witnessing other incarcerated men get released from (and often return to) prison (something they will never get to experience), getting to see first-hand the fate that likely awaits them as they watch others serving LWOP grow old and die in prison, a lack of adequate healthcare in prison and the suffering associated with subpar medical treatment, and a dwindling support network. These drawbacks led the men who were initially sentenced to death and are now serving LWOP to conclude that LWOP may indeed be a fate worse than death. In other words, despite the nearly universal assumption that LWOP is inherently more humane than death, those who have been sentenced to death do not necessarily share this view. As such, replacing capital punishment with LWOP does not necessarily benefit the very people it is intended to benefit and may even impact them *negatively*.

Note

1 The remaining five death row inmates who were in the original sample a decade ago include one who was executed, one who was released, another one found dead in his cell, and two who had already been commuted to sentences that offered the opportunity for parole.

References

Blume, J. H. (2005). Killing the willing: "Volunteers" suicide and competency. *Michigan Law Review, 103*, 939–1009.

Chase, R. (2019, December 5). *Report finds gap in Delaware prison health care system*. Retrieved from AP News: https://apnews.com/article/acdbed6ceabf82aee05b651c64bb3474

Death Penalty Information Center. (2010, May). *Final weighted toplines*. Retrieved from Death Penalty Information Center: https://files.deathpenaltyinfo.org/legacy/documents/topline.DPIC.DPNDP.pdf

Death Penalty Information Center. (2019, November 7). *Execution volunteers*. Retrieved from Death Penalty Information Center: https://deathpenaltyinfo.org/executions/executions-overview/execution-volunteers

Egelko, B. (2014, April 30). *Death Row inmates oppose Prop. 34*. Retrieved September 1, 2021, from SF Gate: https://www.sfgate.com/news/article/Death-Row-inmates-oppose-Prop-34-3891122.php

Eichmann, M. (2019, December 5). *Prison health care in Delaware is not improving, report says*. Retrieved from WHYY: https://whyy.org/articles/prison-health-care-in-delaware-is-not-improving-report-says/

Gill, M. M. (2010). Clemency for lifers: The only road out is the road not taken. *Federal Sentencing Reporter, 23*, 21–26.

Heard, C. (2020). Commentary: Assessing the global impact of the COVID-19 pandemic on prison populations. *Victims & Offenders, 15*, 848–861.

Joy, S. (2014). *Grief, loss, & treatment of death row families*. Lanham, MD: Lexington Books.

Kreager, D. A., Young, J. T., Haynie, D. L., Bouchard, M., Schaefer, D. R., & Zajac, G. (2017). Where "old heads" prevail: Inmate hierarchy in a men's prison unit. *American Sociological Review, 82*, 685–718.

Lomax, D. (2012, April 12). *Death sentence by another name*. Retrieved from Socialist Worker: http://socialistworker.org/2012/04/12/death-sentence-by-another-name

Nellis, A. (2013). Tinkering with life: A look at the inappropriateness of life without parole as an alternative to the death penalty. *University of Miami Law Review, 67*(2), 439–458.

Rauf v. Delaware, 145 A.3d 430 (Delaware Supreme Court August 2, 2016).

Smith, A. (2008). Not "waiving" but drowning: The anatomy of death row syndrome and volunteering for execution. *The Boston University Public Interest Law Journal, 17*, 237–254.

Sykes, G. M. (1958). *The society of captives: A study of a maximum security prison*. Princeton, NJ: Princeton University Press.

Tartaro, C., & Lester, D. (2016). Suicide on death row. *Journal of Forensic Sciences, 61*, 1656–1659.

Wright, J. H. (1991). Life without parole: The view from death row. *Criminal Law Bulletin, 27*, 334–357.

2

Is LWOP Inhumane? The View from Those Serving LWOP

In his book *Doing life: Reflections of men and women serving life sentences*, Zehr (1996) asked approximately 70 Pennsylvania male and female lifers to describe the experience of serving life without parole (LWOP). Their moving responses reveal the profound struggle of living under the crushing weight of the sentence. In vividly bleak similes, the men and women describe the experience as "a black hole of pain and anxiety" (Kimerly Jones as cited in Zehr, 1996, p. 14), "a vacuum" (Gaye Morley as cited in Zehr, 1996, p. 13), "total darkness" (Yvonne Cloud as cited in Zehr, 1996, p. 28), and "a tunnel without light at the end" (Bruce Bainbridge as cited in Zehr, 1996, p. 58), characterizations that conjure images of detachment, disorientation, and darkness. Their descriptions also convey the hardship of enduring and persisting in permanent imprisonment with little relief as reflected in the following observations in which they compare LWOP to:

> A very tall wall that you could continuously climb and never reach to the top.
>
> *(Michael Twiggs as cited in Zehr, 1996, p. 85)*

> Going deep-sea diving. Going all the way down into the depths and losing your oxygen. You're struggling to get to the top. You don't know if you're going to make it, but you never stop struggling.
>
> *(Commer Glass as cited in Zehr, 1996, p. 103)*

> A fire that I can't put out. There's not enough water to put it out, because, no matter how much I try to better myself, it's just not enough.
>
> *(Renee Thomas as cited in Zehr, 1996, p. 43)*

DOI: 10.4324/9781003161783-4

> A whirlpool [that] just about the time you think you'll be able to break free of [it], the water sucks you right back down.
>
> *(Marilyn Dobrolenski as cited in Zehr, 1996, p. 89)*

> A rabbit up in the corner that can't get out. It keeps trying, but eventually it just dies there.
>
> *(Trina Garnett as cited in Zehr, 1996, p. 65)*

The respondents also used language that references LWOP's relation to a formal death sentence as others serving the sentence, scholars, and activists have previously done, for example, "death by incarceration" (Dole, n.d.; Johnson, 1984; Johnson & McGunigall-Smith, 2008; Lempert, 2016); "the extended death penalty" (Irons, 2020, para 2), a "death penalty *replacement* [emphasis in original]" (Lurie, 2015, para 12), and "a silent execution" (May, 2018, para 10). Zehr's subjects agreed that LWOP is tantamount to a death sentence, but a more protracted version of it, as noted in this statement, "A life sentence means that, in effect, you're dead. It's just another form of a death sentence. Instead of having the gall to do it in one fell swoop, you die one day at a time" (Thomas Martin as cited in Zehr, 1996, p. 44).

A central premise of this book is challenging the faulty premise that LWOP is a "lesser" punishment—in terms of severity and suffering—than capital punishment and advancing the argument that it is a "lesser" form of capital punishment in terms of inadequate legal safeguards and the redress of wrongful conviction. Hearing from those with the lived experiences of serving LWOP is a critical dimension of our examination. In the previous chapter, we discussed how those sentenced to death regard LWOP as a worse punishment than death in many respects, and now we turn to the perceptions of those serving LWOP. Ultimately, they agree with the perspectives of the formerly death-sentenced individuals presented in Chapter 1 that for many, LWOP is as painful or potentially more so than a formal death sentence.

Execution and "Execution by Installment":[1] Perceptions of Those Serving Informal and Formal Death Sentences

A limited body of scholarly research has compared the perceptions of individuals serving LWOP and the death penalty and the perceived punitiveness of these two extreme sentences. Thirty years ago, Wright (1991) surveyed 14 individuals sentenced to death in Tennessee. Half of the individuals regarded LWOP as worse than capital punishment, with six of the seven characterizing it as much worse. Follow-up comments centering on the separation from loved ones and the duration of punishment provided insight into why it was perceived as a worse sentence:

> The person must live with his guilt and be separated from his loved ones. The death penalty only ends the offender's suffering! (p. 349)

> When you *know* [emphasis in original] that you would never be with your family and friend[s] again that's worse than death. Why death is only a few seconds away. Life without parole is longer and more painful. (p. 349)

Other studies of men and women serving LWOP also indicate that the penalty is regarded not as a less severe punishment but as an equivalent or even a potentially worse sanction. Benjamin Velasquez, one of the subjects in Zehr's (1996) book, questioned: "Maybe it would have been better if they had just given me the electric chair and ended my life instead of a life sentence, letting me rot away in jail. … I look at the electric chair as more humane than being tortured like this" (p. 86).

In Johnson and McGunigall-Smith's (2008) sample of 22 individuals serving life sentences, eight reported that they would have preferred to have received the death penalty, eight preferred LWOP, and six expressed ambivalence. As with the sentiments expressed by Wright's (1991) sample regarding the degree of suffering over the duration of life imprisonment, one respondent commented that "I think it takes more courage to go on" (p. 333). Similar perceptions exist among women. In their study of females serving life sentences in Georgia, Dye and Aday (2019, p. 60) found that some subjects reported that they would have preferred to have received the death penalty, as demonstrated in the following comments:

> Give me the lethal injection please. Just end my life now. Don't wait and let me die in prison.

> I was afraid of prison and asked for lethal injection. When I got to prison I realized it was worth dying to avoid it.

These sentiments are expanded upon by a female lifer in Michigan who remarked that while she was not given a formal death sentence, she is in fact already dead, "We weren't given death sentences, but we're treated like we're already dead, by society, the justice system, and MDOC [Michigan Department of Corrections]" (Lempert, 2016, p. 15).

In Leigey's (2015) longitudinal study of 25 older people serving sentences of LWOP, some men expressed relief that they did not receive a formal sentence of death because "as long as you have a chance to breathe" there is a hope of release. A similar sentiment was reported by the respondents in Johnson and McGunigall-Smith (2008), despite the fact that a capital conviction is much more likely to be overturned (Baumgartner & Dietrich, 2015). However, others maintained that after decades of serving LWOP and enduring its pains of imprisonment, they would have preferred to have received the death penalty. After serving 22 years of a LWOP sentence, a 67-year-old respondent reported, "Sometimes I wish I would have taken the alternative which was the death penalty … and then I would have been executed. [It] probably would have been

sentenced to a formal sentence of death would actively work to receive a LWOP sentence:

> I never understand why a guy with a death sentence, I never understand why he works so hard for so many years just to get LWOP, so as opposed to them just executing [him]. You want them to torture you? Cause, trust me, if you stay here this long, you'll realize, and if you stay here this long … you've been tortured, you know what I mean, and I think that's a lot more of a sentence than an execution. … I think a guy that's on death row, I think he would be a lot better off if they just went on and executed him as opposed to the LWOP because that's torture. That is cold-blooded torture to stay here.

Even those who believed that life imprisonment should remain a sentencing option stressed that it should be with parole eligibility, and that life sentences were overutilized, costly, and unnecessary given the low likelihood of recidivism, as reflected in the following comments:

> The reason why I think they should have parole is because if they complete all these programs, get educated, and change their way of thinking and [are] willing to do better for themselves and wanting to be productive in society, you should give them hearings to see, and you be the judge, as the board, if they're ready.

> They got some guys in here older lifers that are not dangerous anymore, you know, and I feel that instead of incarcerating them until they die in here, it costs like $37,000, $38,000 a year to keep.

In sum, these qualitative accounts challenge the notion that LWOP is a "lesser" punishment than the death penalty in terms of severity or human suffering.

On "Being Dead While You're Still Alive":[3] A Study of California's Recent Propositions to Abolish the Death Penalty

Recent efforts in California to abolish the death penalty have also led to a deeper appraisal of LWOP, especially by those who would be most impacted if the death penalty was banned. In 2012, death-sentenced individuals were largely opposed to Proposition 34 (Abolition of the Death Penalty Initiative) which aimed to abolish the state's death penalty and install LWOP as the most serious penalty in the state's arsenal (Egelko, 2014). The organization Campaign to End the Death Penalty contacted 220 death-sentenced individuals in the state. Of the 50 who responded to its survey, 47 (94%) opposed the proposition. They, and in particular those who professed innocence, were against the proposed measure because they would lose the additional legal protections (e.g., state-funded attorneys for

their habeas corpus appeals) extended to individuals formally sentenced to death but not to those with LWOP sentences. In explaining their collective position, Kevin Cooper, a death-sentenced individual, commented that passage of Proposition 34 would be "a step backward in our ability to challenge our convictions" (as cited in Egelko, 2014, para 17) because of the reduced legal safeguards. Once again, the perception that perpetual imprisonment was an extended version of the death penalty was raised. For instance, Darrell Lomax (2012), an individual who had been on death row for 15 years, described LWOP as "a death sentence simply being called by another name" (para 2) and "a slow death" (para 18).

While Proposition 34 failed, momentum to abolish California's death penalty persisted. In 2013, the American Civil Liberties Union of Northern California described the horrendous conditions of confinement in its state prisons as evidence in *support* of death penalty abolition (American Civil Liberties Union of Northern California, 2013, para 9):

> Spending even a small amount of time in California's overcrowded, dangerous prisons is not pleasant. Spending thirty years there, growing sick and old, and dying there, is a horrible experience. This is especially true given the unconstitutional failure to provide adequate health care to California's prisoners. Prisoners condemned to die in prison are not given any special treatment and, in fact, have less access to programs than other prisoners. They are housed in high security facilities with few privileges, far away from any relatives, and in crowded group cells. Ironically, people on death row are provided much more comfortable single cells and sometimes gain celebrity and attention just by being there.

In 2016, a similar proposition, Repeal of the Death Penalty Initiative (Proposition 62), was introduced. Spoon Jackson (2016), an individual serving LWOP in California wrote an op-ed condemning the punishment, which he characterized as the death penalty's twin, and encouraged the public to vote against the measure stating that "death can free you from the fate of [a] LWOP death sentence" (para 5). Kenneth E. Hartman (2016), another individual serving LWOP in California explained:

> One of the tricks of LWOP is that it operates under the legal fiction of not being a death sentence, therefore there are no additional appeals, no better quality attorneys, and no higher level of scrutiny. (This is probably the main reason many death row prisoners, who live on hope for an appellate rescue, have opposed ballot measures like Prop 62.). (para 14)

He surmised: "Trading lethal injection executions for lethal terms of imprisonment does not end the death penalty, and this lie needs to be rejected. Life without the possibility of parole is the death penalty, pure and simple" (Hartman,

2016, para 19). In 2016, as in 2012, the proposition to abolish the death penalty failed. Currently, there are 704 individuals serving death sentences in California (Death Penalty Information Center, 2021) and 5,134 serving sentences of LWOP (Nellis, 2021).

The Pains of Permanent Imprisonment: Quantitative and Qualitative Findings

In *The society of captives*, Sykes (1958) described the hardships associated with the carceral experience as the pains of imprisonment: liberty, autonomy, goods and services, heterosexual relationships, and security. A growing body of research, based on both quantitative and qualitative data, has examined the pains of permanent imprisonment and found agreement in the worst facets of the punishment.

Using the same or a slightly modified instrument, several studies have explored the pains of life imprisonment. Despite the different time periods of the studies, countries included, lengths of time served and parole eligibility and demographics (e.g., age, race/ethnicity, etc.), they reveal similarities in the perceived worst pains of perpetual imprisonment. In the first study, Richards (1978) surveyed a sample of 22 individuals incarcerated in England and serving sentences in excess of ten years (including life sentences) on 20 items related to long-term imprisonment (e.g., concerns about mental health, social networks, and conditions of confinement). Two years later, Flanagan (1980) administered the same survey to 49 individuals, all of whom had been incarcerated for at least five years in the US. Sixty percent of the respondents were serving life sentences. In 2015, Leigey and Ryder examined agreement in the pains of imprisonment among 18 men serving LWOP in the US. At the time of the study, all of the men were at least 55 years of age and had been incarcerated for at least 20 years. The following year, Hulley, Crewe, and Wright (2016) examined the pains of imprisonment for 294 men serving life sentences in England and Wales who began their imprisonment before the age of 25. In addition to modifying Richards' instrument by rewording two problems and removing two other problems,[4] Hulley et al. (2016) added 21 problems to their survey.

As can be seen in Table 2.1, when looking at the five worst pains of imprisonment as reported by those with lived experience, some consensus exists, especially with the four analyses that used Richards' instrument or a modified version. Missing somebody was a top pain of imprisonment in all analyses and was the greatest pain in four of the five analyses. Though the exact rank varied, feeling that one's life is being wasted was one of the most problematic aspects across all five analyses. Missing social life appeared as a top pain in four analyses, while feeling sexually frustrated and missing little luxuries were top pains in three analyses. However, with the inclusion of 21 additional problems by Hulley et al. (2016), there was less agreement with the previous studies as three of the greatest pains of imprisonment in this analysis were not included in prior research.

TABLE 2.1 The Worst Pains of Long-Term Imprisonment Across Six Analyses

Richards (1978)	*Flanagan (1980)*	*Leigey and Ryder (2015)*	*Hulley et al. (2016) with Richards' original problems*	*Hulley et al. (2016) with additional problems included*	*Crewe, Hulley, and Wright (2017)*
22 men	49 men	18 men	294 men	294 men	23 women
Missing somebody	Missing somebody	Missing little luxuries	Missing somebody	Missing somebody	Having to follow other people's rules and orders
Feeling that your life is being wasted	Missing social life	Missing social life	Feeling that your life is being wasted	Worrying about people outside	Missing somebody
Feeling sexually frustrated	Worrying about how you will cope when you get out	Missing somebody	Missing social life	Feeling that you are losing the best years of your life	Worrying about people outside
Missing little luxuries	Feeling that your life is being wasted	Feeling that your life is being wasted	Missing little luxuries	Having to follow other people's rules and orders	Not feeling able to completely trust anyone in prison
Missing social life	Feeling sexually frustrated	Wishing you had more privacy	Feeling sexually frustrated	Feeling that your life has been wasted	Thinking about the crime that you committed

Qualitative data also provide insight into the experience of serving LWOP. Joseph Dole (n.d.), incarcerated in Illinois, enumerated its many hardships:

> "Lifers" are denied adequate medical care and often die after years of unnecessary suffering in excruciating pain due to any number of untreated ailments: cancer, hepatitis, diabetes, liver disease, etc. They spend decades in maximum and super maximum-security prisons where daily life is miserable and conditions are often unconstitutionally horrendous. … Waiting to die by imprisonment means decades of disappointment as each appeal is arbitrarily shot down. It means you are forever told you aren't worth rehabilitating. Trying to convince yourself daily that your life has value even while the rest of the world tells you that you're worthless. You spend a lifetime wondering what your true potential really is and yearning for the chance to find out. This is especially unbearable for the wrongfully convicted. … A LWOP sentence means constant contemplation of a wasted life as you hear about your loved ones dying off one after another, a continual despair as to both your inability to aid or comfort those who remain, or accomplish anything significant with your remaining years. (para 9)

Other accounts by lifers confirm Dole's inventory of the major issues associated with LWOP: separation from loved ones (Earnshaw, 2017; Hassine, 2008; Johnson & McGunigall-Smith, 2008; Leigey, 2015; Paluch, 2003; Zehr, 1996), disappointment with sentence appeals and commutation outcomes (Hassine, 2011; Leigey, 2015; Paluch, 2003; Zehr, 1996), societal rejection (Leigey, 2015; Zehr, 1996), inadequate medical care (Leigey, 2015; Paluch, 2003; Willis & Zaitzow, 2015), the unrealized potential of one's life (Leigey, 2015; Zehr, 1996), and dying in prison (Diatchenko, 2015; Leigey, 2015; Zehr, 1996).

Research conducted nearly 80 years ago demonstrated that sentence indeterminacy was associated with greater suffering among incarcerated individuals (Farber, 1944). The indeterminacy of LWOP, not knowing when or how the sentence will end, either through the person's death or a potential reduction in sentence, represents one of the central challenges for those serving it (Leigey, 2015), as reflected in the following comments from Zehr's (1996) subjects:

> I don't have any problem with doing time for the crime I committed. I own up to that. My only problem is how much time should I do? When is it going to end?
>
> *(Bruce Norris as cited in Zehr, 1996, p. 15)*

> It's not having a date. The time I can handle. It's not having numbers at the end of it.
>
> *(Grover Sanger as cited in Zehr, 1996, p. 47)*

> The hardest thing is not knowing when. A date. If you had a date, then you could look for something.
>
> *(John Jay McIntyre as cited in Zehr, 1996, p. 97)*

> The only difference between [a man with a life sentence] and the man on death row is that that man knows the day he is scheduled to die. The lifer lives each day without knowing. But any day can be the end of his life.
>
> *(Robert Hagwood as cited in Zehr, 1996, p. 100)*

> A life sentence means you're incarcerated from the time you're convicted, or the time you're arrested, until whenever the whim of the governor might feel like letting you go. It might be 20 years, 50 years; it might be forever. Might never let you out.
>
> *(David Brown as cited in Zehr, 1996, p. 108)*

Other qualitative accounts underscore the daily struggles of an indeterminate life sentence. Diatchenko (2015), an individual who served 34 years of a LWOP sentence prior to his release, summarized the day-to-day existence of his life as: "Working in the plumbing shop. Going to work every day and doing my thing. Living. Existing. Waiting to die" (para 19).

"An Inescapable Burden": Maturation and Change Under Permanent Punishment

As has been described in the literature, a maturation process occurs for many individuals serving life sentences (Irwin, 2009; Lempert, 2016; Johnson & Leigey, 2020; Zehr, 1996). Irwin (2009) characterized the start as an "awakening," which "begins when lifers fully appreciate that there has been something fundamentally wrong with their former behavior. They realize that *their* [emphasis in the original] actions have brought them to this disastrous end" (p. 66). Maturation, accompanied by self-reflection, can generate self-awareness which can spur on a transformation in both identity and behavior (Johnson & Leigey, 2020; Zehr, 1996). Harry Twiggs, who is now 71 years of age and continues to serve LWOP in Pennsylvania, described how he had changed over his two decades of confinement:

> I was a cocky individual, didn't care anything about anybody but myself—a self-centered person, full of hate, resentments, bitterness, anger. I thought everybody owed me something, and I was planning on taking it from everybody. … I'm 45 years old, and I've been here 23 years. I'm a man who has come to grips with himself and the world around him. I understand that I am only here for a while, and that I should try to make the world a better place than it was when I came here. I feel remorse for the things that I've done in my life, and I want to try to make it up to the people that I've done it to and to society as a whole.
>
> *(as cited in Zehr, 1996, p. 22)*

Other lifers agree that maturation has led to greater wisdom, patience, empathy, and perspective (Johnson & Leigey, 2020; Zehr, 1996). The men in Leigey's longitudinal sample of aging individuals described how they have changed:

> We are not the same inconsiderate people that we used to be when we first got locked up. We have changed for the better. … We're more positive about different things in life, we stop and look before we leap. We think about what we are going to do before we do it. We appreciate ourselves, our lives, and the people that are around us.
>
> I've gotten a lot wiser. I think before I act. I have a chance to look at both sides of the coin … what I would used to [do] is just react before I would think. … I've got a lot grayer, a lot of older, and it changes a person. I believe in that, that it really changes you.

A 62-year-old respondent who had been incarcerated for nearly 30 years maintained that he was proof that a person can change:

> I'm definitely a better person than when I came here. They say that some people can't change or you might have society feel that a person can't

> change, you might have judges, maybe juries, prosecutors that might think that you can't change, but the fact is I'm a living witness that a person can change.

Despite the transformations that many lifers undergo, they are trapped in their punishment, as Irvin Moore, a Pennsylvania lifer described, "like an insect encased in amber" (as cited in Zehr, 1996, p. 11).

While some lifers may engage in disciplinary misconduct at earlier points in their sentences (Crewe, Hulley, & Wright, 2020; Johnson & Dobrzanska, 2005; Leigey, 2015; Nellis, 2012; Sorensen & Wrinkle, 1996; Sorensen, Wrinkle, & Gutierrez, 1998; Willis & Zaitzow, 2015; Zamble, 1992; Zehr, 1996), most desist from violations and seldomly violate prison rules. At first glance it may appear that lifers have the least to lose and would be more inclined to act out, but this is not the reality. As prison is the "involuntary home" of the perpetually incarcerated (Johnson & Dobrzanska, 2005, p. 36), quality of life is highly valued. A good work assignment, decent housing assignment, or additional privileges (e.g., extra visits with family) could be jeopardized by disciplinary misconduct (Johnson & Dobrzanska, 2005; Johnson & Leigey, 2020; Leigey, 2015). As Erin George (2015), who is serving LWOP in Virginia, maintains, "I have far too much to lose to risk getting a ticket for something stupid" (p. 78).

How do lifers survive permanent incarceration? Joseph Miller, a Pennsylvania lifer, offered, "Every day is depressing. Every day is the same. You're just here to die. But yet as life goes on, you live it and you try to make changes and do things, feel human. We all find our own way to be productive" (as cited in Zehr, 1996, p. 38). Productivity takes different shapes. Over the decades of incarceration, many devote their lives to bettering themselves, others, and the prison environment (George, 2015; Hassine, 2008; Kazemian & Travis, 2015; Leigey, 2015; Paluch, 2003; Willis & Zaitzow, 2015; Zehr, 1996). Programs, work, and volunteerism provide a sense of accomplishment, pride, and purpose (George, 2015; Leigey, 2015; Willis & Zaitzow, 2015). James Taylor, a Pennsylvania lifer, explained how he has been able to survive his sentence, "What makes it livable is meaningful activity. I've been very active in pursuing my own growth and development" (as cited in Zehr, 1996, p. 18). They forge lives for themselves under extremely trying circumstances. Through the years of incarceration, many LWOP individuals have earned educational degrees, completed vocational training courses, facilitated groups, assumed greater responsibilities in their work assignments, and been recognized for their humanitarian endeavors. As noted earlier, a hope of release motivates individuals to keep going, day after day, and year after year (Hassine, 2011; Johnson & Dobrzanska, 2005; Leigey, 2015; Lempert, 2016; Seeds, 2021; Willis & Zaitzow, 2015; Zehr, 1996), even though the likelihood of release is extremely low. In the words of one Pennsylvania lifer, "Commutation is an almost fruitless process, but I still hope. As long as I have that, I will keep going" (Betty Heron as cited in Zehr, 1996, p. 68).

Many lifers experience self-growth and transformation and maintain that they are not now who they once were (Johnson & Leigey, 2020; Toch, 2010; Willis & Zaitzow, 2015). A respondent in Leigey's longitudinal sample who is now 74 years old and has been incarcerated for more than four decades reflected, "I know that I'm not the same person that I was in 1977." However, the punishment of LWOP freezes a person to whom they were on the day of the crime (Leigey & Schartmueller, 2019). Erin George (2015) surmised, "The immutable facts behind our incarcerations are an inescapable burden" (p. 216). While they are praised for their accomplishments by correctional staff and clemency boards (Leigey, 2015), evidence of transformation is not enough to alter a LWOP sentence. A punishment of permanent imprisonment is a weight that one individual described as "so hard to get off you" (Letitia Smallwood as cited in Zehr, 1996, p. 98). In fact, the sanction of LWOP was implemented for this very reason. Per its expressed purpose, a person is not meant to be released from prison, and as a result, none of their more recent accomplishments or additional evidence of maturation are required to be taken into consideration in sentence modification. Those serving LWOP express deep frustration that recent evidence of maturation and positive change (e.g., participation in programming and disciplinary behavior)[5] are not given proper consideration at sentence commutation hearings; rather, the crime that they committed decades earlier carries the most weight, as reflected in these comments from Leigey's sample:

> Nobody notices [the] positive changes.
>
> It becomes harder in realizing that no matter how much you change, society is not going to forgive you.
>
> They need to consider what he's done over the past, you know, [number of] years that he's been here.

Female lifers also report a similar frustration as demonstrated in the following comment: "no matter how much I try to better myself, it's just not enough" (Renee Thomas as cited in Zehr, 1996, p. 43). Continuing with this perspective, a respondent in Leigey's sample who had spent more of his life incarcerated than free described this tension: "A person can see a change in themselves in these couple of decades and other people they see the change, but the people that have this hold on you, they just [see]… a murder charge that happened 34 years ago." As a 69-year-old respondent who had served about 20 years told Leigey, "We're still human beings, even though our crimes have us here and [they] took place many, many years ago. They will never change." Although the crime of conviction cannot be changed, many individuals serving LWOP do change. In *Lifers*, Irwin (2009) asserted, "The truth is that whoever they were and whatever crime they committed, the vast majority of lifers become completely different people after serving years in prison" (p. 2).

"An Invisible Entity:" The Experiences of Women Perpetually Incarcerated

According to the most recent statistics from The Sentencing Project, 1 in 15 women overall and 1 in 9 Black or African American women who are currently incarcerated are serving life sentences (Nellis, 2021). Over the last two decades, there has been a precipitous increase in the number of women serving LWOP. From 2008 to 2020, the number of women serving LWOP increased by nearly half (43%). This is especially striking when we consider that the overall number of women incarcerated for a violent offense increased by 2% and the number of men serving LWOP increased by 29% in this same time period (Nellis, 2021).

Similar to the exclusion or underdevelopment of gender in other areas of criminological research, there is much less known about the experiences of women serving life sentences as compared to their male counterparts (but for important exceptions, see Dye & Aday, 2019 and Lempert, 2016). Women serving life sentences have described themselves as living "*in the shadow* [emphasis in original]" of their male counterparts (Howard League for Penal Reform, 1999, p. 8) and being invisible, as noted here: "Women lifers are like an invisible entity. It's like no one knows we're here. You read all the time about the men lifers—their graduations, the things they have. When we graduate, it's not in the papers. We're here, but no one really knows we are here" (Cyd Berger as cited in Zehr, 1996, p. 48).

In one of the earliest recognitions of the increase in female life imprisonment, Genders & Player (1990) examined the experiences of women serving life sentences in England and Wales through the prisms of Sykes' (1958) original pains of imprisonment. However, more recent examinations have explored the gendered pains of life imprisonment, that is, the pains of imprisonment that affect women to a greater extent than their male counterparts. In their study of life-sentence individuals in England and Wales (n=333), Crewe et al. (2017) noted important gender differences in the worst pains of imprisonment and the difficulty of experiencing them. As can be seen in Table 2.1, three of the top pains of imprisonment were the same for men and women, though the exact rank differed: missing somebody, worrying about people outside, and having to follow other people's rules and orders. However, the researchers also noted the pains with the greater gender difference in ranking. Women rated the following pains much higher than men: wishing you had more privacy, losing your self-confidence, not feeling able to completely trust anyone in prison, feeling that you are losing contact with family and friends, feeling that you have no purpose or meaning in your life, and feeling angry with yourself. The pains that men rated higher than women included feeling sexually frustrated, missing social life, feeling frustrated that you are not progressing through the system, and being bored. Importantly, the researchers also noted the severity of the pain (i.e., how difficult it was to experience) was greater for women on all thematic dimensions, with statistical significance noted for "'Anger/Frustration', 'Emotional & Physical Vulnerability', 'Outside Relationships', 'Release Anxiety' and 'Mental Wellbeing'" (Crewe et al., 2017, p. 1365).

As noted earlier, women intensely feel the hardship of the loss of freedom/agency and having to abide by other people's rules and orders (Crewe et al., 2017; Dye & Aday, 2019; George, 2015; Lempert, 2016). Gendered expectations that women are to be docile and obedient add further insight into the sharpness of this pain. Additionally, one of the greatest hardships for women serving life sentences is the separation from their loved ones, especially their children (Dye & Aday, 2019; George, 2015; Lempert, 2016; Zehr, 1996). There is concern over their children's welfare and profound sadness and guilt over their separation (George, 2015; Walker & Worrall, 2000; Zehr, 1996). As Marilyn Dobrolenski, a Pennsylvania lifer explained:

> The hardest thing about a life sentence is being away from my family. My daughter was only two and a half years old when I came to prison. She's now 23. She's grown, and I missed her entire childhood. And my relatives are getting older.
>
> *(as cited in Zehr, 1996, p. 88)*

About half of women who were incarcerated reported that they have never been visited by their minor children since their prison admission (Glaze & Maruschak, 2010). While visits can be a rare source of happiness for an incarcerated mother, they can also be emotionally challenging for both the mother and child alike, especially when it is time to say goodbye at the end of the visit (George, 2015). For women without children, a LWOP sentence is also a barrier in this regard as they mourn the ability to have biological children should they be released (Howard League for Penal Reform, 1999; Walker & Worrall, 2000; Zehr, 1996).

Privacy is another concern of women serving life sentences, and they cited specific examples, such as censorship of mail, close surveillance during visits, strip searches, and menstruation, as instances when it is especially needed (Dye & Aday, 2019; Genders & Player, 1990). An aging female lifer in England described the degradation of being strip-searched by a younger officer:

> One of the worst things about this place is the complete and utter lack of privacy. You get strip-searched about once every two weeks. It's so degrading. As an older woman it's especially awful when you're stripped [by] some of the young officers here—some of them try to be sensitive about it but not all of them.
>
> *(Genders & Player, 1990, p. 53)*

Many women serving life sentences have extensive histories of emotional, physical, and/or sexual abuse which could exacerbate the hardship of various routine indignities in the life of a person incarcerated, for example, strip searches, and observation while showering/undressing (Dye & Aday, 2019; George, 2015; Leigey & Reed, 2010; Lempert, 2016; Zehr, 1996).

Conclusion: Life Without Parole "Picks You Apart"[6]

In sum, the experience of serving LWOP is painful and challenging, as indicated in the words of this Pennsylvania lifer: "I'm not faring well, but I got my life. I ain't living well, but I'm alive" (Calvin Martin as cited in Zehr, 1996, p. 35). Prior research indicates some consensus in the most problematic aspects of LWOP, and that women experience the pains of perpetual imprisonment more severely than men.

As has been argued by critics and those serving the punishment, LWOP is a different iteration of a capital sentence, and its characterization as being a "lesser" punishment only applies in terms of attention and legal safeguards—not in reduced suffering. As a 57-year-old respondent in Leigey's longitudinal sample who had been incarcerated for a quarter of a century surmised about the human and financial costs of LWOP: "All of the people in here, to me, is a terrible waste of life, money, [and] space." Given the pains of imprisonment and the demonstrated likelihood of maturation and change, we assert that perpetual imprisonment is inhumane, and as such, we agree with Johnson and McGunigall-Smith's (2008) contention that "death by incarceration is just as final, just as painful, and just as worthy of the careful scrutiny to which we subject traditional capital sentences" (p. 344).

Notes

1 The full quote from Tyrone Werts, a Pennsylvania lifer, is: "The sentence of life without parole is among the most unjust, most immoral, least effective, cruelest, and most barbaric of our punishments. It is nothing short of execution by installment, the death penalty in slow motion" (as cited in Zehr, 1996, p. 94).

2 This individual died in 2013 after being incarcerated for 36 years.

3 The full statement from Kenneth Hartman (2016), an individual serving LWOP in California, is: "Over the years, I've tried to describe the indescribable. The sense of being dead while you're still alive, the feeling of being dumped into a deep well struggling to tread water until, some 40 or 50 years later, you drown" (para 4).

4 The two problems of being worried about becoming a vegetable and longing for a time in the past were removed and two problems were re-worded. Keeping out of trouble was modified to finding it hard keeping out of trouble and being afraid of going mad was revised to worrying about my mental health.

5 While institutional behavior demonstrates the ability to mature, post-release behavior is also persuasive. Evidence of the extremely low likelihood of recidivism among individuals formerly serving life sentences, including LWOP, indicates that many individuals serving LWOP are not a risk to society (Advisory Committee on Geriatric and Seriously Ill Inmates, 2005; Marquart & Sorensen, 1988; Siegel, 2016; Weisberg, Mukamal, & Segall, 2011). For example, of the 174 who were sentenced to LWOP as juveniles in Philadelphia County, Pennsylvania, and were later released as a result of *Miller*, only two, or a single percent of those released, have been convicted of new offenses, contempt and robbery in the third degree (Daftary-Kapur & Zottoli, 2020).

6 The full statement from Charles Diggs, who continues to serve LWOP in Pennsylvania, is: "It's an ongoing struggle every day to try to make something out of nothing. It picks at you piece by piece. It involves a lot of sadness; it's a stressful situation. It takes a toll on the family. You see things chipping away slowly but surely, and that tears you to pieces. It picks you apart" (as cited in Zehr, 1996, p. 78).

References

Advisory Committee on Geriatric and Seriously Ill Inmates. (2005, June 22). *Report of the advisory committee on geriatric and seriously ill inmates*. Retrieved from Joint State Government Commission: http://jsg.legis.state.pa.us/resources/documents/ftp/publications/2005-40-INMATES%20REPORT.pdf

American Civil Liberties Union of Northern California. (2013, September 24). *The truth about life without parole: Condemned to die in prison*. Retrieved from American Civil Liberties Union of Northern California: https://www.aclunc.org/article/truth-about-life-without-parole-condemned-die-prison

Baumgartner, F. R., & Dietrich, A. W. (2015, March 17). *Most death penalty sentences are overturned. Here's why that matters*. Retrieved from Washington Post: https://www.washingtonpost.com/news/monkey-cage/wp/2015/03/17/most-death-penalty-sentences-are-overturned-heres-why-that-matters/

Crewe, B., Hulley, S., & Wright, S. (2017). The gendered pains of life imprisonment. *British Journal of Criminology*, *57*, 1359–1378.

Crewe, B., Hulley, S., & Wright, S. (2020). *Life imprisonment from young adulthood: Adaptation, identity and time*. London: Palgrave Macmillan.

Daftary-Kapur, T., & Zottoli, T. M. (2020). *Resentencing of juvenile lifers: The Philadelphia experience*. Retrieved from Montclair State University Digital Commons: https://digitalcommons.montclair.edu/cgi/viewcontent.cgi?article=1084&context=justice-studies-facpubs

Death Penalty Information Center. (2021, September 1). *Facts about the death penalty*. Retrieved from Death Penalty Information Center: https://documents.deathpenaltyinfo.org/pdf/FactSheet.pdf

Diatchenko, G. (2015, December 4). *Why it's hard to be a lifer who's getting out of prison*. Retrieved from The Marshall Project: https://www.themarshallproject.org/2015/12/04/why-it-s-hard-to-be-a-lifer-who-s-getting-out-of-prison

Dole, J. (n.d.). *Is life without parole worse than a death sentence?* Retrieved from Prison Writers: https://prisonwriters.com/is-life-without-parole-worse-than-a-death-sentence/

Dye, M. H., & Aday, R. H. (2019). *Women lifers: Lives before, behind, and beyond bars*. New York: Rowman & Littlefield.

Earnshaw, J. (2017, June 13). *Life after life without parole*. Retrieved from The Marshall Project: https://www.themarshallproject.org/2017/06/13/life-after-life-without-parole

Egelko, B. (2014, April 30). *Death Row inmates oppose Prop. 34*. Retrieved September 1, 2021, from SF Gate: https://www.sfgate.com/news/article/Death-Row-inmates-oppose-Prop-34-3891122.php

Farber, M. L. (1944). Suffering and time perspective of the prisoner. *University of Iowa Studies in Child Welfare*, *20*, 155–213.

Flanagan, T. J. (1980). The pains of long-term imprisonment: A comparison of British and American perspectives. *British Journal of Criminology*, *20*, 148–156.

Genders, E., & Player, E. (1990). Women lifers: Assessing the experience. *Prison Journal*, *70*, 46–57.

George, E. (2015). *A woman doing life: Notes from a prison for women* (2nd ed.). (R. Johnson, & A. B. Martin, Eds.) New York: Oxford University Press.

Glaze, L. E., & Maruschak, L. M. (2010, March 3). *Parents in prison and their minor children.* Retrieved from Bureau of Justice Statistics: https://bjs.ojp.gov/content/pub/pdf/pptmc.pdf

Hartman, K. E. (2016, October 23). *Death by another name.* Retrieved from The Marshall Project: https://www.themarshallproject.org/2016/10/23/death-by-another-name

Hassine, V. (2008). *Life without parole: Living in prison today* (4th ed.). (R. Johnson, & A. Dobrzanska, Eds.) New York: Oxford University Press.

Hassine, V. (2011). *Life without parole: Living and dying in prison today* (5th ed.). (R. Johnson, & S. Tabriz, Eds.) New York: Oxford University Press.

Howard League for Penal Reform (1999). *Life in the shadows: Women lifers.* London: Howard League for Penal Reform.

Hulley, S., Crewe, B., & Wright, S. (2016). Re-examining the problems of long-term imprisonment. *British Journal of Criminology, 56,* 769–792.

Irons, P. (2020, June 24). *A prison sentence of life without parole isn't called the death penalty. But it should be.* Retrieved from NBC News: https://www.nbcnews.com/think/opinion/prison-sentence-life-without-parole-isn-t-called-death-penalty-ncna1232018

Irwin, J. (2009). *Lifers: Seeking redemption in prison.* New York: Routledge.

Jackson, S. (2016, October 28). *'No' on Prop 62.* Retrieved from San Francisco Bay View: https://sfbayview.com/2016/10/props-62-and-66-death-penalty-debate-behind-enemy-lines/

Johnson, R. (1984). A life for a life? *Justice Quarterly, 1*(4), 569–580.

Johnson, R., & Dobrzanska, A. (2005). Mature coping among life-sentenced inmates: An exploratory study of adjustment dynamics. *Corrections Compendium, 30*(6), 8–9, 36–38.

Johnson, R., & Leigey, M. E. (2020). The life-course of juvenile lifers: Understanding maturation and development as Miller and its progeny guide juvenile life sentence release decisions. *Journal of Criminal Justice and Law, 3,* 29–46.

Johnson, R., & McGunigall-Smith, S. (2008). Life without parole, America's other death penalty: Notes on life under sentence of death by incarceration. *The Prison Journal, 88,* 328–346.

Kazemian, L., & Travis, J. (2015). Imperative for inclusion of long termers and lifers in research and policy. *Criminology & Public Policy, 14,* 355–395.

Leigey, M. E. (2015). *The forgotten men: Serving a life without parole sentence.* New Brunswick, NJ: Rutgers University Press.

Leigey, M. E., & Reed, K. L. (2010). A woman's life before serving life: Examining the negative pre-incarceration life events of female life-sentenced inmates. *Women & Criminal Justice, 20,* 302–322.

Leigey, M. E., & Ryder, M. A. (2015). The pains of permanent imprisonment: Examining perceptions of confinement among older life without parole inmates. *International Journal of Offender Therapy and Comparative Criminology, 59,* 726–742.

Leigey, M. E., & Schartmueller, D. (2019). The fiscal and human costs of life without parole. *The Prison Journal, 99,* 241–262.

Lempert, L. B. (2016). *Women doing life: Gender, punishment, and the struggle for identity.* New York: New York University Press.

Lomax, D. (2012, November 3). *LWOP: Death sentence by another name – Vote no on 34.* Retrieved from San Francisco Bay View: https://sfbayview.com/2012/11/lwop-death-sentence-by-another-name-vote-no-on-34/

Lurie, S. (2015, June 16). *The death penalty is cruel. But so is life without parole.* Retrieved September 4, 2021, from The New Republic: https://newrepublic.com/article/121943/death-row-crueler-and-more-unusual-penalty-execution

Marquart, J. W., & Sorensen, J. R. (1988). Institutional and postrelease behavior of Furman-commuted inmates in Texas. *Criminology, 26*, 677–693.

May, L. C. (2018, December 31). *Life without parole is 'silent execution'*. Retrieved September 4, 2021, from Scalawag Magazine: https://scalawagmagazine.org/2018/12/life-without-parole-is-silent-execution/

Nellis, A. (2012). *The lives of juvenile lifers: Findings from a national survey*. Washington, DC: The Sentencing Project.

Nellis, A. (2021, February 17). *No end in sight: America's enduring reliance on life imprisonment*. Retrieved March 1, 2021, from Sentencing Project: https://www.sentencingproject.org/publications/no-end-in-sight-americas-enduring-reliance-on-life-imprisonment/

Paluch, J. A. (2003). *A life for a life: Life imprisonment: America's other death penalty*. (T. J. Bernard, & R. Johnson, Eds.) New York: Oxford University Press.

Richards, B. (1978). The experience of long-term imprisonment: An exploratory investigation. *British Journal of Criminology, 18*, 162–169.

Seeds, C. (2021). Hope and the life sentence. *British Journal of Criminology*. DOI: 10.1093/bjc/azab037.

Siegel, R. (2016, February 17). *More than 130 Maryland lifers adjust to freedom after court ruling*. Retrieved September 4, 2021, from NPR: https://www.npr.org/2016/02/17/467118226/more-than-130-maryland-lifers-adjust-to-freedom-after-court-ruling

Sorensen, J., & Wrinkle, R. D. (1996). No hope for parole: Disciplinary infractions among death-sentenced and life-without-parole inmates. *Criminal Justice and Behavior, 23*, 542–552.

Sorensen, J., Wrinkle, R., & Gutierrez, A. (1998). Patterns of rule-violating behaviors and adjustment to incarceration among murderers. *Prison Journal, 78*, 222–231.

Sykes, G. M. (1958). *The society of captives: A study of a maximum security prison*. Princeton, NJ: Princeton University Press.

Toch, H. (2010). "I am not now who I used to be then": Risk assessment and the maturation of long-term prison inmates. *Prison Journal, 90*, 4–11.

Walker, S., & Worrall, A. (2000). Life as a woman: The gendered pains of indeterminate. *Prison Service Journal, 132*, 27–37.

Weisberg, R., Mukamal, D. A., & Segall, J. D. (2011, September). *Life in limbo: An examination of parole release for prisoners serving life sentences with the possibility of parole in California*. Retrieved November 1, 2019, from Stanford Criminal Justice Center: https://law.stanford.edu/wp-content/uploads/sites/default/files/publication/259833/doc/slspublic/SCJC%20Lifer%20Parole%20Release%20Sept%202011.pdf

Willis, A. K., & Zaitzow, B. H. (2015). Doing "life": A glimpse into the long-term incarceration experience. *Laws, 4*, 559–578.

Wright, J. H. (1991). Life without parole: The view from death row. *Criminal Law Bulletin, 27*, 334–357.

Zamble, E. (1992). Behavior and adaptation in long-term prison inmates: Descriptive longitudinal resulys. *Criminal Justice and Behavior, 19*, 409–425.

Zehr, H. (1996). *Doing life: Reflections of men and women serving life sentences*. Intercourse, PA: Good Books.

3

Is LWOP Inhumane? The View from Abroad

Life without parole "is predominantly a US phenomenon" (van Zyl Smit & Appleton, 2019, p. 94). According to the best available evidence, more than 80% of the known LWOP population is incarcerated in the US. While this count includes some nations with missing data, even if the data were complete, the US would almost certainly still account for more than half of the worldwide LWOP population (van Zyl Smit & Appleton, 2019). This is not because the US is a crime-infested wasteland with danger lurking behind every corner; it is because of differences in how LWOP is utilized around the world and the resulting differences in criminal justice policy. In the US, LWOP is imposed with stunning regularity—at the start of 2020, more than one in every 25 sentenced prisoners in the US was serving LWOP (Carson, 2020; Nellis, 2021)—and the US Supreme Court recently reaffirmed the acceptability of sentencing children to death by incarceration (*Jones v. Mississippi*, 2021). Juvenile LWOP (JLWOP) is a direct violation of the United Nations (UN) Convention on the Rights of the Child, which has been ratified by every nation in the world except the US. In contrast, most of the rest of the world considers irreducible life sentences to be violative of basic human rights, for juveniles and adults alike. There is a great deal of irony in this finding given that much of the support for LWOP has come from death penalty abolitionists who argue that capital punishment is inhumane (Barkow, 2012; Gottschalk, 2012; *Harvard Law Review*, 2006; Kleinstuber, Joy, & Mansley, 2016; Ogletree & Sarat, 2012; Seeds, 2018; van Zyl Smit & Appleton, 2019).

By the Numbers

One way to understand how nations perceive different punishments is to look at how often they impose them. van Zyl Smit and Appleton (2019) conducted a worldwide survey of the size of the life-sentenced prison population as of

DOI: 10.4324/9781003161783-5

September 1, 2014, or as close to that date as possible, and they compared those figures to The Sentencing Project's 2016 count (Nellis, 2017) of the life-sentenced population in the US. The results of their research were striking. Whereas the US had 53,290 persons serving LWOP, the entire rest of the Americas, which have more than double the population of the US, had just 222—and more than three quarters of those were incarcerated in Argentina. In fact, just 6,363 persons outside the US were serving *any* life sentence in the Americas. In Europe, which also has a population more than twice that of the US's, the LWOP population was just 2,156 or about 4% the size of the US's LWOP population. Like the distribution of people serving LWOP in the Americas, nearly all of those were incarcerated in a single country (Ukraine). However, due to recent rulings by the European Court of Human Rights (ECtHR) (discussed later), it is likely that the number in Europe will soon drop to zero. In fact, in all of Europe (including Russia and Turkey), there were only 27,213 persons serving *any* life sentence—about *half* the number of people serving LWOP in the US. A comparison of rates is also illuminating. In Europe, there were 3.3 persons serving any type of life sentence for every 100,000 people in the population. In the US, the number just for LWOP was *five times* that at 16.6 per 100,000 (van Zyl Smit & Appleton, 2019).

LWOP and Human Rights Worldwide

So why is the US such an outlier in its use of life and LWOP sentences? Some of this reality can, no doubt, be traced to the US's greater reliance on prison in general than any other country on Earth. The US has the highest incarceration rate on the planet (Walmsley, 2018), so it would make sense that the US also has the highest rate of life-sentenced individuals. However, this does not provide a complete explanation because much of the mass incarceration problem in the US is actually driven by its reliance on life and LWOP sentences (Nellis, 2021); furthermore, while the US is home to around 20% of all known prisoners in the world (Walmsley, 2018), it is home to the *majority* of those serving LWOP (van Zyl Smit & Appleton, 2019). Instead, a better explanation relies on how LWOP is regarded in other countries. During the very period in the late 20th and early 21st centuries when the US was experiencing an increase in support for and use of LWOP, the rest of the world was beginning to challenge LWOP on human rights grounds, and outside of the US, there is now an increasing acceptance that LWOP sentences deny those who receive them their basic human dignity and thus violate their human rights (van Zyl Smit & Appleton, 2019).

International Human Rights Treaties

Following the Second World War, there were concerted efforts to begin using international law to protect human rights, including the rights of prisoners (van Zyl Smit & Appleton, 2019). The Universal Declaration of Human Rights, which was proclaimed by the UN General Assembly in 1948, specifically prohibits torture and "cruel, inhuman, or degrading treatment or punishment" (United Nations, n.d.), and since that time, numerous other international human rights treaties have reiterated the same respect for human dignity, including of those who are incarcerated. Following in the Universal Declaration's footsteps, Article 3 of the European Convention on Human Rights (ECHR), which was adopted in 1950 and came into effect in 1953, prohibits torture and "inhuman or degrading treatment or punishment" (European Court of Human Rights, n.d.). The UN reiterated its opposition to torture and "cruel, inhuman, or degrading treatment or punishment" in 1966 with the International Covenant on Civil and Political Rights, which came into force in 1976 (United Nations Office of the High Commissioner for Human Rights, n.d.). In 1969, the Organization of American States not only echoed the same language but specifically stated that anyone "deprived of their liberty shall be treated with respect for the inherent dignity of the human person" when it adopted the American Convention on Human Rights (ACHR), which entered into force in 1978 (Organization of American States, n.d.). The ACHR then went a step further stating, "Punishments consisting of deprivation of liberty shall have as an essential aim the *reform and social readaptation* of the prisoners" (emphasis added), suggesting that no punishment should deprive the prisoner of the chance to reenter society. The African Charter on Human and Peoples' Rights, adopted in 1981 and entered into force in 1986 (African Commission on Human and Peoples' Rights, n.d.), and the UN Convention against Torture and Other Cruel, Inhuman, or Degrading Treatment or Punishment, which was ratified in 1984 and entered into force in 1987 (Office of the High Commissioner for Human Rights, n.d.), issued the same prohibitions. The constitutions of numerous nations have also adopted the same language (van Zyl Smit & Appleton, 2019).

The 1970s and 1980s: Europe Begins to Question LWOP

Of course, these prohibitions are quite vague and do not specify which punishments qualify as "cruel, inhuman, or degrading," consequently leaving the question of LWOP's humanity open. However, outside of the US, there has been an increasing acceptance over the last 50 years that perpetual imprisonment degrades prisoners, depriving them of their human dignity, and thus violates these international human rights norms. In essence, for the last half century, the US and the rest of the world have been moving in opposite directions when it comes to LWOP. In the 1970s, while many American states were passing LWOP statutes in response to the US Supreme Court's decision in *Furman v. Georgia* (1972) that temporarily banned capital punishment (Garrett, Seale-Carlisle, Modjadidi, & Renberg, 2021; Nellis, 2013), many other nations were beginning to question whether LWOP could comport with the emerging human rights norms. In 1976, as the US Supreme Court was reinstating capital punishment, the European Committee of Ministers declared that "it is inhuman to imprison a person for life without any hope of release. … Nobody should be deprived of the chance of possible release" (cited in van Zyl Smit, 2010, p. 43).

The following year, the Federal Constitutional Court of Germany ruled that LWOP sentences reduce prisoners to "mere tools of the state," turning each into "an object of crime prevention," thus depriving them of their human dignity. The Court went on to note, "If human dignity is understood in this way, then it would be intolerable for the state forcefully to deprive [persons of their] freedom without at least providing them the chance to someday regain their freedom." Therefore, "a humane enforcement of life imprisonment is possible only when the prisoner is given a concrete and realistically attainable chance to regain his or her freedom …; the state strikes at the very heart of human dignity when treating prisoners without regard to the development of their personalities, stripping them of all hope of ever earning their freedom" (cited in Kommers & Miller, 2012, pp. 365–366). As the Court reasoned, "The essence of human dignity is attacked if the prisoner, notwithstanding his personal development, must abandon any hope of ever regaining his freedom" (cited in van Zyl Smit & Appleton, 2019, p. 298). A few years later, in 1981, Norway went a step further than the Germans by abolishing *all* life sentences (van Zyl Smit & Appleton, 2019).

The 1990s: The Debate over LWOP Goes Global

However, the issue of LWOP's permissibility was far from settled, and the debate over the humanity of LWOP sentences continued throughout the 1990s and into the 21st century. In the early 1990s, the UN International Law Commission (ILC) met to draft the Code of Crimes against the Peace and Security of Mankind (van Zyl Smit & Appleton, 2019). During the debates over its drafting, many commissioners, particularly from Latin America, opposed life imprisonment on human rights grounds (van Zyl Smit & Appleton, 2019). Life sentences are prohibited in many Latin American nations, including Brazil, Costa Rica, Colombia, El Salvador, Peru, and Mexico (Henry, 2012). The rationale offered by these nations is that life sentences do not provide individuals with a chance to rehabilitate themselves and thus violate their human rights as enumerated in the ACHR (van Zyl Smit & Appleton, 2019). As Peruvian Commissioner Solari Tudela argued during the ILC's 1991 meeting:

> Life imprisonment did not seem to be compatible with the Latin American legal system. The criterion adopted in the American Convention on Human Rights, for instance, was that penalties should not only be correctional in nature but should also rehabilitate the convicted person so that he could resume his place in society. A more realistic penalty would be imprisonment for a minimum of 10 years and a maximum of 25 years, which was the longest term of imprisonment in many Latin American countries.
>
> *(Yearbook of the International Law Commission 1991:* Summary records of the meetings of the forty-third session 29 April–19 July 1991, 1993, *p. 34)*

By the mid-1990s, however, this debate took a backseat to more pressing and tangible concerns: the UN Security Council needed to decide how to punish those convicted of war crimes and other crimes against humanity in both Yugoslavia and Rwanda. Capital punishment was not an option because its imposition would be vetoed by multiple permanent members of the Security Council, but life sentences were still a possibility. Seeking to avoid the debate over life sentences that had animated the ILC's meetings, the Security Council sidestepped the question of life sentences by permitting the ad hoc tribunals to impose whatever sentences were permitted by the laws of the nations where the crimes took place, except capital punishment (van Zyl Smit & Appleton, 2019). In Rwanda, the maximum penalty was life in prison, but in Yugoslavia, the maximum term of confinement was 30 years; nevertheless, the International Criminal Tribunal for the former Yugoslavia (ICTY) justified life sentences because Yugoslavia did permit the death penalty. Since the ICTY was barred from imposing death sentences, the ICTY reasoned that any sentence less than death would comply with the statute (van Zyl Smit & Appleton, 2019). Whether or not these life sentences would be eligible for parole, however, was a question that was saved for a later date.

The Rome Statute and the 21st Century Consensus of a 25-Year Max

The overarching question of LWOP's compatibility with international human rights law could not be avoided for long, though. In 1998, the UN General Assembly adopted the Rome Statute, which established the International Criminal Court. That statute specifically prohibited LWOP by requiring that all life sentences be reviewed after the prisoner had served 25 years (Rome Statute of the International Criminal Court, 2011). "This twenty-five-year review period has proved to be of wide significance in the debate about an appropriate minimum period for life sentences" (van Zyl Smit & Appleton, 2019, p. 28), and numerous European bodies have since concluded that irreducible life sentences are a violation of fundamental human rights. Although it did not specify that LWOP sentences were prohibited, in 2002, the European Union determined that member states could refuse to execute European arrest warrants if the suspect was at risk of a potential LWOP sentence (Council framework decision of 13 June 2002 on the European arrest warrant and the surrender procedures between Member States, 2002, Article 5 (2)). Then, in 2003, the Council of Europe's Committee of Ministers adopted Recommendation (2003) 22 on conditional release and Recommendation (2003) 23 on the management by prison administrators of life sentence and other long-term prisoners. Together, these documents argued for an explicit right to parole even for those sentenced to life terms. According to Recommendation (2003) 22, "... the law should make conditional release available to all sentenced prisoners, including life-sentence prisoners" (p. 2), and in the Explanatory Memorandum accompanying the recommendation, the Committee of Ministers clearly stated, "Life-sentence prisoners should not be deprived of the hope to be granted release either. Firstly, no one can reasonably argue that all lifers will always remain dangerous to society" (Committee of Ministers, 2003, p. 12). The report accompanying Recommendation (2003)

23 stated that the recommendation "contains the principle that conditional release should be possible for all prisoners … even to life prisoners" (cited in *Vinter and Others v. United Kingdom*, 2013, p. 21).

A few years later, in 2006, the Council of Europe adopted the European Prison Rules, which specified, "*All* detention shall be managed so as to facilitate the reintegration into free society of persons who have been deprived of their liberty" (emphasis added) (Council of Europe, 2006, p. 7). This has been widely interpreted to be a repudiation of LWOP. The following year the Committee for the Prevention of Torture and Inhuman or Degrading Treatment or Punishment (CPT) referred approvingly to the European Prison Rules in its report on Hungary's treatment of prisoners, arguing, "More generally, as regards 'actual lifers', the CPT has serious reservations about the very concept according to which such prisoners, once they are sentenced, are considered once and for all to be a permanent threat to the community and are deprived of any hope of being granted conditional release" (*Report to the Hungarian Government on the visit to Hungary carried out by the European Committee for the Prevention of Torture and Inhuman or Degrading Treatment or Punishment (CPT) from 30 January to 1 February 2007*, 2007, p. 15). Later in the year, the CPT issued a memorandum on "Actual/real life sentences" in which it quoted the Hungarian report to reiterate its opposition to irreducible life sentence and then recommended, among other things, that "Nobody should be forced to die in prison. … No category of prisoners should be stamped as 'likely to spend their natural life in prison'. … Denial of release should never be final. … Not even recalled prisoners should be deprived of hope of release" (Rasmussen, 2007, p. 10). Then, in its 2011 report on the Swiss prison system, the CPT again referred to the European Prison Rules and to Recommendation (2003) 22 of the Committee of Ministers in declaring "that the law should allow for the possibility of all convicted prisoners, including those serving a life sentence, benefiting from conditional release." It continued by concluding "that it is inhuman to imprison someone for life without any real hope of release" (cited in *Vinter and Others v. United Kingdom*, 2013, p. 22).

Vinter and the Abolition of LWOP in Europe

These positions were heavily relied upon by the Grand Chamber of the ECtHR when, in 2013, it issued an authoritative ruling in *Vinter and Others v. United Kingdom* that irreducible life sentences violated Article 3 of the ECHR. According to the Grand Chamber, "there is also now clear support in European and international law for the principle that all prisoners, including those serving life sentences, be offered the possibility of rehabilitation and the prospect of release if that rehabilitation is achieved" (p. 40). In considering the acceptability of LWOP sentences, the judges argued:

> It is axiomatic that a prisoner cannot be detained unless there are legitimate penological grounds for that detention. … However, the balance

> between these justifications for detention is not necessarily static and may shift in the course of the sentence. ... It is only by carrying out a review of the justification for continued detention at an appropriate point in the sentence that these factors or shifts can be properly evaluated. (pp. 39–40)

Using this logic, the Grand Chamber concluded that Article 3 of the ECHR requires that all life sentences be eligible for review and conditional release (*Vinter and Others v. United Kingdom*, 2013). Perhaps most poignantly, in her concurring opinion, Judge Power-Forde argued that LWOP qualifies as a degrading and thus unacceptable punishment because:

> Those who commit the most abhorrent and egregious of acts and who inflict untold suffering upon others, nevertheless retain their fundamental humanity and carry within themselves the capacity to change. Long and deserved though their prison sentences may be, they retain the right to hope that, someday, they may have atoned for the wrongs which they have committed. They ought not to be deprived entirely of such hope. To deny them the experience of hope would be to deny a fundamental aspect of their humanity and, to do that, would be degrading. (p. 53)

The ECtHR's ruling in *Vinter* has had wide significance in Europe and other parts of the world, leading to the abolition of LWOP sentences in many places. For example, in 2015, when posed with the question of whether those convicted and sentenced to life by the ICTY or the International Criminal Tribunal for Rwanda (ICTR) should be eligible for release, Judge Theodor Meron quoted the *Vinter* decision approvingly and determined that a review of the "relevant international legal standards strongly suggests that those sentenced to life imprisonment are not barred from being considered for early release" (*Prosecutor v. Galić*, 2015, § 19). He thus concluded "that a person convicted by the ICTR, the ICTY, or the Mechanism and sentenced to a term of life imprisonment may be considered eligible for early release" (§ 24). The following year, the CPT referenced the *Vinter* decision in a report on life-sentenced prisoners in which it reiterated its view "that to incarcerate a person for life without any real prospect of release is, in its view, inhuman" (European Committee for the Prevention of Torture and Inhuman or Degrading Treatment or Punishment (CPT), 2016, p. 4). Furthermore, the *Vinter* decision set the stage for further rulings by the ECtHR condemning the use of LWOP or *de facto* LWOP sentences in the Netherlands (*Murray v. the Netherlands*, 2016), Lithuania (*Matiošaitis and Others v. Lithuania*, 2017), and, most significantly, in Ukraine (*Petukhov v. Ukraine (No. 2)*, 2019), which at the time of van Zyl Smit and Appleton's (2019) survey housed the vast majority of Europe's LWOP population. As such, LWOP appears close to becoming a punishment of the past in Europe.

Worldwide Impact

The ramifications of this emerging human rights consensus extend far beyond the borders of Europe. As discussed earlier, most Latin American nations have opposed LWOP on human rights grounds for decades (Henry, 2012). Some African nations have also begun to consider LWOP sentences incompatible with emerging human rights norms. As early as 1996, the Namibian Supreme Court affirmed that its constitutional prohibition on "cruel, inhuman or degrading treatment or punishment" did not permit "a sentence which locks the gates of the prison irreversibly for the offender without any prospect whatever of any lawful escape from that condition for the rest of his or her natural life and regardless of any circumstances which might subsequently arise" (*State v. Tcoeib*, 1996, p. 11). Then in 2008, courts in the tiny African island nation of Mauritius, located in the Indian Ocean, followed suit; it was joined by Zimbabwe in 2016 (van Zyl Smit & Appleton, 2019). Also in 2016, courts in Belize, one of the three Latin American nations that utilized LWOP at the time of van Zyl Smith and Appleton's survey, followed the example of European courts in rejecting "LWOP sentences because they do not allow for the prospect of rehabilitation, because they make it effectively impossible for life-sentenced prisoners ever to be released" (van Zyl Smit & Appleton, 2019, pp. 299–300). Adding to this chorus, in 2014, Pope Francis told the International Association of Penal Law that a life sentence was the equivalent of "a hidden death penalty" and called upon Catholics to oppose such sentences as strongly as they oppose capital punishment (Agence France-Presse, 2014). All told, "Numerous international and comparative law materials demonstrate consistent support for life sentences that allow parole review after 25 years" (Nellis, 2013, p. 17).

Final Thoughts

Based upon this review, it is clear that the US's acceptance and growing use of LWOP puts it out of step with the international community. While the US has seen its use of LWOP explode over the last three decades and Americans tend to view LWOP as a humane replacement for capital punishment, the rest of the world has increasingly come to reject LWOP because of its inhumanity. That is, "Contemporary societies have rejected both capital and [death-in-prison (DIP)] sentences as inconsistent with human dignity and violative of human rights. Because of the severity of DIP sentences, they share with capital sentences the condemnation of the international community" (Henry, 2012, p. 79). In brief, the US stands apart.

References

African Commission on Human and Peoples' Rights. (n.d.). *African charter on human and peoples' rights*. Retrieved May 20, 2021, from African Commission on Human and Peoples' Rights: https://www.achpr.org/legalinstruments/detail?id=49

Agence France-Presse. (2014, October 23). *Pope Francis blasts life sentences as 'hidden death penalty'*. Retrieved May 21, 2021, from The Guardian: https://www.theguardian.com/world/2014/oct/23/pope-francis-life-sentence-hidden-death-penalty-torture

Barkow, R. E. (2012). Life without parole and the hope for real sentencing reform. In C. J. Ogletree, & A. Sarat (Eds.), *Life without parole: America's new death penalty?*(pp. 190–226). New York: NYU Press.

Carson, E. A. (2020, October). *Prisoners in 2019.* Retrieved December 31, 2020, from Bureau of Justice Statistics: https://www.bjs.gov/content/pub/pdf/p19.pdf

Committee of Ministers. (2003, September 24). Recommendation Rec (2003) 22 of the Committee of Ministers to Member States on conditional release (parole). Retrieved from https://www.legislationline.org/download/id/1468/file/8c6bd0e8e03dae9eb1870651698a.pdf

Council framework decision of 13 June 2002 on the European arrest warrant and the surrender procedures between Member States. (2002, June 13). Retrieved May 21, 2021, from EUR-Lex: https://eur-lex.europa.eu/legal-content/EN/TXT/?uri=celex%3A32002F0584

Council of Europe. (2006, June). European prison rules. Strasbourg: Council of Europe. Retrieved from https://rm.coe.int/european-prison-rules-978-92-871-5982-3/16806ab9ae

European Committee for the Prevention of Torture and Inhuman or Degrading Treatment or Punishment (CPT). (2016). *Situation of life-sentenced prisoners.* Retrieved May 21, 2021, from Council of Europe: https://rm.coe.int/16806cc447

European Court of Human Rights. (n.d.). *European convention on human rights.* Retrieved May 20, 2021, from European Court of Human Rights: https://www.echr.coe.int/Pages/home.aspx?p=basictexts&c

Furman v. Georgia, 408 U.S. 238 (US Supreme Court 1972).

Garrett, B. L., Seale-Carlisle, T. M., Modjadidi, K., & Renberg, K. M. (2021). Life without parole sentencing in North Carolina. *North Carolina Law Review, 99*, 279–332.

Gottschalk, M. (2012). No way out? Life sentences and the politics of penal reform. In C. Ogletree, & A. Sarat (Eds.), *Life without parole: America's new death penalty?* (pp. 227–281). New York: NYU Press.

Harvard Law Review. (2006). A matter of life and death: The effect of life-without-parole statutes on capital punishment. *Harvard Law Review, 119*, 1838–1854.

Henry, J. S. (2012). Death-in-prison sentences: Overutilized and underscrutinized. In C. J. Ogletree, & A. Sarat (Eds.), *Life without parole: America's new death penalty?*(pp. 66–95). New York: NYU Press.

Jones v. Mississippi, 593 U.S. ___ (US Supreme Court 2021).

Kleinstuber, R., Joy, S., & Mansley, E. A. (2016). Into the abyss: The unintended consequences of death penalty abolition. *University of Pennsylvania Journal of Law and Social Change, 19*, 185–206.

Kommers, D. P., & Miller, R. A. (2012). *The constitutional jurisprudence of the Federal Republic of Germany* (3rd ed.). Durham, NC: Duke University Press.

Matiošaitis and Others v. Lithuania, 22662/13, 51059/13, 58823/13, 59692/13, 59700/13, 60115/13, 69425/13 and 72824/13 (European Court of Human Rights, Second Section August 23, 2017).

Murray v. the Netherlands, 10511/10 (European Court of Human Rights, Grand Chamber April 26, 2016).

Nellis, A. (2013). *Life goes on: The historic rise in life sentences in America.* Washington, DC: The Sentencing Project.

Nellis, A. (2017). *Still life: America's increasing use of life and long-term sentences.* Washington, DC: The Sentencing Project.

Nellis, A. (2021, February 17). *No end in sight: America's enduring reliance on life imprisonment.* Retrieved May 6, 2021, from Sentencing Project: https://www.sentencingproject.org/publications/no-end-in-sight-americas-enduring-reliance-on-life-imprisonment/

Office of the High Commissioner for Human Rights. (n.d.). *Convention against torture and other cruel, inhuman or degrading treatment or punishment.* Retrieved May 20, 2021, from Office of the High Commissioner for Human Rights: https://www.ohchr.org/en/professionalinterest/pages/cat.aspx

Ogletree, C. J., & Sarat, A. (2012). Introduction: Lives on the line: From capital punishment to life without parole. In C. J. Ogletree, & A. Sarat (Eds.), *Life without parole: America's new death penalty?*(pp. 1–24). New York: NYU Press.

Organization of American States. (n.d.). *Multilateral treaties: American convention on human rights "Pact of San Jose, Costa Rica" (B-32).* Retrieved May 20, 2021, from Organization of American States: https://www.oas.org/dil/treaties_b-32_american_convention_on_human_rights_sign.htm

Petukhov v. Ukraine (No. 2), 41216/13 (European Court of Human Rights, Fourth Section September 9, 2019).

Prosecutor v. Galić, MICT-14-83-ES (International Criminal Tribunal for the former Yugoslavia June 23, 2015).

Rasmussen, J. W. (2007, June 27). Actual/real life sentences. Strasbourg: Council of Europe. Retrieved from https://rm.coe.int/090000168069877e

Report to the Hungarian Government on the visit to Hungary carried out by the European Committee for the Prevention of Torture and Inhuman or Degrading Treatment or Punishment (CPT) from 30 January to 1 February 2007. (2007, June 28). Strasbourg: Council of Europe. Retrieved from https://rm.coe.int/1680696b06

Rome Statute of the International Criminal Court. (2011). The Hague, Netherlands: International Criminal Court. Retrieved from https://www.icc-cpi.int/resource-library/documents/rs-eng.pdf

Seeds, C. (2018). Disaggregating LWOP: Life without parole, capital punishment, and mass incarceration in Florida, 1972–1995. *Law & Society Review, 52*, 172–205.

State v. Tcoeib, 1996 (1) SACR 390 (NmS) (Supreme Court of Namibia February 6, 1996).

United Nations Office of the High Commissioner for Human Rights. (n.d.). International covenant on civil and political rights. Retrieved May 20, 2021, from United Nations Office of the High Commissioner for Human Rights: https://www.ohchr.org/en/professionalinterest/pages/ccpr.aspx

United Nations. (n.d.). *Universal declaration of human rights.* Retrieved May 20, 2021, from United Nations: https://www.un.org/en/about-us/universal-declaration-of-human-rights

van Zyl Smit, D. (2010). Outlawing irreducible life sentences: Europe on the brink? *Federal Sentencing Reporter, 23*, 39–48.

van Zyl Smit, D., & Appleton, C. (2019). *Life imprisonment: A global human rights analysis.* Cambridge, MA: Harvard University Press.

Vinter and Others v. United Kingdom, 66069/09, 130/10, and 3896/10 (European Court of Human Rights, Grand Chamber July 9, 2013).

Walmsley, R. (2018, November). *World prison population list.* Retrieved May 22, 2021, from World Prison Brief: https://www.prisonstudies.org/sites/default/files/resources/downloads/wppl_12.pdf

Yearbook of the International Law Commission 1991: Summary records of the meetings of the forty-third session 29 April–19 July 1991 (Vol. 1). (1993). New York: United Nations. Retrieved from https://legal.un.org/ilc/publications/yearbooks/english/ilc_1991_v1.pdf

4

Worse than Death

Innocence and Access to the Courts

Carlos DeLuna, Cameron Todd Willingham, Troy Davis. All executed despite compelling evidence of their innocence, they are the poster children of the anti-death penalty movement. After all, how can we maintain a punishment as irreversible and as permanent as capital punishment when there is such demonstrable evidence of human fallibility leading to innocent people being executed? The thought of such an injustice should send shudders down the spine of even the most ardent proponent of capital punishment, particularly a retributivist, so their plight is a quite persuasive argument against capital punishment and in favor of ending this sanction at any cost. In fact, the risk of wrongful executions turns out to be one of the most effective arguments in garnering support for abolition (Warden, 2012; Wozniak, 2012). But are the innocent really better off with a LWOP sentence rather than a death sentence? On the surface, the answer seems like an obvious yes. After all, LWOP sentences should provide defendants and their allies more time to prove their innocence whereas once someone has been executed, it cannot be undone, even if it is discovered that the execution was in error.

However, this simple, straightforward analysis misses one crucial point: LWOP "sentences receive no heightened judicial attention or scrutiny, which leads to a reduced likelihood that they will be reversed" (Henry, 2012, p. 77). In other words, as tragic as the wrongful executions of DeLuna, Willingham, Davis, and countless others were, if they had been sentenced to LWOP, their cases would have garnered little attention, and they all would have likely died in prison anyway—just in obscurity "because no one makes any effort to reconsider the guilt of" most incarcerated people (Gross, O'Brien, Hu, & Kennedy, 2014, p. 7230). Whereas death sentences are closely scrutinized and receive a substantial amount of attention from both the public and the courts, LWOP sentences "languish in a backwater devoid of procedural protections" (Barkow, 2009, p. 1148).

DOI: 10.4324/9781003161783-6

Consequently, a perverse situation exists whereby being sentenced to death might actually be a legally advantageous predicament for the wrongly convicted. As the *New York Times* explained in regards to Walter McMillian, who spent six years on death row before being exonerated and whose story was chronicled in the book and the film *Just Mercy*, if he had been sentenced to LWOP, "Mr. McMillian might have been another forgotten black inmate in an Alabama prison. … [McMillian's attorney] said only the death sentence had allowed Mr. McMillian to receive adequate representation" (Applebome, 1993, pp. A1, B11). We agree with the assertion that "If McMillian had merely been sentenced to life imprisonment, most likely he would never have been heard from again" (Gross, 1996, p. 498). This is the same sentiment the *Times* proffered nearly a century ago in the infamous Scottsboro Boys case: "A Negro in jeopardy of his life is a potential martyr, but a Negro in jail for the rest of his life for a sordid crime is a forgotten man" (Daniell, 1936, p. E12). Therefore, LWOP is not necessarily a better fate for the wrongly convicted than a death sentence. In this chapter, we will explore this possibility by first providing a brief summary of the legal benefits that are afforded to those under a sentence of death but that are denied to others in prison and then analyzing exoneration rates to see if these legal protections do, in fact, increase the likelihood that those sentenced to death will be exonerated. The results of these analyses strongly suggest that innocent defendants sentenced to LWOP are at *greater risk* of dying in prison than are those sentenced to death. Thus, unless the procedural safeguards currently available only to those on death row are extended to those given a non-capital sentence, replacing capital punishment with LWOP likely *harms* the wrongly convicted.

Super Due Process, Life, and Death

Due to its finality, the Supreme Court has long considered death to be different from other punishments—even life imprisonment. While we take issue with this premise, the result of this logic has been the creation of a separate jurisprudence of death that provides additional procedural safeguards for capital defendants (Steiker & Steiker, 2014). Although these protections only formally apply to the trial and pre-trial stages (Steiker & Steiker, 2014), "[e]verybody knows that direct and collateral review are more painstaking for capital cases than for any others" (Gross, 1996, p. 497). That is, in practice, appellate courts will scrutinize death sentences more closely than any other sentence, including life sentences (Barkow, 2009; *Griffin v. United States*, 1949; Gross, 1996; Liebman, 2000). As Justice Marshall noted in the *Furman* decision—even before most of the extra due process protections were enacted for capital cases—"courts admittedly spend more time with death cases" (*Furman v. Georgia*, 1972, p. 357), and the history of the Supreme Court is full of examples of the Court applying "more exacting appellate review procedures in capital cases than in other criminal cases" (Liebman, 2000, p. 2034) and even taking up cases *because* the defendant was sentence to death. As Barkow (2009) has observed, "Whereas [the Supreme Court's] review of capital sentences is robust, its oversight of noncapital sentences is virtually nonexistent" (p. 1145).

Following this line of thinking, most states now specifically grant those sentenced to death greater access to the courts and more resources to challenge their convictions. As Judge Alex Kozinski of the Ninth Circuit Court of Appeals once noted, "innocent defendants in California are better off with a capital sentence because they will be provided with 'a whole panoply of rights of appeal and review that you don't get in other cases'" (Henry, 2012, p. 77). For example, nearly all death penalty states provide for automatic appellate review of all capital sentences and their underlying convictions directly to the state's court of last resort regardless of whether the defendant actually files an appeal or even desires an appeal, and they typically also engage in a proportionality review to ensure that the sentence is appropriate given the facts of the case, additional scrutiny that is rarely afforded to (and even less likely to be successful for) lesser sentences (Cauthen & Latzer, 2008; Henry, 2012; Johnson, 2020; *Kennedy v. Louisiana*, 2008; Snell, 2007; *Whitmore v. Arkansas*, 1990). Oregon state law, which is not atypical, actually allows for a *ten-part* review process of all death sentences but not for other murder convictions (Kaplan, Collins, & Mayhew, 2016). Additionally, unlike other criminal convictions, nearly all capital sentences are reviewed not just by state appellate courts but also by federal courts via federal habeas corpus petitions (Liebman, 2000, p. 2052; *Whitmore v. Arkansas*, 1990, pp. 174–175).

Furthermore, while the Supreme Court has ruled that the Sixth Amendment only provides a right to state-funded defense counsel for indigent defendants through the first direct appeal (*Ross v. Moffitt*, 1974), due to the publicity and finality of the death penalty, nearly all those sentenced to death are either provided with counsel or gain access to *pro bono* capital defense attorneys until the end. In contrast, nearly all non-capital defendants are forced to represent themselves on any post-appellate collateral attacks or federal habeas corpus petitions, but those sentenced to death typically maintain access to representation throughout the duration of their cases (Banner, 2002; Gross, 1996; Liebman, 2000; Villaume, 2005). On top of this, the additional procedural safeguards in place during capital trials inevitably lead to more issues to be raised on appeal, and the threat of a pending execution incentivizes defense attorneys representing those on death row to drag litigation out as long as possible in order to keep their clients alive—an incentive that does not exist for other clients (Banner, 2002). As a result, reviews of death sentences "take significantly longer to resolve than other types of appeals" (Cauthen & Latzer, 2008, p. 299). These lengthier appeals are important because they provide defendants with more time to discover exculpatory evidence while they still have attorneys and investigators on the outside who are able to search for such evidence, which gives the wrongly convicted a better opportunity to prove their innocence (Dieter, 2014). An extended appellate process also means that courts are more closely scrutinizing the trials for errors, and as a result, they are more likely to discover mistakes. Those who are serving death-in-prison sentences, meanwhile, do not benefit from this additional judicial scrutiny or access to lawyers that those with formal capital sentences receive because "they are the special preserve of defendants who have been sentenced to death and who still face the possibility of execution" (Gross, 1996, p. 500).

Super Due Process and Innocence

The impact of these additional legal protections is hard to ignore. According to the most comprehensive study on the question, between 1973 and 1995, 68% of death sentences were overturned on appeal (Liebman, Fagan, West, & Lloyd, 2000), which stands in sharp contrast to the non-capital reversal rate, which has been estimated to be less than 20% (Henry, 2012)—and according to one estimate, "probably less than 5%," which would make death sentences "7 to 14 times more likely to be reversed than non-capital ones" (Liebman et al., 2002, p. 12). Obviously, many of these reversals are related to procedural errors rather than innocence and many of those granted relief were reconvicted or even resentenced to death, but it is inevitable that this additional scrutiny also ends up benefitting the innocent on death row. In fact, 7% of the death sentences that were overturned between 1973 and 1995 resulted in an acquittal at retrial, and the vast majority of those who were reconvicted received a sentence less than death (Liebman, Fagan, West, & Lloyd, 2000). Overall, a death sentence is far more likely to be overturned than carried out (Baumgartner & Dietrich, 2015; Liebman, 2000),[1] whereas the vast majority of LWOP sentences remain intact (Henry, 2012).

We do not mean to imply that LWOP sentences are never reduced or that wrongly convicted individuals who are not sentenced to death are never discovered. They certainly are—it just occurs proportionally far less often. Given the limited availability of data on sentencing, the statistical rarity of exonerations, and the impossibility of knowing how many innocent individuals are in prison, it is difficult to make any conclusive claims about one's potential for exoneration. However, from the available evidence, it appears that those who are sentenced to death are many times more likely to be exonerated than those serving other sentences, even LWOP sentences. For example, an early analysis of exonerations performed by the National Registry of Exonerations (NRE) found that death sentences imposed from 1992 to 2006 were *nine times* more likely to result in an exoneration than were all homicide convictions over the same time period (Gross & Shaffer, 2012, p. 15). The report further concluded that "the exonerations we know about are 130 times more common for death sentences than for all prison commitments" (Gross & Shaffer, 2012, p. 16).

Of course, since the publication of that report, wrongful convictions have achieved greater public attention and many prosecutors' offices have created conviction integrity units (CIUs) to review questionable convictions (Sutton, 2017). These efforts have led to an increase in the number of exonerations, especially for low-level offenses. Prior to 2012, there was only one year (2000) with at least 100 exonerations. Since 2012, *every year* has seen more than 100 exonerations, and most of these exonerations are now coming from non-death penalty cases (National Registry of Exonerations, 2021). Therefore, to assess whether death row remains a legally advantageous location for the wrongly convicted, we decided to update the findings of the NRE report.

However, to do this, we first needed to identify an appropriate reference group to which to compare death row inmates. The ideal reference group would have the same proportion of wrongly convicted persons in it as death row, but since we cannot know how many persons in prison are factually innocent of the crimes for which they have been convicted, we cannot really know if two different groups have an equal proportion of wrongly convicted individuals in them. Therefore, as we discuss in the methodological appendix for this chapter, we sought a comparison group that was as similar to those sentenced to death as possible. Ideally, this would entail those who were not sentenced to death despite being convicted of a capital offense since they would be the most similar group to those on death row, but unfortunately, there are no data on the number of persons who were convicted of a capital crime but avoided a death sentence or on the number of exonerees who were convicted of capital murder but not sentenced to death. Therefore, as we detail in the methodological appendix for this chapter, we ended up relying on four other reference groups: (1) those sentenced to prison for at least one year, (2) those sentenced to LWOP for any crime, (3) those sentenced to LWOP for murder, and (4) former death row inhabitants. Now, none of these reference groups is perfect, but when combined they provide a pretty good indication of whether the innocent on death row fare better than other wrongly convicted individuals. For readers who are interested in such details, we describe how and why we selected these groups and how we calculated their probability of exoneration in the methodological appendix to this chapter.

Before proceeding with the results of these analyses, a note of caution is necessary. Calculating the likelihood of exoneration is, by necessity, an imprecise exercise. Different data sources cover different time periods, there is a time lag between conviction and exoneration, different sentences have different lengths, we cannot know who will be exonerated in the future or who among those in prison is factually innocent, and it is difficult to find truly equivalent comparison groups, so it is impossible to know with precision how much more likely an innocent death row inmate is to be exonerated than another innocent inmate. Nonetheless, by cobbling together data from different sources, we were able to approximate the differences, and the findings are disquieting—and they should give pause to anyone who has advocated for LWOP because it protects the innocent. Regardless of how we analyzed the data, a death sentence turns out to be more legally advantageous for the innocent, as demonstrated in the following analyses. As such, rather than protecting the innocent, LWOP is sacrificing the many to save the few.

Reference Group 1: All Persons Serving At Least One Year in Prison

First, we compare the exoneration rate for those on death row to everyone sentenced to at least one year in prison. As discussed in the methodological appendix, because the NRE's database includes all known exonerations that have occurred since 1989, we start by looking at the lifetime probability of exoneration, to date, for those convicted from 1989 to 2019, and then because of the increasing attention that has been paid to the issue of wrongful convictions in recent years, we repeat the analysis using only those convictions that occurred from 2012 to 2019. As shown in Table 4.1, both analyses indicate that, to date, those sentenced to death are far more likely to have been exonerated than those serving other prison sentences. For convictions since 1989, to date, death sentences are nearly *81 times more likely* than all new prison commitments to have led to an exoneration (1.151% vs. 0.014%), and for convictions since 2012, death sentences are more than *73 times more likely* to have resulted in an exoneration than all new prison commitments (0.462% vs. 0.006%).[2] It should be noted here that the cumulative number of exonerations will continue to grow as the wrongly convicted have more time to investigate their cases and prove their innocence, so as more time progresses these conclusions could change, especially for the more recent time period. However, the similarity in the results for both the longer and the shorter time periods increases our confidence that these results are picking up a trend that is likely to persist over time.

Reference Group 2: Those Sentenced to LWOP for Any Crime

Of course, comparing those on death row to everyone sentenced to prison is not really a fair comparison because the purpose of our analysis is to determine whether a death sentence or LWOP sentence is more legally advantageous for the wrongly convicted. As the reference group in this analysis includes anyone sentenced to prison for any felony and for any length of time greater than or equal to one year, it may not be a valid proxy for the LWOP population and may not contain as high of a proportion of innocent persons. Therefore, a better comparison is to see whether someone sentenced to LWOP or to death is more likely to be exonerated. Ideally, we would compare those sentenced to death to those sentenced to LWOP for murder, but data on the crime of conviction for those serving LWOP is not available until 2012. Therefore, to be able to include a longer time period in the analysis, we first compare those sentenced to death to everyone sentenced to LWOP, regardless of their crime of conviction.

Unfortunately, data are not available on the cumulative number of LWOP sentences imposed in the nation, so as we discuss in greater detail in the methodological appendix for this chapter, we used the *increase* in the size of the LWOP population between two years as a proxy for the number of new LWOP commitments over the time span. We know this is an undercount since some

TABLE 4.1 Lifetime Exoneration Rate (to Date) for Different Sentences

Year of Conviction	*1989–2019*		*1992–2019*		*2012–2019*			
Sentence	*Death*	*All prison*	*Death*	*LWOP (any crime)*	*Death*	*All prison*	*LWOP (any crime)*	*LWOP for murder*
Total commitments	5,211	12,675,265	4,439	>43,492	433	3,420,878	>6,864	>4,275
Exonerations	60	1,804	47	147	2	215	14	13
Exoneration rate (%)	1.1514	0.0142	1.0588	<0.3380	0.4619	0.0063	<0.2040	<0.3041
Ratio (death/other)	80.90		>3.13		---	73.49	>2.26	>1.52

Notes: All exoneration data come from the National Registry of Exonerations (NRE). The number of death sentences comes from the DPIC's tally of annual death sentences. The number of new prison commitments comes from the BJS's *Prisoners* series. The number of LWOP commitments is tabulated by subtracting the number of people serving LWOP in 1992 and 2012 from the number serving in 2020. This figure is, therefore, incomplete since it assumes no one died or had their LWOP sentence commuted or overturned. For LWOP for murder, the numbers exclude any jurisdiction that did not submit data on crime of conviction in 2012.

people serving LWOP would have died or had their sentences reduced or overturned during this period, so using this number will create an overestimate of the lifetime probability that someone sentenced to LWOP has been exonerated. Nevertheless, we use this number as a starting point because we know if our calculation of death row's lifetime exoneration rate ends up being higher than this overestimate of LWOP's, then the actual lifetime exoneration rate, to date, of those sentenced to death is higher than it is for those sentenced to LWOP. As can be seen in Table 4.1, this turns out to be the case. To date, death sentences imposed since 1992 are *at least* 3.13 times more likely to have led to an exoneration than LWOP sentences implemented over the same period (1.059% vs. 0.338%), and if we restrict the analysis to convictions imposed since 2012, to date, those sentenced to death are *at least* 2.26 times more likely to have been exonerated (0.462% vs. 0.204%).[3] Remember, each of these LWOP calculations is based on the increase in the size of the LWOP population, not the total number of LWOP sentences imposed, which is, obviously, larger than the total growth in LWOP, so these calculations overestimate LWOP's actual exoneration rate and thus underestimate how much more likely death row inhabitants are to be exonerated.

Due to this shortcoming, we also decided to use The Sentencing Project's data to calculate the *annual* exoneration rate for both sentences in each year for which the size of the LWOP population is known. That is, we calculated the percentage of prisoners who started the year serving each respective sentence who were exonerated during that calendar year. This enables us to generate a more precise comparison between the two sentences, but as we discuss in the methodological appendix, using annual data introduces a great deal of randomness into the analysis, which reduces the reliability of any results. Nonetheless, because using these data allows us to know the precise size of the population of potential exonerees, we felt that this analysis could further illuminate the differences in the exoneration potential between those on death row and those serving LWOP. The results of this analysis mostly confirm the findings from the analysis using lifetime data: those on death row are substantially more likely to be exonerated than are those sentenced to "death by incarceration."

As seen in Table 4.2, there were no death row exonerations in 2016, which highlights the randomness of the annual data because there were six death row exonerations in 2015 and five in 2017. Given the annual average of less than four death row exonerations per year since 1973 (Death Penalty Information Center, n.d.c), we have to be extremely careful to avoid drawing too broad of a conclusion from annual data. Nevertheless, despite this caveat, the combined picture from these five years of data strongly suggest that an innocent person on death row is more likely to be able to correct the miscarriage of justice than an innocent person serving LWOP. The data indicate that someone on death row at the start of 2003 was nearly *57 times* more likely to be exonerated during that year than someone who started the year serving LWOP (0.337% vs. 0.006%). In 2008, those who began the year on death row were *ten times* more likely

TABLE 4.2 Annual Exoneration Rate for Those on Death Row and Those Serving LWOP

Year of Exoneration	*2003*		*2008*		*2012*			*2016*			*2020*		
Sentence	*Death row*	*LWOP (any crime)*	*Death row*	*LWOP (any crime)*	*Death row*	*LWOP (any crime)*	*LWOP for murder*	*Death row*	*LWOP (any crime)*	*LWOP for murder*	*Death row*	*LWOP (any crime)*	*LWOP for murder*
Inmates at year start	3,562	33,633	3,215	40,174	3,065	49,081	29,155	2,872	53,290	38,493	2,563	55,945	41,364
Exonerations that year	12	2	4	5	3	6	4	0	11	10	6	24	24
Exoneration rate (%)	0.3369	0.0059	0.1244	0.0124	0.0979	0.0122	0.0137	0.0000	0.0206	0.0260	0.2341	0.0429	0.0580
Ratio (death/LWOP)		56.65		10.00	---	8.01	7.13	---	0.00	0.00	---	5.46	4.03

Notes: The death row population comes from the Bureau of Justice Statistics' *Capital Punishment* series, which lists the death row population as of December 31 of the previous year. The LWOP population comes from the Sentencing Project's reports on life sentences and is supposed to represent the LWOP population as of January 1 of the year. Data on the number of exonerations comes from the National Registry of Exonerations. For LWOP for murder, all numbers exclude any jurisdiction that did not submit data on crime of conviction.

to be exonerated by the end of the year than those serving LWOP (0.124% vs. 0.012%). In 2012, those on death row were *eight times* more likely to be exonerated (0.098% vs. 0.012%), and in 2020, death row inhabitants had more than *five times* the probability of being exonerated (0.234% vs. 0.043%).

Reference Group 3: Those Serving LWOP for Murder

Now, comparing exoneration rates for death sentences to all LWOP sentences is less than ideal since not everyone serving LWOP was convicted of murder while everyone sentenced to death was, but as mentioned earlier, there are no data on the crime of conviction for those serving LWOP until 2012. Therefore, we are only able to compare the exoneration rate of those on death row to those serving LWOP for murder, which is a more appropriate comparison, for a few years. As we discuss in the methodological appendix to this chapter, due to the nature of the NRE's data we could not restrict the analysis just to those convicted of capital murder or even first-degree murder, so we are comparing those sentenced to LWOP for *any degree* of murder to those sentenced to death. As shown in Table 4.1, to date, those sentenced to death since 2012 are *at least* 1.5 times more likely to have been exonerated than those sentenced to LWOP for a murder since 2012.[4] Of course, as noted earlier, since we rely on the increase in the number of persons serving LWOP for murder rather than new commitments, we know that our calculation overestimates the exoneration rate for those serving LWOP, so in reality, the difference between the two exoneration rates is even greater.

As with those sentenced to LWOP for any crime, due to the imprecise nature of our calculation of the lifetime probability of exoneration, we also look at the annual exoneration rate for those serving LWOP for murder in 2012, 2016, and 2020. The results of this analysis are reported in Table 4.2, and they indicate that in 2012, those on death row (0.098%) were more than *seven times* more likely to be exonerated than those serving LWOP for murder (0.014%). As mentioned earlier, in 2016, there were no death row exonerations, but in 2020, there were six (0.234%), giving those who began the year on death row four times the chance of being exonerated by the end of the year than those serving LWOP for murder (0.058%). Although these results are slightly less dramatic than the ones comparing death sentences to all LWOP sentences, even factoring in the oddity of 2016, the disparities are clear: death sentences appear far more likely to result in exonerations than LWOP sentences, including LWOP sentences stemming from murder convictions.

Reference Group 4: Former Death Row Inhabitants

Lastly, thanks to data published by Gross et al. (2014), we are also able to compare the exoneration rate of those on death row to the exoneration rate of those who were initially removed from death row for a reason other than an exoneration or death. Out of our four reference groups, this is probably the best one since both

TABLE 4.3 Exoneration Rate for Death Row and Former Death Row Inmates as of December 31, 2004

Status	*N*	*Exonerations*	*Percentage*
On death row at case conclusion	4,797	107	2.23%
Removed from death row prior to conclusion	2,685	10	0.37%

Source: Data come from Gross et al. (2014)

groups were initially sentenced to death,[5] and it is also a good indication of the likely outcome for current death row inmates if their sentences are replaced with LWOP. Unfortunately, the most recent data are now quite dated, so we cannot be certain that the same trend remains true today. Nonetheless, the results paint the same picture as in the earlier analyses. According to the data, which are shown in Table 4.3, as of December 31, 2004, there were 4,797 people who either remained on death row until their case concluded (death or exoneration) or were still on death row. Of these, 107 had been exonerated, which is an exoneration rate of 2.23% or one out of every 45 people on death row. On the other hand, there were 2,685 individuals who were removed from death row without dying or being exonerated. Only ten of these individuals, or 0.37% (one out of every 269), were subsequently exonerated (Gross, O'Brien, Hu, & Kennedy, 2014, p. 7231). In other words, those sentenced to death are *six times more likely* to be exonerated if they remain on death row than if they are re-sentenced prior to exoneration.

Conclusion

Given the stunningly high known error rate for death sentences, the very real risk of executing the innocent—a serious injustice that has no doubt occurred in the US—is one of the most compelling arguments against the death penalty. Yet, despite the fact that wrongful convictions are endemic to the entire justice system, this same fear has not generated the same level of opposition to LWOP sentences—or death by incarceration. This contradiction is particularly troubling since death-sentenced individuals are afforded greater access to the courts, which then apply additional scrutiny to death sentences, meaning that erroneous convictions are less likely to be discovered when the defendant does not face an execution. Although it impossible to construct perfect comparison groups because of the limited data availability and an inability to know if the proportion of wrongful convictions is equivalent across different groups of prisoners (since it is impossible to know which inmates are, in fact, innocent), the evidence that does exist strongly suggests that the innocent on death row are in a better legal position to prove their innocence than any other group of prisoners.

No matter how we analyzed the data, death row inmates were more likely to be exonerated than the comparison group. Even assuming that wrongful convictions are more common in capital cases, it is unlikely that differences of the magnitude identified in our analyses can be accounted for solely by a higher proportion of innocent people on death row. The additional attention that death sentences invoke clearly benefits the innocent on death row. Even among those sentenced to death, exonerations were *six times* more likely for those still on death row than they were for those removed from death row prior to exoneration. As such, the data that are available (limited though they may be) strongly suggest that, from a legal perspective, LWOP is actually worse than death for the innocent because their innocence is more likely to be discovered if they are scheduled to be executed than if they are simply sentenced to die in prison.

To be clear, these findings are hardly an endorsement of the death penalty. On the contrary, these findings should shatter the illusion that the American criminal justice system is effectively diverting the innocent out of the system and illustrate that additional oversight is also needed in non-capital cases. One out of every 49 death sentences that has been imposed since 1973 has been overturned due to the defendant's innocence,[6] and these are just the errors we know about. The actual error rate for death sentences has been estimated to be more than double the known error rate (Gross, O'Brien, Hu, & Kennedy, 2014). Yet, as this chapter has shown, it is highly probable that the innocent who are sentenced to death are in the best position to prove their innocence and therefore have the most success doing so, as mentioned by the Maryland Commission on Capital Punishment (2008): "Had those same defendants been sentenced to life imprisonment, or a term of years, their cases might not have been reviewed as carefully and by so many different parties. As a result, some of the injustices with which the public has recently become acquainted might not have been corrected" (p. 188). In this regard, LWOP is not an improvement over the death penalty for the innocent.

This chapter illustrates that while our death sentencing system is horribly (and probably irredeemably) broken, the super due process protections afforded to those who are sentenced to death at least work better than the rest of the system does. Capital punishment represents an extremely small subset of the overall criminal justice apparatus—a tiny and select subgroup of criminal convictions—yet, we have nonetheless discovered nearly 200 wrongly condemned persons in the last half-century just among this miniscule sample. Imagine how many more we would find if we gave the same attention and judicial review to non-capital cases. Therefore, super due process protections should be expanded to all incarcerated people. Otherwise, innocent individuals sentenced to LWOP will remain in a *worse* legal position than they would have been if they had been sentenced to be executed. All those convicted of crimes deserve a thorough review of their cases to try to catch as many mistakes as possible, but as it currently stands, only inhabitants of death row are entitled to this protection. As such, the only way LWOP could possibly be construed as a better outcome for a factually innocent defendant than a death sentence is if the additional court access and scrutiny that are currently reserved for those on death row are expanded to allow those serving LWOP to access them as well.

There is an obvious trade off here, though. If more defendants are suddenly able to access the courts for post-conviction proceedings, without a dramatic expansion of the court system's capacity, the system would quickly become overwhelmed, which would likely lead to lower reversal rates (Liebman et al., 2002). Therefore, to truly be effective, expanded due process protections also require a substantial investment of money and resources, which is one of the reasons death sentences are so much more expensive than life sentences (see Chapter 5). Such an investment would, therefore, eat into the financial argument in favor of LWOP that many abolitionists make. In other words, it is simply not tenable to be simultaneously concerned about innocence and cost. Considering cost was one of the rationales proffered by many of the states that have abolished the death penalty in the 21st century (Warden, 2012), it should come as no surprise that none of these states have granted additional due process protections to those serving LWOP, which means that those who were wrongly convicted of murder in those states are probably worse off now than they were prior to abolition. In other words, to prevent the execution of a few innocent people, we have likely condemned far more innocent people to die in prison.

Methodological Appendix

To determine whether those sentenced to death are more likely to be exonerated than those sentenced to LWOP, we first needed to identify an appropriate reference group. Unfortunately, it is impossible to know how many people sent to prison or to death row are actually innocent of the crimes for which they have been convicted, and defendants charged with different offenses may not be equally likely to be wrongfully convicted. In fact, wrongful convictions are probably *more* likely in murder—especially capital murder—cases than they are in other cases (Gross, 1996). Murders, particularly gruesome ones, generate greater publicity and thus more pressure on police to solve the crime—even in the absence of any probative evidence. They are also less likely to have living witnesses or victims to assist the police or to contradict errors, which means police are more likely to rely on incentivized informants or coercive interrogation techniques, both of which provide notoriously unreliable evidence, or to fabricate evidence altogether. The incentive for jailhouse snitches to lie or for the real culprits to divert attention away from themselves are typically greater in murder cases as well since the police are likely to offer bigger favors to informants and the peril to the real killers is greater in homicide cases—especially well publicized capital murder cases. The same pressures police experience are also felt by prosecutors, who may be less likely to dismiss shaky homicide cases. In fact, prosecutors lose a greater proportion of homicide trials than other trials, which suggests that juries do vet out at least some of the innocent defendants but also that prosecutors tend to take weaker homicide cases to trial than they do for other cases, which increases the odds of a wrongful conviction (Gross, 1996).

Then, of course, there are distinctive features of capital trials that may tip the scales toward conviction. First, the same publicity and public pressures that influence police and prosecutors may influence jurors as well, making them more likely to convict (Gross, 1996). Second, hearing the details of a heinous crime during trial may prejudice jurors in the direction of conviction. Third, social science studies have demonstrated that the death qualification process itself distorts the jury pool in two ways that increase the likelihood of conviction. The death qualification process tends to eliminate more liberal potential jurors, leaving behind jurors who are more pro-prosecution and conviction-prone to begin with while simultaneously causing jurors to begin thinking about punishment prior to the guilt stage of the trial—a fact that causes them to already think about the defendant as guilty (Fitzgerald & Ellsworth, 1984; Fleury-Steiner, 2004; Haney, 1984; Haney, 1997; Haney, Hurtado, & Vega, 1994; Haney, Sontag, & Costanzo, 1994; Sandys, Walsh, Pruss, & Cunningham, 2014; Young, 2004). Lastly, the bifurcated capital trial design distracts defense counsel from the guilt stage since they need to spread their quite limited resources across both the guilt and sentencing phases, and it may be strategically advantageous to focus more on the punishment stage, thus reducing the quality of representation in the guilt stage (Gross, 1996). Therefore, it is possible that death row exonerations are more likely simply because wrongful convictions are more common in capital cases.

Due to these factors, it was necessary to construct comparison groups that would be as similar to those sentenced to death as possible in terms of the likelihood of being wrongfully convicted. Thus, the ideal comparison group would be those convicted of a capital offense but not sentenced to death since there is little reason to suspect that those sentenced to death are more likely to be innocent than their counterparts who were also convicted of capital crimes but ended up with a non-capital sentence. If anything, we would expect the opposite to be true. Research with capital jurors indicates that the number one reason they would vote against a death sentence is "lingering doubts about the defendant's guilt" (Garvey, 1998, p. 1563). Additionally, when juries are unable to reach a unanimous verdict on guilt (i.e., the cases with reasonable doubt), they will often reach a compromise verdict in which the holdouts will agree to vote guilty in exchange for the pro-death jurors agreeing to vote for a life sentence (Bowers, Sandys, & Steiner, 1998). Lastly, the fear of receiving a death sentence may coerce innocent capital defendants into pleading guilty in exchange for a life sentence (Gross, 1996). Those who are tried, obviously, are more likely to be acquitted than those who plead guilty, which should reduce wrongful convictions among those who go to trial relative to those who plead guilty, and guilty pleas are, obviously, less likely to lead to a death sentence than trials. All of these factors suggest that those who are convicted of capital offenses but avoid a death sentence are *more* likely to be innocent than the ones sentenced to death. As such, if death row inmates are more likely to be exonerated than convicted capital defendants who are *not* sentenced to death, this would be compelling evidence that the extra post-trial scrutiny afforded to death sentences is critical for helping uncover wrongful convictions that would have never been discovered otherwise. Unfortunately, data that would allow us to make this comparison simply do not exist. We do not know how many defendants were convicted of a capital offense but avoided a death sentence, nor do we know how many of those people were subsequently exonerated.

One way to try to overcome this shortcoming would be to compare the likelihood of exoneration from death row to the likelihood of exoneration for all others convicted of murder. Then, we would at least be comparing individuals convicted of the same offense and thus many of the pressures that produce wrongful convictions will be present in both groups. Unfortunately, the Bureau of Justice Statistics (BJS) stopped reporting the number of convictions by crime in 2006, which means we could not update the National Registry of Exonerations' (NRE) 2012 report that found that those sentenced to death from 1992 to 2006 were exonerated at *nine times* the rate of all individuals convicted of murder in this time span (Gross & Shaffer, 2012). While that comparison is telling, wrongful convictions have been gaining increasing attention in recent years, and more non-capital convictions are now being overturned. Therefore, it is unclear if these conclusions remain true today.

As such, we sought to update these findings using the most recent possible data and the most similar possible reference groups. Based upon the available data, we identified four potential comparison groups: (1) those sentenced to prison for at least one year, (2) those serving LWOP sentences, (3) those serving LWOP sentences for murder, and (4) those who were sentenced to death and subsequently had their death sentence overturned without having their conviction overturned. None of these reference groups is perfect, but they are the best available comparison groups, and when considered together, they are able to provide a fairly reliable indicator of whether the legal protections afforded to those sentenced to death benefit the wrongly convicted. Of these four reference groups, the first is, obviously, the least similar to death row inhabitants, but since those sentenced to LWOP do not receive any additional procedural protections that other prisoners do not receive, this reference group at least provides a good starting point. Furthermore, this is the largest reference group, so it provides a fairly stable and thus reliable estimate of one's potential for exoneration if not sentenced to death. The second group, "those serving LWOP sentences" is less similar to those sentenced to death than the third group, "those serving LWOP sentences for murder," but since there are no data on the crime of conviction for those serving LWOP prior to 2012, we decided to include this group as well so we could include longer time frames in our analysis. Lastly, the fourth group is probably the best proxy for those convicted of capital offenses but not sentenced to death since they were also convicted of a capital crime but are no longer facing the threat of an execution. This group is also a good approximation of the likely outcome for those on death row if the death penalty is abolished and replaced with LWOP. We chose not to rely solely on this comparison, because it does contain some flaws. First, those who have been removed from death row represent only a fraction of those who were convicted of capital crimes but who are not facing a potential execution since most of those convicted of capital crimes are not sentenced to death in the first place (see Chapter 5). Therefore, this group may not be representative of all those convicted of capital offenses but not sentenced to death. In fact, because their cases have already undergone court scrutiny and their sentences have already been overturned while their convictions have remained intact, one could argue that this group may be less likely to be innocent than others convicted of capital crimes or even those convicted of non-capital murder. Thus, it may not be as good of a comparison as it initially appears. Secondly, the only available data on this group are now quite outdated (i.e., year-end 2004), so we cannot tell if the findings remain applicable today. Lastly, the size of this group is substantially smaller than the other reference groups, which reduces the stability and therefore the reliability of the results. In other words, none of our reference groups are perfect, and as our comparisons get more valid, the reliability of our results decreases. Therefore, we felt it was important to perform all four comparisons to see if they each told the same story.

Data and Calculations

To calculate the exoneration rate for each of our comparison groups, we divided the number of exonerees in the group by the size of the group. To determine these values, we relied on the sources described next and used the most recent available data as of September 30, 2021.

Death Sentences and Death Row Population

There are two potential sources of data on the cumulative number of death sentences imposed: the BJS's *Capital Punishment* series and the Death Penalty Information Center (DPIC)'s tabulation of the number of national death sentences by year. These counts do not align, but the DPIC states, "We only count the number of 'new sentences,' i.e., we do not recount individuals who were sentenced to death in a previous year, had their sentences overturned, and were resentenced in the current year" (Death Penalty Information Center, n.d.a). Therefore, to avoid double counting the same person for the same crime, we elected to count the number of death sentences using the DPIC data. Although we know there were 18 death sentences imposed in 2020 (Death Penalty Information Center, 2020), we have excluded 2020 from our count for two reasons. First, at the time of our analysis, we did not yet have a count for any of our reference groups in 2020, and second, as of this writing, no one sentenced to death in 2020 has yet had time to be exonerated.

We derived our number of death row exonerations from the NRE's online database. Because the NRE's database only includes known exonerations that have occurred since 1989, we limited our pool of potential exonerees to those sentenced to death since the beginning of 1989. This restriction ensures we do not miss any exonerations from our pool of potential exonerees. Because the earliest available LWOP data are from 1992, we also created a group that includes only those sentenced to death since the start of 1992 for comparison with those serving LWOP. Finally, because wrongful convictions have received more attention in recent years and the number of exonerations has been increasing, especially for lower-level offenses (National Registry of Exonerations, 2021; Sutton, 2017), we also created a third "death sentences" group, which includes only those death sentences imposed in 2012 or later. We chose 2012 as our cut-off for two reasons. First, 2011 was the last year in which the number of exonerations in the NRE database fell below 100, and second, 2012 is the first year for which data are available on the crime of conviction for those serving LWOP.

To determine the number of these persons who were exonerated, we counted the number of individuals in the NRE database who were convicted in 1989 or later and sentenced to death (regardless of when the exoneration took place). We then cross-checked these data with the DPIC's Innocence Database. In the time period of interest, there are eight exonerations that appear in the DPIC data that do not appear in the NRE data (three of them for convictions since 2012). It is not clear why this discrepancy exists. There is also one death row exoneration in the NRE data that does not appear in the DPIC data. This is likely because that exoneration involves an individual who was convicted of six homicides and sentenced to death and then subsequently had his convictions vacated after DNA evidence linked one of those killings to a serial killer who had confessed to that crime. However, despite the evidence suggesting that all six murders were probably committed by the same person, the defendant was reconvicted on the other five counts and sentenced to LWOP (National Registry of Exonerations, 2020). Due to the reconvictions, this individual does not meet the DPIC's standards to be considered an exoneree. To maintain consistency in the counting of exonerations across all comparison groups, we relied on the NRE's data to tabulate the number of death row exonerations. We then repeated this process for sentences imposed since 1992 and those imposed since 2012. Although we rely on the NRE's data to produce our comparisons, in the interest of transparency, we also provided information in the endnotes describing what the lifetime exoneration rate for death sentences would be if we had relied on the DPIC dataset.

As we discuss further, we also tabulated the likelihood that someone on death row at the end of one calendar year would be exonerated during the subsequent calendar year—what we call the annual exoneration rate. Due to the availability of LWOP data, we calculated this rate for exonerations that took place in 2003, 2008, 2012, 2016, and 2020, so we needed to know the size of the death row population at the end of 2002, 2007, 2011, 2015, and 2019. Data on the size of the death row population at the end of a year is derived from the BJS's annual *Capital Punishment* report. It reports the death row population on the last day of the year the report covers *and* the immediately preceding year to show the change in the composition of death row. This means the number of prisoners under a sentence of death at the end of a particular year appears in two different reports. However, these two numbers do not always match; therefore, to account for the probability that the discrepancy exists because the BJS was able to get more accurate or up-to-date data, we utilized the more recent report to obtain the size of the death row population (i.e., to obtain the death row population at the end of 2007, we used the reported death row population for December 31, 2007, in the BJS's 2008 *Capital Punishment* report rather than its 2007 report).

The number of death row exonerations during a given year again comes from the NRE's database on exonerations and includes anyone who was exonerated during the calendar year of interest, regardless of when the conviction took place, and whose sentence was death. Because of how long it takes the wrongly convicted to prove their innocence, there is no record of anyone being sentenced to death and then exonerated in the same calendar year, so none of these exonerations include someone who was not on death row at the end of the previous year. We also cross-checked these data with the DPIC's Innocence Database, and the numbers matched for all five years.

All Persons Sentenced to At Least One Year in Prison

For the universe of potential exonerees from prison, we used all new court commitments to prison for a term of at least one year. These data come from the BJS's *Prisoners* series and are available via the BJS's online *Corrections Statistical Analysis Tool*. For this count, we only included *new* court commitments, not all prison admissions since many admissions are the result of someone violating the terms of parole, and we did not want to count someone twice for the same offense. At the time of data collection, the most recent year in the BJS dataset was 2019, and, as we mentioned above, the NRE database includes all known exonerations that have taken place since 1989. Therefore, our universe of potential exonerees is anyone sentenced to prison for at least one year for a new crime from the start of 1989 to the end of 2019 (as of this writing, no one sentenced to prison for at least one year more recently than 2019 has yet been exonerated anyway).

As with death row exonerations, the count of exonerations comes from the NRE's online database, and it includes anyone in the database whose conviction is from 1989 to 2019 and who was sentenced to at least one year. We then repeated this process for convictions since the start of 2012 to see if the greater attention now being paid to wrongful convictions produces different conclusions for these more recent convictions.

A couple notes of caution about this reference group are necessary. First, not all prison sentences are the same length. Since most people do not seek exoneration after they have been released or after a wrongly convicted loved one has passed away, those with shorter sentences are less likely to be exonerated simply because they have less time (and less incentive) to prove their innocence, so we cannot attribute differences in the probability of being exonerated entirely to the additional legal protections death-sentenced inmates receive. Second, although we consider this calculation the lifetime probability of exoneration, it is actually the lifetime probability as of the date of data collection. People who are currently sentenced to prison will continue to be exonerated in the future; consequently, this rate will change as more wrongful convictions are discovered.

LWOP Sentences and Population

To create more equivalent comparison groups, we next compared the exoneration potential of those sentenced to death to that of individuals sentenced to LWOP. We recognize that using those sentenced to LWOP for murder is an even better reference group, but data on crime of conviction for those sentenced to LWOP is not available until 2012. Therefore, to include longer time periods, we started by tabulating an estimate of the exoneration rate for everyone sentenced to LWOP, regardless of the crime for which they were convicted. Unfortunately, to our knowledge, there is no published count on the number of new LWOP commitments as there is for new death sentences or new court commitments to prison. Therefore, we utilized two data sources to attempt to approximate this number. First, the 1992 *Sourcebook of Criminal Justice Statistics* lists the number of persons serving LWOP as of September 30, 1992. Second, The Sentencing Project has published a count of the number of persons serving LWOP in 2003, 2008, 2012, 2016, and 2020. According to Ashley Nellis (personal communication, August 24, 2020) of The Sentencing Project, these counts represent the LWOP population as of the final day of the previous year. Therefore, while we do not know how many persons received a LWOP sentence in a given time period, we could calculate the *increase* in the size of the LWOP population between two reports. As such, the pool of potential lifetime LWOP exonerees is defined as the increase in the size of the LWOP population from September 30, 1992, to December 31, 2019. As with our other reference groups, we also repeated the process for the period beginning at the start of 2012 to assess whether more recent convictions continue to demonstrate the same pattern as the older ones. We know that these numbers will both be smaller than the total number of new LWOP commitments during the periods in question since some people serving LWOP sentences died while others had their sentences overturned or shortened, but it at least produces a *minimum* number of new LWOP commitments. Therefore, readers should be aware that the exoneration rate that this universe of potential exonerees produces is an overestimate of the true lifetime likelihood that someone sentenced to LWOP has been exonerated.

Again, the count of exonerees from this group comes from the NRE's database and includes any exoneree who was convicted from 1992 to 2019 and sentenced to LWOP. It should be noted that since the count of LWOP in 1992 is from September 30, it is possible that a few of the exonerations from 1992 convictions come from individuals who are outside our pool of potential exonerees. There are only six total LWOP exonerations from convictions that occurred in 1992, so this problem should not substantively affect the results, but to the extent that it does, it could inflate the exoneration rate of LWOP admissions even further. As with our other analyses, we then repeated this process for convictions from 2012 to 2019.

Because the available data on LWOP do not permit a more precise calculation of the lifetime probability of exoneration from a LWOP sentence, we also calculated the *annual* exoneration rate of those serving LWOP. This is defined as the percentage of persons serving LWOP at the start of a calendar year who were exonerated during that calendar year, so the size of our pool of potential LWOP exonerees in a given year is the total number of people serving LWOP in that year according to The Sentencing Project. As mentioned above, the Sentencing Project report these data for 2003, 2008, 2012, 2016, and 2020, so we looked at the annual exoneration rate in each of these five years. The number of exonerations for each of these years is the number of people in the NRE database who were sentenced to LWOP and exonerated in the year of interest (regardless of when they were convicted). As with death sentences, there is no record of anyone being sentenced to LWOP and exonerated in the same year, so all of those included in our count of exonerees were also included in our pool of potential exonerees.

A note of caution is necessary here as well. Using annual data introduces a great deal of randomness and volatility into the analysis, especially for statistically rare events like exonerations, so it is important not to generalize too much from the findings produced by this analysis. The lifetime data are clearly a much better way to assess which group is more likely to be exonerated, but since the available data provide a precise size of the LWOP population at the beginning of certain years and thus enable us to generate a precise tabulation of the likelihood that someone serving LWOP at the start of a year would be exonerated during that year, we included the annual data to get a more complete picture of the exoneration potential of both those sentenced to LWOP and to death.

LWOP for Murder

In 2012, The Sentencing Project began collecting data on the crime of conviction for those serving LWOP. Therefore, we repeated our tabulation for both the lifetime and annual LWOP exoneration rates described above for the time periods since 2012 using *just* those sentenced to LWOP for murder. Unfortunately, the NRE's database does not specify which degree of murder an exoneree was convicted of, so we could not limit the analysis solely to those convicted of first-degree murder. Therefore, for this analysis, our pool of potential LWOP for murder exonerees includes all those serving LWOP for *any* degree of murder. These data were provided to us by Ashley Nellis (personal communication, August 21, 2020, and June 24, 2021) of The Sentencing Project. However, crime of conviction was not submitted by five states (Florida, Hawaii, Illinois, Tennessee, and Virginia) or the federal government in 2012, so these six jurisdictions were excluded from our calculation of the lifetime probability of exoneration, and no LWOP for murder exoneration from any of these jurisdictions was factored into the calculation. As it turns out, as of this writing, no one convicted in 2012 or later and sentenced to LWOP has yet been exonerated in any of the jurisdictions with missing data, so by excluding these six jurisdictions (since we do not know what the change in the LWOP for murder population was), this calculation inflates the lifetime exoneration rate of those sentenced to LWOP for murder even more than it already is.

We also excluded any jurisdiction that did not provide data on crime of conviction from the three calculations of the annual exoneration rate of those serving LWOP for murder (2012, 2016, and 2020). This includes the six jurisdictions discussed above for 2012 along with Virginia and the federal system in 2016. All jurisdictions reported crime of conviction data in 2020. Because of these missing data, we ended up excluding two exonerations in 2012 (one from Illinois and one from Virginia) and one in 2016 (from Virginia).

Current and Former Death Row Inhabitants

The biggest flaw with each of the aforementioned comparisons is that we do not know how many individuals in the reference groups were convicted of a *capital* murder, and so, for the reasons discussed earlier, we cannot be sure they are equally likely to have been wrongly convicted. Therefore, since data on the number of capital murder convictions that have not resulted in a death sentence are unavailable, for our final analysis, we decided to compare the exoneration rate of former death row inhabitants to current death row inhabitants. For this comparison, we utilized data published by Gross, O'Brien, Hu, and Kennedy (2014). In their paper, they listed the case status as of December 31, 2004, for everyone sentenced to death between 1973 and 2004. The current death row inhabitants group includes everyone sentenced to death during this time frame who either remained on death row until the conclusion of their case (either death or exoneration) or was still on death row as of year-end 2004. This group consists of everyone who was executed, who died on death row without being executed, who was still on death row, and who was exonerated while still facing a potential death sentence. To maintain a consistent comparison, we used these same data to tabulate the size of the comparison group, former death row inhabitants. This group includes those who were "removed from death row but not exonerated" and those "exonerated, not under threat of execution." To ensure we were using a consistent comparison, we did not rely on the NRE's database to determine the number of exonerees from each group. Instead, we used the number of exonerations for each group provided by Gross et al. (2014).

Notes

1 From 1973 to the end of 2020, there were 8,752 death sentences imposed in the US (Death Penalty Information Center, n.d.a). As of year-end 2020, 1,529 of those individuals (17.5%) had been executed (Death Penalty Information Center, n.d.b; Snell, 2021) and 2,469 people (28.2%) remained on death row (Snell, 2021). Of those, two have since

been exonerated (Death Penalty Information Center, n.d.c) (and others have no doubt had their sentences overturned without being exonerated), but even if everyone else ends up being executed (which is highly improbable), less than half of death sentences imposed between 1973 and 2020 will end up being carried out.

2 We restricted our analysis to those exonerations in the NRE database; however, there are additional death row exonerations that appear in the DPIC's Innocence Database. It is not clear why this discrepancy exists, but if we were to use the DPIC data instead of the NRE data to calculate the death row exoneration rate, those sentenced to death since 1989 would be 90 times more likely to be exonerated than all persons sentenced to at least one year in prison, and those sentenced to death since 2012 would be 181 times more likely to be exonerated.

3 If we use the DPIC Innocence Database instead, the lifetime exoneration rate of those sentenced to death since 1992 is 1.216%, which is at least 3.60 times greater than the lifetime probability of someone sentenced to LWOP since 1992 being exonerated, and the lifetime probability of exoneration for someone sentenced to death since 2012 is 1.155%, which is 5.66 times greater than the highest possible lifetime LWOP exoneration rate over this same period.

4 If we use the DPIC Innocence Database instead, the lifetime death row exoneration to date is 3.80 times greater than the highest possible LWOP for murder exoneration rate. It should also be noted here that we excluded five states and the federal government from our analysis because they did not report crime of conviction in 2012. None of these jurisdictions has yet had anyone exonerated who was convicted since 2012 and sentenced to LWOP. Therefore, if we were able to factor in the increase in the number of persons serving LWOP for murder in those jurisdictions, the lifetime exoneration rate for those sentenced to LWOP for murder would decline even further, so we are quite confident that someone sentenced to death is more likely to be exonerated than someone sentenced to LWOP for murder.

5 Although, as we discuss in the methodological appendix, it is possible that former death row inmates are less likely to be innocent since they have already had their cases scrutinized.

6 As of year-end 2021, 8,770 death sentences had been imposed since 1973. Of those, 180 (2.05%) have resulted in an exoneration (Death Penalty Information Center, n.d.c).

References

Applebome, P. (1993, March 3). Alabama releases man held on death row for six years. *New York Times*, pp. A1, B11. Retrieved July 23, 2020, from New York Times: https://www.nytimes.com/1993/03/03/us/alabama-releases-man-held-on-death-row-for-six-years.html

Banner, S. (2002). *The death penalty: An American history*. Cambridge, MA: Harvard University Press.

Barkow, R. E. (2009). The court of life and death: The two tracks of constitutional sentencing law and the case for uniformity. *Michigan Law Review, 107*, 1145–1205.

Baumgartner, F. R., & Dietrich, A. W. (2015, March 17). *Most death penalty sentences are overturned. Here's why that matters.* Retrieved from Washington Post: https://www.washingtonpost.com/news/monkey-cage/wp/2015/03/17/most-death-penalty-sentences-are-overturned-heres-why-that-matters/

Bowers, W. J., Sandys, M., & Steiner, B. D. (1998). Foreclosed impartiality in capital sentencing: Jurors' predispositions, guilt-trial experience, and premature decision making. *Cornell Law Review, 83*, 1476–1556.

Cauthen, J. N., & Latzer, B. (2008). Why so long? Explaining processing time in capital appeals. *The Justice System Journal, 29*, 298–312.

Daniell, F. R. (1936, January 26). Bitterness is added to Scottsboro Case. New York Times, p. E12.

Death Penalty Information Center. (2020, December 16). *The death penalty in 2020: Year end report.* Retrieved December 18, 2020, from Death Penalty Information Center: https://files.deathpenaltyinfo.org/reports/year-end/YearEndReport2020.pdf

Death Penalty Information Center. (n.d.a). *Death sentences in the United States since 1977.* Retrieved December 21, 2021, from Death Penalty Information Center: https://deathpenaltyinfo.org/facts-and-research/sentencing-data/death-sentences-in-the-united-states-from-1977-by-state-and-by-year

Death Penalty Information Center. (n.d.b). *Execution database.* Retrieved December 21, 2021, from Death Penalty Information Center: https://deathpenaltyinfo.org/executions/execution-database

Death Penalty Information Center. (n.d.c). *Innocence database.* Retrieved December 21, 2021, from Death Penalty Information Center: https://deathpenaltyinfo.org/policy-issues/innocence-database

Dieter, R. C. (2014). The issue of costs in the death penalty debate. In J. R. Acker, R. M. Bohm, & C. S. Lanier (Eds.), *America's experiment with capital punishment: Reflections on the past, present, and future of the ultimate penal sanction* (pp. 595–609). Durham, NC: Carolina Academic Press.

Fitzgerald, R., & Ellsworth, P. C. (1984). Due process vs. crime control: Death qualification and jury attitudes. *Law and Human Behavior, 8*, 31–51.

Fleury-Steiner, B. (2004). *Jurors' stories of death: How America's death penalty invests in inequality.* Ann Arbor, MI: University of Michigan Press.

Furman v. Georgia, 408 U.S. 238 (US Supreme Court 1972).

Garvey, S. P. (1998). Aggravation and mitigation in capital cases: What do jurors think? *Columbia Law Review, 98*, 1538–1576.

Griffin v. United States, 336 U.S. 704 (US Supreme Court 1949).

Gross, S. R. (1996). The risks of death: Why erroneous convictions are common in capital cases. *Buffalo Law Review, 44*, 469–500.

Gross, S. R., & Shaffer, M. (2012, June). *Exonerations in the United States, 1989–2012: Report by the National Registry of Exonerations.* Retrieved June 29, 2020, from National Registry of Exonerations: http://www.law.umich.edu/special/exoneration/Documents/exonerations_us_1989_2012_full_report.pdf

Gross, S. R., O'Brien, B., Hu, C., & Kennedy, E. H. (2014). Rate of false conviction of criminal defendants who are sentenced to death. *Proceedings of the National Academy of Sciences of the United States of America, 111*, 7230–7235.

Haney, C. (1984). On the selection of capital juries: The biasing effects of the death-qualification process. *Law and Human Behavior, 8*, 121–132.

Haney, C. (1997). Commonsense justice and capital punishment: Problematizing the 'will of the people'. *Psychology, Public Policy, and Law, 3*, 303–337.

Haney, C., Hurtado, A., & Vega, L. (1994). 'Modern' death qualification: New data on its biasing effects. *Law and Human Behavior, 18*, 619–633.

Haney, C., Sontag, L., & Costanzo, S. (1994). Deciding to take a life: Capital juries, sentencing instructions, and the jurisprudence of death. *Journal of Social Issues, 50*, 149–176.

Henry, J. S. (2012). Death-in-prison sentences: Overutilized and underscrutinized. In C. J. Ogletree, & A. Sarat (Eds.), *Life without parole: America's new death penalty?* (pp. 66–95). New York: NYU Press.

Johnson, D. T. (2020). *The culture of capital punishment in Japan.* Cham, Switzerland: Palgrave Macmillan.

Kaplan, A. B., Collins, P. A., & Mayhew, V. L. (2016, November 16). *Oregon's death penalty: A cost analysis*. Retrieved December 21, 2020, from Lewis & Clark Law School: https://law.lclark.edu/live/files/22888-oregons-death-penalty-a-cost-analysis-2016

Kennedy v. Louisiana, 554 U.S. 407 (US Supreme Court 2008).

Liebman, J. S. (2000). The overproduction of death. *Columbia Law Review, 100*, 2030–2156.

Liebman, J. S., Fagan, J., Gelman, A., West, V., Davies, G., & Kiss, A. (2002, February 11). *A broken system II: Why there is so much error in capital cases, and what can be done about it*. Retrieved July 15, 2020, from Columbia Law School: http://www2.law.columbia.edu/brokensystem2/report.pdf

Liebman, J. S., Fagan, J., West, V., & Lloyd, J. (2000). Capital attrition: Error rates in capital cases, 1973–1995. *Texas Law Review, 78*, 1839–1865.

Maryland Commission on Capital Punishment. (2008, December 12). *Final report to the General Assembly*. Retrieved January 13, 2021, from Maryland State Archives: https://msa.maryland.gov/megafile/msa/speccol/sc5300/sc5339/000113/012000/012331/unrestricted/20100208e.pdf

National Registry of Exonerations. (2020, February 12). *Hubert Geralds, Jr.* Retrieved July 8, 2021, from National Registry of Exonerations: https://www.law.umich.edu/special/exoneration/Pages/casedetail.aspx?caseid=3795

National Registry of Exonerations. (2021, July 4). *Exonerations by year: DNA and non-DNA*. Retrieved July 4, 2021, from National Registry of Exonerations: http://www.law.umich.edu/special/exoneration/Pages/Exoneration-by-Year.aspx

Ross v. Moffitt, 417 U.S. 600 (US Supreme Court 1974).

Sandys, M., Walsh, S. M., Pruss, H., & Cunningham, D. (2014). Stacking the deck for guilt and death: The failure of death qualification to ensure impartiality. In J. R. Acker, R. M. Bohm, & C. S. Lanier (Eds.), *America's experiment with capital punishment: Reflections on the past, present, and future of the ultimate penal sanction* (3rd ed., pp. 393–423). Durham, NC: Carolina Academic.

Snell, T. L. (2007, January 30). *Capital punishment, 2005*. Retrieved July 15, 2020, from Bureau of Justice Statistics: https://www.bjs.gov/content/pub/pdf/cp05.pdf

Snell, T. L. (2021, December). *Capital punishment, 2020–statistical tables*. Retrieved December 21, 2021, from Bureau of Justice Statistics: https:// bjs.ojp.gov/content/pub/pdf/cp20st.pdf

Steiker, C. S., & Steiker, J. M. (2014). Judicial developments in capital punishment law. In J. R. Acker, R. M. Bohm, & C. S. Lanier (Eds.), *America's experiment with capital punishment: Reflections on the past, present, and future of the ultimate penal sanction* (3rd ed., pp. 77–100). Durham, NC: Carolina Academic.

Sutton, L. (Ed.). (2017). *Innocent: The fight against wrongful convictions*. New York: Time.

Villaume, A. C. (2005). "Life without parole" and "virtual life sentences": Death sentences by any other name. *Contemporary Justice Review, 8*, 265–277.

Warden, R. (2012). How and why Illinois abolished the death penalty. *Law and Inequality, 30*, 245–286.

Whitmore v. Arkansas, 495 U.S. 149 (US Supreme Court 1990).

Wozniak, K. H. (2012). Legislative abolition of the death penalty: A qualitative analysis. *Studies in Law, Politics, and Society, 57*, 31–70.

Young, R. L. (2004). Guilty until proven innocent: Conviction orientation, racial attitudes, and support for capital punishment. *Deviant Behavior, 25*, 151–167.

5

The Price of Life

The Financial Burden of LWOP

Perhaps counterintuitively, studies have consistently demonstrated that capital punishment is more expensive than life in prison (Dieter, 2014). This reality turns out to be one of the most compelling and effective rationales used by abolitionists in their efforts to get states to repeal capital punishment (Chammah, 2014; Warden, 2012). However, this argument overlooks two critical facts. First, one of the primary reasons capital punishment is so expensive is that it provides defendants with additional procedural safeguards, such as a second state-funded defense attorney, more qualified defense counsel, more extensive pre-trial preparation, more pre-trial litigation, and greater post-conviction appellate scrutiny, which are all designed to prevent or correct wrongful convictions and are thus all *good and necessary expenditures* (Cook, 2009; Kaplan, Collins, & Mayhew, 2016). In other words, abolishing capital punishment *for the purpose of cutting costs* is not necessarily a step toward justice. On the contrary, the shift from capital punishment to LWOP has *increased* the number of individuals sentenced to die in prison while providing fewer procedural protections for the accused.

Second, the studies examining the cost of capital punishment typically compare the cost of a capital trial to a non-capital murder trial or the cost of maintaining capital punishment to the cost of sentencing those same individuals to LWOP. Yet, LWOP is not simply replacing capital punishment; it is being used far more frequently than capital punishment ever was and for a wider variety of offenses, thereby ensnaring many individuals who would never have been death-eligible in the first place. Only around 64% of those serving LWOP in 2020 were convicted of first-degree murder (Nellis, personal communication, April 21, 2021), and, of course, even most people convicted of first-degree murder are not eligible for a death sentence. Between the reinstatement of capital punishment in 1973 and the end of 2020, there were 8,752 different individuals sentenced to death in the US (Death Penalty Information Center, n.d.a).

DOI: 10.4324/9781003161783-7

In contrast, there were more than *six times* that number of people—55,945—serving death by incarceration sentences in 2020. In the early 1990s, as LWOP was about to begin its dramatic expansion, there were only around 2,500 individuals on death row in the US (Greenfield, 1992), and even at its highest population, in 2000, death row only possessed 3,593 condemned individuals (Snell, 2001), which means LWOP is now being used for offenses that would have never resulted in a death sentence. As such, even though each LWOP sentence costs less than each death sentence, it is possible that, due to its greater scale, LWOP could still impose a greater cost burden on the system. In this chapter, we explore this possibility, and the results of our analyses reveal that, in all likelihood, the cost of LWOP exceeds that of capital punishment.

To be clear, this conclusion is not an endorsement of capital punishment; rather, it is further evidence of the central thesis of this book: LWOP is not necessarily an improvement over capital punishment from either a fiscal or human costs perspective. Therefore, death penalty abolition should include abolition of death by incarceration, not an expansion of it, and abolition should not come at the expense of due process protections. Otherwise, as bad as capital punishment is, LWOP will end up being worse.

Yes, Death Sentences Cost More than Life Sentences

State-level studies have repeatedly found that sentencing people to death or even just seeking an execution imposes a larger financial burden than sentencing those same individuals to life. In fact, this conclusion is nearly universal among the studies performed (Oklahoma Death Penalty Review Commission, 2017). Now, there is no precise, nationwide estimate for the cost of capital punishment since not all states' death penalty systems have been studied, and states experience different costs depending on how their systems are structured, how much actors in the system are compensated, and how often the state uses the death penalty (Dieter, 2013; Dieter, 2014). However, one review of 15 state-level studies revealed that seeking the death penalty costs approximately $700,000 more, on average, than not seeking it (Oklahoma Death Penalty Review Commission, 2017, p. 227). Due to the heightened level of prison security and appellate scrutiny dedicated to condemned inmates, these costs are not recouped by executing a few offenders. If anything, they increase even further.

For example, in one of the most comprehensive studies of the death penalty's cost, Roman et al. (2008) found that seeking a single death sentence in Maryland cost nearly $1.8 million over the lifetime of the case, even if the defendant was not sentenced to death, while a capital-eligible case in which the death penalty was not sought cost around $1.1 million, still a hefty amount but not nearly as much as a case in which the death penalty was sought. If a death sentence was imposed, the associated costs ballooned to over $3 million per case. Roman and his colleagues (2008) concluded that for cases tried from 1978 to 1999, the death penalty ended up costing Maryland taxpayers $186 million more than if *those same cases* had been pursued non-capitally. A similar analysis in Washington state determined that the average cost of pursing a death sentence was approximately $3.1 million while the cost of not seeking a death sentence for an aggravated first-degree murder was considerably less, at around $2 million (Collins, Boruchowitz, Hickman, & Larrañaga, 2016). In neighboring Oregon, including the cost of incarceration, a trial that resulted in a death sentence cost approximately $900,000 more than an aggravated murder trial that did not result in a death sentence (Kaplan, Collins, & Mayhew, 2016). These conclusions are not limited to coastal "blue" states either. An analysis of Nebraska's death penalty determined that each capital prosecution cost nearly $1.5 million more than a similar LWOP prosecution (Goss, Strain, & Blalock, 2016).

Even studies conducted by state legislative bodies, rather than academics, have reached the same conclusion. In Nevada, the Legislative Auditor found that "the death penalty, from arrest through the end of incarceration, costs about $532,000 more than other murder cases" (State of Nevada Legislative Auditor, 2014, p. 10). Specifically, a non-capital murder case cost the state around $775,000 whereas an execution cost the state about $1 million, a capital case that did not result in a death sentence had a $1.2 million price tag, and a death sentence that did not result in an execution cost approximately $1.3 million. Indiana's Legislative Services Agency (2015) looked at the cost of sentencing 124 offenders who were eligible for the death penalty in that state and determined that, including the cost of incarceration, seeking the death penalty cost $789,581 per jury trial and $433,702 per guilty plea while the costs associated with seeking LWOP were $185,422 and $164,928, respectively.

Studies that estimate the statewide rather than the per-case cost of capital punishment have reached substantively similar conclusions. In 2000, the *Palm Beach Post* published an estimate that, compared to the cost of sentencing all those convicted of first-degree murder to LWOP, Florida was spending an extra $51 million per year to have capital punishment (Date, 2000). An academic analysis of California's death penalty determined that from the reinstatement of capital punishment in 1978 through 2010, Californians had spent an additional $4 billion on the death penalty relative to the cost of abolition (Alarcón & Mitchell, 2011). Meanwhile, a study in North Carolina concluded that if there was no capital punishment in fiscal years 2005 and 2006, the state would have spent a total of $21.6 million less (Cook, 2009), and another analysis determined that if Illinois had abolished capital punishment in 2000, by mid-year-2010, it would have saved *at least* $150 million (Bienen, 2010). The New Jersey Death Penalty Study Commission (2007) was unable to quantify the precise costs associated with either punishment but did conclude, "The costs of the death penalty are greater than the costs of life in prison without parole ..." (p. 31).

These facts have been instrumental in convincing many states to abolish capital punishment in recent years (Chammah, 2014; Collins, Boruchowitz, Hickman, & Larrañaga, 2016; Dieter, 2014; Warden, 2012). When Nebraska's conservative unicameral legislature voted to override the governor's veto and (temporarily, it turns out) repeal capital punishment in 2015, cost was one of its main concerns (Berman, 2015). As State Senator Colby Coash, who co-sponsored the repeal bill stated, "I've said frequently, if any other program was as inefficient and as costly as this has been, we would've gotten rid of it a long time ago" (Berman, 2015, para 13). In announcing Connecticut's repeal of capital punishment in 2012, Governor Daniel Malloy pointed to the fact that "the people of this state pay for appeal after appeal" as one of the reasons supporting the decision (Ariosto, 2012, para 5). While advocating for New Mexico's abolition bill in 2009, the bill's sponsor, Representative Gail Chasey, argued that abolishing capital punishment would save the state money (CNN, 2009), and after the legislature passed the bill, Governor Bill Richardson told reporters that capital punishment's cost was one of his major reasons for signing it (Boyd, 2009).

But Those Costs Save Lives

This discussion of costs, however, overlooks the reason *why* capital cases cost so much more and simply assumes that those additional expenditures are inherently wasteful. Yes, some of these expenses are related to the penalty phase of the trial and the additional investigation that accompanies it and to the segregated housing for those on death row, both of which would be unnecessary without capital punishment, but not all of these extra expenditures are "wasteful" as some have characterized them (for further elaboration, see Kleinstuber, Joy, & Mansley, 2016). As mentioned earlier, much of the additional cost associated with capital cases is the result of additional due process protections afforded to capital defendants: more qualified defense counsel, more vigorous representation (e.g., more defense filings and pre-trial motions), a second defense attorney, more experts, more appellate rights, greater appellate scrutiny, and a higher proportion of cases being overturned on appeal (Barkow, 2009; Cauthen & Latzer, 2008; Cook, 2009; Dieter, 2014; Gross, 1996; Kaplan, Collins, & Mayhew, 2016; Liebman et al., 2002). These features should not be thought of as "wasteful" or in negative terms; they are necessary to prevent and correct errors and thus are *good due process measures* that should be accessible to *all* criminal defendants. In fact, it is deeply ironic that the two primary impetuses for death penalty abolition have been "awareness of the inevitability of death penalty mistakes and the fiscal implications of maintaining" capital punishment (Warden, 2012, p. 285) since these are two contradictory concerns. It is the very expenses of capital punishment that have enabled our awareness of and ability to correct those mistakes.

It has been well documented that the quality of indigent defense in the US is appallingly low, with most public defenders being overworked, underfunded, and under-resourced, all of which contributes to wrongful convictions (Alexander, 2012; Canon, 2015; Godsey, 2017; Norris, Bonventre, & Acker, 2018; Reiman & Leighton, 2013). If anything, Americans should be spending *more* on indigent defense, not less, but abolishing capital punishment *for the purpose of saving money* is almost guaranteed to make the situation *worse*. As Jonathan Gradess testified before the Maryland Commission on Capital Punishment:

> If the death penalty is abolished, it is unlikely that the unique procedural protections that apply in capital cases will be held to apply in life without parole cases. In the four years since New York has had life without parole as the exclusive punishment for first-degree murder, this has been the case. There has been no revision of the statutes to provide for specialized services in life without parole cases. Nor has a broader right to counsel emerged or a more extensive right to appeal. And no greater procedural protections have been articulated by the courts. The experiences in Massachusetts and Michigan, both of which have only life without parole as the most severe penalty for murder, is similar.
>
> *(Maryland Commission on Capital Punishment, 2008, p. 54)*

Likewise, "The imposition of 'life without parole' in Massachusetts, while subject to strict due process and legal/constitutional scrutiny, has never been hamstrung by the extraordinary constitutional review that death cases rightfully receive ..." (Scott Harshbarger as cited in Maryland Commission on Capital Punishment, 2008, p. 54). In his analysis of North Carolina's death penalty, Cook (2009) pointed out that one reason capital punishment costs more than LWOP is because "If these cases had been sentenced to LWOP rather than death, the opportunities to pursue post-conviction appeals would have been sharply curtailed" (p. 25). In other words, abolishing capital punishment to "save money" will reduce the protections available to defendants, and as our analysis in the previous chapter revealed, it will also make it harder for the wrongly convicted to get justice.

This fact is not an argument against abolishing capital punishment. It is simply a recognition that saving money is not inherently good and that abolishing capital punishment without extending access to the due process protections currently available only to capital defendants does not benefit the cause of justice. There are lots of problems with capital punishment, but the extra scrutiny given to capital cases is not one of them. In fact, it is quite perverse to argue that capital punishment should be abolished because it affords defendants too many costly protections, especially while being simultaneously concerned about wrongful convictions. Super due process is the one positive aspect of capital punishment in America. We should not be eliminating it; rather, we should be making it accessible to all defendants. As we detailed in the previous chapter, these super due process protections are potentially lifesaving, and getting rid of them essentially guarantees that *more* people, including more innocent people, will die in prison.

To the extent that these protections help prevent or overturn wrongful convictions, they may even *save* money. Obviously, it is impossible to know how many wrongful convictions these protections prevent since we cannot know what the outcome of a trial would have been if the defendant had fewer due process protections, but we do know that wrongful convictions are expensive, both in terms of money and crimes committed. Wrongful convictions require the state to imprison an innocent person who should not be in prison, and upon discovery, they often require the state to compensate the wrongly convicted (Norris, Bonventre, & Acker, 2018). When a conviction occurs that should not have, the state has to bear the cost of appeals that should not have been necessary, and if that conviction is overturned, the state often must bear the expense of a re-trial that could have been prevented if those errors were caught in the original trial. Additionally, a recent analysis concluded that each "true perpetrator" who remains free due to a wrongful conviction "commits an average of 3.1 crimes during his or her period of wrongful liberty" and that "the wrongful convictions that occur each year would ultimately enable true perpetrators to commit between 21,824 and 41,664 additional crimes" (Norris, Weintraub, Acker, Redlich, & Bonventre, 2020, p. 375). In other words, the money spent on extra due process protections may not just help protect innocent defendants from wrongful convictions, it may also help protect society from future crimes. Given the expenses associated with both crime and wrongful convictions, depending on the extent to which super due process prevents wrongful convictions, it has the potential to save the state money, but even if it does not save money, preventing even a few wrongful convictions and the associated crimes is reason enough to maintain—and even extend—these additional procedural protections. Doing this properly—that is, ensuring all defendants are entitled to these protections—will wipe out any cost-savings associated with abolishing capital punishment.

And There Are More Life Sentences

The other major problem with the cost analyses discussed earlier is that they do not account for LWOP's larger scale. A single death sentence is, without question, more costly than a single LWOP sentence, which means simply replacing capital punishment with LWOP would undoubtedly save states money. Yet, this is not what is happening. As capital punishment has been declining, death by incarceration has been expanding at a far faster rate, ensnaring offenders who were never eligible for a death sentence in the first place. Based on The Sentencing Project's survey of the various state departments of correction, in 2020, there were 55,945 individuals serving a formal LWOP sentence (Nellis, 2021). There are also tens of thousands of persons serving life with parole who will never be released and 42,353 persons serving terms of at least 50 years (a "virtual life sentence") (Nellis, 2021). In addition, there are an unknown number of individuals who have already died while serving LWOP, so this number is an undercount of the total scale of LWOP. Nevertheless, this number is still more than *six times greater* than the 8,752 people who have been sentenced to death between the reinstatement of capital punishment in 1973 and the end of 2020 (Death Penalty Information Center, n.d.a), nearly *twenty-three times* greater than the size of death row (2,469) at year-end 2020 (Snell, 2021), and *nearly thirty-seven* times the 1,529 executions carried out between reinstatement and the end of 2020 (Death Penalty Information Center, n.d.b; Snell, 2021). As such, it seems likely that any cost savings associated with abolishing or reducing the use of capital punishment could be eclipsed by the increasing costs associated with the exponential expansion of LWOP that has been occurring over the past three decades. In the remainder of this chapter, we analyze whether this hypothesis is true.

Because there are different ways of conceptualizing the costs of both sentences, to assess this hypothesis, we utilize four different analyses to estimate the cost of LWOP relative to the cost of capital punishment while accounting for the greater scale of LWOP. First, we look at how the ratio of capital punishment-to-LWOP costs compares to the ratio of usage for both penalties. Second, we estimate the overall cost of both sentencing regimes on both a per annum and lifetime basis. Third, to account for the fact that anyone sentenced to death or to LWOP would still be sent to prison even in a less punitive penal environment, we estimate the "extra" cost both sentences impose on the system above and beyond what would have been spent punishing the same offenders less severely. Lastly, we look at the cost associated with the aging of the inmate population that has accompanied the expansion of LWOP and how this compares to the cost of capital punishment. As each of these analyses indicate, due to the greater scale of LWOP, its cost is almost certainly greater than the cost of capital punishment.

Data on Costs

The cost of both LWOP and capital punishment differs across different states, so although there have been many state-level studies, there is no precise, nationwide estimate of the cost of either sanction (Dieter, 2013; Dieter, 2014). Therefore, to determine which sentence costs taxpayers more money, we produce our own estimate of the total cost of each sentence. Starting with capital punishment, to ensure that we are generating an estimate that captures *at least* the full cost of capital punishment (and that likely overestimates its cost), we rely on the study that produced the largest difference in cost between a capital and a non-capital trial, which is Roman et al.'s (2008) study of Maryland's death penalty. Using inflation-adjusted 2007 dollars, Roman et al. (2008) discovered that a death sentence costs an average of $3,017,000, a capital trial that does not result in a death sentence costs an average of $1,793,000, and the average non-capital murder trial costs $1,103,000. To maintain a consistent comparison with the cost of LWOP, we re-adjust these figures into 2020 dollars, which comes to $3,771,250, $2,241,250, and $1,378,750, respectively. It is these revised figures we use to calculate both the total cost of capital punishment and the projected nationwide savings from death penalty abolition. Remember, this is the highest estimate, and studies from other states report lower costs for capital punishment. Therefore, using this figure likely overestimates the cost of capital punishment.

Like with capital punishment, the cost to incarcerate someone also differs dramatically across states. Unlike with capital punishment, however, there are fairly reliable tabulations of the per-prisoner cost of incarceration in most jurisdictions. The most recent of these calculations, which we use to estimate the total cost of LWOP, comes from a survey of state prison budgets in 2015 performed by the Vera Institute of Justice (Mai & Subramanian, 2017). Five states did not respond to the survey, so for each of those five states, we imputed the overall mean cost per prisoner.[1] For prisoners in the federal system, we used the federal Bureau of Prisons' calculation of the cost of incarcerating each inmate in fiscal year 2018 (Hyle, 2019). We then adjusted each of these figures to 2020 dollars to generate a more accurate assessment of the current cost of LWOP. This adjustment only accounts for inflation; it does not reflect any changes in correctional budgets that may have taken place. We then used The Sentencing Project's published report on the number of persons serving LWOP in 2020 in each jurisdiction to calculate how much each jurisdiction was spending to incarcerate those serving LWOP in 2020. Of course, this calculation is limited to an estimate of the cost to house those serving LWOP; it does not consider any other costs, like the cost of appeals, that LWOP might generate. For the purpose of this analysis, however, we want to produce as conservative of an estimate as possible so as not to risk overestimating the cost of LWOP. Therefore, we limit our analysis *just to* the cost of incarcerating those sentenced to LWOP.

The Cost Ratio of Death to LWOP Is Outweighed by LWOP's Greater Use

We begin by looking to see if the ratio of capital punishment's cost to LWOP's cost is greater than the ratio of LWOP's usage to capital punishment's usage. If so, this would suggest that even though LWOP is used more often, it nonetheless costs less than capital punishment; if not, it would suggest the opposite. With the exception of Indiana, where capital cases cost more than four times non-capital murder cases (Legislative Services Agency, 2015), most analyses of the cost of LWOP and capital punishment find that, including the cost of incarceration, capital cases cost one-and-a-half to two times what it costs to sentence the *same individuals* to LWOP. This means we could potentially sentence two individuals to LWOP for the cost of a single capital trial and thus could potentially save money by replacing capital punishment with LWOP as long as the number of people being sentenced to LWOP is less than *double* the size of the population being diverted away from a capital trial due to the presence of LWOP.

Obviously, it is impossible to know for certain how many people *would have been* subjected to a capital trial but for the emergence of LWOP, but we can calculate how many additional death sentences there would have been if capital punishment had maintained the same pace as it had during its peak in the early-to-mid 1990s. We can then use this knowledge to estimate how many fewer capital trials are taking place each year. Beginning with death sentences, as shown in Table 5.1, from 1991–1996, the US averaged 296 death sentences per year. By the late 2010s (2015–2020), that average dropped by 88% to 35.5 death

TABLE 5.1 Ratio of LWOP to Capital Punishment

Metric	*Value*
Average death sentences per year, 1991–1996	296
Average death sentences per year, 2015–2020	35.5
Decline in average yearly death sentences between 1991–1996 and 2015–2020	88.0%
Decline in average yearly murders between 1990–1995 and 2014–2019	34.5%
Reduction in yearly death sentences not attributable to decline in murders	158.2
Estimated yearly reduction in capital trials not attributable to decline in murders	632.8
Total increase in LWOP population between 1992 and 2020	43,492
Average increase in LWOP per year, 1992–2020	1,553.3
Ratio of average yearly increase in LWOP to the estimated yearly reduction in capital trials not attributable to the decline in murders	**2.46**

sentences per year—or 260.5 fewer annual death sentences. Unfortunately, there is no record on the number of capital trials that did not result in a death sentence that have taken place, and the few state-level studies that have been done indicate that the death sentence-to-capital trial ratio varies dramatically across different states. For example, from 1973 to 2014, prosecutors in Nebraska secured 27.7% of the death sentences they sought (Goss, Strain, & Blalock, 2016), and over a two-year period in North Carolina, 31.0% of capital trials produced a death sentence (Cook, 2009). Similarly, over a 22-year period in Maryland, 34.6% of capital trials resulted in a death sentence (Roman, Chalfin, Sundquist, Knight, & Darmenov, 2008), and 39.8% of death notices filed in Washington state between 1981 and 2014 produced a death sentence (Collins, Boruchowitz, Hickman, & Larrañaga, 2016). Meanwhile, researchers in California estimated that *half* of the state's capital trials led to a death sentence (Alarcón & Mitchell, 2011), and in Indiana, out of eight capital jury trials, six defendants (75%) were sentenced to death (Legislative Services Agency, 2015). As such, in order to generate an estimate that likely *over*estimates the cost of capital punishment, we assume that 25% of capital trials result in a death sentence, which is lower than any state-level calculation thus far produced, and that all death sentences are the result of a jury trial. We know this is not true, but doing so, again, allows us to generate a figure that overestimates the number of capital trials and thus the cost of capital punishment.

Using this assumption, there would have been 1,042 fewer capital trials each year in the late 2010s than in the early 1990s. Of course, from 1990–1995 to 2014–2019 (due to the amount of preparation time, most capital trial take place the year after the murder), the annual number of murders fell by 34.5% (Federal Bureau of Investigation, n.d.), which means there were fewer potential capital trials in the latter period simply due to the decline in the number of murders. Therefore, we can estimate that approximately 39.3% of the decline in death sentences (34.5% ÷ 88.0% = 39.3%) is attributable to the reduction in homicides. That leaves 60.7% attributable to other causes. The existing literature suggests that neither the passage of LWOP statutes nor the increase in the number of

LWOP sentences have meaningfully contributed to the reduction in death sentences over the last quarter century (*Harvard Law Review*, 2006; Miao, 2020). Rather, other causes, such as declining public support for capital punishment and more stringent appellate review, likely played a much larger role than LWOP (*Harvard Law Review*, 2006). Therefore, it would be inaccurate to attribute all or even most of this remaining decline in death sentences to the rise of LWOP. Nevertheless, to produce as generous of an estimate as possible of the cost savings plausibly attributable to replacing capital punishment with LWOP, we assume the remaining reduction in the number of death sentences is entirely attributable to the increasing use of LWOP, which would mean that LWOP was responsible for 158.2 fewer death sentences (260.5 x 60.7% = 158.2) and, using our 25% death sentencing rate assumption, 632.8 fewer capital trials per year.

However, as seen in Table 5.1, between 1992 and 2020, the size of the LWOP population increased by 43,492 persons (Nellis, 2013; Nellis, 2021), or by about 1,553.3 persons per year—nearly *2.5 times* the absolute maximum number of capital trials plausibly prevented by the increasing use of LWOP. We have to remember that this ratio is, without a doubt, an underestimate since we used an extremely conservative estimate of the number of LWOP sentences and a very generous estimate of the number of capital trials potentially prevented by LWOP. In reality, the increase in the number of people serving LWOP is less than the total number of people sentenced to LWOP over this period since some people serving a LWOP sentence during this period died, and we know that factors other than LWOP and the reduction in the number of murders also contributed to the decline in the number of death sentences. In fact, LWOP likely played, *at most*, only a small role in the declining use of the death penalty (*Harvard Law Review*, 2006; Miao, 2020). Additionally, based on the studies reviewed earlier, our estimate of four capital trials per death sentence is likely an overcount. In other words, the actual ratio of LWOP sentences to capital trials prevented by LWOP is likely to be several times greater than our estimate, which makes it clear that the greater scale of LWOP eclipses the potential cost-savings associated with abolishing capital punishment. If LWOP was confined *solely* to individuals who would have otherwise faced a death sentence, then it would save money relative to capital punishment, but it is obvious that this is not what has happened. People who were never at risk of a death sentence are now being sentenced to die in prison, thus erasing any potential cost-savings associated with abolition.

Total Cost of LWOP Is Greater than Total Cost of Death

Turning our attention to the total cost generated by each sentencing regime, we can use the same assumptions as before to estimate that the 8,752 death sentences imposed in the US between 1973 and 2020 were accompanied by approximately 26,256 capital trials in which the death sentence was not imposed. Using the cost estimates produced by Roman et al.'s (2008) study, we estimate that these cases cost US taxpayers around $91.85 billion in total—or about $1.91 billion per year on average—a daunting sum indeed! Of course, this calculation is almost certainly an overestimate since it assumes that only 25% of capital trials result in a death sentence, which seems like a low estimate that, in turn, overestimates the number of capital trials. It also assumes that all capital cases are resolved via a jury trial, which we know is not true, and cases resolved via a plea bargain cost substantially less (Cook, 2009; Death Penalty Advisory Committee, 2014; Legislative Services Agency, 2015). However, the total cost of LWOP—even using conservative estimates—still tops this amount.

Simply multiplying the annual cost per prisoner in each jurisdiction by the number of persons serving LWOP in that jurisdiction and then summing those products generates a total cost for LWOP of $1.94 billion in 2020—slightly more than the average annual cost of capital punishment since 1973. However, this calculation is actually a huge underestimate because it does not account for the fact that those serving LWOP are going to be older, on average, than those who are eligible for release from prison. Elderly individuals who are incarcerated have increased medical and security needs that drive up the cost of incarceration. Most studies suggest that it costs two to three times more to imprison those over the age of 50 than it does to house the average person in prison (American Civil Liberties Union, 2012; Henrichson & Delaney, 2012); although, some researchers have suggested that due to a lack of data, this is actually an underestimate of how expensive incarcerating the elderly is (Ahalt, Trestman, Rich, Greifinger, & Williams, 2013). Nevertheless, to generate a more conservative estimate, we assume that imprisoning someone who is over the age of 50 costs the state twice as much as the average per-prisoner cost of incarceration.

To incorporate this cost, though, we need to know the age distribution of the LWOP population so we know how many people generate the additional costs associated with age. This information is not publicly reported, but The Sentencing Project's most recent report (Nellis, 2021) indicates what percentage of those serving any type of life or virtual life sentence in each state were over the age of 55 in 2020. Since, by definition, those serving LWOP are less likely to be released than those serving other life terms, it is safe to assume that the LWOP population skews even older than the rest of the lifer population. Nevertheless, to ensure we are generating an overly conservative estimate of LWOP's cost, we assume that the percentage of those serving LWOP who are elderly in each state and thus cost double to imprison is the same as the percentage of lifers who are over the age of 55 in that state. For the three jurisdictions with missing data (Virginia, West Virginia, and the federal Bureau of Prisons), we used mean replacement. As shown in Table 5.2, accounting for the advanced age of the LWOP population in this manner raises our estimate of the cost *just to incarcerate* those serving LWOP in 2020 to nearly $2.59 billion or about $674 million *more* than the average annual cost of capital punishment since 1973.

Looking at the annual cost of each sentence, however, is only part of the picture. It tells us the short-term expenses but not the long-term ones associated with each sentence. Depending on how long LWOP sentences last, they could

TABLE 5.2 Total Cost of LWOP and Capital Punishment

	Annual cost	*Lifetime cost*
LWOP	$2,587,540,017	$106,619,225,571
Capital punishment	$1,913,588,333	$91,852,240,000
Cost difference	$673,951,683	$14,766,985,571

Note: Costs in 2020 dollars, rounded to the nearest dollar; due to rounding, totals may not add up exactly.

still save the state money in the long run. Therefore, to get a fuller picture of the total cost of each sanction, we also examine the *lifetime* cost of the two sentences. Unfortunately, generating an estimate of the lifetime cost of LWOP is significantly more challenging than calculating the annual cost of LWOP because the former requires us to know the average age at admission for those serving LWOP and the average life expectancy of someone serving LWOP. Because neither of these data points is known, we use what is known to make some reasonable inferences that allow us to generate a realistic approximation for both numbers. For age at admission, the Bureau of Justice Statistics (BJS) reports that the median age of admission for *all* prisoners in 2013 was 32 (Carson & Sabol, 2016). State-level studies of LWOP have revealed that the average age at conviction for those serving LWOP in North Carolina was also 32 (Garrett, Seale-Carlisle, Modjadidi, & Renberg, 2021), and in Louisiana, it was 28.9 (Leigey & Schartmueller, 2019). Similarly, the FBI's Uniform Crime Report indicates that the median age range of someone arrested for homicide (the most common crime for those serving LWOP) is consistently 30–39 (the published data do not indicate a more specific age) (Federal Bureau of Investigation, n.d.) and that the arrest rate for murder peaks during the ages of 17–21 before declining rapidly (Snyder, Cooper, & Mulako-Wangota, 2017a). As such, we feel confident estimating that the average age of someone sentenced to LWOP is no greater than 35 years, so we use this as our average age of admission for those serving LWOP.

To determine how long a typical LWOP sentence is likely to last, we begin by using life expectancy projections from the Centers for Disease Control and Prevention (CDC). According to the most recently published data from the CDC, the life expectancy of 35-year-old males in the US is an additional 43.3 years (Arias & Xu, 2020). Of course, those who end up in prison are generally poorer and less healthy than the rest of the population, which could reduce their life expectancy (Patterson, 2010), and the experience of being in prison has also been shown to reduce life expectancy (Patterson, 2013; Wildeman, 2016). Furthermore, those serving LWOP are disproportionately Black (Nellis, 2021), and 35-year-old Black males have a life expectancy of only 39.5 more years (Arias & Xu, 2020). One study, however, did find that Black males in prison have a *lower* mortality rate than nonincarcerated Black males (Patterson, 2010), so prison might not have much of an overall effect on the life expectancy of those serving LWOP. Additionally, studies of the cost of capital punishment typically assume the average LWOP sentence will last 40 years (Hoppe, 1992; Oklahoma Death Penalty Review Commission, 2017; Roman, Chalfin, Sundquist, Knight, & Darmenov, 2008), as do The Sentencing Project's projections of the length of LWOP (Mauer, King, & Young, 2004; Nellis, 2017). However, to account for the possibility that prison might reduce life expectancy and to produce a conservative estimate of the cost of LWOP, we assume that the average LWOP prisoner dies at age 70, after serving 35 years.

As seen in Table 5.2, using these assumptions produces a lifetime cost estimate of more than $106.6 billion *just to incarcerate* the 55,945 individuals currently serving LWOP, which is nearly $14.8 billion *more* than the *total* cost of capital punishment since 1973. Keep in mind that both this estimate and the estimate of the annual cost of LWOP sentences only consider the cost of incarceration for those currently serving LWOP, not the overall costs of LWOP. Neither estimate includes the cost of trials, attorneys, appeals, or any LWOP sentences that ended prior to 2020, nor do these estimates consider costs associated with "virtual life sentences." Therefore, they significantly underestimate the cost of LWOP. It should also be noted that because our estimate of the annual cost of LWOP relies on fewer assumptions and more known facts, it is substantially more reliable than our estimate of the lifetime costs. However, because we were unable to generate an estimate of the costs associated with the LWOP sentences that came to an end prior to 2020 and because we assumed those sentenced to LWOP were older and would therefore serve less time than is probably true, it is reasonable to conclude that our estimate of the lifetime cost of LWOP is an even bigger underestimate than our estimate of the annual costs. Additionally, because we used the highest reported estimate of the cost of a capital trial and almost certainly overestimated the number of capital trials, our calculation of the cost of capital punishment is very likely an overestimate.

Comparing Cost Savings from Abolition to the "Extra" Cost of Non-Capital LWOP

Of course, even without the expansion of LWOP, both those who have been sentenced to LWOP and those who received death sentences would have received prison sentences, and many of them would still be in prison even if LWOP were abolished. Therefore, it is arguably unfair to compare the *total* cost of each sentencing regime since this calculation includes costs that would have been borne anyway even if less severe sentences were being used. Therefore, a better comparison may be to examine the additional costs each sentence entails relative to some less severe sanction. It is to these "extra" costs that we now turn. Unfortunately, making this comparison is not a straightforward process because we do not know how long those sentenced to LWOP or to death would serve in the absence of either sanction. Therefore, to produce our estimates, we relied upon what is known to make some reasonable counter-factual assumptions. Other assumptions were also plausible, so we will do our best to highlight what

TABLE 5.3 "Extra" Cost of LWOP and Capital Punishment

Average annual "extra" cost of capital punishment 1973–2020	$908,020,000
Maximum possible capital punishment cost savings in 2020 due to the decline in capital punishment since 1996	$996,000,000
Estimated minimum "extra" cost of LWOP in 2020	$928,063,910
Estimated maximum "extra" cost of LWOP in 2020	$1,066,796,426

Note: Costs in 2020 dollars, rounded to the nearest dollar.

assumptions we made and why so readers can judge for themselves how reasonable our assumptions are and how much weight to give to our results.

We start by estimating how much less money the US would have spent from 1973 to 2020 if capital punishment did not exist during these years. If we again use John Roman et al.'s (2008) calculation of the extra costs imposed by charging a defendant with a capital crime rather than proceeding non-capitally and make the same assumption as before that 25% of capital cases result in a death sentence, between 1973 and 2020, capital punishment cost nearly $43.6 billion more than it would have to simply sentence those same offenders to LWOP. As shown in Table 5.3, averaged over 48 years, that comes to $908 million per year. Of course, it could be argued that it is not fair to use the average annual cost of capital punishment over the past 48 years because the number of death sentences is already declining due to the rise of LWOP. While we do not believe the evidence supports this argument (c.f., *Harvard Law Review*, 2006; Miao, 2020), we should at least consider this possibility. So, using the same assumptions as earlier, if the number of death sentences issued each year had remained at 315, as it was during 1996, the peak year for death sentences, capital punishment would have cost $1.57 billion more per year than proceeding non-capitally against the same defendants. However, as we discussed earlier, it is unreasonable to assume that death sentences would have remained at their 1996 peak since the number of murders declined, leaving fewer available murder defendants to prosecute. From 1995 to 2019, the number of murders in the US declined by 30.9% (Federal Bureau of Investigation, n.d.). If the number of death sentences had fallen by the same percentage, there would have been approximately 218 death sentences in 2020. In actuality, there were 18 (Death Penalty Information Center, 2020). Obviously, some of this difference was caused by declining support for capital punishment and by the COVID-19 pandemic that shuttered many courts for large parts of 2020 (Death Penalty Information Center, 2020; *Harvard Law Review*, 2006), but even if we were to assume that all of this difference was caused by LWOP's growth, that means that *at most*, it is plausible that the expansion of LWOP prevented 200 death sentences and (using the 25% death sentence rate estimate from above) 800 total capital trials in 2020, which would produce savings of $996 million, as shown in Table 5.3.

Therefore, it is reasonable to conclude that even if the expansion of LWOP played a significant role in the death penalty's decline over the last quarter century, it helped to produce death penalty-related cost savings somewhere in the range of $900 million to $1 billion per year. But how much additional cost is LWOP generating by continuing to incarcerate people who in earlier generations would have already been released? This is difficult to know with any precision because we cannot know which individuals serving LWOP would have been released had they not been sentenced to LWOP. However, we do know that prior to the 1970s, those serving life sentences were routinely released after a decade or two (Garrett, Seale-Carlisle, Modjadidi, & Renberg, 2021; Gottschalk, 2012; Harvard Law Review, 2006; Nellis, 2013; Seeds, 2018) and that paroled lifers and released elderly inmates have extremely low recidivism rates (Advisory Committee on Geriatric and Seriously Ill Inmates, 2005; Anderson, 2019; California Department of Corrections and Rehabilitation, 2013; Justice Policy Institute, 2018; Millemann, Bowman-Rivas, & Smith, 2017; Rosenfeld, Wallman, & Fornango, 2005; State of New York Department of Corrections and Community Supervision, 2016; van Zyl Smit & Appleton, 2019; Weisberg, Mukamal, & Segall, 2011). It is also plausible (though not likely according to the evidence) that without the decline in the use of capital punishment, more of those sentenced to LWOP for capital offenses would have received a death sentence. Therefore, it seems reasonable to conclude that individuals who are over the age of 55 and serving LWOP for *non-capital* crimes could be safely released and likely would have been released if it was not for the increasing use of LWOP against non-capital defendants. Thus, the cost incurred by continuing to incarcerate this population is what we are considering to be the "extra" cost that LWOP imposes on the prison system.

To generate this estimate, we first needed to determine who among those serving LWOP was, in fact, eligible for a death sentence. This information is not known, but we do know that nearly 36% of those serving LWOP were convicted of a crime less serious than first-degree murder and were thus definitely not eligible for a death sentence (Nellis, personal communication, April 21, 2021). Therefore, we used the crime of conviction counts for each state's LWOP population that was generated by The Sentencing Project (Nellis, personal communication, June 23, 2021) to count everyone convicted of a crime less serious than first-degree murder as a non-capital LWOP inmate. Additionally, we know that most first-degree murders are not capital murders, which means that the majority of those serving LWOP for first-degree murder were also not death eligible and so should also be added to our count of non-capital LWOP inmates. Because we do not know what the exact proportion of this group is, though, we created a range of possible estimates by calculating what the size of the non-capital LWOP population would be if we assume that between 25% and 40% of those serving LWOP for first-degree murder were convicted of a capital offense. Then, to determine how many of those serving LWOP for non-capital offenses were over the age of 55, we assumed that the proportion of elderly inmates was roughly equivalent between the capital and non-capital groups. Because elderly individuals cost more to imprison, to figure out how much these "extra" inmates cost each jurisdiction, we then multiplied our range by double the cost of the average prisoner in each jurisdiction.

As shown, summing the results indicates that, in 2020, it cost US taxpayers between $928 million and $1.07 billion to incarcerate elderly individuals serving LWOP for non-capital offenses. These are individuals who, in all likelihood, could be safely released in the absence of LWOP. The results, therefore, suggest that the death penalty-related cost savings potentially attributable to LWOP's expansion are, at best, equivalent or nearly equivalent to the extra cost burden LWOP's expansion imposes on the system by not releasing elderly individuals who were not convicted of a capital offense. In interpreting this conclusion, it is important to keep in mind that the nature of the question we are trying to answer forced us to rely upon some counter-factual assumptions. Other assumptions were also plausible, and using different assumptions would have produced different results. However, we tried to rely on assumptions that would *over*estimate the death-penalty related cost savings attributable to LWOP while also *under*estimating the "extra" cost imposed by LWOP. For example, our comparison assumes that any decline in capital punishment can be attributed to either LWOP's expansion or the reduction in murders; yet as we mentioned earlier, the existing evidence suggests very little, if any, of this reduction is the result of LWOP (*Harvard Law Review*, 2006; Miao, 2020). We also base our calculation on an assumption that there are four capital trials for every death sentence. This is probably an overestimate that inflates the cost of capital punishment. In addition, we use the highest estimated difference in the cost of a capital versus a non-capital trial; in most states, the difference is probably smaller. Thus, our calculation of the potential cost savings LWOP produces is almost certainly too high. When it comes to LWOP's costs, our estimate that between 60% and 75% of those serving LWOP for first-degree murder did not commit a capital murder is probably an underestimate that leads to an undercount of the number of persons serving LWOP for non-capital crimes, and as we have already discussed, the majority of those convicted of capital crimes also do not receive a death sentence and would probably not have been sentenced to death even without LWOP as an option. In the absence of LWOP, each of those individuals could *also* be released when they reach an advanced age. Finally, we also used a very conservative estimate of the proportion of those serving LWOP for non-capital crimes who are elderly, we used 55 rather than 50 as the cut-off for elderly, and we *only* factored in the cost of incarceration for those individuals, not the cost of any additional appeals or lawsuits they may generate.

Therefore, it appears likely that, *at best*, the cost savings produced by the death penalty's decline are canceled out or nearly canceled out by the increasing costs associated with LWOP's expansion and that, in all probability the "extra" costs of LWOP's expansion exceed the cost savings of death penalty abolition. This suggests that unless LWOP's use is restricted only to defendants who would have previously faced a potential death sentence, abolishing capital punishment is unlikely to produce more than negligible cost savings. In other words, because

LWOP has a much wider reach than capital punishment, at this point, arguments that attempt to justify LWOP on fiscal grounds appear to be dubious.

LWOP Has Contributed to the Aging of the Prison Population

The previous analyses attempted to incorporate the additional cost imposed by incarcerating elderly persons serving LWOP who would likely have been released in earlier decades, but they do not account for the overall aging of the prison population that has occurred commensurate with the growth in LWOP. Obviously, not all of this growth is directly due to LWOP, but by raising the sentencing ceiling, LWOP has enabled a whole host of punitive sanctions and thus increased the length of time all those sentenced to prison can expect to serve, which has increased the average age of the overall prison population (Carson & Sabol, 2016; Pew Charitable Trusts, 2015). It is widely accepted that after one's mid-20s, one's criminal propensity begins to decline precipitously (Hirschi & Gottfredson, 1983; Snyder, Cooper, & Mulako-Wangota, 2017b; Sweeten, Piquero, & Steinberg, 2013) and that older inmates pose a very small risk of recidivism (Advisory Committee on Geriatric and Seriously Ill Inmates, 2005; Anderson, 2019; California Department of Corrections and Rehabilitation, 2013; Justice Policy Institute, 2018; Millemann, Bowman-Rivas, & Smith, 2017; Rosenfeld, Wallman, & Fornango, 2005; State of New York Department of Corrections and Community Supervision, 2016; van Zyl Smit & Appleton, 2019; Weisberg, Mukamal, & Segall, 2011)—yet, as discussed above, it is more expensive to incarcerate them.

According to the BJS, in 1991, 3.4% of US prisoners were 55 or older (Gilliard & Beck, 1998). By the end of 2019, that proportion had nearly *quadrupled* to 13.1% (Carson, 2020)! The Vera Institute of Justice reported that in 2015, the average inmate cost $33,274 to incarcerate (Mai & Subramanian, 2017). Adjusting for inflation, that would be about $36,601 in 2020 dollars, but as we have previously mentioned, elderly people cost at least twice as much to incarcerate (American Civil Liberties Union, 2012; Human Rights Watch, 2012). As shown in Table 5.4, the number of sentenced prisoners at year-end 2019 was 1,380,427 which means that incarcerating those over the age of 55 cost US taxpayers more than $13.2 billion in 2019. If the number of prisoners under the age of 55 were to remain the same as was actually reported in 2019 but the proportion of those in prison who are over the age of 55 had remained unchanged between 1991 and

TABLE 5.4 Extra Cost of the Aging Prison Population, 2019

Total sentenced prisoners	1,380,427
Approximate size of 55+ prison population	180,836
Per-person cost to incarcerate those 55+	$73,202
Total cost to incarcerate 55+ prison population	$13,237,696,929
Number of "extra" 55+ persons in prison	138,614
Cost of "extra" 55+ prison population	$10,146,955,274

Note: All numbers rounded to nearest whole number, costs in 2020 dollars.

2019, then there would have been nearly 139,000 fewer elderly people in prison in 2019, for a cost savings of more than \$10.1 billion! Recall that we calculated that *at most*, capital punishment has cost US taxpayers \$1.91 billion per year, on average, since 1973, or about \$8.2 billion *less* than the annual cost burden imposed by the increasing proportion of elderly persons serving prison sentences, which has been enabled by the dramatic growth in LWOP since the early 1990s. Even if we estimate the annual cost of capital punishment using the peak year for death sentences (315 in 1996), we get an annual cost of \$3.3 billion, which is still \$6.8 billion less than the cost of incarcerating the surplus number of 55-plus-year-old inmates that has been generated by increasing punitiveness.

Summary

No matter how we calculate the cost of LWOP, the incarceration costs alone encountered by the rapid expansion of LWOP *at least* offset the cost savings we can expect from abolishing capital punishment, and in most of our analyses, they exceed those cost savings. As such, LWOP is *not* a money saver, and any argument to abolish capital punishment due to its cost should also include abolishing or greatly limiting the use of death by incarceration. Keep in mind that the comparisons in the preceding analyses utilize an *extremely* conservative estimate of the cost of "death in prison" sentences while using the *highest* published estimate of the cost of capital punishment and an extremely generous estimate of the number of capital trials, and they still indicate that LWOP is more expensive than capital punishment—not because death sentences are cheaper than life sentences but because "death by incarceration" is being used far more prolifically than capital punishment ever was. This should not be misconstrued as an argument for retaining or reinstating capital punishment. Instead, this analysis is showing that LWOP is not necessarily an improvement, especially if the goal of abolition is to save money. If we continue to sentence non-capital defendants to die in prison as the trade-off for abolishing capital punishment, then we will not save any money. Of course, if LWOP was *only* used in what were formerly capital cases, then shifting from capital punishment to LWOP would save the state money, but that is not what has happened. LWOP is being used substantially more often and for a wider variety of offenses than the death penalty ever was—including for nonviolent crimes. In fact, nearly 36% of those serving LWOP in 2020 were convicted of a crime *less severe* than first-degree murder (and even most first-degree murderers are not eligible for a death sentence), and more than a quarter (26.0%) were not even convicted of a homicide offense (Nellis, personal communication, April 21, 2021), so it is clear that despite serving the same basic function as death, LWOP casts a far wider net and thus costs the state far more money.

Furthermore, many of the additional costs associated with capital punishment are the result of the additional procedural protections afforded to capital defendants and are thus a *good thing*. We agree with abolitionists that capital punishment is bad policy and should be abolished, but we disagree with accomplishing abolition at the expense of defendants' due process rights. On the contrary, we advocate for *increasing* the protections for defendants and the funding available for indigent defense. As such, the goal of abolition should not be to cut costs, and the cost of capital punishment should not be used as a reason to repeal it. In fact, it is quite grotesque to suggest that capital punishment should be repealed for the purpose of limiting defendants' procedural protections, which is essentially what the argument that capital punishment is too expensive is saying. Saving money by reducing due process rights is not a step toward justice and will simply result in more innocent persons being sentenced to die in prison.

Note

1 We do not believe this decision will greatly affect the results as three of these states have less than 100 individuals serving LWOP, and combined, these five states account for 3.6% of the total LWOP population.

References

Advisory Committee on Geriatric and Seriously Ill Inmates. (2005, June 22). *Report of the Advisory Committee on Geriatric and Seriously Ill Inmates.* Retrieved from Joint State Government Commission: http://jsg.legis.state.pa.us/resources/documents/ftp/publications/2005-40-INMATES%20REPORT.pdf

Ahalt, C., Trestman, R. L., Rich, J. D., Greifinger, R. B., & Williams, B. A. (2013). Paying the price: The pressing need for quality, cost, and outcomes data to improve correctional health care for older prisoners. *Journal of the American Geriatrics Association, 61*(11), 2013–2019.

Alarcón, J. A., & Mitchell, P. M. (2011). Executing the will of the voters?: A roadmap to mend or end the California legislature's multi-billion-dollar death penalty debacle. *Loyola of Los Angeles Law Review, 44,* S41–S224.

Alexander, M. (2012). *The new Jim Crow: Mass incarceration in the age of colorblindness* (Revised ed.). New York: New Press.

American Civil Liberties Union. (2012, June). *At America's expense: The mass incarceration of the elderly.* Retrieved December 31, 2020, from American Civil Liberties Union: https://www.aclu.org/files/assets/elderlyprisonreport_20120613_1.pdf

Anderson, J. L. (2019). Recidivism of paroled murderers as a factor in the utility of life imprisonment. *Current Issues in Criminal Justice, 31*(2), 255–268.

Arias, E., & Xu, J. (2020, November 17). *United States life tables, 2018.* Retrieved January 9, 021, from Centers for Disease Control and Prevention: https://www.cdc.gov/nchs/data/nvsr/nvsr69/nvsr69-12-508.pdf

Ariosto, D. (2012, April 25). *Connecticut becomes 17th state to abolish death penalty.* Retrieved December 30, 2020, from CNN: https://www.cnn.com/2012/04/25/justice/connecticut-death-penalty-law-repealed/index.html

Barkow, R. E. (2009). The court of life and death: The two tracks of constitutional sentencing law and the case for uniformity. *Michigan Law Review, 107,* 1145–1205.

Berman, M. (2015, May 27). *Nebraska lawmakers abolish the death penalty, narrowly overriding governor's veto.* Retrieved December 30, 2020, from Washington Post: https://www.washingtonpost.com/news/post-nation/wp/2015/05/27/nebraska-lawmakers-officially-abolish-the-death-penalty/

Bienen, L. B. (2010). Capital punishment in Illinois in the aftermath of the Ryan commutations: Reforms, economic realities, and a new saliency for issues of cost. *Journal of Criminal Law and Criminology*, *100*, 1301–1402.

Boyd, D. (2009, March 17). *Thinking it over.* Retrieved January 13, 2021, from Albuquerque Journal: https://www.abqjournal.com/news/state/17104545077newsstate03-17-09.htm

California Department of Corrections and Rehabilitation. (2013). *Lifer parolee recidivism report.* Sacramento, CA: California Department of Corrections and Rehabilitation.

Canon, G. (2015, July 27). *Can a public defender really handle 700 cases a year?* Retrieved June 28, 2021, from Mother Jones: https://www.motherjones.com/politics/2015/07/aclu-lawsuit-public-defense-fresno-california/

Carson, E.A. (2020, October). *Prisoners in 2019.* Retrieved December 31, 2020, from Bureau of Justice Statistics: https://www.bjs.gov/content/pub/pdf/p19.pdf

Carson, E. A., & Sabol, W. J. (2016, May). *Aging of the state prison population, 1993–2013.* Retrieved January 9, 2021, from Bureau of Justice Statistics: https://www.bjs.gov/content/pub/pdf/aspp9313.pdf

Cauthen, J. N., & Latzer, B. (2008). Why so long? Explaining processing time in capital appeals. *The Justice System Journal*, *29*, 298–312.

Chammah, M. (2014, December 17). *The slow death of the death penalty.* Retrieved January 13, 2021, from Marshall Project: https://www.themarshallproject.org/2014/12/17/the-slow-death-of-the-death-penalty

CNN. (2009, March 18). *New Mexico governor repeals death penalty in state.* Retrieved December 30, 2020, from CNN: https://www.cnn.com/2009/CRIME/03/18/new.mexico.death.penalty/index.html

Collins, P.A., Boruchowitz, R. C., Hickman, M. J., & Larrañaga, M.A. (2016). An analysis of the economic costs of seeking the death penalty in Washington State. *Seattle Journal for Social Justice*, *14*(3), 727–779.

Cook, P.J. (2009). Potential savings from abolition of the death penalty in North Carolina. *American Law and Economics Review*, *11*(2), 498–529.

Date, S.V. (2000, January 4). The high price of killing killers. Palm Beach Post, p. 1A.

Death Penalty Advisory Committee. (2014, February 13). *Report of the Judicial Council Death Penalty Advisory Committee.* Retrieved December 22, 2020, from Kansas Judicial Council: https://kansasjudicialcouncil.org/Documents/Studies%20and%20Reports/2015%20Reports/death%20penalty%20cost%20report%20final.pdf

Death Penalty Information Center. (2020, December 16). *The death penalty in 2020: Year end report.* Retrieved December 18, 2020, from Death Penalty Information Center: https://files.deathpenaltyinfo.org/reports/year-end/YearEndReport2020.pdf

Death Penalty Information Center. (n.d.a). *Death sentences in the United States since 1977.* Retrieved January 13, 2021, from Death Penalty Information Center: https://deathpenaltyinfo.org/facts-and-research/sentencing-data/death-sentences-in-the-united-states-from-1977-by-state-and-by-year

Death Penalty Information Center. (n.d.b). *Execution database.* Retrieved January 12, 2021, from Death Penalty Information Center: https://deathpenaltyinfo.org/executions/execution-database

Dieter, R. C. (2013, October). *The 2% death penalty: How a minority of counties produce most death cases at enormous cost to all.* Retrieved December 21, 2020, from Death Penalty Information Center: https://files.deathpenaltyinfo.org/legacy/documents/TwoPercentReport.pdf

Dieter, R. C. (2014). The issue of costs in the death penalty debate. In J. R. Acker, R. M. Bohm, & C. S. Lanier (Eds.), *America's experiment with capital punishment: Reflections on the past, present, and future of the ultimate penal sanction* (3rd ed., pp. 595–609). Durham, NC: Carolina Academic.

Federal Bureau of Investigation. (n.d.). *Crime data explorer*. Retrieved January 9, 2021, from https://crime-data-explorer.app.cloud.gov/explorer/national/united-states/shr

Garrett, B. L., Seale-Carlisle, T. M., Modjadidi, K., & Renberg, K. M. (2021). Life without parole sentencing in North Carolina. *North Carolina Law Review, 99*, 279–332.

Gilliard, D. K., & Beck, A. J. (1998, August). *Prisoners in 1997*. Retrieved January 8, 2021, from Bureau of Justice Statistics: https://www.bjs.gov/content/pub/pdf/p97.pdf

Godsey, M. (2017). *Blind injustice: A former prosecutor exposes the psychology and politics of wrongful convictions*. Oakland, CA: University of California Press.

Goss, E., Strain, S., & Blalock, J. (2016, August 15). *The economic impact of the death penalty on the state of Nebraska: A taxpayer burden?* Retrieved December 22, 2020, from Death Penalty Information Center: https://files.deathpenaltyinfo.org/legacy/files/pdf/The-Economic-Impact-of-the-Death-Penalty-on-the-State-of-Nebraska.pdf

Gottschalk, M. (2012). No way out? Life sentences and the politics of penal reform. In C. Ogletree, & A. Sarat (Eds.), *Life without parole: America's new death penalty?* (pp. 227–281). New York: NYU Press.

Greenfield, L. A. (1992, October). *Capital punishment 1991*. Retrieved January 2, 2021, from Bureau of Justice Statistics: https://www.bjs.gov/content/pub/pdf/cp91.pdf

Gross, S. R. (1996). The risks of death: Why erroneous convictions are common in capital cases. *Buffalo Law Review, 44*, 469–500.

Harvard Law Review. (2006). A matter of life and death: The effect of life-without-parole statutes on capital punishment. *Harvard Law Review, 119*, 1838–1854.

Henrichson, C., & Delaney, R. (2012, July 20). *The price of prisons: What mass incarceration costs taxpayers*. Retrieved December 31, 2020, from Vera Institute of Justice: http://www.vera.org/sites/default/files/resources/downloads/price-of-prisons-updated-version-021914

Hirschi, T., & Gottfredson, M. (1983). Age and the explanation of crime. *American Journal of Sociology, 89*, 552–584.

Hoppe, C. (1992, March 8). Executions cost Texas millions. Dallas Morning News, p. 1A.

Human Rights Watch. (2012, January). *Old behind bars: The aging prison population in the United States*. Retrieved January 9, 2021, from Human Rights Watch: https://www.hrw.org/sites/default/files/reports/usprisons0112webwcover_0_0.pdf

Hyle, K. (2019, November 19). Annual determination of average cost of incarceration fee (COIF). *Federal Register, 84*(223), 63891–63892. Retrieved June 14, 2021, from https://www.govinfo.gov/content/pkg/FR-2019-11-19/pdf/2019-24942.pdf

Justice Policy Institute. (2018, November). *The Ungers, 5 years and counting: A case study in safely reducing long prison terms and saving taxpayer dollars*. Retrieved October 30, 2019, from Justice Policy Institute: http://www.justicepolicy.org/uploads/justicepolicy/documents/The_Ungers_5_Years_and Counting.pdf

Kaplan, A. B., Collins, P. A., & Mayhew, V. L. (2016, November 16). *Oregon's death penalty: A cost analysis*. Retrieved December 21, 2020, from Lewis & Clark Law School: https://law.lclark.edu/live/files/22888-oregons-death-penalty-a-cost-analysis-2016

Kleinstuber, R., Joy, S., & Mansley, E. A. (2016). Into the abyss: The unintended consequences of death penalty abolition. *University of Pennsylvania Journal of Law and Social Change, 19*, 185–206.

Legislative Services Agency. (2015, April 13). *Fiscal impact statement: LS 6092*. Retrieved December 22, 2020, from Indiana General Assembly: http://iga.in.gov/legislative/2015/bills/senate/8#document-8e4c35a4

Leigey, M. E., & Schartmueller, D. (2019). The fiscal and human costs of life without parole. *The Prison Journal, 99*, 241–262.

Liebman, J. S., Fagan, J., Gelman, A., West, V., Davies, G., & Kiss, A. (2002, February 11). *A broken system II: Why there is so much error in capital cases, and what can be done about it.*

Retrieved July 15, 2020, from Columbia Law School: http://www2.law.columbia.edu/brokensystem2/report.pdf

Mai, C., & Subramanian, R. (2017, May). *The price of prisons: Examining state spending trends, 2010–2015.* Retrieved January 2, 2021, from Vera Institute of Justice: https://www.vera.org/downloads/publications/the-price-of-prisons-2015-state-spending-trends.pdf

Maryland Commission on Capital Punishment. (2008, December 12). *Maryland Commission on Capital Punishment: Final report to the General Assembly.* Retrieved January 13, 2021, from Maryland State Archives: https://msa.maryland.gov/megafile/msa/speccol/sc5300/sc5339/000113/012000/012331/unrestricted/20100208e.pdf

Mauer, M., King, R. S., & Young, M. C. (2004, May). *The meaning of 'life': Long prison sentences in context.* Retrieved January 9, 2021, from Sentencing Project: file:///C:/Users/RKLEINS/Downloads/The-Meaning-of-Life-Long-Prison-Sentences-in-Context.pdf

Miao, M. (2020). Replacing death with life? The rise of LWOP in the context of abolitionist campaigns in the United States. *Northwestern Journal of Law & Public Policy, 15*, 173–223.

Millemann, M., Bowman-Rivas, R., & Smith, E. (2017). Releasing older prisoners. In E. Luna (Ed.), *Reforming Criminal Justice: Punishment, Incarceration, and Release* (Vol. 4, pp. 325–340). Phoenix, AZ: Arizona State University.

Nellis, A. (2013). *Life goes on: The historic rise in life sentences in America.* Washington, DC: The Sentencing Project.

Nellis, A. (2017). *Still life: America's increasing use of life and long-term sentences.* Washington, DC: The Sentencing Project.

Nellis, A. (2021, February 17). *No end in sight: America's enduring reliance on life imprisonment.* Retrieved March 1, 2021, from Sentencing Project: https://www.sentencingproject.org/publications/no-end-in-sight-americas-enduring-reliance-on-life-imprisonment/

New Jersey Death Penalty Study Commission. (2007, January). *New Jersey Death Penalty Study Commission Report.* Retrieved January 13, 2021, from New Jersey Legislature: https://www.njleg.state.nj.us/committees/dpsc_final.pdf

Norris, R. J., Bonventre, C. L., & Acker, J. R. (2018). *When justice fails: Causes and consequences of wrongful convictions.* Durham, NC: Carolina Academic Press.

Norris, R. J., Weintraub, J. N., Acker, J. R., Redlich, A. D., & Bonventre, C. L. (2020). The criminal cost of wrongful convictions: Can we reduce crime by protecting the innocent? *Criminology & Public Policy, 19*(2), 367–388.

Oklahoma Death Penalty Review Commission. (2017, March). *The report of the Oklahoma Death Penalty Review Commission.* Retrieved December 21, 2020, from Constitution Project: https://archive.constitutionproject.org/wp-content/uploads/2017/05/OKDPRC_Final.pdf

Patterson, E. J. (2010). Incarcerating death: Mortality in U.S. state correctional facilities, 1985–1998. *Demography, 47*(3), 587–607.

Patterson, E. J. (2013). The dose–response of time served in prison on mortality: New York state, 1989–2003. *American Journal of Public Health, 103*(3), 523–528.

Pew Charitable Trusts. (2015, November). *Prison time surges for federal inmates.* Retrieved January 13, 2021, from Pew Charitable Trusts: www.pewtrusts.org/~/media/assets/2015/11/prison_time_surges_for_federal_inmates.pdf

Reiman, J., & Leighton, P. (2013). *The rich get richer and the poor get prison: Ideology, class, and criminal justice* (10th ed.). Upper Saddle River, NJ: Routledge.

Roman, J., Chalfin, A., Sundquist, A., Knight, C., & Darmenov, A. (2008, March). *The cost of the death penalty in Maryland.* Retrieved December 23, 2020, from Urban Institute: https://www.urban.org/sites/default/files/publication/31526/411625-The-Cost-of-the-Death-Penalty-in-Maryland.PDF

Rosenfeld, R., Wallman, J., & Fornango, R. (2005). The contribution of ex-prisoners to crime rates. In J. Travis, & C. Visher (Eds.), *Prisoner Reentry and Crime in America* (pp. 80–104). New York: Cambridge University Press.

Seeds, C. (2018). Disaggregating LWOP: Life without parole, capital punishment, and mass incarceration in Florida, 1972–1995. *Law & Society Review, 52*, 172–205.

Snell, T. L. (2001, December). *Capital punishment 2000.* Retrieved January 2, 2021, from Bureau of Justice Statistics: https://www.bjs.gov/content/pub/pdf/cp00.pdf

Snell, T. L. (2021, December). *Capital punishment, 2020–statistical tables.* Retrieved December 21, 2021, from Bureau of Justice Statistics: https://bjs.ojp.gov/content/pub/pdf/cp20st.pdf

Snyder, H. N., Cooper, A. D., & Mulako-Wangota, J. (2017a, August). *Arrest rates by age for murder and non-negligent manslaughter.* Retrieved March 1, 2021, from Bureau of Justice Statistics Arrest Data Analysis Tool: https://www.bjs.gov/index.cfm?ty=datool&surl=/arrests/index.cfm#

Snyder, H. N., Cooper, A. D., & Mulako-Wangota, J. (2017b, August). *Arrest rates by age for violent crime index offenses.* Retrieved May 17, 2021, from Bureau of Justice Statistics: https://www.bjs.gov/index.cfm?ty=datool&surl=/arrests/index.cfm#

State of Nevada Legislative Auditor. (2014, November 17). *Performance audit: Fiscal cost of the death penalty: 2014.* Retrieved December 22, 2020, from Nevada Legislature: https://www.leg.state.nv.us/Division/audit/Full/BE2014/Costs%20of%20Death%20Penalty,%20LA14-25,%20Full.pdf

State of New York Department of Corrections and Community Supervision. (2016, December). *2012 inmate releases: Three year post-release follow-up.* Retrieved February 7, 2019, from http://www.doccs.ny.gov/Research/Reports/2017/2012_releases_3yr_out.pdf

Sweeten, G., Piquero, A. R., & Steinberg, L. (2013). Age and the explanation of crime, revisited. *Journal of Youth and Adolescence, 42*, 921–938.

van Zyl Smit, D., & Appleton, C. (2019). *Life imprisonment: A global human rights analysis.* Cambridge, MA: Harvard University Press.

Warden, R. (2012). How and why Illinois abolished the death penalty. *Law and Inequality, 30*, 245–286.

Weisberg, R., Mukamal, D. A., & Segall, J. D. (2011, September). *Life in limbo: An examination of parole release for prisoners serving life sentences with the possibility of parole in California.* Retrieved November 1, 2019, from Stanford Criminal Justice Center: https://law.stanford.edu/wp-content/uploads/sites/default/files/publication/259833/doc/slspublic/SCJC%20Lifer%20Parole%20Release%20Sept%202011.pdf

Wildeman, C. (2016). Incarceration and population health in wealth democracies. *Criminology, 54*(2), 360–382.

6

LWOP as Racial Control

In their arguments, opponents of capital punishment often point out the presence of racial bias in its application (American Civil Liberties Union, 2012). While the effectiveness of this as a legal strategy is up for debate (c.f., *McCleskey v. Kemp*, 1987; Peffley & Hurwitz, 2007), the reality of capital punishment's discriminatory application has been well documented (Grosso, O'Brien, Taylor, & Woodworth, 2014). Simply put, studies consistently find that those accused of killing white victims are more likely to be sentenced to death, and in some jurisdictions, Black defendants who kill white victims are at the highest risk of a death sentence (Grosso, O'Brien, Taylor, & Woodworth, 2014). It does not follow from this conclusion, however, that LWOP is any less discriminatory. In fact, the evidence suggests that LWOP may be even *more* discriminatory than capital punishment.

For example, according to the most recent data, Black and African American people (alone or in combination) account for 14% of the US population (US Census Bureau, 2021), 33% of those serving a prison sentence in the US (Carson, 2021), and 41% of those on death row (Snell, 2021), but they represent 55% of those serving LWOP (Nellis, 2021, p. 18)! This disparity is even greater when looking at those sentenced to LWOP for nonviolent crimes and for crimes committed as children. According to the American Civil Liberties Union (ACLU) (2014), nationwide, nearly two thirds (65.4%) of those serving LWOP for nonviolent offenses are Black, and overall, people of color account for a staggering four fifths (82.2%) of those serving LWOP for nonviolent crimes. In some states, these differences are even greater. In Louisiana, for example, 91% of prisoners serving LWOP for a nonviolent crime are Black (American Civil Liberties Union of Louisiana, 2013). Juvenile LWOP (JLWOP) also mirrors these disproportions. More than three fifths (62%) of the JLWOP population is Black, and Black juveniles arrested for an interracial murder are far more likely to receive a LWOP sentence than their white counterparts are (Rovner, 2021).

DOI: 10.4324/9781003161783-8

While some of these disparities may be attributable to differences in criminal involvement among different racial groups, the existing evidence suggests that, on the whole, these disparities are neither legally justifiable nor an accidental byproduct of an otherwise race-neutral system. That is, much of these differences are attributable to *public policy decisions* rather than the actual level of threat posed by different racial and ethnic groups. Remember, as we have discussed throughout this book, LWOP sentences are really just "semantically disguised sentences of death" (Villaume, 2005, p. 266) or what some have referred to as "death by incarceration" (Johnson & McGunigall-Smith, 2008). The death penalty's role as a form of racial control has been well-documented (Banner, 2002; Kleinstuber, 2016a; Marquart, Ekland-Olson, & Sorensen, 1994; McFeely, 1997), and as an extension of the death penalty, LWOP suffers from the same racial biases. The method of death may be different, but the way the system operates is not. Furthermore, even if LWOP were not a type of death sentence, the crimes punishable with lifetime imprisonment clearly target the behaviors of the poorest, most marginalized members of society rather than equally—or sometimes more—harmful actions performed by wealthier, more powerful members of society. Lastly, since it is unjust to impose LWOP on *children*, the disproportionate use of JLWOP against children of color is *inherently* discriminatory regardless of the behavior of those being punished. In other words, the available evidence suggests that rather than eliminating it, LWOP is supplementing capital punishment's racial control function, and given LWOP's far greater scale, this means that LWOP has the potential to have a far more detrimental impact on racial equality than capital punishment does.

The Death Penalty Is Racial Control and LWOP Is the Death Penalty

Throughout the US's history, the death penalty has been used more as a tool of racial control than crime control. There is very little evidence that the death penalty reduces homicide rates (Nagin & Pepper, 2012), but there is a great deal of evidence that it is applied in a racially biased manner, especially when the defendant is Black and the victim is white (Grosso, O'Brien, Taylor, & Woodworth, 2014). African Americans convicted of murder are also 50% more likely to be innocent than other prisoners convicted of murder and are more likely to be the victims of official misconduct—especially, again, when the victim is white (Gross, Possley, & Stephens, 2017)—which suggests that it is easier to convict a Black defendant with less evidence, particularly in interracial cases. All of this suggests that the death penalty—like lynching before it—is actually a tool for maintaining existing racial hierarchies rather than for preventing murder. In the words of Marquart et al. (1994), "Slavery, criminal justice, lynchings, and capital punishment are historically closely intertwined in the United States" (p. 185).

This statement may sound radical, but consider a few facts. Following the abolition of slavery, the use of lynching as a tool of racial terrorism increased in the American south, and its use was most prominent in locations where white Americans felt the most threatened by African Americans (Tolnay & Beck, 1995). Although the use of lynching began to fall into disfavor in the 1930s (Marquart et al., 1994), "The hundred-a-year lynchings of the 1890s were matched by similar numbers of legal executions in the 1930s," causing critics to coin the phrase "legal lynching" (McFeely, 1997, para 14). Not surprisingly, these executions were rife with racial bias, and, critically, these biases were most pronounced in executions for rape (which remained legal until 1977). The archetypal lynching victim was a Black man accused of raping a white woman, a pattern that remained once legal executions replaced lynching (Foerster, 2012). As Banner (2002) has documented, executions for rape were concentrated almost entirely in the former Confederacy, and 91% of those executed for rape between 1870 and 1950 were Black. In contrast, not a single white man has ever been executed in the US for raping a Black woman (McGuire, 2010). These patterns were also evident in executions for other crimes, with Black Americans being executed at much higher rates that white Americans (Banner, 2002).

Although this indicates that "The death penalty was a means of racial control" (Banner, 2002, p. 230) in previous generations, it does not necessarily mean it remains so. After all, the Supreme Court struck down existing capital sentencing statutes in 1972 because they were arbitrary and capricious and then approved new statutes in 1976 that were designed to eliminate racial biases (*Furman v. Georgia*, 1972; *Gregg v. Georgia*, 1976). Yet, the available evidence suggests that the Court largely failed in its endeavor. Dozens of studies have concluded that the death penalty still discriminates against those who kill white victims, especially Black defendants who kill white victims (Grosso, O'Brien, Taylor, & Woodworth, 2014). More importantly, however, the modern death penalty is used more frequently in states that utilized lynching more often during the Reconstruction period, and as the proportion of Black residents in a state increases, its propensity to use capital punishment also increases (Jacobs, Carmichael, & Kent, 2005)—just as the propensity to lynch increased in response to the political threat posed by Black Americans during Reconstruction (Blalock, 1967).

This racial bias is even detectable at the local and individual levels. As a report from the Death Penalty Information Center has shown, most death sentences and executions in the modern era originated in just two percent of American counties, and only 15% of US counties have had anyone executed since 1976 (Dieter, 2013). Fleury-Steiner, Kaplan, and Longazel (2015) refer to these areas as "racist localisms" because of they have histories of white terrorism and "zones of racial exclusion" designed to fortify racial boundaries. Additionally, individual attitudes toward capital punishment are strongly tied to race. For more than half a century, public opinion polls have shown that African Americans are far less likely to support capital punishment than their white counterparts (Cochran & Chamlin, 2006), and the latest data from Pew indicate that although this gap appears to be narrowing, white Americans remain more likely to support the death penalty than Black Americans by around 14 percentage points

(63% vs. 49%) (Pew Research Center, 2021).[1] The reason for these differences appears to be rooted in racial prejudice as numerous studies have concluded that support for the death penalty among white Americans is strongly tied to racial prejudice (Barkan & Cohn, 1994; Bobo & Johnson, 2004; Soss, Langbein, & Metelko, 2003; Unnever & Cullen, 2007). In fact, when white Americans learn that the death penalty discriminates against African Americans, they tend to become *more supportive* of it (Peffley & Hurwitz, 2007).

All of these facts support the claims of those who view capital punishment as "legal lynching," and at first glance would appear to support the abolitionists' position that LWOP is a better alternative than executions. However, we have to remember that LWOP is not distinct from capital punishment. Much like legal executions replaced extra-judicial lynching in the early 20th century, LWOP is now simply replacing the death penalty (and then some), and like capital punishment fulfilled the same function as lynching, LWOP fulfills the same function as the death penalty. Yes, LWOP does not involve any executions, but it is still a death sentence. Capital punishment and LWOP are two sides of the same coin and are cut from the same cloth. As we have already detailed extensively, LWOP is a type of death sentence. Both sentences seek to permanently eliminate the accused from society, depriving them of their freedom and, ultimately, their lives. That is, regardless of whether one is sentenced to death or LWOP, they will live out the rest of their days in prison, deprived of any of the existential features of life that make it worth living. In the same way that death by electrocution, death by hanging, and death by lethal injection are just different methods of achieving the same outcome, death by execution and death by incarceration are the same sentence—they are just not acknowledged as such. Therefore, if capital punishment is a form of racial control, then as the death penalty in disguise, so too is LWOP.

The obvious rebuttal to this line of reasoning is that, unlike capital punishment, LWOP is often imposed as a mandatory punishment, which should eliminate racial biases. However, eliminating discretion in the sentencing decision does not eliminate discretion; it simply shifts it from the publicity of open court to the privacy of prosecutorial charging decisions. This likely *increases* the amount of racial bias while simultaneously making it harder to detect. There are also some states that impose LWOP in a discretionary manner for some crimes, and the Supreme Court has mandated that JLWOP be discretionary (*Miller v. Alabama*, 2012). Therefore, it is quite plausible that LWOP is utilized in the same racially biased manner as capital punishment. Unfortunately, in contrast to the research on capital punishment, the study of LWOP is still in its infancy, which means there is very little empirical research examining racial bias in the use of LWOP. The limited evidence that does exist, though, suggests that LWOP is plagued with the same racial biases as capital punishment and perpetuates the same racial control function. After all, the increase in the use of LWOP is not connected to increases in crime; it is connected to policy changes (Mauer, King, & Young, 2004). For example, in a separate work, Coldsmith and Kleinstuber

(Under Review) found that, nationwide, use of LWOP at the state level is not impacted by the state's violent crimes rates, and in North Carolina, where LWOP is the mandatory minimum penalty for first-degree murder, Garrett, Seale-Carlisle, Modjadidi, and Renberg (2021) discovered that the county-level use of LWOP actually *declines* when the county's homicide rate increases and that past use of LWOP in a county is a strong predictor of its present use. These facts suggest that LWOP is not being used for crime control purposes; its use is driven by prosecutorial discretion and political goals.

So, what are these political goals, and how are prosecutors exercising their discretion? Well, according to the same study in North Carolina, there is a significant race-of-victim effect in use of LWOP sentences that is "consistent with research on death sentencing patterns" (Garrett et al., 2021, p. 285). Specifically, counties that experienced more Black homicide victims were less likely to utilize LWOP, suggesting that, just like in capital cases, the lives of Black victims are not valued as highly as the lives of white victims (Garrett et al., 2021). Similarly, the nationwide data on exonerations have shown that non-capital exonerees convicted of killing white victims were 54% more likely to be sentenced to life (as opposed to a prison term shorter than life), which suggests that "the pattern of harsh sentencing for murder convictions with white victims and lighter sentencing for those with black victims is not restricted to death sentences" (Gross et al., 2017, p. 5). Among juvenile offenders, where courts have the most discretion, Black youths arrested for murder are nearly *twice* as likely to receive a LWOP sentence than white juveniles arrested for murder (Mills, Dorn, & Hritz, 2016, pp. 577–578). When looking just at interracial murders, Black children who are arrested for killing white victims are *more than three times* (3.25) more likely than white youths arrested for killing Black victims to receive a LWOP sentence (Rovner, 2021, p. 4),[2] which again shows that the racial biases that have been well documented among death sentences also exist for LWOP sentences. These findings are not confined to murder cases either. Habitual offender laws (discussed in greater detail later), which are a big driver of LWOP populations, also appear to be implemented in a racially-biased manner. In California, a study of 171,000 incarcerated people found that, after controlling for legally relevant variables, African Americans were 47% more likely to receive a sentence for a third strike than whites. This discrepancy increased for offenses that can be charged as either felonies or misdemeanors and for less serious (i.e., drug and property) offenses—that is, when prosecutors have greater discretion (Chen, 2008). This pattern also appears in the federal court system. A recent study of federal sentencing patterns over an eight-year period found that, after controlling for legally relevant variables, Black defendants were 58% more likely to receive a LWOP sentence than white defendants. As suggested above, this outcome appears to be the result of harder-to-detect *prosecutorial* discretion. The study did not identify any bias in judicial decisions to impose LWOP. Rather, Black defendants were more likely to receive a LWOP sentence because they were more likely to be placed into a sentencing guideline cell that made them eligible for LWOP, were more likely to be convicted at trial (instead of via a plea bargain), were less likely to receive a downward departure, and were more likely to receive a mandatory minimum sentence (Johnson, Spohn, & Kimchi, 2021). These factors are all the result of discretionary decisions made by prosecutors in the pre-trial stages, shielded from public scrutiny.

LWOP Targets the Disadvantaged

Beyond the realities that LWOP is implemented in a racially-biased manner, the crimes that are eligible for LWOP in the first place also target the behaviors of disadvantaged groups while overlooking similarly harmful activities by privileged groups. As Quinney (1970) has pointed out, "Crime is a definition of behavior that is conferred on some persons by others" (p. 15). This means that *even if LWOP operated without any racial bias*, it would still function as a form of racial control because of which deaths get defined as murder, who gets defined as a "habitual offender," and the use of LWOP against some drug offenders.

What Is Murder?

One of the most obvious critiques of the claim that LWOP is a form of racial control is the fact that the majority of those serving LWOP were convicted of murder, which seems like a legitimate and race-neutral use of LWOP. After all, murder is the most serious crime, so it should get the most severe punishment. As long as similarly-situated defendants get treated the same (they do not, but assuming for a moment they did), how could punishing murderers with LWOP be racist? If some groups happen to commit murder more often, that does not make the law racist, and in the US, 51.1% of homicides reported to police from 1980 to 2019 involved African American suspects (Puzzanchera, Chamberlin, & Kang, 2020). Viewed in this light, the racial disparities in the LWOP population do not appear as problematic. However, one has to realize that what society defines as murder is not objective; this definition is rife with racial and class bias. Murder is usually defined as a direct interpersonal attack or a one-on-one act where an individual or a group of individuals physically attacks and kills another specific individual or group of individuals. Knowingly refusing to correct serious safety violations that lead to the deaths of dozens of workers—like the Upper Big Branch mine collapse or BP's *Deepwater Horizon* oil rig explosion in 2010—is not defined as murder even though the latter places more people in danger and leads to more deaths.

To repeat a question posed by Reiman and Leighton (2013), "Why do 10 dead miners amount to an 'accident' and a 'tragedy,' and 6 dead commuters a 'mass murder'?" (p. 66). After all, in the example they present, the mine owners repeatedly violated the Mine Safety Act, exposing the workers to danger while hiding these violations from inspectors, and as they document, Americans are far more likely to be killed or injured by unsafe working conditions that could have been prevented than they are to be attacked by another individual. Furthermore, corporate crimes cost society *far more* than all the street crimes reported in the FBI's Uniform Crime Report, yet corporate criminals are treated *far more* leniently (Reiman & Leighton, 2013). While it is true that corporate executives may not intend the harms their decisions cause, they nevertheless make those decisions *knowing* that their decisions place people in avoidable danger—often scores of people—and they make these decisions "out of cool reckoning" (to save money) rather than during the heat of the moment the way many interpersonal crimes occur (Reiman & Leighton, 2013), but when these decisions lead to someone's death, no one is charged with murder or sentenced to die in prison. In fact, causing the death of an employee by *willfully* violating safety laws is only a misdemeanor (Reiman & Leighton, 2013). On the other hand, accomplices in robberies-gone-bad who never intended for anyone to get hurt and who took no active part in bringing about the victim's death are routinely charged with first-degree murder under felony murder and accomplice liability statutes and then sentenced to die in prison (Robinson, 2012). Therefore, the deaths we define as "murder" and thus the defendants who are eligible for a LWOP sentence reflect existing racial and class hierarchies.

Who Is a Habitual Offender?

In addition to the growing use of LWOP for those convicted of murder, one of the biggest drivers of LWOP's growth has been the implementation of habitual offender statutes, commonly referred to as "three strikes" laws (Ogletree & Sarat, 2012; Spohn, 2014; Tonry, 2014; Tonry, 2016). In the abstract, these laws make intuitive sense. Habitual offenders are responsible for the majority of criminal acts (Wolfgang, Figlio, & Sellin, 1972), so locking them up seems like a logical—and race-neutral—means of incapacitating the most dangerous offenders. However, what this logic overlooks is that the crimes that are counted as "strikes" do not need to be violent, and they are almost exclusively street crimes like burglary and robbery that are primarily committed by the underprivileged rather than white collar crimes like worker safety violations or wage theft that typically cause more harm to society but are also typically committed by "upstanding" members of society. As Reiman and Leighton (2013) have discussed, "The fact is that the label 'crime' is not used in America to name all or the worst of the actions that cause misery and suffering to Americans. It is reserved primarily for the dangerous actions of the poor" (p. 66). And due to the racialized nature of poverty and inequality in American society, this also means it is reserved primarily for the actions of Black and Hispanic Americans. This is not to suggest that street crimes do not pose a threat to society. They certainly do, but as we have already discussed, other behaviors that are either not labeled as crimes or are not treated as harshly *also* pose a threat to society—often even a greater threat. Like with murder, the typical "strikable" offense is an interpersonal crime in which a perpetrator physically attacks a specific and identifiable victim—although, as mentioned earlier, the triggering offense does not always need to be violent.

What this mean is that someone convicted of three low-level street crimes might wind up in prison for the rest of their life while the maximum possible penalty for "Willful and repeated violations" of workplace safety laws—even ones "that pose a substantial probability of death or serious physical harm to workers"—is a $70,000 fine (Michaels, 2010). For example, to support a heroin addiction, 37-year-old Leandro Andrade stole approximately $150 worth of video cassettes, but due to three prior convictions for nonviolent residential burglary (all of which had occurred on the same day, twelve years prior to the theft of the video tapes), he was sentenced to 50 years to life (at his age, the functional equivalent of LWOP) under California's three strikes law (Chemerinsky, 2004; Lockyer v. Andrade, 2003). Andrade's plight is not unique. Stories like his can be found all over the nation. In Louisiana, Dale Wayne Green received a LWOP sentence for selling $20 worth of marijuana to an undercover police officer due to a prior conviction for attempted possession of cocaine that had occurred nine years earlier and another one for simple robbery that occurred eight years earlier (*Louisiana v. Green*, 2003). Hershel Miles was sentenced to LWOP under Mississippi's three strikes law following a conviction for forgery and petit larceny; his prior convictions included four burglaries, one robbery, and one cocaine sale (*Miles v. Mississippi*, 2003). Perhaps most egregiously, a 22-year-old man in Florida received a LWOP sentence for robbing a sandwich shop because the crime occurred less than three years after his release from prison for an earlier drug conviction (Nellis, 2010).

In contrast to these LWOP sentences for relatively minor street crimes, prior to the *Deepwater Horizon* explosion that killed eleven workers in 2010 (and spewed millions of gallons of oil into the Gulf of Mexico), the oil rig's owner, BP, repeatedly flaunted workplace safety laws. In the three years prior to the explosion, BP had been cited for 760 "egregious, willful" violations of Occupational Safety and Health Administration (OSHA) rules—the highest level of culpability. Those violations had led to 30 deaths, more than 200 injuries, and a 200,000-gallon oil spill in Alaska (Thomas, Jones, Cloherty, & Ryan, 2010). However, no one at BP was charged as a habitual offender, and no one saw any prison time (Grimm, 2019; Larino, 2019; Pavlo, 2015; Pavlo, 2018). Instead, the company was fined $4.5 billion (Krauss & Schwartz, 2012) or about one third of the $14 billion profit the company reported in 2009 (the year before the explosion) (Graham, 2010)—and less than one fifth of the $25.7 billion profit the company recorded in 2011 (the year before the fine was levied) (Macalister, 2012). Similarly, wage theft, where employers do not pay workers for all the hours they work, pay them below minimum wage, or do not pay them properly for overtime, is almost never prosecuted even though the practice harms far more people and costs workers several times more than all property crimes reported to the FBI combined (Darby, 2019; Meixell & Eisenbrey, 2014). On the rare occasion when it is prosecuted, it is typically treated as a misdemeanor, and repeat offenders are certainly never charged under three strikes laws (Jamieson, 2015; Kucera, 2012). For example, for stealing $230,000 worth of wages from his workers, the owner of nine Papa John's franchises in New York only received a 60-day jail sentence (Jamieson, 2015).

Both the business executives and the petty criminals described earlier are repeat offenders who pose a threat to society, but the executives clearly pose a greater threat. Yet, only the street criminals (who are far more likely to be poor, urban, and Black) are defined as "habitual offenders" and sentenced to die in prison. As a result, habitual offender laws end up exacerbating LWOP's already existing racial disparities. For example, in North Carolina, 62% of those serving LWOP for homicide are Black, but 81% of those serving LWOP as habitual offenders are Black (Nellis, 2021, p. 28). Similarly, three quarters of those sentenced to LWOP under Mississippi's habitual offender statute are Black, and among those whose third strike was a nonviolent offense, the proportion of African Americans is even greater (Nellis, 2021, p. 29).

Death in Prison for Drugs?

At the age of 28, Theresa Wilson sold a prescription bottle that contained a 3.45-ounce liquid mixture containing morphine to an undercover police officer for $150. Although she had no prior felony convictions, the drug-addicted mother of two was nonetheless sentenced to die in prison (*Wilson v. State*, 2001). Courts upheld this grossly disproportionate sentence because in 1991, the US Supreme Court upheld a LWOP sentence against Ronald Harmelin, a first-time felon convicted of possessing 672 grams of cocaine. In the Court's opinion, Justice Scalia argued that Harmelin's grotesquely harsh sentence was constitutionally permissible because such "penalties may be cruel, but they are not unusual" (*Harmelin v. Michigan*, 1991, p. 994). In other words, such overly severe penalties are constitutionally acceptable precisely *because* they are so common.

Now, drug abuse and addiction are, of course, serious social problems that need to be addressed, but that does not mean they need to be treated as *criminal justice* problems rather than *public health* crises. After all, a prison cell seems like a particularly ineffective way of treating drug addiction, and trying to deter drug addicts seems like an exercise in futility. Yet, prison is the method the US chose for dealing with the drug problem, and as the aforementioned anecdotes demonstrate, many states are also sentencing first-time, nonviolent drug offenders to *die* in prison. According to the most recent data, there were 1,668 persons serving LWOP for a drug offense in 2020, which accounts for nearly 3% of all those serving LWOP and *at least* 38% (and possibly up to 71%) of those serving LWOP for nonviolent offenses (Nellis, personal communication, April 21, 2021).[3] Therefore, it is prudent to ask why US policymakers chose this route rather than some other path for addressing the issue of drug abuse, and the answer to that question suggests that the Drug War was not motivated by a concern over drug abuse but by a desire to reassert control over a "threatening"

Black population in the wake of the advancements made during the Civil Rights Movement (Alexander, 2012; Wacquant, 2000).

This phenomenon has been extensively documented by other scholars, so we will only provide a cursory overview here. Suffice it to say that it is no accident that the War on Drugs started shortly after the passage of the Civil Rights Act. Lyndon Johnson's signature on the law caused white southerners to abandon their traditional allegiance to the Democratic Party and essentially become free agents. Throughout the Civil Rights Movements, opponents linked the movement with crime and opposition to the movement with calls for "law and order." This enabled Richard Nixon to exploit southern discontent with integration efforts during the 1968 presidential campaign through the use of carefully selected code words or dog whistles that focused on "crime," "disorder," and "lawlessness" that had already come to be associated with African Americans during the turmoil of the Civil Rights Movement and related social unrest. As Nixon's domestic policy chief, John Ehrlichman, explained, the "subliminal appeal to the anti-black voter was always present in Nixon's statements and speeches" (as cited in Alexander, 2012, p. 44). This messaging, which became known as the "Southern Strategy," was stunningly effective, transforming the once uniformly Democratic South into a Republican stronghold for generations (Alexander, 2012; Beckett & Sasson, 2004).

Once Nixon took office, he needed to make some effort to follow up on his campaign promise of cracking down on crime, so he declared a "War on Drugs," describing illicit drugs as "public enemy number one" (as cited in Alexander, 2012, p. 48). Not surprisingly, given the anti-Black messaging in Nixon's campaign speeches and his appeal to the poor white voters who felt the most threatened by racial equality, this war became a means of maintaining white supremacy by primarily targeting communities of color. Again, as John Ehrlichman explained in a 1994 interview:

> We knew we couldn't make it illegal to be either against the war or black, but by getting the public to associate the hippies with marijuana and blacks with heroin, and then criminalizing both heavily, we could disrupt those communities. We could arrest their leaders, raid their homes, break up their meetings, and vilify them night after night on the evening news. Did we know we were lying about the drugs? Of course we did.
>
> *(as cited in Baum, 2016, para 2)*

Although the War on Drugs began as a rhetorical war, given this emphasis, once it was transformed into a literal war, the primary victims of that war were, unsurprisingly, Black and Hispanic.

If one were to gauge the extent of the drug problem by looking at the composition of American prisons, one could be forgiven for concluding that this is a plague that predominantly affects communities of color, but drug use does not disproportionately impact Black or Hispanic communities. Drug enforcement, however, does. Surveys consistently demonstrate that African Americans, Hispanics, and whites use illicit drugs at roughly equal rates (Substance Abuse and Mental Health Services Administration, n.d.). Yet, 54% of prisoners whose most serious offense is a drug crime are Black or Hispanic (Carson, 2021). So, there is no question that the War on Drugs has targeted people of color and has functioned as a form of racial control. This has to do with the drugs we choose to criminalize and the way we enforce those drug laws. Drugs that are more prominent in poor communities of color, like heroin and crack, tend to be criminalized with severe penalties while drugs that are more common among wealthier whites, like alcohol or powder cocaine, are either legal or treated more leniently (Alexander, 2012; Donziger, 1996). The infamous 100:1 crack-to-powder sentencing disparity that has been discussed at length by others is probably the most notorious example of this, but there are countless others. For example, Alexander (2012) has shown that despite the fact that drunk driving posed a far greater threat to public safety than crack addiction, it was crack possession rather than drunk driving that elicited punitive criminal justice responses. Although there were crackdowns on driving under the influence, the penalties typically entailed fines, short jail stints, and license suspensions; it did not involve decades in prison.

On top of this, among the drugs that are outlawed, enforcement of those laws is racially biased. Even when controlling for behavior, police officers are more likely to stop and search Black and Hispanic drivers and pedestrians, and when they do search people of color, they are *less likely* to discover contraband, which suggests that police need less suspicion to initiate searches against people of color (Alexander, 2012; Harris, 2002; New York Civil Liberties Union, 2014; Stanford Open Policing Project, 2021). Drug law enforcement also tends to be concentrated in poor, urban communities of color rather than in more affluent (and politically powerful) neighborhoods or college dormitories (Alexander, 2012; Beckett, Nyrop, & Pfingst, 2006; Beckett, Nyrop, Pfingst, & Bowen, 2005). It is for these reasons that despite using marijuana at similar rates, Black Americans are 3.64 times more likely to be arrested for marijuana possession than white Americans (American Civil Liberties Union, 2020), and Black men are thirteen times more likely than white men to be sent to state prison for any drug crime (Alexander, 2012). As such, the entire War on Drugs is a form of racial control, and by sentencing nonviolent drug offenders to die in prison, LWOP becomes the most powerful tool in that war and thus also becomes a tool of racial control.

Juvenile LWOP

As we will discuss in much greater detail in Chapter 8, due to their cognitive immaturity, juveniles have diminished culpability, which renders JLWOP inherently unjust. As such, if this inherently unjust sanction is imposed more often on one group than another, then the policy is *de facto* discriminatory—regardless of the behavior of those being punished. That is, if society creates a punishment that is unjust because it is exceedingly harsh, it is irrelevant if one group engages in the activity that is subject to the punishment more than another group because the punishment is not serving any legitimate crime control function. If a punishment cannot be justified by any legitimate goal of punishment, then arbitrarily utilizing it against behaviors that some groups happen to commit more than others is inherently discriminatory. Think of it this way: since imposing the death penalty on jaywalkers would be overly harsh, thus serving no legitimate sentencing goal, if Black people happen to jaywalk more often than white people, then executing jaywalkers would be racist because doing so becomes a means of targeting Black people, not controlling crime.

Therefore, if JLWOP is imposed on Black youths more than white ones, the punishment is racially biased *even if* Black youth are more likely to be arrested for LWOP-eligible offenses, and the data are pretty clear that juveniles of color are more likely to be sentenced to LWOP than white youth. In fact, "Non-whites are overrepresented among the JLWOP population in ways perhaps unseen in any other aspect of our criminal justice system. This kind of disparity harkens back to the inequitable sentencing practices that developed during the Jim Crow Era" (Mills et al., 2016, pp. 579–580). For example, prior to abolishing JLWOP, every juvenile sentenced to LWOP in Texas was Black or Hispanic (Mills et al., 2016). In Illinois, Louisiana, and North Carolina, greater than 80% of the JLWOP population consists of people of color while in Pennsylvania, people of color represent just 22.1% of the overall state population but 79.5% of the JLWOP population (Mills et al., 2016). Nationwide, *more than three fifths* (62%) of those serving JLWOP are African American (Rovner, 2021)—nearly *two-and-a-half times* the number of white youths serving JLWOP (Mills et al., 2016).

Conclusion: A War on Which Crimes?

The composition of our prisons—including the LWOP population—is not an accurate reflection of those who pose the most threat to society. Rather, it is the result of *decisions* made by those who write the laws, those who enforce the law, those who determine guilt and innocence, and those who impose sentence. It has been widely demonstrated that there is racial bias that disadvantages people of color at *each* of these decision points (Alexander, 2012; Kleinstuber, 2016b), and so the racial disparities in the LWOP population are more the result of these *public policy decisions* than it is the result of the differing levels of threat different racial and ethnic groups pose to society. Of course, we need to temper this conclusion a little bit. To date, there is very little research specifically examining whether LWOP is imposed in a racially-biased manner, so more research is still needed before any definitive claims can be made about the relationship between LWOP and race. However, the evidence that does exist strongly suggests that LWOP can be added to the list of "closely intertwined" phenomena that have historically been used to control minority populations and thus to maintain existing racial hierarchies.

As part of the so-called "War on Crime," American police forces have gained access to surplus military equipment, such as grenade launchers, M-16 rifles, night vision goggles, helicopters, and drones (Alexander, 2012), and as a result, they have been increasingly outfitting themselves like an occupying army rather than as civil servants. However, these military resources and tactics have been almost exclusively deployed against poor communities of color. As Barak, Leighton, and Cotton (2018) have observed:

> Generally, with the crimes of the powerless, the governmental legal agents wage "wars" like the ones on illicit drugs or undocumented families and have "zero tolerance" for a range of petty crimes. Such acts receive a disproportionate priority with investigations, surveillance, arrest, and prosecutions and during what is likely to be a negotiated settlement (plea bargain). When convicted, perpetrators are typically sentenced to prison or placed on probation. Either way, the poor and powerless are disproportionately represented as "common criminals" or the "dangerous class," and they are treated accordingly.
>
> By contrast, many crimes of the very powerful are "beyond incrimination" or not subject to the criminal law in the first place because of lobbying and donations to politicians. Thus, the possibility of criminal liability and prison does not even exist. Police do not investigate, and it is a regulatory matter to be dealt with by a fine and a consent decree. Even when there is an actual crime, offenders can receive a "deferred prosecutorial agreement," which means charges will be dropped if there is no additional wrongdoing. (pp. 88–89)

If the acts that are targeted for LWOP sentences do not reflect an objective accounting of the acts that pose the most danger to society, then "it is sensible to conclude that" these sentences are being "applied for reasons that lie with the decision makers and not in the realm of objective dangers" (Reiman & Leighton, 2013, p. 74). And what could those reasons be? Well, if the police are being outfitted and deployed like an army into poor communities of color, if the use of LWOP is not responsive to crime rates, and if LWOP sentences are being disproportionately doled out to people of color, it is not a stretch to conclude that this reason is racial control rather than crime control. Remember, African Americans represent about 14% of the US population (US Census Bureau, 2021) and 33% of sentenced prisoners (Carson, 2021) but a staggering 55% of those serving LWOP (Nellis, 2021) and 62% of those serving JLWOP (Rovner, 2021)—which are both *greater than* the 41% of death row that is Black or African American (Snell, 2021). Of course, the entire American criminal justice system could aptly be described as a mechanism of racial and class control, but LWOP, as the most extreme feature of that system, is the most powerful weapon in the arsenal of that control mechanism and therefore fulfills that racial control function in its own right.

Notes

1 In 2018, the gap in Pew's survey was 23 percentage points (59–36%) (Oliphant, 2018), and in 2016, white Americans were nearly twice as likely as likely to support capital punishment than black Americans (57–29%) (Oliphant, 2016). Gallup's 2021 survey found a gap of 14 percentage points in death penalty support (59–45%) between white people and people of color (Jones, 2021), but Gallup does not provide more specific comparisons, and historically African Americans have been less supportive of capital punishment than Asians or Hispanics.

2 According to Rovner (2021), 23.2% of juvenile arrests for murder involve a Black suspect and a white victim, but 42.4% of JLWOP sentences involve this combination. On the other hand, although white youths accused of killing Black victims make up 6.4% of juvenile murder arrests, they only represent 3.6% of JLWOP sentences. Dividing these ratios ((42.4/23.2)÷(3.6/6.4)) produces a disproportion of 3.25.

3 We provide a range here because there are 2,048 individuals serving LWOP for "other" crimes (Nellis, personal communication, April 21, 2021). Although this "other" category contains "some violent offenses in it," it is unknown precisely how many of these crimes are violent (Nellis, personal communication, March 1, 2021).

References

Alexander, M. (2012). *The new Jim Crow: Mass incarceration in the age of colorblindness* (Revised ed.). New York: New Press.

American Civil Liberties Union. (2012). *The case against the death penalty*. Retrieved June 3, 2021, from American Civil Liberties Union: https://www.aclu.org/other/case-against-death-penalty

American Civil Liberties Union. (2014, October 27). *Written submission of the American Civil Liberties Union on racial disparity in sentencing*. Retrieved from American Civil Liberties Union: www.aclu.org/sites/default/files/assets/141027_iachr_racial_disparities_aclu_submission_0.pdf

American Civil Liberties Union. (2020). *A tale of two countries: racially targeted arrests in the era of marijuana reform*. Retrieved April 9, 2021, from American Civil Liberties Union: https://www.aclu.org/sites/default/files/field_document/marijuanareport_03232021.pdf

American Civil Liberties Union of Louisiana. (2013, November). *A living death: Life without parole for nonviolent offenses*. Retrieved June 26, 2020, from American Civil Liberties Union of Louisiana: https://www.laaclu.org/sites/default/files/field_documents/2013_Report_Life_Without_Parole_Louisiana_1.pdf

Banner, S. (2002). *The death penalty: An American history*. Cambridge, MA: Harvard University Press.

Barak, G., Leighton, P., & Cotton, A. (2018). *Class, race, gender, & crime* (5th ed.). New York: Roman & Littlefield.

Barkan, S. E., & Cohn, S. F. (1994). Racial prejudice and support for the death penalty by whites. *Journal of Research in Crime and Delinquency*, *31*, 202–209.

Baum, D. (2016, April). *Legalize it all: How to win the war on drugs*. Retrieved May 16, 2021, from Harper's Magazine: https://harpers.org/archive/2016/04/legalize-it-all/

Beckett, K., & Sasson, T. (2004). *The politics of injustice: Crime and punishment in America* (2nd ed.). Thousand Oaks, CA: Sage.

Beckett, K., Nyrop, K., & Pfingst, L. (2006). Race, drugs, and policing: Understanding disparities in drug delivery arrests. *Criminology*, *44*, 105–137.

Beckett, K., Nyrop, K., Pfingst, L., & Bowen, M. (2005). Drug use, drug arrests, and the question of race: Lessons from Seattle. *Social Problems*, *52*, 419–441.

Blalock, J. H. (1967). *Toward a theory of minority-group relations*. New York: John Wiley & Sons.
Bobo, L. D., & Johnson, D. (2004). A taste for punishment: Black and white Americans' views on the death penalty and the war on drugs. *Du Bois Review, 1*(1), 151–180.
Carson, E. A. (2021, December). *Prisoners in 2020—statistical tables*. Retrieved December 21, 2021, from Bureau of Justice Statistics: https:// bjs.ojp.gov/content/pub/pdf/p20st.pdf
Chemerinsky, E. (2004, January 1). *Life in prison for shoplifting: Cruel and unusual punishment*. Retrieved May 12, 2021, from American Bar Association: https://www.americanbar.org/groups/crsj/publications/human_rights_magazine_home/human_rights_vol31_2004/winter2004/irr_hr_winter04_shoplifting/
Chen, E. Y. (2008). The liberation hypothesis and racial and ethnic disparities in the application of California's three strikes law. *Journal of Ethnicity in Criminal Justice, 6*, 83–102.
Cochran, J. K., & Chamlin, M. B. (2006). The enduring racial divide in death penalty support. *Journal of Criminal Justice, 34*, 85–99.
Coldsmith, J., & Kleinstuber, R. (Under Review). Fighting crime or needless time? Disentangling the reciprocal effects of life without parole and violent crime using structural equation models.
Darby, L. (2019, November 8). *Is your employer stealing from you?* Retrieved June 13, 2021, from GQ: https://www.gq.com/story/wage-theft
Dieter, R. C. (2013, October). *The 2% death penalty: How a minority of counties produce most death cases at enormous cost to all*. Retrieved February 3, 2014, from Death Penalty Information Center: http://www.deathpenaltyinfo.org/documents/TwoPercentReport.pdf
Donziger, S. R. (Ed.). (1996). *The real war on crime: The report of the national criminal justice commission*. New York: Harper Perennial.
Fleury-Steiner, B., Kaplan, P., & Longazel, J. (2015). Racist localisms and the enduring cultural life of America's death penalty: Lessons from Maricopa County, Arizona. *Studies in Law, Politics, and Society, 66*, 63–85.
Foerster, B. J. (2012). *Race, rape, and injustice: Documenting and challenging death penalty cases in the Civil Rights Era*. (M. Meltsner, Ed.) Knoxville, TN: University of Tennessee Press.
Furman v. Georgia, 408 U.S. 238 (US Supreme Court 1972).
Garrett, B. L., Seale-Carlisle, T. M., Modjadidi, K., & Renberg, K. M. (2021). Life without parole sentencing in North Carolina. *North Carolina Law Review, 99*, 279–332.
Graham, N. (2010, May 27). *BP's profits far outweigh the cost of cleaning up Gulf oil spill*. Retrieved May 18, 2021, from HuffPost: https://www.huffpost.com/entry/bps-profits-far-outweigh_n_591992
Gregg v. Georgia, 428 U.S. 153 (US Supreme Court 1976).
Grimm, A. (2019, July 18). *BP oil spill: Criminal cases largely unresolved 5 years after Deepwater Horizon blowout*. Retrieved May 18, 2021, from NOLA.com: https://www.nola.com/news/environment/article_ac227f5c-e019-51c4-a248-416e1339a3b0.html
Gross, S. R., Possley, M., & Stephens, K. (2017, March 7). *Race and wrongful convictions in the United States*. Retrieved May 7, 2021, from National Registry of Exonerations: https://www.law.umich.edu/special/exoneration/Documents/Race_and_Wrongful_Convictions.pdf
Grosso, C. M., O'Brien, B., Taylor, A., & Woodworth, G. (2014). Race discrimination and the death penalty: An empirical and legal overview. In J. R. Acker, & C. S. Lanier (Eds.), *America's experiment with capital punishment: Reflections on the past, present, and future of the ultimate penal sanction* (3rd ed., pp. 525–576). Durham, NC: Carolina Academic Press.
Harmelin v. Michigan, 501 U.S. 957 (US Supreme Court 1991).
Harris, D. A. (2002). *Profiles in injustice: Why racial profiling cannot work*. New York: New Press.
Jacobs, D., Carmichael, J. T., & Kent, S. L. (2005). Vigilantism, current racial threat, and death sentences. *American Sociological Review, 70*, 656–677.

Jamieson, D. (2015, November 19). *Papa John's franchisee gets jail time for failing To pay full wages.* Retrieved June 13, 2021, from HuffPost: https://www.huffpost.com/entry/papa-johns-wage-theft_n_564a16e9e4b045bf3df02826

Johnson, R., & McGunigall-Smith, S. (2008). Life without parole, America's other death penalty: Notes on life under sentence of death by incarceration. *The Prison Journal, 88*, 328–346.

Johnson, B. D., Spohn, C., & Kimchi, A. (2021). Life lessons: Examining sources of racial and ethnic disparity in federal life without parole sentences. *Criminology, 59*, 704–737.

Jones, J. M. (2021, November 18). *Death penalty support holding at five-decade low.* Retrieved December 20, 2021, from Gallup: https://news.gallup.com/poll/357440/death-penalty-support-holding-five-decade-low.aspx

Kleinstuber, R. (2016a). Discrimination and the death penalty. In I. Šimonović (Ed.), *Death penalty and the victims* (pp. 111–127). New York: United Nations Office of the High Commissioner for Human Rights.

Kleinstuber, R. (2016b). McCleskey and the lingering problem of "race". In D. P. Keys, & R. J. Maratea (Eds.), *Race and the death penalty: The legacy of McCleskey v. Kemp* (pp. 37–48). Boulder, CO: Lynne Rienner.

Krauss, C., & Schwartz, J. (2012, November 15). *BP will plead guilty and pay over $4 billion.* Retrieved January 2, 2013, from New York Times: https://www.nytimes.com/2012/11/16/business/global/16iht-bp16.html

Kucera, B. (2012, April 5). *Minnesota contractor charged with wage theft.* Retrieved June 13, 2021, from People's World: https://www.peoplesworld.org/article/minnesota-contractor-charged-with-wage-theft/

Larino, J. (2019, July 18). *Jury acquits BP exec accused of lying about oil spill flow.* Retrieved May 18, 2021, from NOLA.com: https://www.nola.com/news/crime_police/article_106be61d-5c1b-52c8-947f-ca994aa428d2.html

Lockyer v. Andrade, 538 U.S. 63 (US Supreme Court 2003).

Louisiana v. Green, 839 So.2d 970 (Court of Appeal of Louisiana, Second Circuit 2003).

Macalister, T. (2012, February 7). *BP's $25bn annual profit sees confidence and dividends soar.* Retrieved May 18, 2021, from The Guardian: https://www.theguardian.com/business/2012/feb/07/bp-announces-25bn-annual-profit

Marquart, J. W., Ekland-Olson, S., & Sorensen, J. R. (1994). *The rope, the chair, and the needle: Capital punishment in Texas, 1923–1990.* Austin, TX: University of Texas Pres.

Mauer, M., King, R. S., & Young, M. C. (2004, May). *The meaning of 'life': Long prison sentences in context.* Retrieved January 9, 2021, from Sentencing Project: file:///C:/Users/RKLEINS/Downloads/The-Meaning-of-Life-Long-Prison-Sentences-in-Context.pdf

McCleskey v. Kemp, 481 U.S. 279 (US Supreme Court 1987).

McFeely, W. S. (1997, November). *A legacy of slavery and lynching: The death penalty as a tool of social control.* Retrieved from The Champion: http://www.nacdl.org/CHAMPION/ARTICLES/97nov03.htm

McGuire, D. L. (2010). *At the dark end of the street: Black women, rape, and resistance – a new history of the Civil Rights Movement from Rosa Parks to the rise of Black Power.* New York: Alfred A. Knopf.

Meixell, B., & Eisenbrey, R. (2014, September 11). *An epidemic of wage theft is costing workers hundreds of millions of dollars a year.* Retrieved June 13, 2021, from Economic Policy Institute: https://www.epi.org/publication/epidemic-wage-theft-costing-workers-hundreds/

Michaels, D. (2010, March 16). *Testimony of David Michaels before the Subcommittee on Workforce Protections, The Committee on Education and Labor, U.S. House of Representatives.* Retrieved May 9, 2021, from Occupational Safety and Health Administration: https://www.osha.gov/news/testimonies/03162010

Miles v. Mississippi, 2002-KA-01134-COA (Court of Appeals of Mississippi 2003).
Miller v. Alabama, 567 U.S. 460 (US Supreme Court 2012).
Mills, J. R., Dorn, A. M., & Hritz, A. C. (2016). Juvenile life without parole in law and practice: Chronicling the rapid change underway. *American University Law Review, 65*, 535–605.
Nagin, D. S., & Pepper, J.V. (Eds.). (2012). *Deterrence and the death penalty*. Washington, DC: National Academies Press.
Nellis, A. (2010). Throwing away the key: The expansion of life without parole sentences in the United States. *Federal Sentencing Reporter, 23*, 27–32.
Nellis, A. (2021, February 17). *No end in sight: America's enduring reliance on life imprisonment*. Retrieved May 6, 2021, from Sentencing Project: https://www.sentencingproject.org/publications/no-end-in-sight-americas-enduring-reliance-on-life-imprisonment/
New York Civil Liberties Union. (2014, August 19). *Stop-and-frisk during the Bloomberg administration (2002–2013)*. Retrieved May 16, 2021, from New York Civil Liberties Union: https://www.nyclu.org/sites/default/files/publications/stopandfrisk_briefer_2002-2013_final.pdf
Ogletree, C. J., & Sarat, A. (2012). Introduction: Lives on the line: From capital punishment to life without parole. In C. J. Ogletree, & A. Sarat (Eds.), *Life without parole: America's new death penalty?*(pp. 1–24). New York: NYU Press.
Oliphant, J. B. (2016, September 29). *Support for death penalty lowest in more than four decades*. Retrieved June 3, 2021, from Pew Research Center: https://www.pewresearch.org/fact-tank/2016/09/29/support-for-death-penalty-lowest-in-more-than-four-decades/
Oliphant, J. B. (2018, June 11). *Public support for the death penalty ticks up*. Retrieved May 7, 2021, from Pew Research Center: https://www.pewresearch.org/fact-tank/2018/06/11/us-support-for-death-penalty-ticks-up-2018/
Pavlo, W. (2015, November 6). *Government drops obstruction charges against former BP engineer Kurt Mix*. Retrieved May 18, 2021, from Forbes: https://www.forbes.com/sites/walterpavlo/2015/11/06/government-drops-obstruction-charges-against-former-bp-engineer-kurt-mix/?sh=7d066ef920e9
Pavlo, W. (2018, January 8). *Two years after ruling, BP engineer still carries burden of prosecution*. Retrieved May 18, 2021, from Forbes: https://www.forbes.com/sites/walterpavlo/2018/01/08/two-years-after-ruling-bp-engineer-still-carries-burden-of-prosecution/?sh=2f573a074f70
Peffley, M., & Hurwitz, J. (2007). Persuasion and resistance: Race and the death penalty in America. *American Journal of Political Science, 51*(4), 996–1012.
Pew Research Center. (2021, June 2). *Most Americans favor the death penalty despite concerns about its administration*. Retrieved June 3, 2021, from Pew Research Center: https://www.pewresearch.org/politics/2021/06/02/most-americans-favor-the-death-penalty-despite-concerns-about-its-administration/
Puzzanchera, C., Chamberlin, G., & Kang, W. (2020, November 16). *Easy access to the FBI's Supplementary Homicide Reports: 1980–2019*. Retrieved June 7, 2021, from Office of Juvenile Justice and Delinquency Prevention: https://www.ojjdp.gov/ojstatbb/ezashr/
Quinney, R. (1970). *The social reality of crime*. Boston: Little, Brown.
Reiman, J., & Leighton, P. (2013). *The rich get richer and the poor get prison: Ideology, class, and criminal justice* (10th ed.). Upper Saddle River, NJ: Routledge.
Robinson, P. H. (2012). Life without parole under modern theories of punishment. In C. J. Ogletree, & A. Sarat (Eds.), *Life without parole: America's new death penalty?* (pp. 138–166). New York: NYU Press.
Rovner, J. (2021, May 24). *Juvenile life without parole: An overview*. Retrieved September 3, 2021, from Sentencing Project: https://www.sentencingproject.org/publications/juvenile-life-without-parole/

Snell, T. L. (2021, December). *Capital punishment, 2020–statistical tables*. Retrieved December 21, 2021, from Bureau of Justice Statistics: https:// bjs.ojp.gov/content/pub/pdf/cp20st.pdf

Soss, J., Langbein, L., & Metelko, A. R. (2003). Why do white Americans support the death penalty? *Journal of Politics*, *65*(2), 397–421.

Spohn, C. (2014). Twentieth-century sentencing reform movement: Looking backward, moving forward. *Criminology & Public Policy*, *13*, 535–545.

Stanford Open Policing Project. (2021). *Findings*. Retrieved May 18, 2021, from Stanford Open Policing Project: https://openpolicing.stanford.edu/findings/

Substance Abuse and Mental Health Services Administration. (n.d.). *Substance abuse and mental health data archive*. Retrieved May 16, 2021, from Substance Abuse and Mental Health Services Administration: https://pdas.samhsa.gov/#/

Thomas, P., Jones, L. A., Cloherty, J., & Ryan, J. (2010, May 27). *BP's dismal safety record*. Retrieved January 2, 2013, from ABC News: https://abcnews.go.com/WN/bps-dismal-safety-record/story?id=10763042

Tolnay, S. E., & Beck, E. M. (1995). *A festival of violence: An analysis of southern lynchings, 1882–1930*. Urbana and Chicago, IL: University of Illinois Press.

Tonry, M. (2014). Remodeling American sentencing: A ten-step blueprint for moving past mass incarceration. *Criminology & Public Policy*, *13*, 503–533.

Tonry, M. (2016). *Sentencing fragments: Penal reform in America, 1975–2025*. New York: Oxford University Press.

Unnever, J. D., & Cullen, F. T. (2007). The racial divide in support for the death penalty: Does white racism matter? *Social Forces*, *85*(3), 1281–1301.

US Census Bureau. (2021, August 12). *Race and ethnicity in the United States: 2010 Census and 2020 Census*. Retrieved August 18, 2021, from US Census Bureau: https://www.census.gov/library/visualizations/interactive/race-and-ethnicity-in-the-united-state-2010-and-2020-census.html

Villaume, A. C. (2005). "Life without parole" and "virtual life sentences": Death sentences by any other name. *Contemporary Justice Review*, *8*, 265–277.

Wacquant, L. (2000). The new 'peculiar institution': On the prison as surrogate ghetto. *Theoretical Criminology*, *4*, 377–389.

Wilson v. State, 830 So. 2d 765 (Court of Criminal Appeals of Alabama 2001).

Wolfgang, M. E., Figlio, R. M., & Sellin, T. (1972). *Delinquency in a birth cohort*. Chicago: University of Chicago Press.

Part II

Examining the Tough-on-Crime Case for LWOP

7

LWOP and the War on Crime

For those concerned about the problem of crime, LWOP may seem like a logical solution. After all, for decades, conservatives have championed more cops, more prisons, and more punitive sentencing as the way to fight crime (Beckett & Sasson, 2004; Peterson, 1945), and it is sensible to conclude that more severe punishments ought to deter more people from committing crime. If that fails, at least longer prison terms will keep criminals off the streets for longer, preventing them from being able to harm society. From this perspective, then, LWOP seems like a reasonable policy response to a serious social problem. However, deterrence theory also argues that the certainty of punishment is a more potent deterrent than its severity is, and decades of criminological research support this proposition (Beccaria, 1963; Nagin, 2013; Travis, Western, & Redburn, 2014). As the National Research Council has summarized, pretty much every review of the deterrence literature has found that more severe sentences do not reduce crime (Travis, Western, & Redburn, 2014). In addition, there is widespread agreement among criminologists that criminal offending typically peaks during late adolescence and early adulthood and then declines rapidly after around the age of 25 years (Hirschi & Gottfredson, 1983; Snyder, Cooper, & Mulako-Wangota, 2017; Sweeten, Piquero, & Steinberg, 2013). This would suggest that increasing the length of punishment beyond this crime-prone age range is unlikely to produce much, if any, reduction in crime since older persons are unlikely to commit crime anyway, and studies have repeatedly found that paroled lifers and others who are elderly when they are released from prison have extremely low recidivism rates (Advisory Committee on Geriatric and Seriously Ill Inmates, 2005; Anderson, 2019; California Department of Corrections and Rehabilitation, 2013; Justice Policy Institute, 2018; Mauer, King, & Young, 2004; Millemann, Bowman-Rivas, & Smith, 2017; Rosenfeld, Wallman, & Fornango, 2005; State of New York Department of Corrections and Community Supervision, 2016; van Zyl Smit & Appleton, 2019; Weisberg, Mukamal, & Segall, 2011).

DOI: 10.4324/9781003161783-10

So, is LWOP really going to be an effective weapon in the fight against crime? Although the deterrence literature consistently indicates that increasing the length of already lengthy prison terms does not reduce crime (Nagin, 2013; Travis, Western, & Redburn, 2014), as we discussed throughout Part I of this book, LWOP is more like a type of death sentence than a term of years, so it is not clear if these findings can be generalized to LWOP. Unfortunately, turning to the death penalty literature also does not help us answer this question because, as the National Research Council has summarized, "… research to date … is not informative about whether capital punishment decreases, increases, or has no effect on homicide rates" (Nagin & Pepper, 2012, p. 2). The reason for these inconclusive results is that the statistical rarity of executions combined with the highly unstable nature of homicide rates produces highly unreliable statistical estimates in which even slight variations in model specification or conceptualization of the independent variable produce vastly different results (Berk, 2005; Cohen-Cole, Durlauf, Fagan, & Nagin, 2009; Donohue & Wolfers, 2005; Donohue & Wolfers, 2009; Land, Teske, & Zheng, 2009; Nagin & Pepper, 2012; Shepherd, 2005). Because these problems are inherent in the data, some researchers have suggested that there are no "methodological tools that are likely to overcome the multiple challenges that face researchers" trying to determine whether capital punishment deters homicide (Chalfin, Haviland, & Raphael, 2013, p. 41). LWOP, however, is not statistically rare, which enables it to overcome many of the statistical problems that have plagued death penalty studies (for more details, refer to Kleinstuber & Coldsmith, 2020). Therefore, we can subject LWOP to more reliable empirical analyses in an effort to determine if it, specifically, has any impact on violent crime, and that is the focus of this chapter.

As we discuss in greater detail in the methodological appendix to this chapter, to account for the various plausible ways LWOP and violent crime rates may interact, we run a variety of statistical models to see if we are able to detect any effect of LWOP on violent crime. We begin by investigating whether the enactment of a LWOP statute reduces violent crime, and then we proceed to investigate whether using LWOP more often results in lower rates of violent crime. The overall conclusion from each of these analyses is that LWOP is unlikely to be an effective method of reducing violent crime. Although some states experienced a reduction in violent crime after enacting a LWOP statute, most did not, and increasing the proportion of life sentences that are ineligible for parole does not produce a statistically significant reduction in violent crime rates in *any* of the models that we run.

Enactment of LWOP Statutes and Violent Crime

We begin our analysis by seeking to determine whether implementing a LWOP statute is associated with reductions in violent crime. To do so, we use interrupted time series analyses using generalized least-squares regression. For details on how and why we constructed these models, please refer to this chapter's methodological appendix. It is important to recognize that these models utilize a quasi-experimental approach in which each state serves as its own control. That is, because the introduction of a LWOP statute is the experimental treatment, the "control" group is the state prior to implementing LWOP and the "experimental" group is the state after implementing LWOP. To get a fuller picture of the violent crime trends in each state before and after implementation and to reduce the impact of a potentially aberrant year, we look at five years of data pre- and post-implementation. While these models produce a good comparison between a state before and after the introduction of an experimental condition (in this case, the enactment of a LWOP statute), they presume that other factors that could affect violent crime rates change slowly enough that they could not create a sudden change in violent crime rates or change the trajectory of those crime rates timed to the same year that LWOP was implemented. This means that these models are susceptible to errors when outside factors, such as a severe recession or higher system level trends, cause sudden shocks to the system that have a lasting or trend-altering impact on the outcome of interest. Therefore, to highlight where such errors are the most likely to show up in the results, we will also discuss the results in the context of changes in the national crime rate.

Beginning with the states that first applied a LWOP statute in the 1970s or 1980s, Table 7.1 and Figure 7.1 indicate that the results of these legislative experiments were really a mixed bag during these two decades. Looking first at the change in the violent crime rate in the year in which LWOP was implemented (represented by b_2 in Table 7.1), we see that five states (Arkansas, South Dakota, Wyoming, Maryland, and Vermont) experienced statistically significant declines in violent crime in the year they first imposed LWOP, one state (Oregon) saw a statistically significant increase in violent crime, and the remaining nine states did not experience a statistically significant change. Turning to the change in the violent crime trend line from pre- to post-implementation (represented by b_3 in Table 7.1), after enacting a LWOP statute, five states (Arkansas, South Dakota, Rhode Island, Wyoming, and Vermont) saw the slope of their violent crime trend lines decline significantly relative to the trend line that existed prior to the imposition of the law. However, four states (Missouri, Connecticut, Maryland, and Oklahoma) saw statistically significant *increases* in the slope of their trend lines relative to what they were prior to LWOP's implementation. The remaining six states did not experience a statistically significant change in the relative slope of their trend lines. In other words, in some places, imposing a LWOP statute was associated with reductions in violent crime, in other places, it initiated increases in violent crime, and in still others, it had no noticeable relationship with violent crime. This leads us to conclude that during this time period, LWOP probably did nothing. Other factors were likely driving these changes since a policy is unlikely to have a positive effect in one state while having a negative effect in another state and no detectable effect at all in yet another state. However, this was also during a time of generally rising crime rates. The national violent crime rate (excluding rape, which as we explain in the methodological appendix is excluded for both conceptual and methodological

TABLE 7.1 Interrupted Time-Series Analyses Using Generalized Least-Squares Regressions on Violent Crime Rates for the States Implementing LWOP in the 1970s and 1980s

State	*LWOP implementation year*	b_0	b_1	b_2	b_3
New Hampshire	1974	44.21***	6.89***	−1.23	1.02
		(3.22)	(0.99)	(7.99)	(1.83)
Arkansas	1976	215.35***	26.66***	−51.35*	−24.40**
		(10.71)	(2.88)	(18.04)	(6.82)
Hawaii	1976	168.19**	1.21	39.19	6.09
		(36.47)	(12.55)	(36.43)	(14.11)
California	1978	530.00***	36.76***	26.78	−31.57
		(6.72)	(6.04)	(49.96)	(15.29)
Illinois	1978	558.92***	18.64	44.39	−10.07
		(31.15)	(11.62)	(54.79)	(18.24)
South Dakota	1978	139.58***	12.29	−54.57*	−24.72*
		(21.82)	(7.45)	(21.26)	(8.28)
Rhode Island	1979	270.80***	14.44*	50.90	−25.79*
		(6.23)	(4.85)	(39.14)	(10.07)
Alabama	1981	371.15***	9.08	−11.33	5.01
		(6.74)	(4.30)	(39.45)	(15.00)
Wyoming	1982	216.44***	48.66***	−225.47***	−45.05***
		(6.13)	(4.04)	(20.91)	(7.25)
Missouri	1984	518.95***	−13.49	−2.10	40.13**
		(18.80)	(6.87)	(26.59)	(8.58)
Oregon	1984	475.61***	−12.87	77.06*	14.08
		(13.04)	(6.13)	(23.29)	(6.79)
Connecticut	1985	407.14***	−11.53	13.05	40.65***
		(19.17)	(6.26)	(21.97)	(7.68)
Maryland	1987	788.73***	−2.01	−50.98*	47.83***
		(18.70)	(6.21)	(17.97)	(6.14)
Vermont	1987	91.26***	10.85**	−24.69*	−18.20***
		(6.23)	(2.30)	(9.28)	(2.68)
Oklahoma	1988	378.27***	2.62	20.49	35.73***
		(8.23)	(3.19)	(14.86)	(5.13)

Notes: Semirobust Standard Errors reported in parentheses below the coefficients.

b_0: Estimated Initial Violent Crime Rate

b_1: Annual Change in the Violent Crime Rate Prior to LWOP's Implementation

b_2: Change in the Violent Crime Rate in the Initial Year of LWOP's Implementation

b_3: Annual Change in Violent Crime Rate After LWOP's Implementation Relative to the Pre-implementation Trend

*$p \leq 0.05$, **$p \leq 0.01$, ***$p \leq 0.001$ (two-tailed tests)

reasons), measured in crimes per 100,000 population, doubled from 344.8 in 1970 to 688.6 in 1990. Therefore, those states that saw decreases after implementing LWOP were, essentially, bucking the trend, and it is plausible that enacting LWOP is the phenomenon that helped them do so. Similarly, those states that did not experience a statistically significant change may have been able to avoid the nationwide surge due to LWOP's implementation.

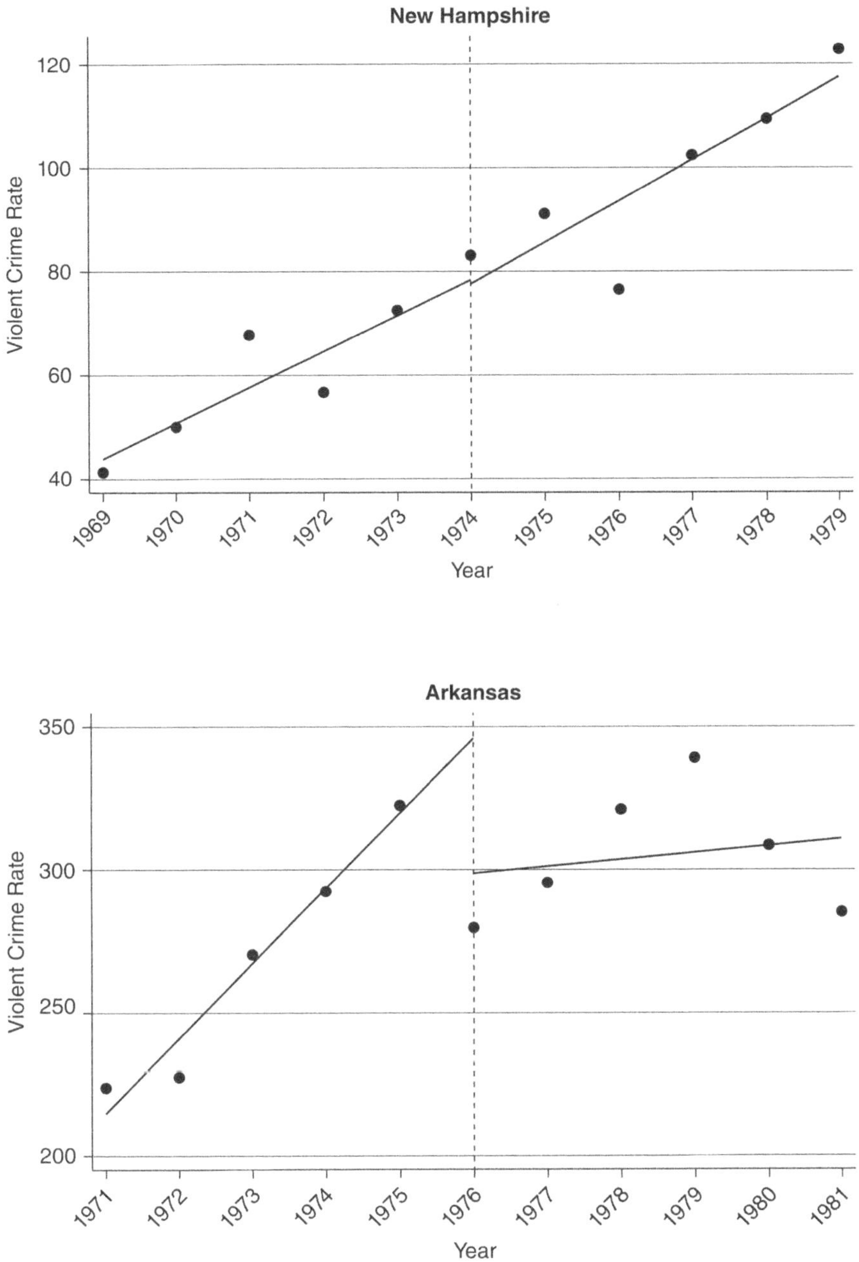

FIGURE 7.1 Trends in Violent Crime Rates Before and After LWOP Implementation in the 1970s and 1980s *(Continued)*

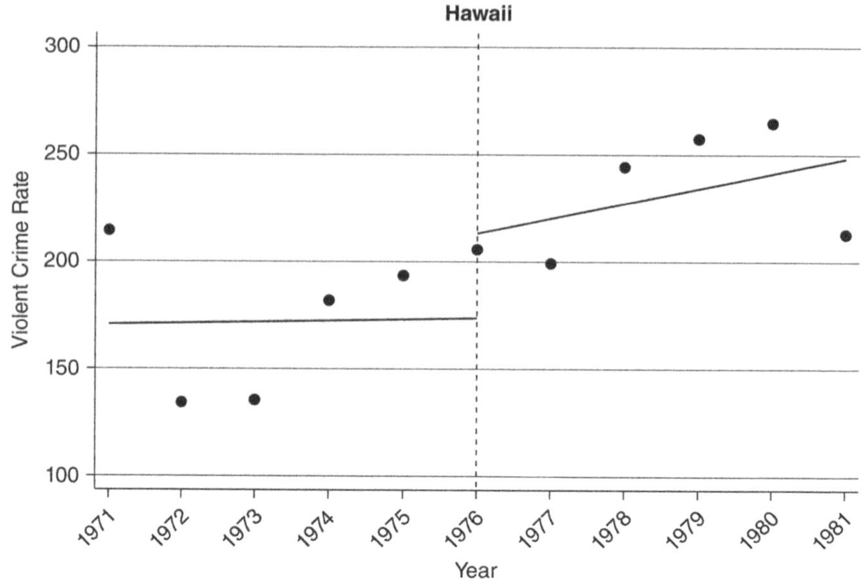

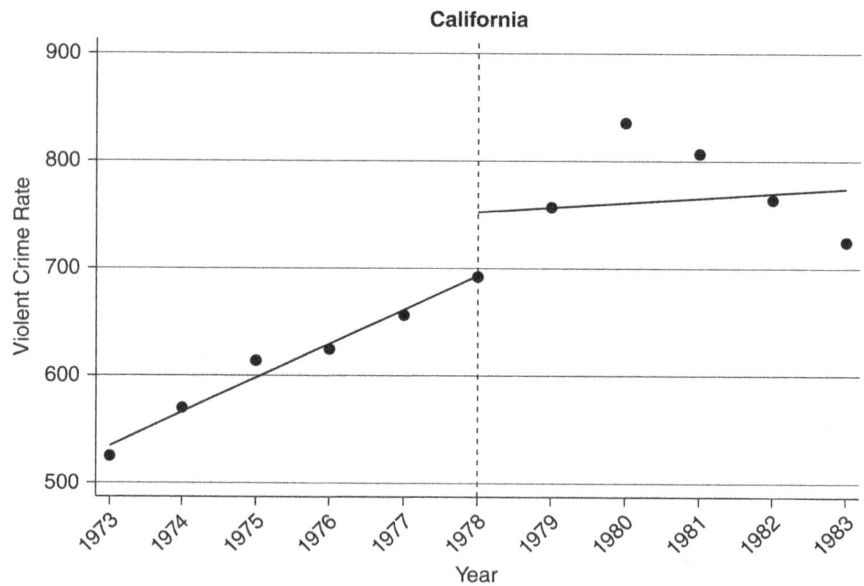

FIGURE 7.1 *(Continued)*

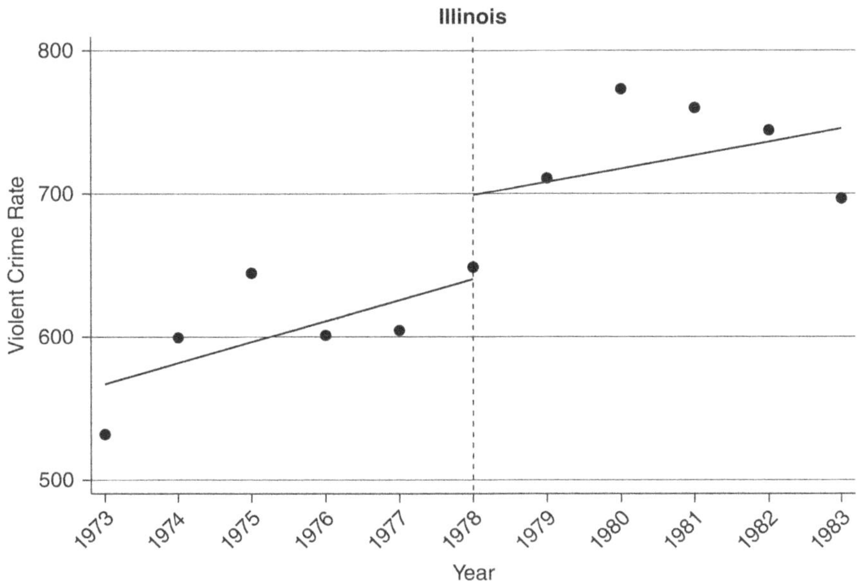

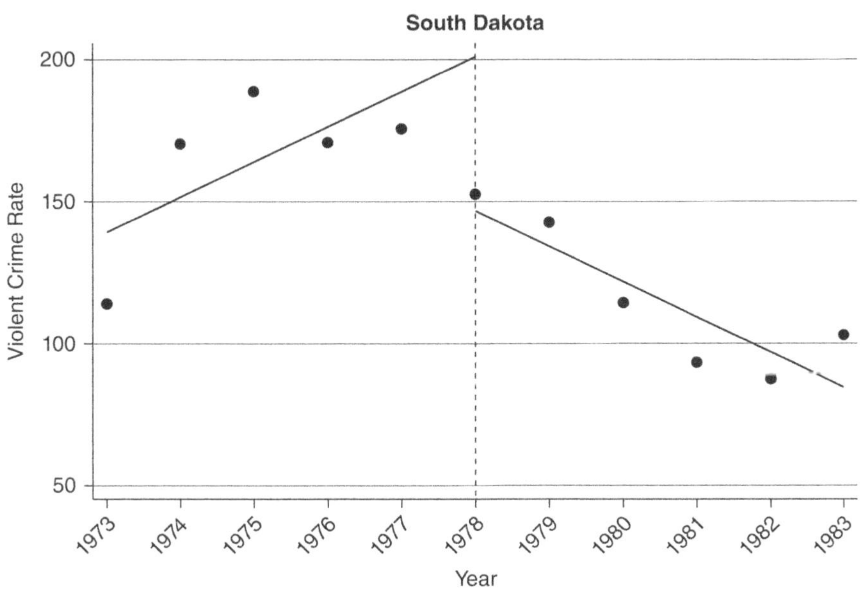

FIGURE 7.1 *(Continued)*

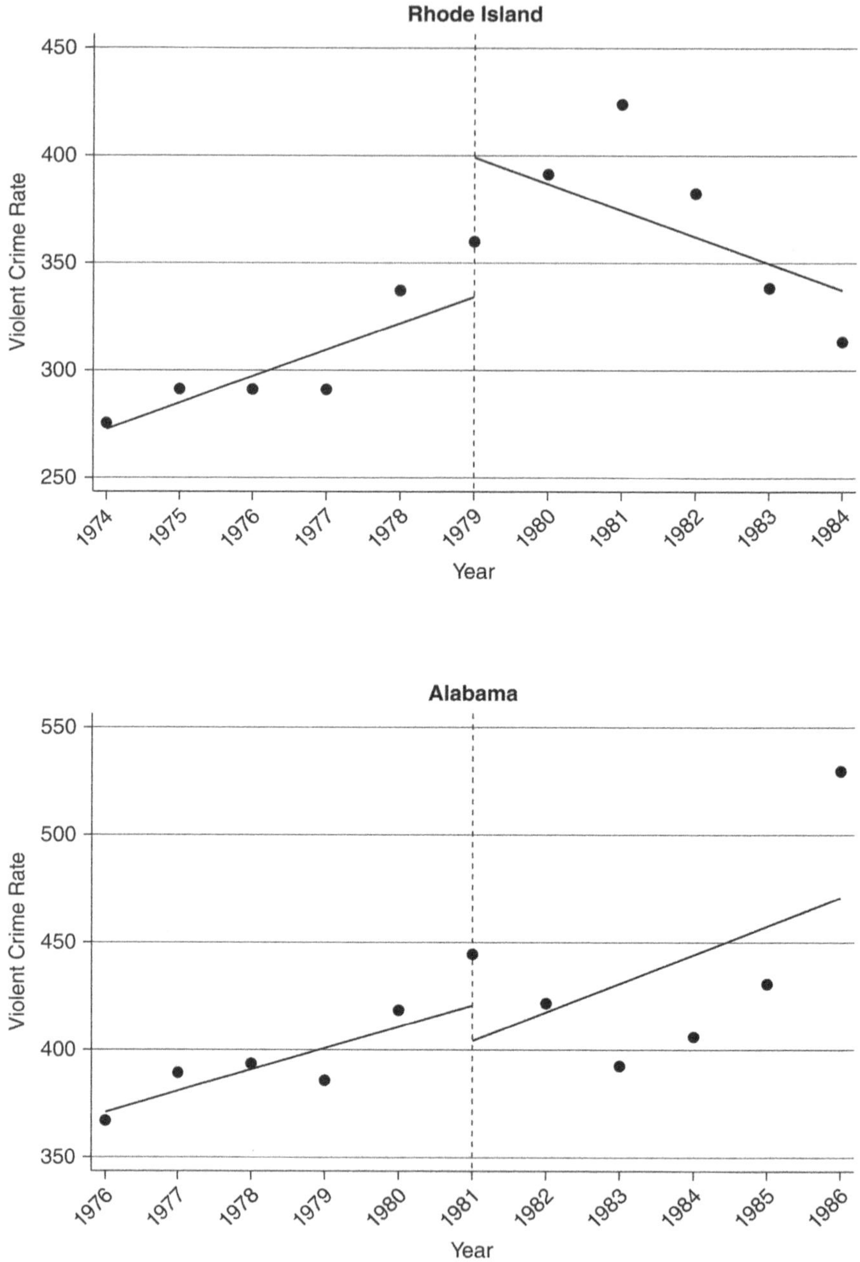

FIGURE 7.1 *(Continued)*

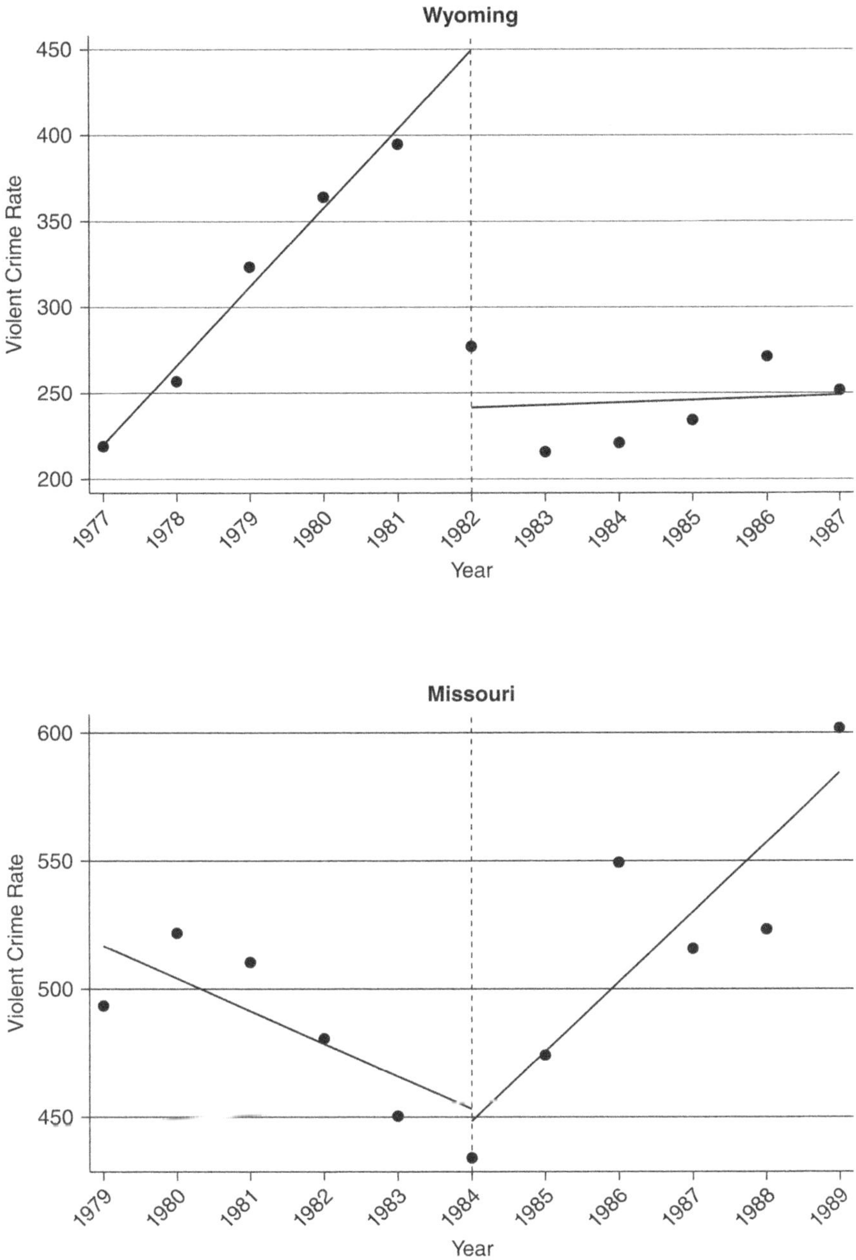

FIGURE 7.1 *(Continued)*

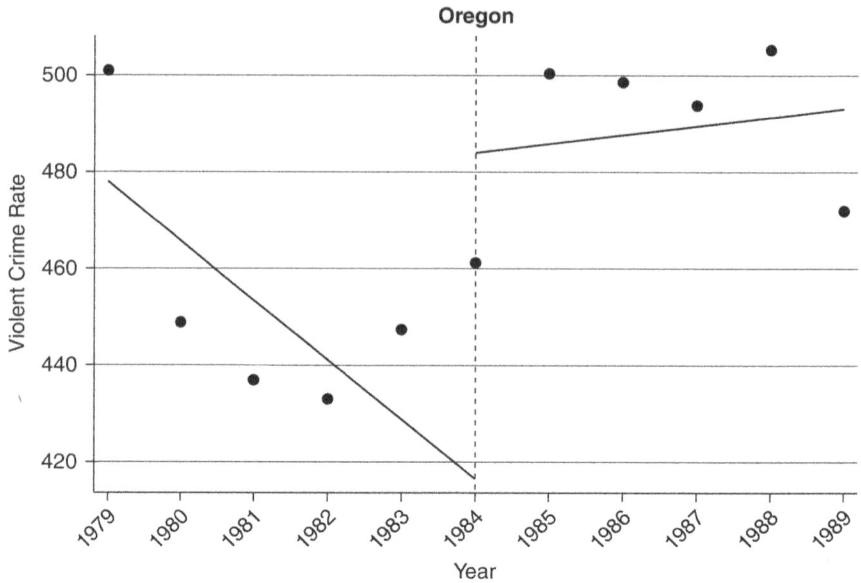

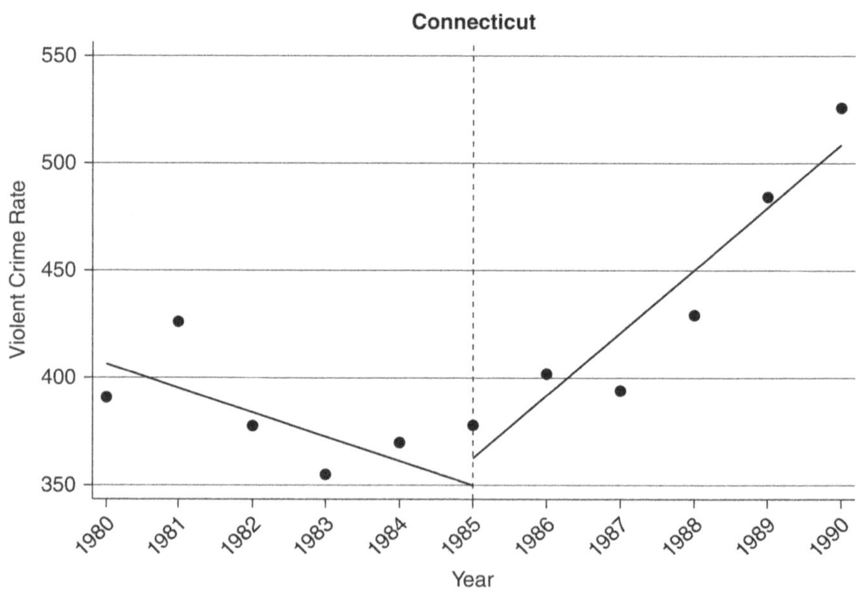

FIGURE 7.1 *(Continued)*

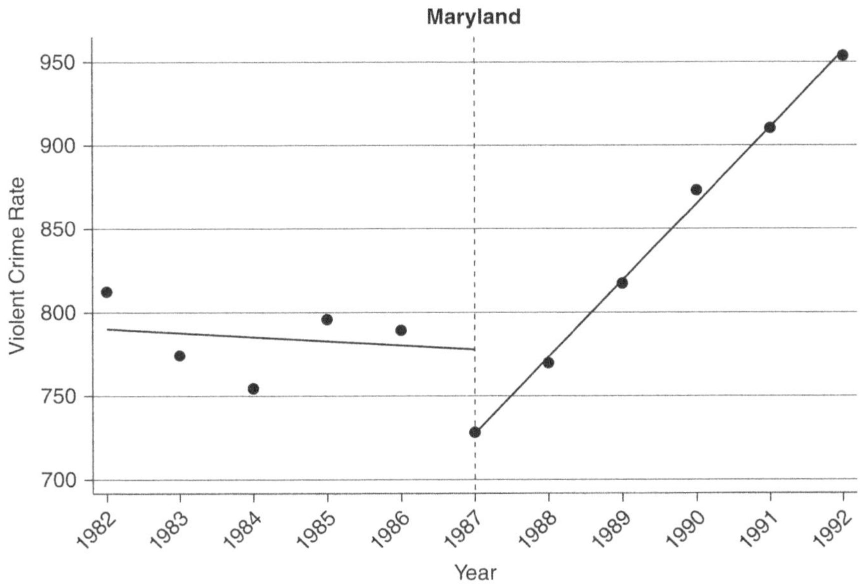

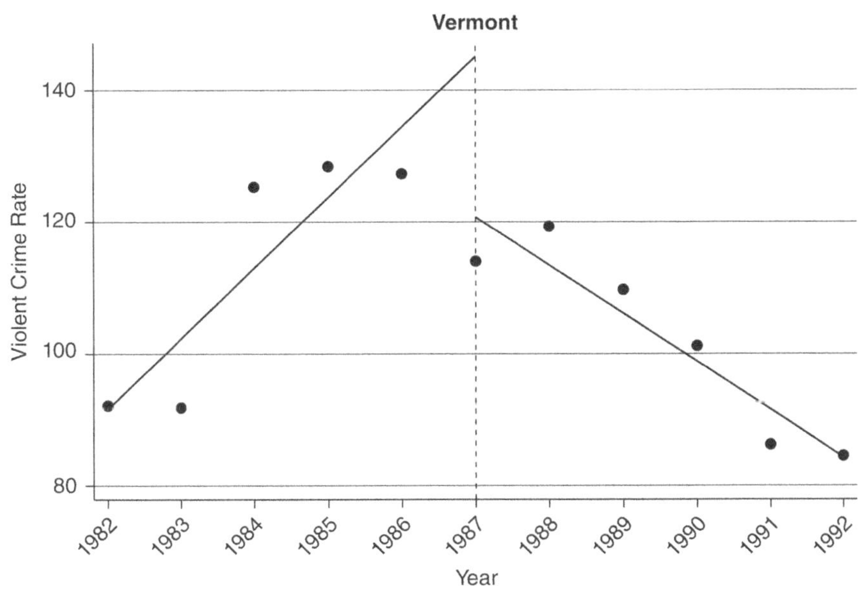

FIGURE 7.1 *(Continued)*

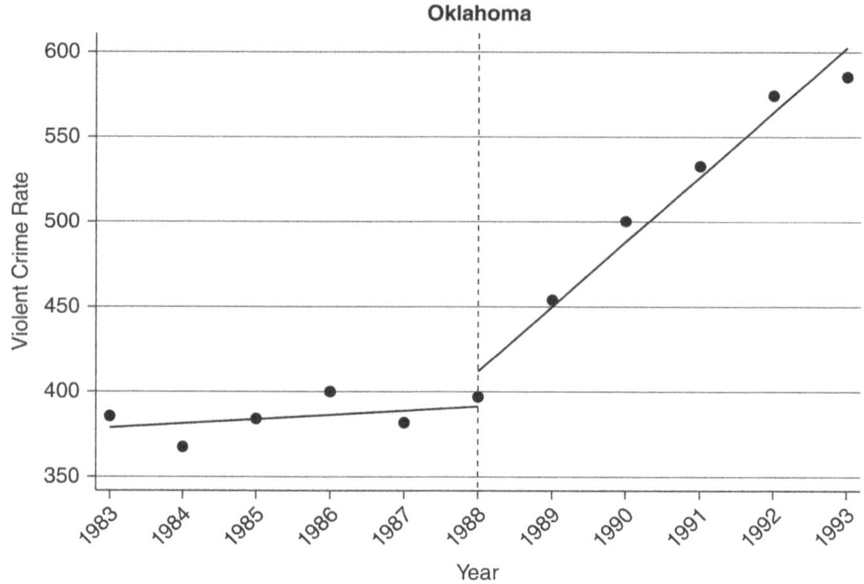

FIGURE 7.1 *(Continued)*

In the 1990s, however, the national context changed dramatically. After peaking at 715.9 violent crimes (excluding rape) per 100,000 in 1991, crime rates plummeted during the decade, falling by 33.7% to 474.5 violent crimes (excluding rape) per 100,000 in 2000. Therefore, in this national environment, we would expect to see the crime rate falling in states that enacted LWOP regardless of whether LWOP was responsible for the change. Yet, as can be seen in Table 7.2 and Figure 7.2, while we found this was the case in some places, it was not a consistent pattern. Twenty states implemented LWOP during the final decade of the 20th century, and among those, just five (Washington, Florida, Louisiana, North Carolina, and New York) saw their violent crime rates drop in the year they imposed the law. On the other hand, even in this national environment that should favor finding a deterrent effect, two states (Minnesota and Kentucky) experienced an *increase* in violent crime during the initial year of LWOP enactment. Most states in this time period did not experience a statistically significant change in their violent crime rates in the first year of LWOP enactment. Turning to the five-year trend lines, however, reveals a more consistent pattern. Here, after imposing LWOP, the majority of states (12: Minnesota, Arizona, Georgia, Washington, Florida, Indiana, Louisiana, North Carolina, Virginia, Ohio, South Carolina, and Tennessee) saw the slope of their trend lines decrease relative to the pre-implementation trend line. Only one state (Kentucky) saw the relative slope of its trend line *increase* after enacting LWOP. The remaining states saw no statistically significant change. These results suggest that LWOP may very well be responsible for producing lower rates of violent crime in the 1990s. At the same time, violent crime was going down nationwide, including in states that did not enact LWOP during this decade, so the models may just be picking up on the national trend.

TABLE 7.2 Interrupted Time-Series Analyses Using Generalized Least-Squares Regressions on Violent Crime Rates for the States Implementing LWOP in the 1990s

State	*LWOP implementation year*	b_0	b_1	b_2	b_3
Minnesota	1992	250.55***	6.27***	16.51**	−8.10***
		(2.04)	(0.51)	(3.86)	(1.04)
Utah	1992	210.40***	9.43***	−11.15	0.52
		(1.92)	(1.54)	(7.53)	(2.11)
Arizona	1993	563.68***	18.01***	42.52	−45.37***
		(9.70)	(3.51)	(18.78)	(5.30)
Georgia	1993	652.32***	14.35	−51.41	−39.27**
		(21.19)	(8.33)	(27.06)	(8.21)
Washington	1993	404.26***	14.96***	−24.23*	−31.94***
		(5.41)	(1.75)	(9.22)	(2.91)
Florida	1994	1121.29***	10.40	−80.25*	−61.57***
		(31.56)	(10.91)	(29.22)	(11.39)
Indiana	1994	395.30***	20.70	24.76	−50.59*
		(25.69)	(10.71)	(40.52)	(14.81)
Louisiana	1994	775.21***	59.29***	−86.19**	−116.36***
		(17.53)	(6.06)	(23.45)	(9.63)
North Carolina	1994	544.32***	30.82**	−78.04*	−50.37***
		(16.90)	(7.12)	(26.34)	(7.07)
Virginia	1994	299.97***	13.24*	−30.69	−21.79**
		(12.36)	(4.89)	(16.52)	(5.12)
Wisconsin	1994	224.17***	7.17	−8.10	−11.88
		(13.38)	(5.20)	(17.40)	(5.26)
Montana	1995	130.49***	4.45	−34.24	10.21
		(7.59)	(2.04)	(24.60)	(7.29)
New Jersey	1995	613.38***	−6.21*	−4.69	−25.34
		(3.47)	(1.95)	(42.62)	(11.98)
New York	1995	1176.55***	−48.82***	−157.42**	−2.21
		(12.51)	(7.52)	(31.82)	(7.55)
Ohio	1995	493.22***	−11.64	−2.00	−21.05*
		(15.63)	(5.59)	(17.99)	(6.29)
South Carolina	1995	900.66***	15.94*	−5.51	−55.11***
		(19.12)	(6.41)	(33.56)	(9.60)
Tennessee	1995	645.12***	19.14*	−4.39	−35.61**
		(19.32)	(8.07)	(29.31)	(8.94)
Iowa	1997	285.35***	3.10	−22.98	10.31
		(11.94)	(7.40)	(34.08)	(7.31)
North Dakota	1997	58.73***	0.85	−6.31	−2.01
		(1.09)	(0.54)	(4.50)	(1.12)
Kentucky	1998	436.27***	−44.78***	65.99**	34.37***
		(7.79)	(4.30)	(18.94)	(3.95)

Notes: Semirobust Standard Errors reported in parentheses below the coefficients.

b_0: Estimated Initial Violent Crime Rate

b_1: Annual Change in the Violent Crime Rate Prior to LWOP's Implementation

b_2: Change in the Violent Crime Rate in the Initial Year of LWOP's Implementation

b_3: Annual Change in Violent Crime Rate After LWOP's Implementation Relative to the Pre-implementation Trend

*$p \leq 0.05$, **$p \leq 0.01$, ***$p \leq 0.001$ (two-tailed tests)

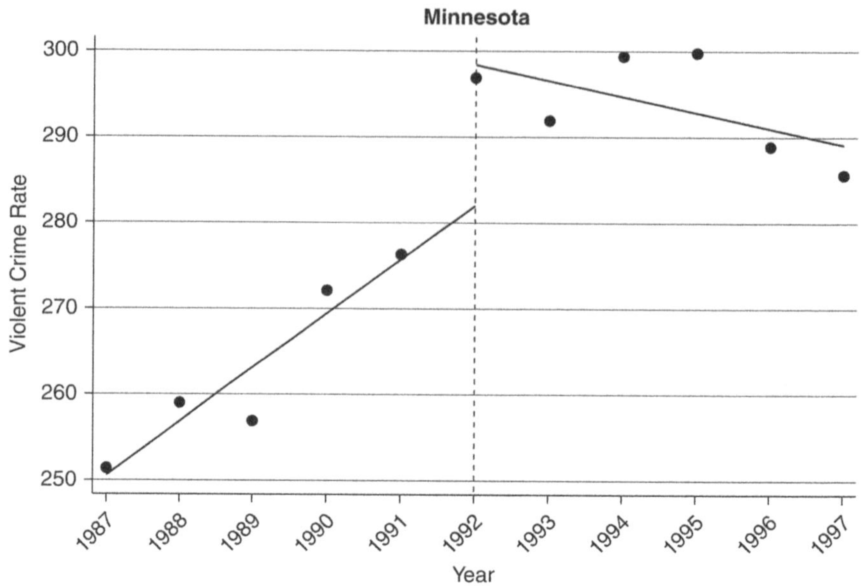

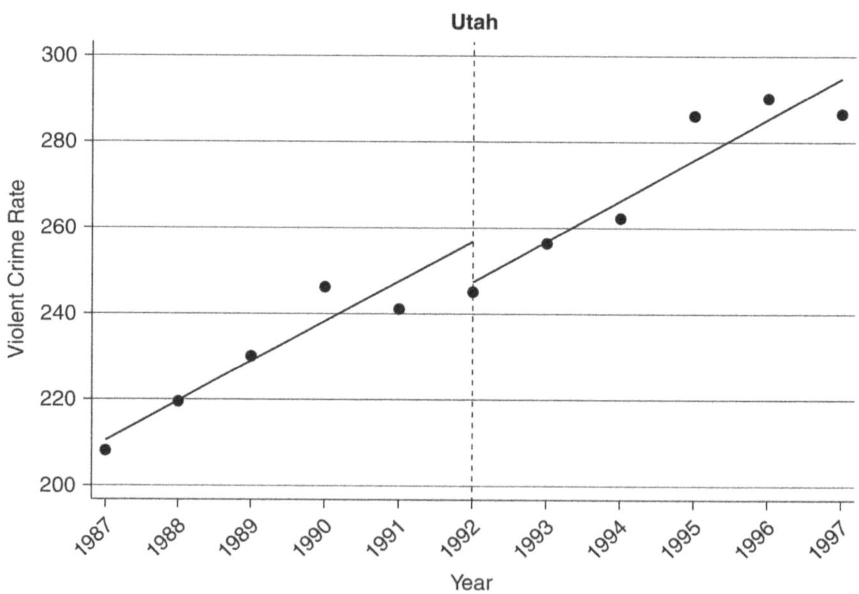

FIGURE 7.2 Trends in Violent Crime Rates Before and After LWOP Implementation in the 1990s *(Continued)*

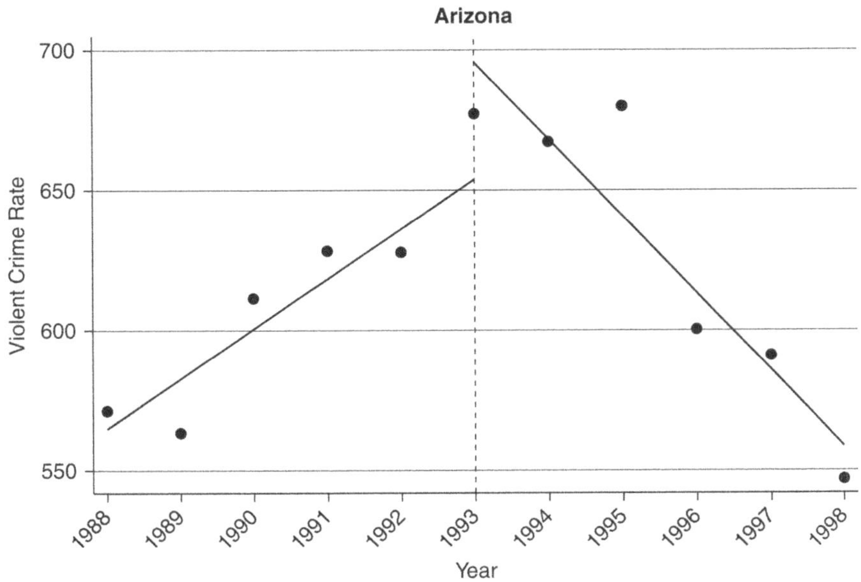

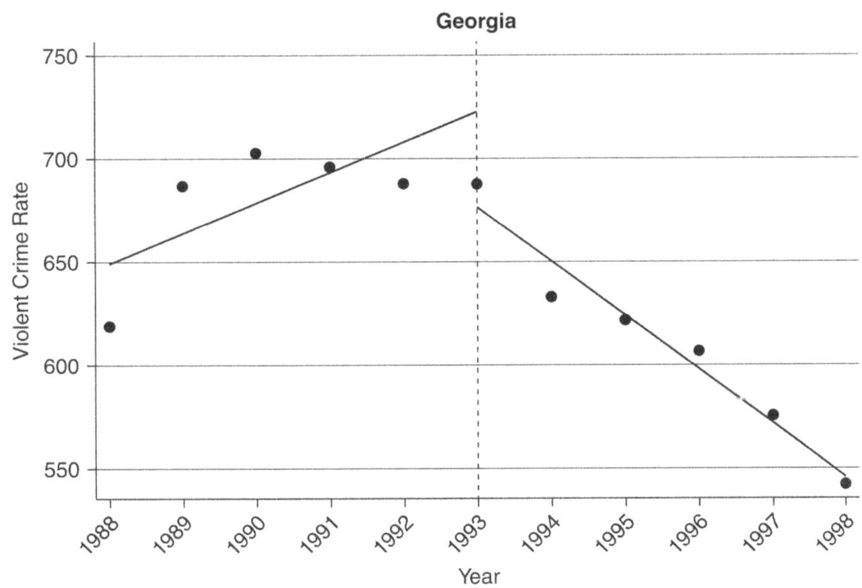

FIGURE 7.2 *(Continued)*

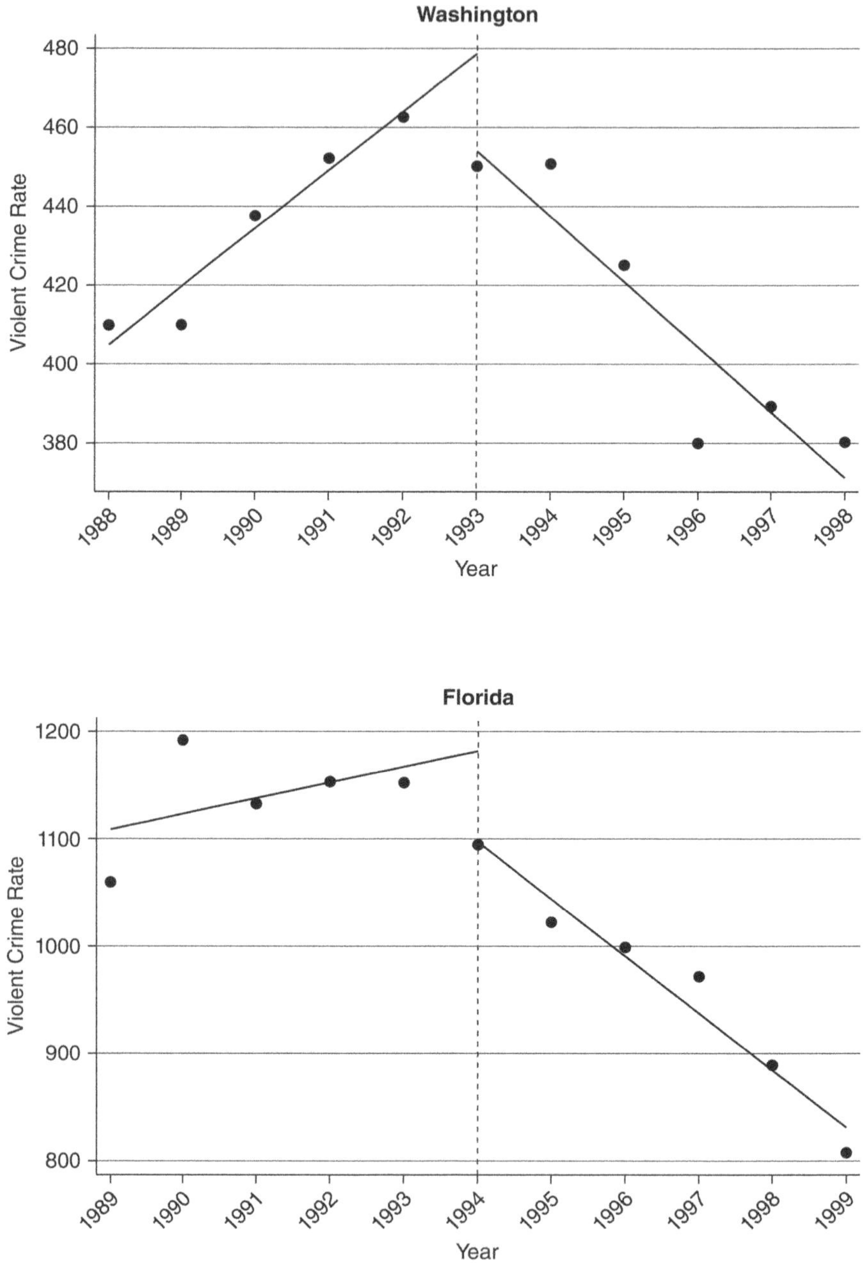

FIGURE 7.2 *(Continued)*

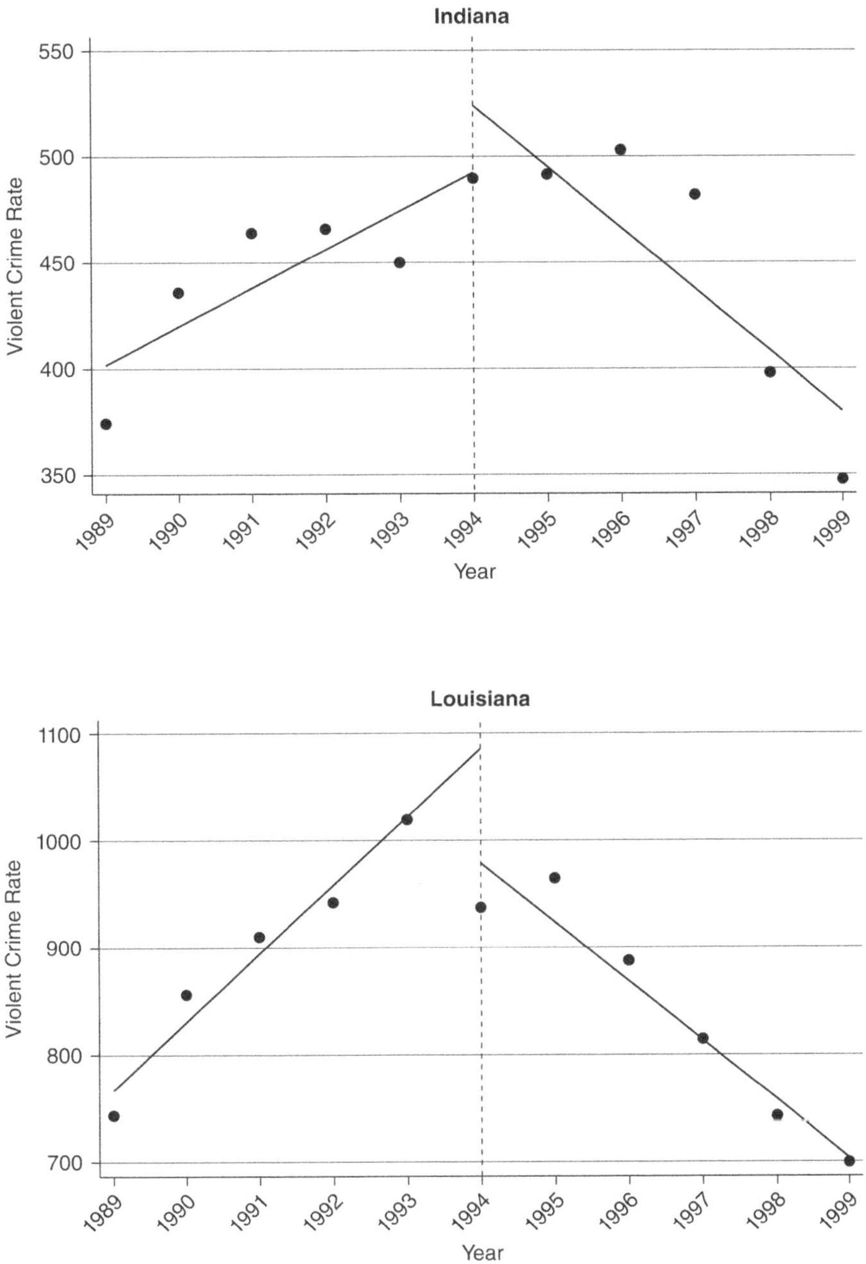

FIGURE 7.2 *(Continued)*

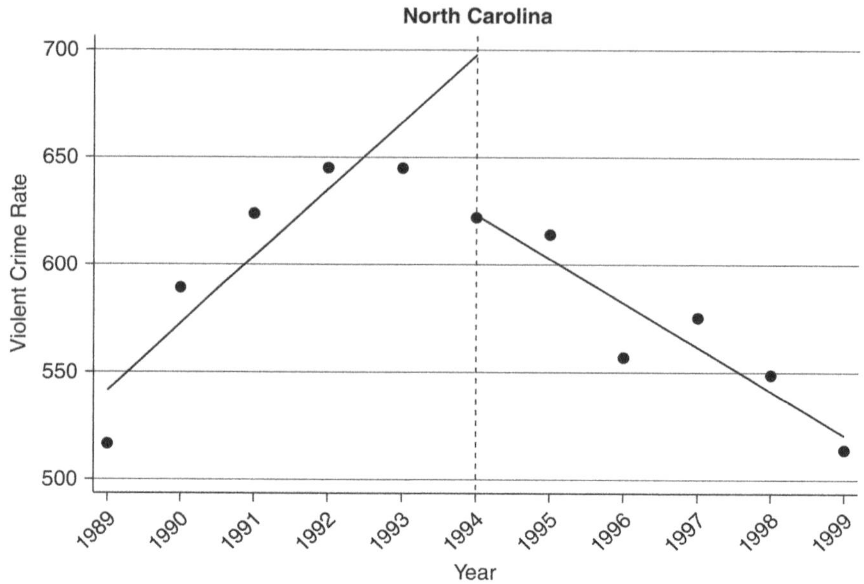

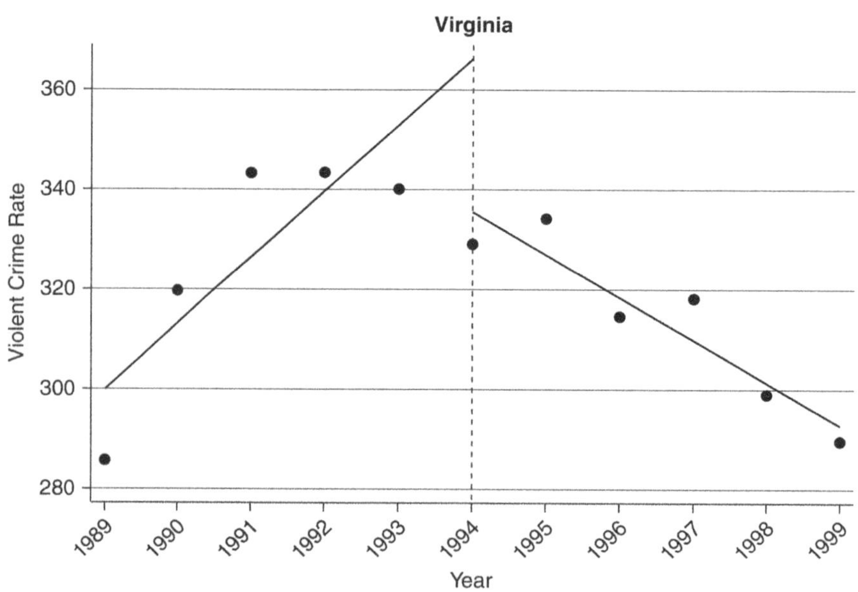

FIGURE 7.2 *(Continued)*

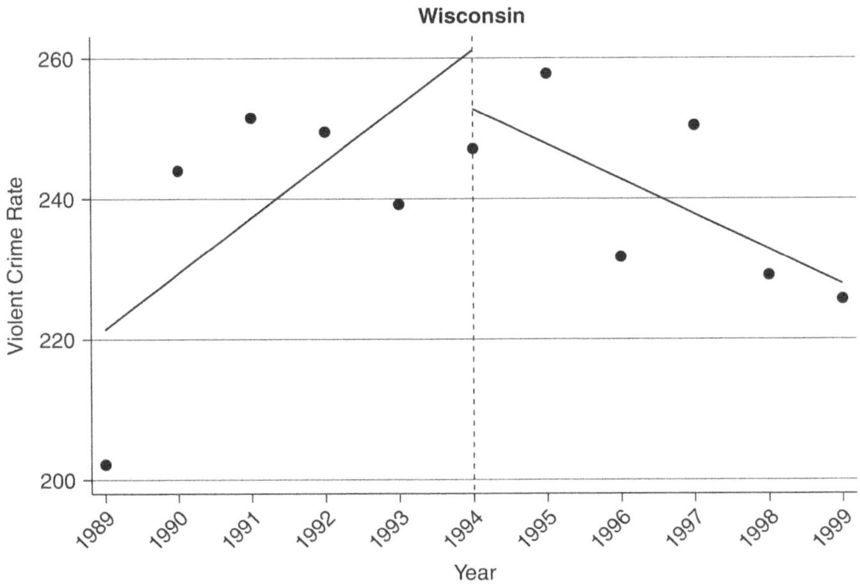

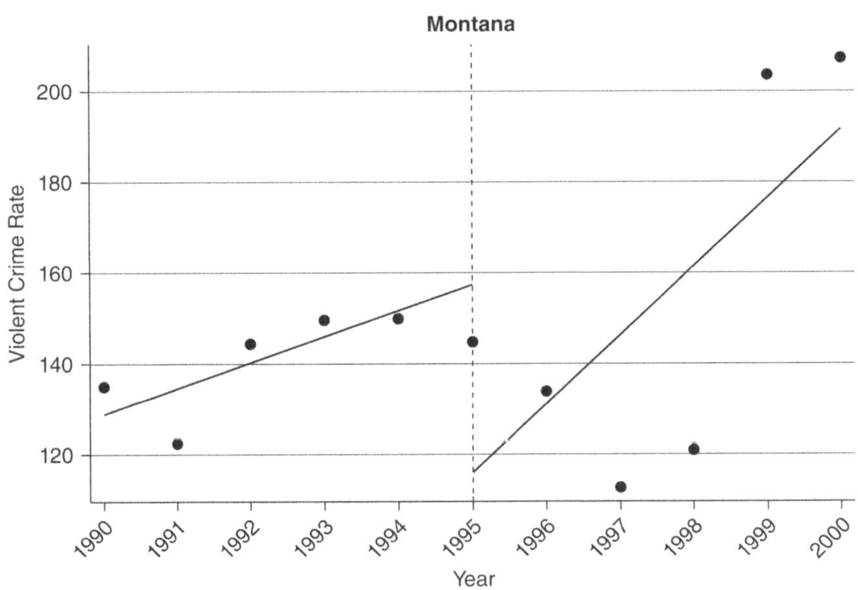

FIGURE 7.2 *(Continued)*

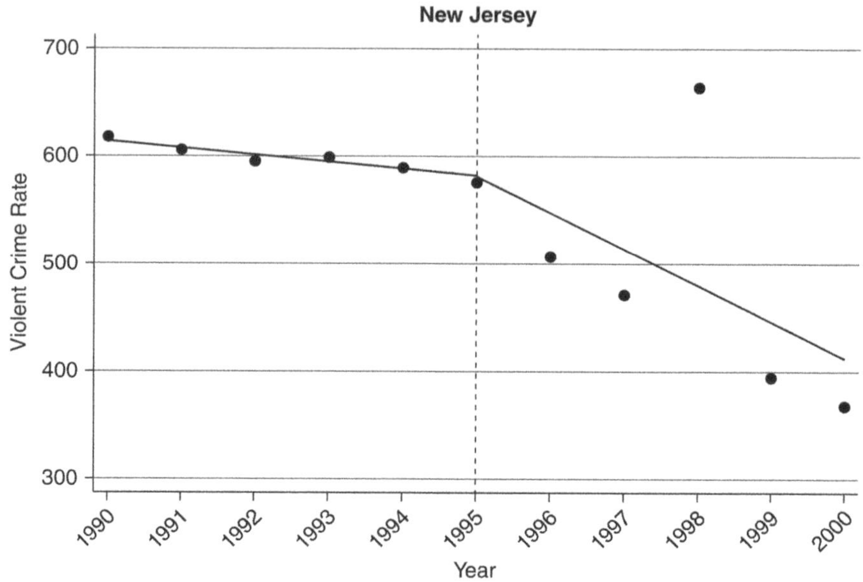

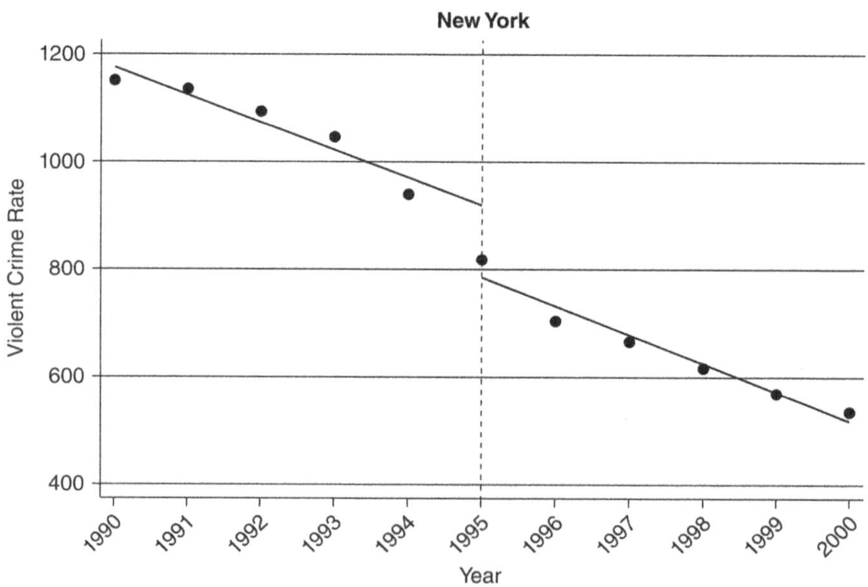

FIGURE 7.2 *(Continued)*

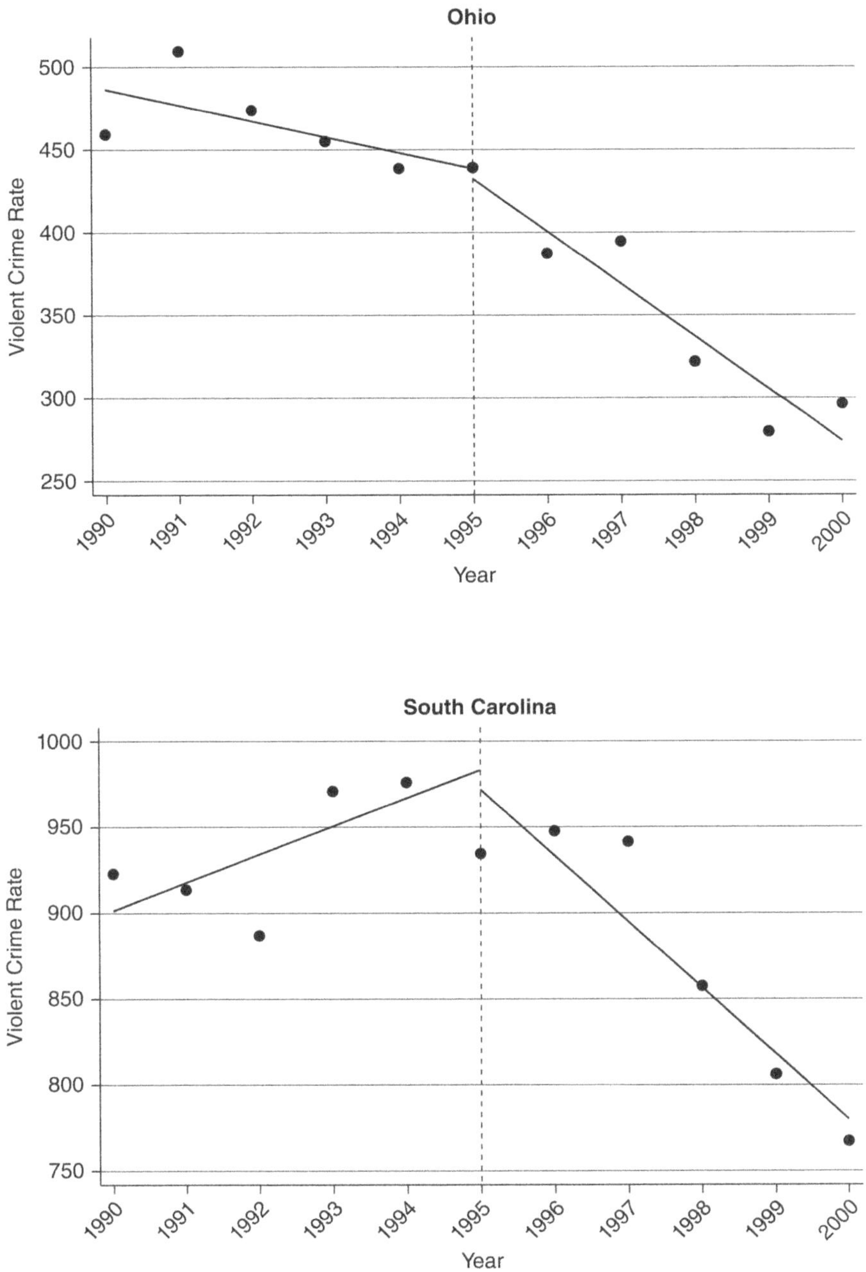

FIGURE 7.2 *(Continued)*

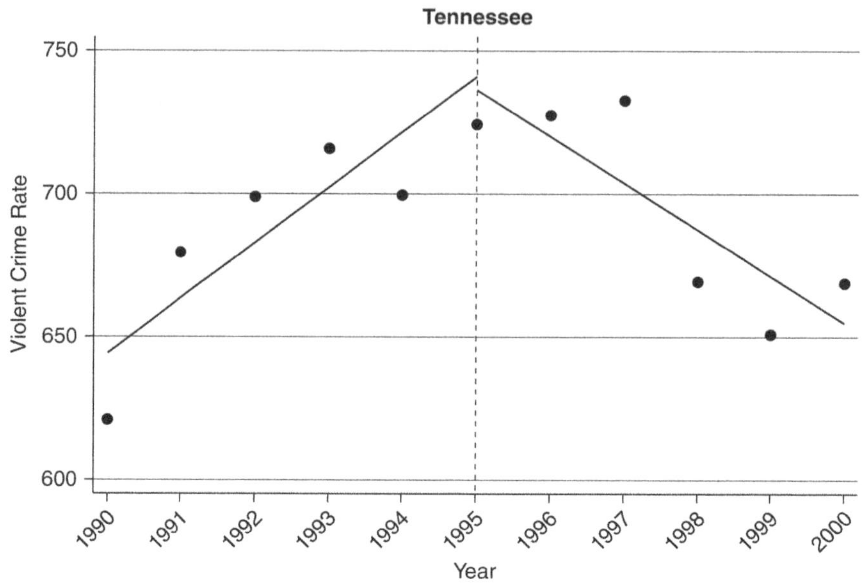

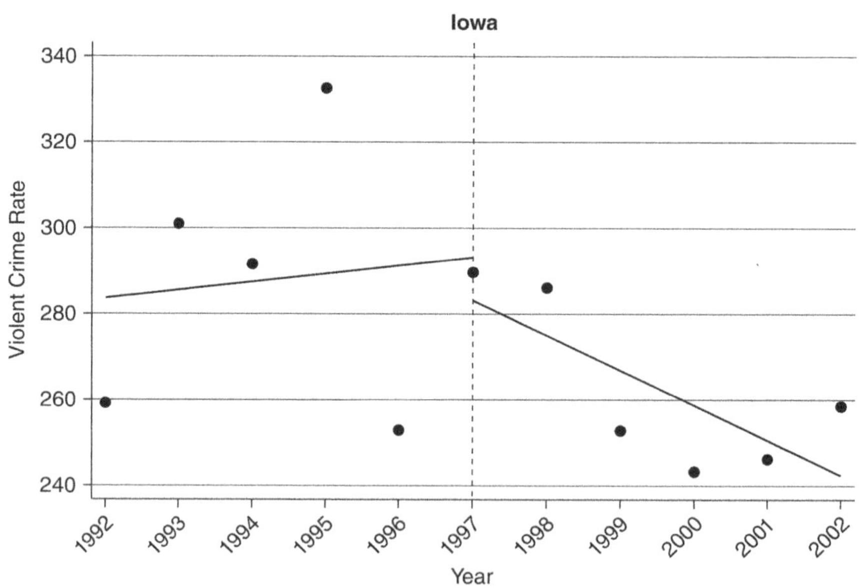

FIGURE 7.2 *(Continued)*

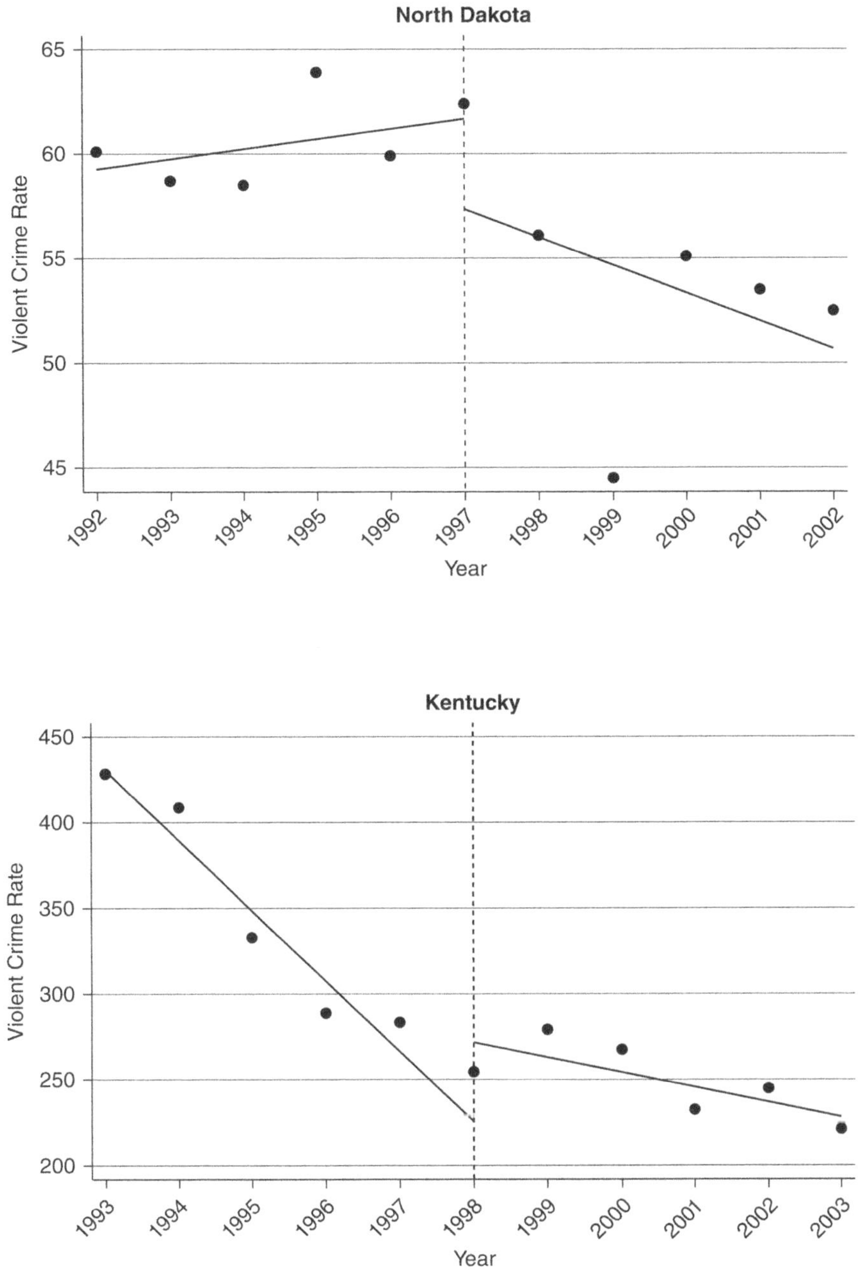

FIGURE 7.2 *(Continued)*

Therefore, to complete our analysis of the impact of enacting LWOP statutes on violent crime rates, we look at the states that implemented LWOP in the first decade of the 21st century. Compared to the two earlier time periods, the national violent crime rate was relatively flat, falling 20.6% from 2000 to 2010. So, crime rates were still falling, but not as rapidly as they were in the 1990s. As such, this decade provides the most neutral test of LWOP's efficacy, but even if LWOP did not do anything, we would still expect those states that implemented LWOP during this period to experience reductions in their violent crime rates. Yet, as show in Table 7.3 and Figure 7.3, that did not happen. Despite the overall downward trend in violent crime during this period, Delaware saw its violent crime rate *increase* in the year it initially implemented LWOP, and both Nebraska and Delaware saw the relative slope of their five-year trend lines *increase* after they enacted LWOP. These findings suggest that, in these states anyway, not only did LWOP fail to produce reductions in violent crime, it quite possibly did the opposite, driving crime rates up. None of the other states experienced statistically significant changes in their violent crime rates after implementing LWOP, but the magnitude of most of the post-implementation coefficients is *positive*, again suggesting that if they are detecting a real change, that change is in

TABLE 7.3 Interrupted Time-Series Analyses Using Generalized Least-Squares Regressions on Violent Crime Rates for the States Implementing LWOP in the 2000s

State	*LWOP implementation year*	b_0	b_1	b_2	b_3
Colorado	2002	323.38***	−6.92	24.66	12.00
		(8.17)	(3.37)	(16.64)	(6.48)
Nebraska	2002	448.48***	−40.72***	31.06	36.81**
		(23.61)	(7.89)	(23.69)	(8.17)
Delaware	2003	697.63***	−38.14***	82.58*	51.43***
		(4.25)	(3.48)	(32.10)	(8.63)
Idaho	2004	218.25***	−1.97	1.01	0.87
		(3.36)	(1.26)	(5.23)	(1.74)
Kansas	2004	347.89***	2.09	−7.09	4.53
		(5.96)	(2.61)	(18.12)	(5.63)
Texas	2005	523.86***	−2.08	−15.21	−10.76
		(16.30)	(5.64)	(16.89)	(6.87)
New Mexico	2009	612.03***	−3.77	−34.58	−3.99
		(15.84)	(5.14)	(17.18)	(6.52)

Notes: Semirobust Standard Errors reported in parentheses below the coefficients.

b_0: Estimated Initial Violent Crime Rate

b_1: Annual Change in the Violent Crime Rate Prior to LWOP's Implementation

b_2: Change in the Violent Crime Rate in the Initial Year of LWOP's Implementation

b_3: Annual Change in Violent Crime Rate After LWOP's Implementation Relative to the Pre-implementation Trend

*$p \leq 0.05$, **$p \leq 0.01$, ***$p \leq 0.001$ (two-tailed tests)

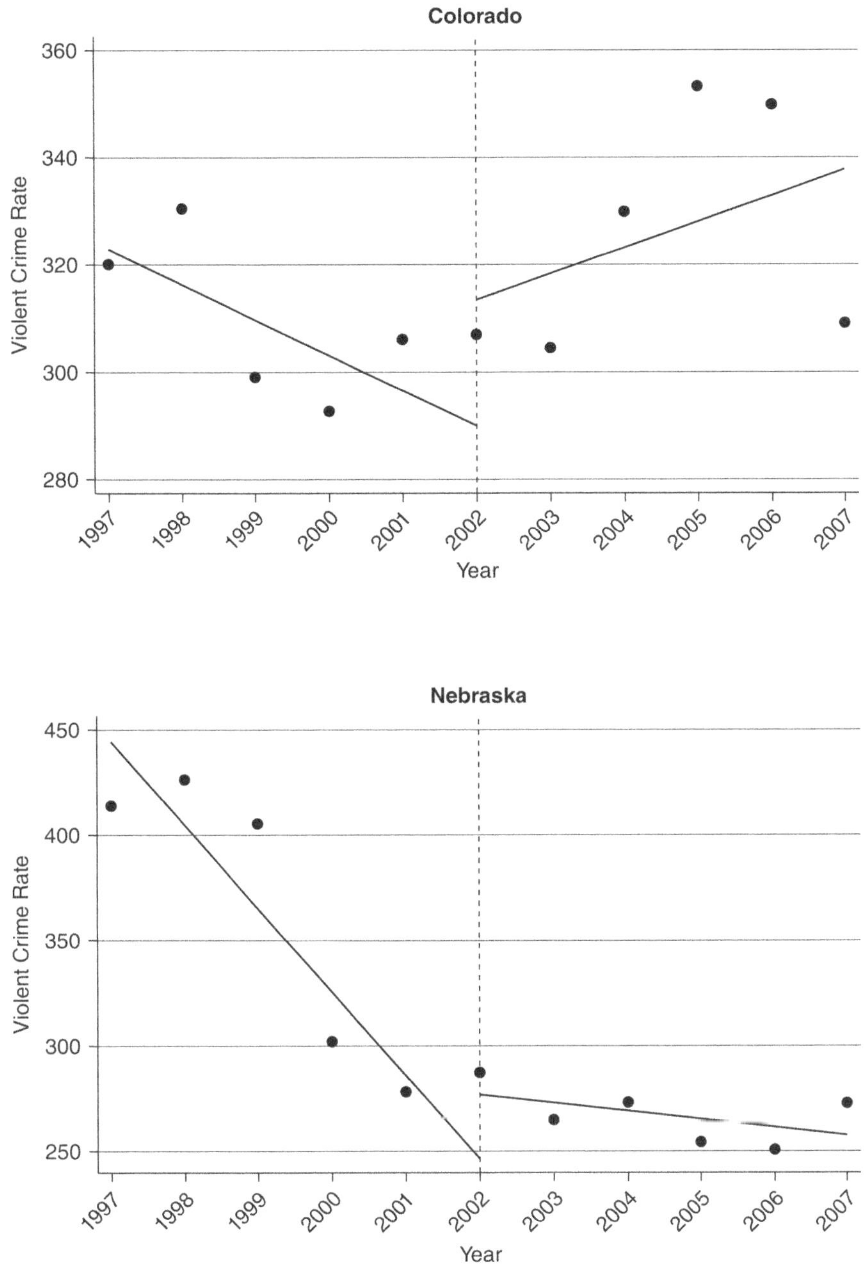

FIGURE 7.3 Trends in Violent Crime Rates Before and After LWOP Implementation in the 2000s *(Continued)*

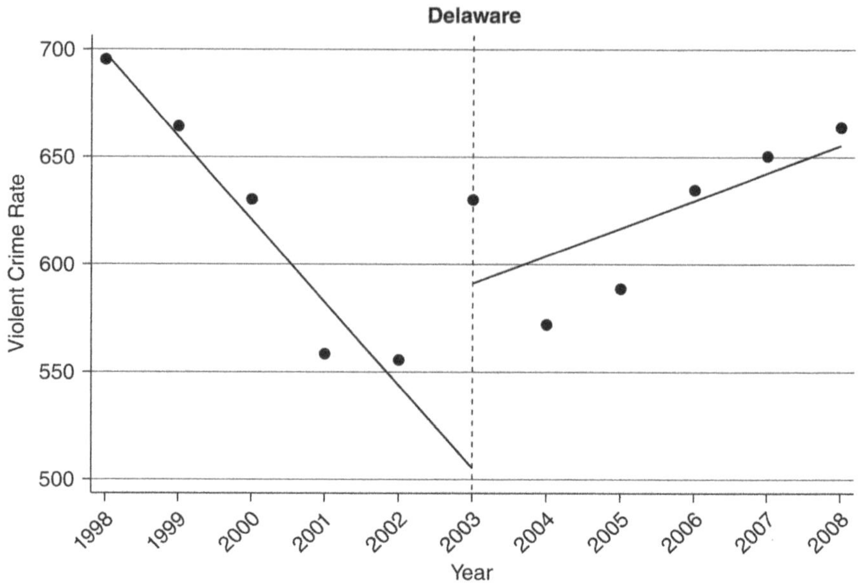

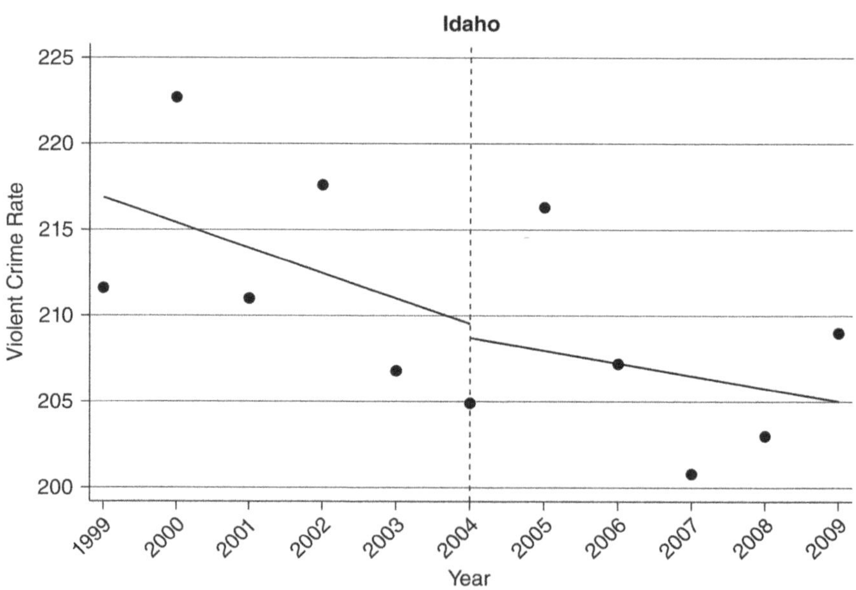

FIGURE 7.3 *(Continued)*

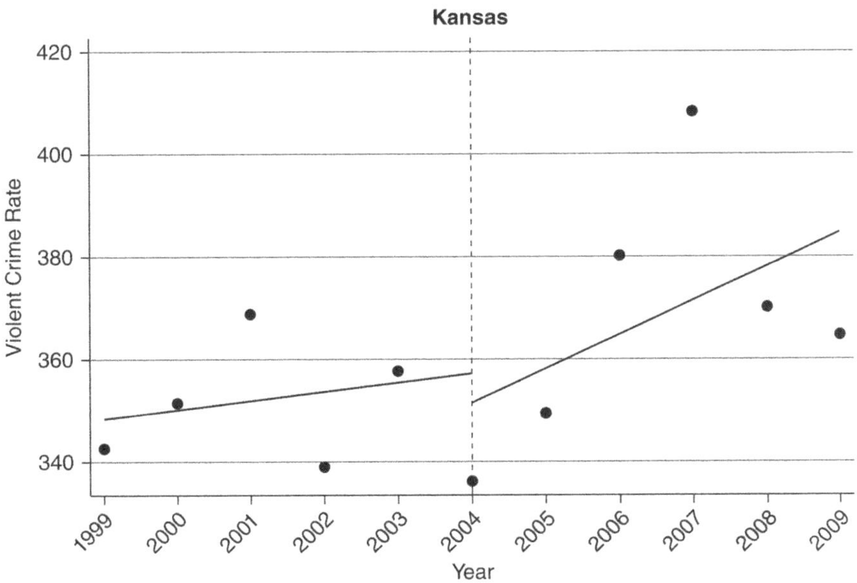

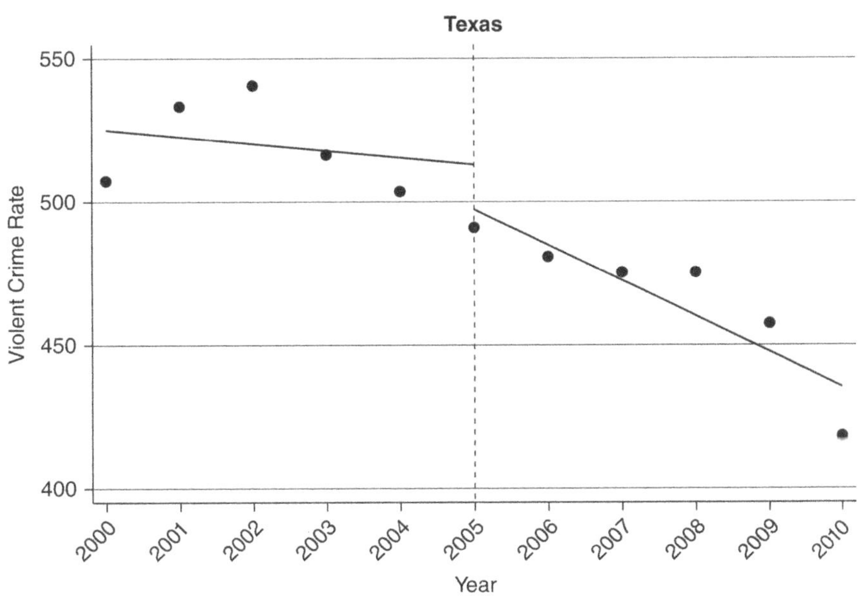

FIGURE 7.3 *(Continued)*

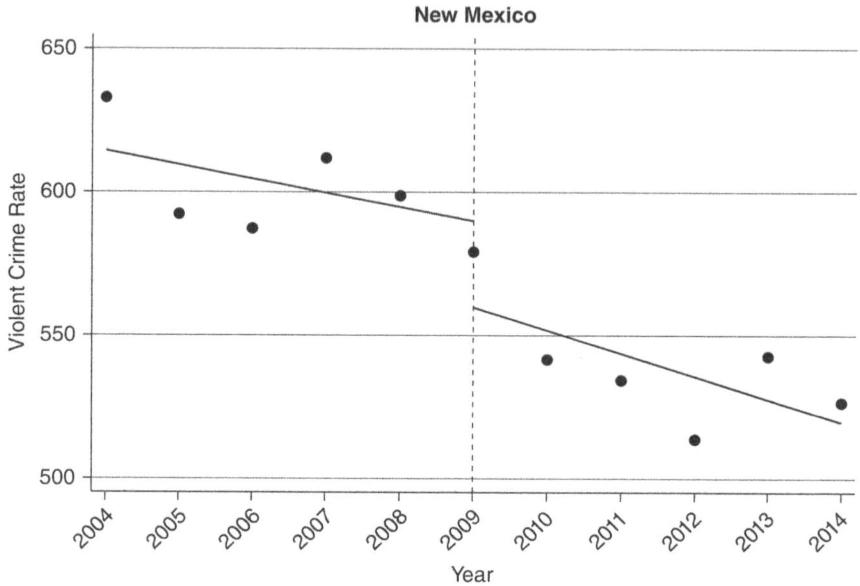

FIGURE 7.3 *(Continued)*

the wrong direction. Only two states, Texas and New Mexico, saw the relative slope of their trend lines decline post-LWOP implementation, but neither of those changes was statistically significant, and in Texas, Figure 7.3 makes it clear that their downward trend began two years *before* LWOP was enacted, so LWOP could not have caused it.

So, what are we to make of these results? Essentially, the results, as summarized in Table 7.4, indicate that in some places at some points in time, the implementation of a LWOP statute is associated with reductions in violent crime while in other places and other time periods, it is associated with increases in violent crime, and in still others, it is unrelated to violent crime. To be more specific, of the 42 states that have enacted LWOP since 1970, just 10 experienced significant declines in violent crime in the year they implemented LWOP while four experienced significant increases. The remaining 28 states did not see a statistically significant change in their violent crime rates in the year they enacted LWOP. In looking at the five-year trend lines, 17 states' post-implementation trend lines

TABLE 7.4 Number of States Experiencing Each Result

	Statistically significant decrease	*No statistically significant change*	*Statistically significant increase*
Year LWOP was Implemented	10	28	4
Relative Change in 5-Year Trend	17	18	7

Note: Statistical significance is indicated in Tables 7.1 through 7.3 and begins with a p value less than or equal to 0.05.

indicated reductions in crime relative to the pre-implementation trend line, 7 states had a post-implementation trend line that showed an increase in crime relative to the pre-implementation trend line, and the remaining 18 states did not experience a statistically significant change in their trend lines after enacting LWOP. In other words, there is no consistent relationship between the enactment of a LWOP statute and violent crime rates, which suggests that merely enacting a LWOP statute is not, by itself, enough to impact violent crime. Perhaps most tellingly, despite a national trend that may have influenced the results in a way that would favor finding a deterrent effect, in the 2000s, we discovered a brutalization effect instead. During this period, even in the absence of a new LWOP statute, we would have expected to see crime go down, but in those states that implemented such statutes during that decade, crime did *not* go down, and in some of them, it actually went up! If the mere presence of a LWOP statute was sufficient to lower violent crime, we should not have seen the amount of violent crime increase after the law was passed, especially not in a national environment where crime was going down. However, it is possible that these mixed results are due to states utilizing LWOP differently. Perhaps some states used LWOP more often than other states, which could explain why different states got different results. Therefore, in the next section, we turn to analyzing whether states that *use* LWOP more often have better success at producing lower violent crime rates than states that use it less often.

The Effect of Using LWOP More Frequently on Violent Crime

In the preceding analysis, we found that the mere enactment of a LWOP statute does not appear to be sufficient to produce reductions in violent crime. This could be because a state needs to do more than simply make LWOP an available sentencing option to alter the behavior of its residents. It may need to utilize the sanction frequently enough to produce a deterrent and/or incapacitation effect, so in the following analyses, we seek to determine whether states that use LWOP more often experience lower rates of violent crime or bigger reductions in their violent crime rates. We do this by first examining whether there is any detectable bivariate correlation between the use of LWOP and violent crime. We then proceed to multivariate statistical techniques that allow us to control for other potential causal variables.

Before proceeding to the analyses, however, it is necessary to briefly discuss how we measured a state's use of LWOP and what this measurement means. On the surface, this seems fairly straightforward. After all, The Sentencing Project has published reports tabulating the number of people serving LWOP in each state in 2003, 2008, 2012, 2016, and 2020, so we could just use those numbers to indicate how often a state uses LWOP. However, even in the absence of LWOP, nearly every person who has received a LWOP sentence would have received some other prison sentence, so we are not really interested in the *absolute* effect of LWOP. We are interested in its *marginal* effect. To summarize this distinction succinctly, the absolute effect of a punishment is the total amount of crime reduction it accomplishes without regard for how much of that reduction could be accomplished by lesser sanctions. The marginal effect is the additional effect the punishment has above and beyond the effect of some lesser sanction. By way of example, when students in one of our classes are asked if they have ever sped while driving, nearly all students raise their hands. When asked if they would speed if the punishment for speeding was life in prison, suddenly all students say they would no longer speed. Thus, the *absolute* effect of a life sentence on speeding—at least among the students asked—is 100% crime reduction. However, when those same students are asked if they would speed if the penalty for speeding was 30 years in prison, still no one raises their hand. Therefore, the *marginal* effect of sentencing speeders to life in prison relative to the effect of a 30-year sentence is zero because the same amount of crime reduction could be accomplished with the lesser penalty (and most probably, by a penalty far less severe).

For our analysis of LWOP, since we acknowledge that most of those sentenced to LWOP would probably get *some* prison time even if LWOP did not exist, we are really interested in whether LWOP produces any *marginal* effect. Thus, we measure a state's use of LWOP by the proportion of the state's life-sentenced population that is ineligible for parole ("LWOP per life"). This should tell us the marginal effect of LWOP relative to life *with* parole. If denying lifers eligibility for parole has any ability to reduce violent crime, then states that deny a greater proportion of their life-sentenced population eligibility for parole should have lower rates of violent crime. On the contrary, if denying lifers parole eligibility does not produce any additional crime reduction beyond that which is accomplished by parole-eligible life sentences, then we would expect there to be no difference between states that deny a large proportion and those that deny a small proportion of lifers the opportunity to seek early release through parole. Because, as of this writing, data on violent crime rates are not yet available for 2021, for the analyses in this chapter, we only rely on the LWOP data through 2016.

The Bivariate Correlation

We begin our analysis simply, by looking at the bivariate correlation between "LWOP per life" and violent crime rates to see if there is a *prima facia* case for suspecting that reducing the proportion of lifers who are eligible for parole can reduce violent crime. The results, which are reported in Table 7.5, show that there is no significant relationship between "LWOP per life" and violent crime rates in any of the years for which both LWOP and violent crime data are available. On its face, then, this would suggest that denying more life-sentenced individuals the opportunity to seek parole is likely to be an ineffective means of lowering violent crime rates. However, we need to take these results with a healthy grain of salt. These correlations simply look at the bivariate relationship between "LWOP per life" and violent crime rates without controlling for

TABLE 7.5 Correlations between LWOP as a Proportion of All Persons Serving Life and Violent Crime Rates

Data wave	*Correlation coefficient*	*Significance level*
2003–2004	−0.0636	0.6675
2008–2009	−0.0284	0.8499
2012–2013	−0.0330	0.8199
2016–2017	−0.0836	0.5636

Notes: LWOP as a Proportion of All Persons Serving Life is measured in the first year of the data wave, while the Violent Crime Rate is measured in the second year of the data wave.

possible confounding factors. Perhaps the relationship between LWOP and violent crime is reciprocal or is being masked by some third variable. Therefore, to fully explore the relationship between LWOP and violent crime rates, we need to investigate these possibilities.

Examining Potential Reciprocal Causation

The first issue that must be addressed before reaching any conclusions about the impact of LWOP on violent crime rates is the potential existence of a phenomenon referred to as reciprocal causation or simultaneity, which suggests that in addition to the potential effect LWOP may have on violent crime, it is also possible that the violent crime rate could affect how often LWOP gets used. In essence, when crime rates are higher, there are more defendants eligible to receive a LWOP sentence and the political pressure to get tougher on criminals may also increase, so violent crime rates could be driving the frequency with which LWOP gets used (Levitt, 1996; Marvell & Moody, 1994; Nagin, 2013; Spelman, 2000). In fact, according to one study, one of the primary factors that influences incarceration rates is the violent crime rate (Spelman, 2009), so this is a legitimate concern. Since these predicted effects operate in opposing directions (increasing crime should drive up LWOP usage while increasing LWOP usage should reduce crime), the true impact of LWOP on violent crime rates could be getting masked by the reciprocal effect of violent crime on LWOP (Levitt, 1996; Spelman, 2000; Spelman, 2009).

Therefore, before proceeding further, it is necessary to test for this possibility. To do so, we utilized two separate but related statistical techniques: cross-lagged paned models and maximum likelihood estimated cross-lagged panel models with fixed effects. The results of those analyses, which are reported in a separate work (Coldsmith & Kleinstuber, Under Review), suggested that "LWOP per life" and violent crime do *not* have a reciprocal relationship. To be more specific, in the data available to us, violent crime rates did not have a statistically detectable effect on the future percentage of lifers who are ineligible for parole in any of the models that we ran, and, importantly, the results *also* showed that "LWOP per life" was not correlated with future violent crime rates. Taken together, these findings indicate that the frequency with which those sentenced to life are denied parole eligibility is not influenced by the violent crime rate *and* that LWOP is no more effective than life with parole at controlling violent crime (Coldsmith & Kleinstuber, Under Review). However, like with the previous analysis, it is important not to read too much into these results. The small sample size (i.e., 50 states) reduces the explanatory power of those models and limits the number of control variables we were able to include. Therefore, now that we have established that LWOP and violent crime rates are unlikely to be reciprocally related, we can pool our years of data using pooled time series models to increase the explanatory power of our models, thus making any effect LWOP may have on violent crime rates easier to detect while also allowing us to include more control variables.

Pooled Time Series Results

To account for several different plausible ways LWOP may influence violent crime rates, we ran four different pooled time series models. For details on what variables were included in these models and how the models were constructed, please refer to this chapter's methodological appendix. The results of these analyses are reported in Table 7.6. Beginning with Model 1, we sought to determine if the proportion of all life sentences that are LWOP sentences in one year impacts the violent crime rate in the subsequent calendar year. The results of that analysis indicate that "LWOP per life" does not have a statistically significant effect on violent crime rates in the following year, which suggests that moving from life with parole to LWOP sentences will not produce less violent crime.

However, this model could be underestimating the effect of LWOP because it does not consider the possibility of diminishing returns. Put succinctly, society typically imprisons the most serious offenders first, which means that the first person punished should produce a greater reduction in crime than the second, who should produce more of a reduction than the third, and so on (Levitt, 2004). If this is true, it would create a non-linear relationship between LWOP and violent crime rates in which initial increases in LWOP reduce violent crime while subsequent increases either do not reduce crime or have a much smaller influence on violent crime. To model this possibility, we re-ran Model 1 with the addition of a squared term, which was designed to capture the potentially bending, parabolic—rather than strictly linear—relationship between LWOP and violent crime. The results of that analysis, which are reported in Model 2 in Table 7.6, show that neither the LWOP variable nor its square are statistically significant, and the Wald Test for Joint Significance, which is designed to test for the joint significance of the linear and quadratic effects of the LWOP variables, shows that the joint effect of the two variables is also non-significant ($F = 0.45$, $p \geq 0.6391$). In other words, regardless of whether the strictly linear or the quadratic models better represent reality, denying more life-sentenced individuals the opportunity to be released on parole does not appear to result in measurably lower violent crime rates.

TABLE 7.6 Ordinary Least-Squares Regressions of LWOP as a Proportion of All Persons Serving Life and Controls on Violent Crime Rates and Change in Violent Crime Rates

	Violent crime rates				*Change in violent crime rates*			
	Model 1		*Model 2*		*Model 3*		*Model 4*	
Independent Variables	b	β	b	β	b	β	b	β
LWOP per Life	−21.050	−0.043	3.492	0.007	39.609*	0.483*	39.638	0.484
	(39.633)		(54.713)		(19.419)		(26.067)	
LWOP per Life²			−88.825	−0.072			−0.105	−0.001
			(118.994)				(41.821)	
College	0.104	0.004	0.238	0.009	−0.544	−0.127	−0.544	−0.127
	(3.200)		(3.252)		(1.250)		(1.263)	
18–24	−2.628	−0.013	−1.857	−0.009	6.748	0.198	6.749	0.198
	(14.846)		(15.166)		(6.097)		(6.132)	
25–34	10.354	0.070	10.824	0.073	8.038	0.326	8.039	0.326
	(12.340)		(12.330)		(5.970)		(5988)	
Non-white	−1.155	−0.095	−1.025	−0.084	−0.162	−0.080	−0.162	−0.080
	(3.113)		(3.113)		(1.905)		(1.910)	
Population (thousands)	−0.035*	−1.627*	−0.036*	−1.660*	0.004	1.071	0.004	1.070
	(0.014)		(0.014)		(0.005)		(0.005)	
Poverty	−1.348	−0.029	−1.092	−0.024	−0.704	−0.091	−0.704	−0.091
	(4.337)		(4.383)		(2.369)		(2.396)	
Employed	−2.406	−0.073	−2.100	−0.064	−0.790	−0.145	−0.789	−0.145
	(4.394)		(4.448)		(1.939)		(1.969)	
Police per capita	15.659	0.062	16.196	0.064	−3.458	−0.083	−3.457	−0.083
	(17.351)		(16.921)		(8.587)		(8.584)	
Firearm Suicide	−0.248	−0.021	−0.229	−0.019	0.063	0.032	0.063	0.032
	(1.668)		(1.632)		(0.554)		(0.557)	
Three Strikes Law	−51.092	−0.169	−55.825	−0.185	−3.430	−0.068	−3.435	−0.068
	(28.449)		(29.780)		(12.654)		(12.804)	
Right to Carry Law	27.938	0.082	28.354	0.083	5.140	0.090	5.141	0.090
	(15.401)		(15.218)		(5.143)		(5.181)	
y-intercept	369.377***		370.179***		−1.364		−1.363	
	(70.652)		(69.852)		(36.044)		(36.185)	
State-Years	195		195		195		195	

Notes: Unstandardized (b) and standardized (β) coefficients reported for each model. Robust Standard Errors are reported in parentheses below the unstandardized coefficients. All continuous independent variables are mean centered. Included, but not shown, are dummy variables for 49 of the 50 states to control for time invariant state-level characteristics as well as dummy variables for 3 of the 4 years to control for national level time trends.

*$p \leq 0.05$, **$p \leq 0.01$, ***$p \leq 0.001$ (two-tailed tests)

Yet, before concluding that the data indicate there is no relationship between LWOP and violent crime, we need to recognize that not all states start with the same violent crime rate, and this could potentially influence the results of these two models. Therefore, an arguably more neutral and thus fairer test of LWOP's effect on violent crime would be to see if greater use of LWOP produces greater *reductions* in the violent crime rate (regardless of its starting point). To account for this possibility, we re-ran the first two models using the *change* in the violent crime rate from the year in which the LWOP data were collected to the following calendar year as the outcome variable. The results of the strictly linear model, which are reported in Model 3 of Table 7.6, indicate that LWOP may actually be producing a *brutalization* effect. To be more specific, the data indicate that relative to a scenario in which all life-sentenced individuals in a state are eligible for parole, if no life-sentenced individuals in that state were eligible for parole, the state would expect to experience a year-over-year *increase* of about 39.6 additional violent crimes per 100,000 state residents. Keep in mind that Model 3 is measuring the *change* in the violent crime rate, so it is telling us that regardless of where their violent crime rates started, holding all other variables constant, states that have a higher proportion of lifers serving LWOP can expect to see their violent crime rates go up in the subsequent calendar year. What this means is that if a state were to re-sentence everyone serving LWOP to life with parole, it would expect to see steeper declines or slower increases in its violent crime rate than if it maintained LWOP.

In Model 4, we added a squared term to account for the possibility of diminishing returns. The results of that model indicate that neither "LWOP per life" nor its square have a statistically significant effect on violent crime rates. Likewise, the Wald Test for Joint Significance showed that the variables were also not jointly significant ($F = 2.39$, $p \geq 0.0960$), thus suggesting that the proportion of lifers who are ineligible for parole does not impact the trajectory of violent crime. Overall, then, the results of each of these analyses suggests that using LWOP instead of life with parole will not produce lower rates of violent crime.

Conclusion

In this chapter, we explored the possibility that LWOP might be justifiable as an effective weapon in the war against crime. We ran numerous statistical tests in an attempt to detect a crime-reducing effect of LWOP. When examining the results holistically, it becomes clear that LWOP does not produce measurably lower crime rates and thus cannot be justified on these grounds. We began our inquiry by testing to see if implementing a LWOP statute reduces violent crime rates. That analysis produced inconsistent results. In some states, after LWOP was enacted, crime went down, but in most states, it stayed the same, and in several others, it went up. It would be illogical to suggest that LWOP was responsible for reductions in some states, increases in other states, and did nothing in others. Therefore, we concluded that merely placing a LWOP statute on the books is insufficient, in and of itself, to reduce crime.

However, that does not necessarily mean LWOP is ineffective. These inconsistent findings could be the result of different states using LWOP with varying frequency. Therefore, we then proceeded to use several different statistical models to investigate whether there is a relationship between the frequency with which a state denies those sentenced to life terms the possibility of parole and violent crime rates. In *none* of those analyses were we able to find any evidence that a higher proportion of the life-sentenced population being denied eligibility for parole resulted in lower rates of violent crime or greater reductions in violent crime. In fact, the only statistically significant result we found suggested that, if anything, greater use of LWOP may actually *increase* crime. These results held up under various model specifications, including those designed to account for reciprocal causation, those designed to account for diminishing returns, and ones using various measures of violent crime. Therefore, these results are quite robust and provide fairly compelling evidence that LWOP is no more effective than life *with* parole, which means that LWOP cannot be justified for crime-control purposes.

However, we do have one final note of caution. Our measurement of how often a state uses LWOP relative to all life sentences was based on the proportion of lifers serving LWOP in each state. Yet, this is not a perfectly accurate measure of the phenomenon of interest for two reasons. First, due to parole releases of those serving life with parole, it could be over-counting the ratio of LWOP-to-life sentences imposed in a state. As long as states release parole-eligible lifers at roughly equal rates, though, this variable should still capture the relative frequency with which each state uses LWOP. Second, because life sentences last so long, the LWOP-to-life ratio may be reflective of sentencing practices that occurred decades ago that have since been modified. Yet, it is reasonable to suspect that current sentencing practices may have a stronger influence on behavior than present populations. Unfortunately, there are no publicly accessible data on the number of new LWOP or life commitments at the state level. Although we could estimate the number for LWOP by using the increase in the size of the LWOP population, this strategy does not work for life with parole sentences due to the possibility of parole releases. Therefore, the LWOP-to-life proportion is the best proxy we have for how frequently a state uses LWOP relative to life with parole. To overcome this shortcoming in our research, we encourage future researchers to collect data on new life sentences imposed and then see if our results can be replicated.

Methodological Appendix

Variables Included in the Analyses

The dependent variable, or the outcome we are interested in explaining, for the analyses in this chapter is either the violent crime rate or the change in the violent crime rate. While studies of capital punishment's deterrent power rely on murder rates for their dependent variable, we focused on violent crime rates more generally because, unlike capital punishment, LWOP is applied for a variety of crimes, not just murder. Although LWOP has also been applied for nonviolent offenses, the vast majority of those serving LWOP were convicted of a violent crime, and most of the remaining individuals serving LWOP were convicted of drug offenses (Nellis, 2017), which are not accurately recorded in police reports. Therefore, it makes little sense to limit our analyses strictly to homicide or to expand them beyond violent crimes (for more details on this point, see Kleinstuber and Coldsmith, 2020 and Coldsmith and Kleinstuber, Under Review).

To calculate each state's violent crime rate, we used the number of murders, robberies, and aggravated assaults per 100,000 state residents as reported in the FBI's annual Uniform Crime Report (UCR). While the FBI and most other measures of the violent crime rate also include rape in their tabulation, we excluded this component of violent crime for both methodological and conceptual reasons. Methodologically, rape suffers from massive underreporting and other measurement errors (Breiding et al., 2014; Morgan & Kena, 2018; Truman & Planty, 2012), which vary considerably based on cultural and contextual differences across states (Rennison, Dragiewicz, & DeKeseredy, 2013). As a result, the rate of rape reported by the FBI in the URC is a highly inaccurate measure with substantial and systematic differences in the degree of inaccuracy between the states. Thus, including rape in our measure of the violent crime rate would generate a great deal of statistical noise and could potentially create systematic bias in our results. Conceptually, prior to 2013, the FBI only counted "forcible rapes" in which the victim was female. Starting in 2013, the FBI revised its definition of rape to be more in line with modern cultural and legal understandings of rape by removing both the force and the female victim requirements. As a result, the conceptual meaning of the rape component of the violent crime rate shifted in the middle of our analytical period, meaning the concept captured, however imperfectly, by the measure of rape in the UCR is different before and after 2013. Consequently, including rape in our violent crime rate measures would require us to remove the last wave of data from our analyses. Due to both of these problems with the tabulation of rape in the UCR, we excluded rape from our measure of the violent crime rate.

Although violent crime is the concept we are interested in measuring, for each of our analyses, we operationalized this variable slightly differently. First, in the quasi-experimental analyses, we measure the violent crime rate at 11 time periods: 5 years prior to LWOP's implementation, the year LWOP was implemented, and 5 years after LWOP's implementation. Using eleven years' worth of data on the dependent variable allows for both pre- and post- implementation trends to be established while preventing both random measurement error and outlying datapoints from being overly influential in the models. As the number of time periods included in an interrupted time series increases, so does the statistical power of the model (Zhang, Wagner, & Ross-Degnan, 2011), although it is equally important not to lengthen the time periods to include points historically inconsistent with the underlying trend being considered in the analysis (Bernal,

Cummins, & Gasparrini, 2017). Additionally, having a balanced design (i.e., the number of years before and after the intervention are the same) has been found to increase the power of interrupted time series analyses, at least in a simulated analysis of health data (Zhang, Wagner, & Ross-Degnan, 2011). We believe that the balanced five-year periods pre- and post-intervention included in our interrupted time series models balance the need for statistical power with concerns over including data from periods experiencing dramatically different underlying trends. Then, in the pooled time series models, we measure the dependent variable in two different ways. In the first two models, we use the violent crime rate measured in the calendar year following the measurement of the LWOP population. In the last two models, the dependent variable is measured as the change in the violent crime rate, which is calculated by subtracting the violent crime rate in the year that the number of people serving LWOP was measured from the violent crime rate in the subsequent calendar year. Calculating the change in violent crime rate in this way allows positive values to indicate increases and negative values to indicate decreases. So, while each of the analyses presented in this chapter is focused on state-level violent crime rates, how we operationalized that outcome differs in important ways across our various analyses.

The independent variable, the one that is hypothesized to cause a certain outcome, in these analyses is LWOP. Again, however, we measured this slightly differently in each of our analyses. In the quasi-experimental models, the experimental treatment is the implementation of a LWOP statute, as reported by the Death Penalty Information Center. In states such as California where the LWOP statute was passed in one year and then implemented in a subsequent year, the intervention is considered to begin during the year in which the law took effect rather than in the year in which it was passed. In states where LWOP was introduced for different crimes in different years, the treatment year was determined on a case-by-case basis. For New Mexico, which introduced LWOP for two-time sex offenders in 1997 and as a death penalty replacement in 2009, we selected 2009 as the treatment year, since the initial introduction of LWOP was limited to a crime which is not included in our outcome variable. Using 1997 as the treatment year would have heavily favored a finding of no effect of LWOP's implementation, so using 2009 as the treatment year provides a fairer test of the effect LWOP is likely to have on the violent crime rate. For Virginia, the other state for which the Death Penalty Information Center indicates two separate statutes implementing LWOP, we selected the treatment year as 1994, the year LWOP was first introduced, rather than 1995, the year LWOP was added as an alternative to the death penalty. We made this decision in order to pick up any effect implementation of the initial statute had on violent crime rates. In this case, the addition of a second statute in the following year should, if anything, increase the impact of LWOP on this state's violent crime rate.

For the pooled time series analyses, we were interested in whether *using* LWOP more frequently would result in less violent crime. However, because nearly everyone sentenced to LWOP would have received some prison sentence even in the absence of LWOP, we are really interested in whether LWOP produces a *marginal* effect relative to the effect of life with parole. Therefore, we measure a state's use of LWOP as the proportion of the formally-life sentenced population who are ineligible for parole. In the models that include a quadratic term, we simply multiply the "LWOP per life" measure by itself to generate its square. Both the total life population and the LWOP population for each state are taken from The Sentencing Project' various reports on life sentences. These reports are available for 2003, 2008, 2012, and 2016 (2020 is also available but was omitted because violent crime data are not yet available for 2021). It is important to note that virtual life sentences (i.e., sentences that are so long that no one can reasonably be expected to survive them) are not included in the data employed in these analyses. While we consider virtual life sentences to be an important and pressing issue in criminology, there is simply a lack of agreement over what in fact counts as a virtual life sentence (Barkow, 2012; van Zyl Smit & Appleton, 2019), and, more pragmatically, there is also a scarcity of data on virtual life sentences. The Sentencing Project started releasing data on virtual life sentences in 2016, but as of this writing, there is still not a sufficient number of years with virtual life sentence data available to perform the type of analyses performed in this chapter.

Finally, we must consider the control variables included in the pooled time series analyses. Due to the small number of observations inherent in doing state-level analyses, we were limited in the number of control variables we could include. Therefore, we had to be judicious in selecting variables that could represent the demographic, economic, and criminal justice environments of each state. To do so, we selected variables that are standard controls in the formal death penalty literature: age, education, race/ethnicity, and population to represent each state's demographics; poverty and employment to control for economic conditions; and police presence, firearm suicides, and the presence of three strikes and right to carry laws to capture the criminal justice context (Dezhbakhsh & Shepherd, 2006; Katz, Levitt, & Shustorovich, 2003; Kovandzic, Vieraitis, & Boots, 2009; Zimmerman, 2004; Zimmerman, 2006).

Demographically, it is well-established that criminal offending peaks in adolescence and early adulthood and then declines rapidly thereafter (Hirschi & Gottfredson, 1983; Sweeten, Piquero, & Steinberg, 2013). Therefore, we included the percentage of the resident population of a state which is 18–24 years old (18–24) and 25–34 years old (25–34) as control variables. Due to the strong negative association between educational attainment and crime (Dennison & Swisher, 2019; Groot & van den Brink, 2010; Lochner, 2004; Lochner & Moretti, 2004; Nordin, 2018), we also control for the percentage of a state's noninstitutionalized population age 25 years and older which has obtained a bachelor's degree or higher (college). Also, because there is a consistent correlation between the racial composition of a state and the officially reported violent crime rate (Rosich, 2007; Schleiden, Soloski, Milstead, & Rhynehart, 2020), it has become standard practice for quantitative criminological studies to control for the disparate impact of race on violent crime rates (Steffensmeier, Feldmeyer, Harris, & Ulmer, 2011). As such, we also control for the percentage of a state's population who are people of color (non-white). Finally, to control for differences in offending patterns due to a state's size, we control for the population of each state measured in thousands of state residents (population).

Next, to measure the economic climate of each state, we control for the percentage of the state's population that lives in poverty (poverty) and the noninstitutionalized civilian population that is 16 years old or older which is employed in a civilian job (employed) as reported by the Bureau of Labor Statistics. Although the empirical connection between economic conditions and violent crime rates is not settled (Aaltonen, MacDonald, Martikainen, & Kivivuori, 2013; Chiricos, 1987; Cook, 2010; Raphael & Winter-Ebmer, 2001; Rosenfeld, 2018), we want to guard against omitted variable bias and therefore include these variables in order to capture the aggregate economic environment in the state. Specifically, we include a measure of poverty because of the longstanding relationship between poverty and crime found throughout the criminological literature (Hipp & Yates, 2011; Hsieh & Pugh, 1993). Although most studies utilize the unemployment rate to capture the economic context, we feel the employment rate is a better measure of a state's economic health because the size of the labor force (the denominator in the unemployment rate calculation) fluctuates with the economic environment while the size of the working-age population (the denominator in the employment rate calculation) does not (Bureau of Labor Statistics, 2015).

Finally, the criminal justice context of each state can play an important role in determining its violent crime rate. Specifically, because policing has been found to reduce the violent crime rate (Levitt, 1997; Levitt, 2002), we control for the risk of apprehension using the number of police officers per hundred thousand state residents (police per capita) as reported by the FBI's online *Crime Data Explorer.* The percentage of suicides in a state that are committed with a firearm (firearm suicide) is based on data from the Center for Disease Control and Prevention's (CDC) *National Center for Health Statistics Compressed Mortality File* and are included as a proxy for the rate of firearm ownership because direct data on the prevalence of firearm ownership has not been available at the state level since 2004 and the firearm suicide-to-suicide ratio has been shown to be a reliable proxy for the percentage of households with a firearm (Azrael, Cook, & Miller, 2004; National Research Council, 2005). While controversial, most studies examining the relationship have shown that the prevalence of firearm ownership is positively associated with violent crime rates (Moore & Bergner, 2016; National Research Council, 2005; RAND, 2018). Finally dummy variables indicating the presence of three strikes (three strikes law) and right to carry laws (right to carry law) are included since large bodies of literature indicate that they may have an impact on violent crime rates, although the results of the studies on right to carry laws are more mixed than are the results of studies focused on three strikes laws. Both measures are based on information from the National

Criminal Justice Reference Service (NCJRS) and are coded as the presence of the law equals 1 and the absence of the law equals 0.

Analytic Strategies

We began our investigation of the crime fighting potential of LWOP by examining the effect of enacting a LWOP statute on the violent crime rate in each state that enacted such a statute between 1970 and today. As discussed above, we do so by examining the eleven-year period surrounding the implementation of a LWOP statute in each of the 42 states that implemented such laws during this time period. Specifically, we construct a dataset for each state that consists of the violent crime rate in the five years prior to implementation, the year of implementation, and the five years after implementation. We then conduct an interrupted time series analysis on each of these state datasets using the user created *itsa* command in Stata 17 with the *prais*, *vce(robust)*, and *rhotype(tscorr)* options to conduct generalized least-squares (GLS) regressions with semirobust standard errors and p-values based on the autocorrelation of the residuals (Linden, 2015). Interrupted time series analyses are a form of quasi-experimental design in that the time period prior to intervention acts as a control for the post-intervention period (Campbell & Stanley, 1963; Huitema & McKean, 2000; Linden, 2015). In these analyses, the implementation of a LWOP statute acts as the introduction of an experimental condition within a state, which should alter the pre-intervention trend if the treatment is having a causal effect on the outcome of interest. Unlike pure experiments however, interrupted time series analyses are not applied to randomly chosen subjects in carefully controlled conditions. As a result, three important assumptions at the core of these models must be recognized (Kontopantelis, Doran, Springate, Buchan, & Reeves, 2015). First, it is assumed that the pre-intervention trend line would have continued uninterrupted into the future without the introduction of the experimental treatment, which in this case is the implementation of a LWOP statute. Second, it is assumed that there are no other interventions which could explain any deviation from the pre-intervention trend line other than the intervention being investigated. Third, the general characteristics of the population being studied, in this case the characteristics of the state, are assumed to be constant through the time period of the study, or at least, the characteristics change slowly and steadily enough that they could not account for any sudden changes observed in the outcome variable timed approximately with the introduction of the treatment. Because the interrupted time series analyses conducted in this chapter are single case or single-group analyses, which occur when there is only one case under investigation in the interrupted time series analysis, another important constraint on the models must be recognized. In this type of interrupted time series analysis, there is no control group against which to compare the results to generate an understanding of what would have occurred had the intervention not taken place. Because the national context does shift over time, we have broken these analyses up by decade, lumping together states that implemented a LWOP statute during the crime wave of the 1970s and 1980s, states that implemented a LWOP statute during the great crime decline of the 1990s, and states that implemented a LWOP statute during the first decade of the 21st century. So, while there is no true control group against which to statistically examine the results, we can deepen our understanding of the results by considering the results of the analysis for a single state in the context of other states implementing a similar policy during the same national context and against the trends seen more generally at the national level.

The bivariate correlations included in this chapter are calculated to examine the relationship between LWOP per life and the violent crime rate (excluding rape) in the following calendar year. To avoid problems of non-independence that would be generated if we pooled the data and ran a single correlation, a separate correlation is computed for each of the waves of the LWOP per life measure and its corresponding measure of the violent crime rate. These correlations were calculated using the *pwcorr* command in Stata 17 with the *sig* option in order to additionally generate the calculated significance level of the calculated correlation coefficient.

The pooled time series models are designed to investigate the marginal effect of LWOP on violent crime rates controlling for a standard set of control variables from the death penalty literature while also increasing the statistical power of the models by pooling the data and thus increasing the sample size. Pooling violent crime rates over the four data waves results in a nearly normal distribution of the dependent variable, which is demonstrated by a skewness score of 0.55. Similarly, the skewness of the distribution of change in the violent crime rate for the pooled data is −0.45, again indicating a nearly normally distributed dependent variable. As both of these scores fall within typically accepted tolerances for normality (Garson, 2012), we run the analyses focused on these two dependent variables using Ordinary Least-Squares (OLS) regressions with robust standard errors using the *regress* command in Stata 17 with the *r* option. The *b* option is also included to generate the beta or standardized regression coefficients along with the unstandardized ones generated by the *regress* command. To account for the fact that we are pooling data from the same states over four data waves, we also include dummy variables for 49 of the 50 states and for three of the four years, making our analyses fixed effects models as well. In effect, these state and year dummy variables allow us to account for time invariant state-level effects as well as national level trends that are time dependent (Allison, 2009; Rabe-Hesketh & Skrondal, 2012). Finally, to reduce the multicollinearity between "LWOP per life" and its square in the quadratic models, we mean center all of the continuous independent variables. To keep the models consistent, we do this for all of the pooled time series analyses, which also makes the y-intercept of these models interpretable as the estimated violent crime rate for these state-years when all the continuous independent variables are at their mean and the dummy variables are all zero.

References

Aaltonen, M., MacDonald, J. M., Martikainen, P., & Kivivuori, J. (2013). Examining the generality of the unemployment-crime association. *Criminology, 51*, 561–594.

Advisory Committee on Geriatric and Seriously Ill Inmates. (2005, June 22). *Report of the Advisory Committee on Geriatric and Seriously Ill Inmates*. Retrieved from Joint State Government Commission: http://jsg.legis.state.pa.us/resources/documents/ftp/publications/2005-40-INMATES%20REPORT.pdf

Allison, P. D. (2009). *Fixed effects regression models*. Thousand Oaks, CA: Sage.

Anderson, J. L. (2019). Recidivism of paroled murderers as a factor in the utility of life imprisonment. *Current Issues in Criminal Justice, 31*(2), 255–268.

Azrael, D., Cook, P. J., & Miller, M. (2004). State and local prevalence of firearms ownership measurement, structure, and trends. *Journal of Quantitative Criminology, 20*, 43–62.

Barkow, R. E. (2012). Life without parole and the hope for real sentencing reform. In C. J. Ogletree, & A. Sarat (Eds.), *Life without parole: America's new death penalty?* (pp. 190–226). New York: NYU Press.

Beccaria, C. (1963). *On crimes and punishments*. (H. Paolucci, Trans.) New York: Macmillan.

Beckett, K., & Sasson, T. (2004). *The politics of injustice: Crime and punishment in America* (2nd ed.). Thousand Oaks, CA: Sage.

Berk, R. (2005). New claims about executions and general deterrence: Déjà vu all over again? *Journal of Empirical Legal Studies, 2*, 303–330.

Bernal, J. L., Cummins, S., & Gasparrini, A. (2017). Interrupted time series regression for the evaluation of public health interventions: A tutorial. *International Journal of Epidemiology*, 348–355.

Breiding, M. J., Smith, S. G., Basile, K. C., Walters, M. L., Chen, J., & Merrick, M. T. (2014, September 5). *Prevalence and characteristics of sexual violence, stalking, and intimate partner victimization – National Intimate Partner and Sexual Violence Survey, United States, 2011*. Retrieved October 11, 2018, from Centers for Disease Control and Prevention: https://www.cdc.gov/mmwr/preview/mmwrhtml/ss6308a1.htm?s_cid=ss6308a1_e#Table1

Bureau of Labor Statistics. (2015, October 8). *How the government measures unemployment*. Retrieved August 8, 2020, from https://www.bls.gov/cps/cps_htgm.htm

California Department of Corrections and Rehabilitation. (2013). *Lifer parolee recidivism report*. Sacramento, CA: California Department of Corrections and Rehabilitation.

Campbell, D. T., & Stanley, J. C. (1963). *Experimental and quasi-experimental designs for research*. Boston, MA: Houghton Mifflin Company.

Chalfin, A., Haviland, A. M., & Raphael, S. (2013). What do panel studies tell us about a deterrent effect of capital punishment? A critique of the literature. *Journal of Quantitative Criminology, 29*, 5–43.

Chiricos, T. G. (1987). Rates of crime and unemployment: An analysis of aggregate research evidence. *Social Problems, 34*, 187–212.

Cohen-Cole, E., Durlauf, S., Fagan, J., & Nagin, D. (2009). Model uncertainty and the deterrent effect of capital punishment. *American Law and Economics Review, 11*, 335–369.

Coldsmith, J., & Kleinstuber, R. (Under Review). Fighting crime or needless time? Disentangling the reciprocal effects of life without parole and violent crime using structural equation models.

Cook, P. J. (2010). Property crime–yes; violence–no: Comment on Lauritsen and Heimer. *Criminology & Public Policy, 9*, 693–697.

Dennison, C. R., & Swisher, R. R. (2019). Postsecondary education, neighborhood disadvantage, and crime: An examination of life course relative deprivation. *Crime & Delinquency, 65*, 215–238.

Dezhbakhsh, H., & Shepherd, J. M. (2006). The deterrent effect of capital punishment: Evidence from a "judicial experiment". *Economic Inquiry, 44*, 512–535.
Donohue, J. J., & Wolfers, J. (2005). Uses and abuses of empirical evidence in the death penalty debate. *Stanford Law Review, 58*, 791–845.
Donohue, J. J., & Wolfers, J. (2009). Estimating the impact of the death penalty on murder. *American Law and Economics Review, 11*, 249–309.
Garson, G. D. (2012). *Testing statistical assumptions*. Asheboro, NC: Statistical Associates Publishing.
Groot, W., & van den Brink, H. M. (2010). The effects of education on crime. *Applied Economics, 42*, 279–289.
Hipp, J. R., & Yates, D. K. (2011). Ghettos, thresholds, and crime: Does concentrated poverty really have an accelerating increasing effect on crime? *Criminology, 49*(4), 955–990.
Hirschi, T., & Gottfredson, M. (1983). Age and the explanation of crime. *American Journal of Sociology, 89*, 552–584.
Hsieh, C.-C., & Pugh, M. D. (1993). Poverty, income inequality, and violent crime: A meta-analysis of recent aggregate data studies. *Criminal Justice Review, 18*(2), 182–202.
Huitema, B. E., & McKean, J. W. (2000). Design specification issues in time-series intervention models. *Educational and Psychological Measurement, 60*(1), 38–58.
Justice Policy Institute. (2018, November). *The Ungers, 5 years and counting: A case study in safely reducing long prison terms and saving taxpayer dollars*. Retrieved October 30, 2019, from Justice Policy Institute: http://www.justicepolicy.org/uploads/justicepolicy/documents/The_Ungers_5_Years_and_Counting.pdf
Katz, L., Levitt, S. D., & Shustorovich, E. (2003). Prison conditions, capital punishment, and deterrence. *American Law and Economics Review, 5*, 318–343.
Kleinstuber, R., & Coldsmith, J. (2020). Is life without parole an effective way to reduce violent crime? An empirical assessment. *Criminology & Public Policy, 19*, 617–651.
Kontopantelis, E., Doran, T., Springate, D. A., Buchan, I., & Reeves, D. (2015). Regression based quasi-experimental approach when randomisation is not an option: Interrupted time series analysis. *British Medical Journal, 350*. Retrieved from https://www.bmj.com/content/350/bmj.h2750
Kovandzic, T. V., Vieraitis, L. M., & Boots, D. P. (2009). Does the death penalty save lives? New evidence from state panel data, 1977 to 2006. *Criminology & Public Policy, 8*, 803–843.
Land, K. C., Teske Jr., R. H., & Zheng, H. (2009). The short-term effects of executions on homicides: Deterrence, displacement, or both? *Criminology, 47*, 1009–1043.
Levitt, S. D. (1996). The effect of prison population size on crime rates: Evidence from prison overcrowding litigation. *The Quarterly Journal of Economics, 111*, 319–351.
Levitt, S. D. (1997). Using electoral cycles in police hiring to estimate the effect of police on crime. *American Economic Review, 87*, 270–290.
Levitt, S. D. (2002). Using electoral cycles in police hiring to estimate the effects of police on crime: Reply. *American Economic Review, 92*, 1244–1250.
Levitt, S. D. (2004). Understanding why crime fell in the 1990s: Four factors that explain the decline and six that do not. *Journal of Economic Perspectives, 18*, 163–190.
Linden, A. (2015). Conducting interrupted time-series analysis for single- and multiple-group comparisons. *The Stata Journal, 15*(2), 480–500.
Lochner, L. (2004). Education, work, and crime: A human capital approach. *International Economic Review, 45*, 811–843.
Lochner, L., & Moretti, E. (2004). The effect of education on crime: Evidence from prison inmates, arrests, and self-reports. *American Economic Review, 94*, 155–189.
Marvell, T. B., & Moody, C. J. (1994). Prison population growth and crime reduction. *Journal of Quantitative Criminology, 10*, 109–140.

Mauer, M., King, R. S., & Young, M. C. (2004, May 1). *The meaning of "life": Long prison sentences in context*. Retrieved from Sentencing Project: https://www.sentencingproject.org/publications/the-meaning-of-life-long-prison-sentences-in-context/

Millemann, M., Bowman-Rivas, R., & Smith, E. (2017). Releasing older prisoners. In E. Luna (Ed.), *Reforming criminal justice: Punishment, incarceration, and release* (Vol. 4, pp. 325–340). Phoenix, AZ: Arizona State University.

Moore, M. D., & Bergner, C. M. (2016). The relationship between firearm ownership and violent crime. *Justice Policy Journal, 13*(1). Retrieved from http://www.cjcj.org/uploads/cjcj/documents/jpj_firearm_ownership.pdf

Morgan, R. E.& Kena, G. (2018, October). *Criminal victimization, 2016: Revised*. Retrieved November 24, 2018, from Bureau of Justice Statistics: https://www.bjs.gov/content/pub/pdf/cv16re.pdf

Nagin, D. S. (2013). Deterrence in the twenty-first century. *Crime & Justice, 42*, 199–263.

Nagin, D. S., & Pepper, J.V. (Eds.). (2012). *Deterrence and the death penalty*. Washington, DC: National Academies Press.

National Research Council. (2005). *Firearms and violence: A critical review*. Washington, DC: National Academies Press.

Nellis, A. (2017). *Still life: America's increasing use of life and long-term sentences*. Washington, DC: The Sentencing Project.

Nordin, M. (2018). Does eligibility for tertiary education affect crime rates? Quasi-experimental evidence. *Journal of Quantitative Criminology, 34*, 805–829.

Peterson, V. W. (1945, April). *'Case dismissed': The unreasonable leniency of American justice*. Retrieved July 22, 2021, from The Atlantic: https://www.theatlantic.com/magazine/archive/1945/04/case-dismissed-unreasonable-leniency-american-justice/309204/

Rabe-Hesketh, S., & Skrondal, A. (2012). *Multilevel and longitudinal modeling using Stata* (3rd ed., Vols. II, Categorical responses, counts, and survival). College Station, TX: Stata Press.

RAND. (2018, March 2). *The relationship between firearm prevalence and violent crime*. Retrieved from https://www.rand.org/research/gun-policy/analysis/essays/firearm-prevalence-violent-crime.html.

Raphael, S., & Winter-Ebmer, R. (2001). Identifying the effect of unemployment on crime. *Journal of Law & Economics, 44*, 259–283.

Rennison, C. M., Dragiewicz, M., & DeKeseredy, W. S. (2013). Context matters: Violence against women and reporting to police in rural, suburban and urban areas. *American Journal of Criminal Justice, 38*, 141–159.

Rosenfeld, R. (2018). Studying crime trends: Normal science and exogenous shocks. *Criminology, 56*, 5–26.

Rosenfeld, R., Wallman, J., & Fornango, R. (2005). The contribution of ex-prisoners to crime rates. In J. Travis, & C. Visher (Eds.), *Prisoner reentry and crime in America* (pp. 80–104). New York: Cambridge University Press.

Rosich, K. J. (2007). *Race, ethnicity, and the criminal justice system*. Washington DC: American Sociological Association. Retrieved August 7, 2020, from https://www.asanet.org/sites/default/files/savvy/images/press/docs/pdf/ASARaceCrime.pdf

Schleiden, C., Soloski, K. L., Milstead, K., & Rhynehart, A. (2020). Racial disparities in arrests: A race specific model explaining arrest rates across black and white young adults. *Child & Adolescent Social Work Journal, 37*(1), 1–14.

Shepherd, J. M. (2005). Deterrence versus brutalization: Capital punishment's differing impacts among states. *Michigan Law Review, 104*, 203–254.

Snyder, H. N., Cooper, A. D., & Mulako-Wangota, J. (2017, August). *Arrest rates by age for violent crime index offenses*. Retrieved May 17, 2021, from Bureau of Justice Statistics: https://www.bjs.gov/index.cfm?ty=datool&surl=/arrests/index.cfm#

Spelman, W. (2000). What recent studies do (and don't) tell us about imprisonment and crime. *Crime and Justice*, *27*, 419–494.

Spelman, W. (2009). Crime, cash, and limited options: Explaining the prison boom. *Criminology & Public Policy*, *8*, 29–77.

State of New York Department of Corrections and Community Supervision. (2016, December). *2012 inmate releases: Three year post-release follow-up*. Retrieved February 7, 2019, from http://www.doccs.ny.gov/Research/Reports/2017/2012_releases_3yr_out.pdf

Steffensmeier, D., Feldmeyer, B., Harris, C. T., & Ulmer, J. T. (2011). Reassessing trends in black violent crime, 1980–2008: Sorting out the "Hispanic Effect" in Uniform Crime Reports arrests, National Crime Victimization Survey offender estimates, and U.S. prisoner counts. *Criminology*, *49*, 197–251.

Sweeten, G., Piquero, A. R., & Steinberg, L. (2013). Age and the explanation of crime, revisited. *Journal of Youth and Adolescence*, *42*, 921–938.

Travis, J., Western, B., & Redburn, S. (2014). *The growth of incarceration in the United States: Exploring causes and consequences*. Washington, DC: National Academies Press.

Truman, J. L., & Planty, M. (2012, October). *Criminal victimization, 2011*. Retrieved November 24, 2018, from Bureau of Justice Statistics: https://www.bjs.gov/content/pub/pdf/cv11.pdf

van Zyl Smit, D., & Appleton, C. (2019). *Life imprisonment: A global human rights analysis*. Cambridge, MA: Harvard University Press.

Weisberg, R., Mukamal, D. A., & Segall, J. D. (2011, September). *Life in limbo: An examination of parole release for prisoners serving life sentences with the possibility of parole in California*. Retrieved November 1, 2019, from Stanford Criminal Justice Center: https://law.stanford.edu/wp-content/uploads/sites/default/files/publication/259833/doc/slspublic/SCJC%20Lifer%20Parole%20Release%20Sept%202011.pdf

Zhang, F., Wagner, A. K., & Ross-Degnan, D. (2011). Simulation-based power calculation for designing interrupted time series analyses of health policy interventions. *Journal of Clinical Epidemiology*, *64*, 1252–1261.

Zimmerman, P. R. (2004). State executions, deterrence, and the incidence of murder. *Journal of Applied Economics*, 7, 163–193.

Zimmerman, P. R. (2006). Estimates of the deterrent effect of alternative execution methods in the United States: 1978–2000. *American Journal of Economics and Sociology*, *65*, 909–941.

8

Is LWOP Just Retribution or Cruel and Unusual Punishment?

In 1953, Joe Ligon participated in a string of robberies in which two people were killed. He has admitted his involvement in the crimes but has denied doing the killings. Nevertheless, due to accomplice liability and felony murder statutes, it did not matter. The illiterate 15-year-old was convicted of murder and sentenced to die in prison. Sixty-eight years later, at age 83, Ligon was eventually released due to a series of court rulings and an agreement from the Philadelphia District Attorney (Melamed, 2021). Despite his eventual release, Ligon's case epitomizes one of the major problems with the way LWOP is utilized in the US: it is being imposed far too often, for far too many offenses, and on offenders whose crimes do not warrant such a severe penalty.

Although we have shown in the previous chapters that LWOP is unlikely to serve any utilitarian goal, for many, the justification for LWOP does not rest on any perceived or potential utility the punishment may possess. Rather, it is justified on retributive grounds. That is, some argue that LWOP is the only just form of retribution for serious offenders who *deserve* such a severe sentence and the only way to provide closure for the victims of serious offenses or their survivors. Of course, unlike the utilitarian goals of punishment, which can have their efficacies empirically assessed, the justness of retribution as a punishment philosophy cannot be empirically assessed because this determination relies on value judgments. However, the degree to which a particular punishment, in practice, comports with the basic tenets of retribution or helps to provide closure for victims can be assessed, and as LWOP is currently being utilized in the US, it fails to do either. On the contrary, as the Ligon case illustrates, LWOP is often disproportionately harsh, and the best available evidence also suggests that victims (and their survivors) are not best served by retribution. Instead, retribution tends to perpetuate suffering by creating a cycle of revenge that does not benefit victims.

DOI: 10.4324/9781003161783-11

LWOP Violates the Core Principles of Retribution

The punishment rationale of retribution is fairly straightforward. It suggests that criminals deserve to be punished for harming society and that failure to do so is unfair to the rest of society, which has followed the law. That is, to maintain a sense of justice, criminals need to get what is coming to them—their "just deserts." Most people would view it as unjust if someone who had committed a crime, especially a serious crime, was permitted to continue walking around without suffering any consequences. Even children recognize the unfairness of not punishing rule breakers. In fact, the Model Penal Code indicates that retribution should be the primary consideration in determining the punishment of criminal offenders (American Law Institute, 2017; Robinson, 2012). As such, LWOP seems as though it could be justified for serious crimes regardless of its utility. However, the philosophy of retribution also requires punishment to match the moral blameworthiness of the offender and to be proportional to both the harm done and the severity of the offense (American Law Institute, 2017; Robinson, 2012). Furthermore, offenders need to be ranked based upon these characteristics—that is, offenders need to be placed into their proper ordinal ranking such that more serious offenses and offenders receive more serious punishments than less serious offenses and offenders. As currently practiced in the US, LWOP fails to achieve those goals.

First, as a type of death sentence—death by incarceration—LWOP is tied for the most serious sanction that can be imposed. Therefore, to comply with the requirements of retribution, it needs to be reserved *only* for the most serious offenders—those who are major participants in aggravated and intentional killings. Yet, unlike capital punishment, "many of the offenses on which LWOP sentences are based ... do not involve intentional killings ... and thus are not appropriate under a desert analysis for this most serious sentence" (Robinson, 2012, p. 145). When it comes to capital punishment, the Supreme Court has explicitly stated that it cannot be used in cases where the victim did not die (*Kennedy v. Louisiana*, 2008), but as we have discussed throughout this book, no similar restriction exists for LWOP. In fact, more than a third of those serving LWOP in the US were convicted of crimes less serious than first-degree murder, more than a quarter were sentenced for crimes other than homicide, and between 2,340 and 4,388 (or around four to eight percent) are serving LWOP for *nonviolent* offenses (Nellis, personal communication, April 21, 2021).[1] Any way you slice it, sentences of this magnitude for non-homicides are clearly disproportionate to the severity of the offense. By punishing these crimes with the same sentence that murder elicits, such a prolific use of LWOP violates the fundamental tenet of retribution that the most serious offenses receive harsher punishments than less serious ones. In fact, imposing LWOP on such a wide variety of offenses trivializes important differences in blameworthiness (Robinson, 2012). Murderers are more blameworthy than thieves and should be treated as such.

Second, even among those convicted of homicide, LWOP is still typically grossly disproportionate to the offender's culpability or moral blameworthiness. Again, when it comes to capital punishment, the Supreme Court has ruled that it cannot be imposed as an automatic punishment for any crime, even first-degree murder (*Woodson v. North Carolina*, 1976). Rather, sentencing bodies are required to hold a separate punishment trial in which they exercise what is known as "guided discretion" to evaluate the convicted individual's culpability and blameworthiness so that executions are reserved for the "worst of the worst" (*Gardner v. Florida*, 1977; *Gregg v. Georgia*, 1976; *Woodson v. North Carolina*, 1976). To accomplish this, states are required to enumerate a list of statutory aggravators, at least one of which must be present *in addition to* the elements of first-degree murder before someone convicted of first-degree murder is even eligible for a death sentence (*Gregg v. Georgia*, 1976; *Ring v. Arizona*, 2002). The determination of whether or not one of these statutory aggravators is present must be made by a jury unanimously and beyond a reasonable doubt (*Ring v. Arizona*, 2002). Thus, a *capital murder* is a more serious offense than first-degree murder that requires additional elements to be present, such as the killing of a police officer or a young child. Yet, even the presence of a capital murder is not enough to ensure a death sentence. In fact, the majority of those convicted of capital murder are not sentenced to death. Once the sentencing body determines that a defendant is death-eligible, it is then required to consider all aggravating and mitigating factors presented and render a decision as to whether the defendant should be executed (*Gregg v. Georgia*, 1976; *Lockett v. Ohio*, 1978). States differ in the mechanism by which this is accomplished and the specific questions that are asked of jurors, but the Court has explicitly stated that sentencers may not "refuse to consider, *as a matter of law*, any relevant mitigating evidence" (*Eddings v. Oklahoma*, 1982, p. 114).

Although the literature suggests that these procedures are not particularly effective at reducing arbitrariness or limiting death sentences to just the "worst of the worst" (Acker, Bohm, & Lanier, 2014; Baldus, Woodworth, & Pulaski, 1990; *Callins v. Collins*, 1994, pp. 1145–1146; Keys & Maratea, 2016; Kleinstuber, 2016; Mandery, 2016; McCord, 2006), they at least indicate that the Court realizes that some murders are more serious than others and thus should be treated differently. These procedures also end up limiting the number of capital murder convictions that produce a death sentence to less than half (see Chapter 5). As the functional equivalent of a death sentence, from a retributive perspective, the same procedural and substantive standards would need to be met before imposing a LWOP sentence; yet, no similar requirements exist for death by incarceration sentences, at least not for adults. In fact, in many states, LWOP is a mandatory sentence for some offenses, and once convicted of these offenses, defendants have no opportunity to reduce their sentence through the presentation of mitigating factors that may be relevant for determining their culpability or moral blameworthiness (Garrett, 2020; Nellis, 2010; Nellis, 2017). In 2016, around *two thirds* of those serving LWOP for first-degree murder were given a mandatory LWOP sentence with no opportunity to present potentially relevant mitigating circumstances (Nellis, 2017). This proportion was not reported in 2020, but even if it declined to 60%, this would mean that around *three quarters* of those serving death by incarceration were either convicted of a crime less serious than first-degree murder or were given a mandatory sentence and thus do not qualify as the "worst of the worst" as would be required for a formal death sentence.[2]

Third, taking this concern a step further, current LWOP practice does not take into consideration the potentially dramatic variations in the culpability and blameworthiness of co-conspirators. Rather, accomplice liability statutes assign the same level of culpability to all participants in a crime, which means that minor participants can—and often do—receive the same sanction as the most serious participants, with little to no consideration of their actual level of complicity (Decker, 2008; Girgis, 2013; Legal Information Institute, n.d.). Furthermore, the felony murder rule makes those who participate in a felony that contributes to someone's death guilty of first-degree murder, even if death was not contemplated or intended (Birdsong, 2006; Justia, 2018). Combining these two provisions means that a minor participant in an underlying felony that results in someone getting killed (say, the getaway driver in a robbery turned murder or the lookout in a drug deal gone bad) is technically guilty of capital murder. In capital cases like these, however, the Supreme Court has expressed some reservations about allowing such minor participants to be executed. In *Enmund v. Florida* (1982), the Court ruled that it was unconstitutionally cruel and unusual punishment to impose a death sentence against an accomplice "who does not himself kill, attempt to kill, or intend that a killing take place or that lethal force will be employed" (p. 797). However, five years later, the Court ruled that accomplices who did not intend to kill could still be sentenced to death if they played a major role in the crime and displayed "reckless disregard for human life" (*Tison v. Arizona*, 1987, p. 138). The combined result of these rulings is a murky criterion that suggests that those who were not directly involved in the killing or planning the killing cannot be executed unless they were a major participant in the crime. While the line between a "major" and a "minor" participant remains unclear, there is at least some recognition by the Court that these two types of participants have different levels of culpability and thus should receive different punishments.

Yet, the Court has made no such distinction for death by incarceration sentences for adults, which means that minor participants who had no intention of causing death or even knowledge that a death might take place can be sentenced to die in prison. Such sentences—even if they do take into consideration other mitigating circumstances—are clearly disproportionate in that they treat individuals with vastly different levels of criminal intent—and thus culpability and moral blameworthiness—the same (Girgis, 2013). Despite this reality, many people have been sentenced to die in prison because they played a minor role in someone else's crime. For example, on his sixteenth birthday, Robert Holbrook accepted 500 dollars from local drug dealers to serve as a lookout during what they claimed would be a drug deal. Unfortunately, a rival drug dealer's wife was killed during the exchange, and even though he was not present during the killing and had no knowledge that someone could get killed, Holbrook was sentenced to LWOP (Young, 2016).

Both the Holbrook and Ligon cases also illustrate the fourth problem with LWOP from a retributive perspective: its use against juveniles. Due to their immaturity, lack of cognitive development, and susceptibility to peer pressure, the Supreme Court has recognized that juveniles are not as culpable as adults and has thus prohibited the use of capital punishment on anyone who was under the age of 18 at the time of the offense (*Roper v. Simmons*, 2005). For the same reasons, from a retributive perspective, it would also be inappropriate to sentence children to die in prison. As the American Medical Association (AMA) and other relevant professional organizations have succinctly summarized, "In sum, the conclusion of the scientific research is that … adolescents as a group are less able than adults to moderate risky behavior or control impulses" because their brains are less developed in precisely those areas responsible for such functions (Brief for the AMA et al. as Amici Curiae in Support of Respondent, *Roper v. Simmons*, 2005).

Specifically, adolescents have a more active limbic system, which is responsible for emotions, than adults, particularly in the amygdala, which is responsible for aggression. At the same time, they have a less active and less developed frontal lobe, which is responsible for higher order thought, long-term planning, and the regulation of emotional impulses. These realities leave juveniles less capable of controlling their impulses, engaging in moral reasoning and risk assessment, regulating their emotions, and performing proper cost-benefit analyses. Furthermore, the very structure of adolescent brains makes them more emotionally volatile, aggressive, and susceptible to both stress and peer pressure. Because the parts of their brains that are responsible for cost-benefit analysis are not yet fully developed, juveniles tend to overvalue short-term rewards and undervalue long-term consequences, which leads to risk-taking behavior, including reckless or drunk driving, unsafe sexual behavior, drug use, and criminal offending. These realities are exacerbated in the presence of stress, peer pressure, and strong emotions. While these factors impair everyone's ability to think clearly and rationally, adolescents' brains, which privilege emotional responses over rational ones, make them particularly vulnerable to these influences. As such, juveniles are, quite literally, less capable of conforming to the law and avoiding the temptations of crime because their brains are less developed than adults' brains in precisely those regions responsible for impeding risk taking, impulsivity, and short-term gratification and enabling moral reasoning, emotional regulation, risk assessment, and rational planning (Brief for the AMA et al. as Amici Curiae in Support of Respondent, *Roper v. Simmons*, 2005). It is worth noting here that these developmental patterns are not restricted to humans; adolescents from a wide range of animal species exhibit an increase in risk-taking and sensation-seeking behaviors and a stronger proclivity to associate with peers relative to their older or younger counterparts (Spear, 2003). In other words, juveniles are simply physically incapable of forming the same level of criminal intent as adults, and because their brains are still maturing, they are also, by definition, more amenable to prosocial behavioral changes (Monahan, Steinberg, & Piquero, 2015; Steinberg & Scott, 2003).

To make matters worse, brain research indicates that, *biologically*, teens are more susceptible to peer pressure (Steinberg, 2004; Steinberg, 2007). Peer pressure, meanwhile, has been shown to further diminish adolescents' self-control while group settings and the presence of peers tends to increase risk-taking behavior among teens (Ash, 2012; Steinberg, 2007). On top of this, the activities that stimulated adolescents when they were younger often cease to thrill them, leading to a transient condition that is qualitatively similar to, but less intense than, a disorder known as "reward-deficiency syndrome," which has been linked to drug addiction, sensation seeking, and other behavioral problems (Spear, 2000). This can cause teens to engage in riskier and more stimulating activities in search of the same levels of excitement, and this often includes crime. It is not that adolescents do not know right from wrong or are incapable of rational thought; rather, as David Fassler, a clinical professor in the child psychiatry department at the University of Vermont Larner College of Medicine, explains, "... particularly when confronted with stressful or emotional decisions, [adolescents] are more likely to act impulsively, on instinct, without fully understanding or analyzing the consequences of their actions" (as cited in Ritter, 2007, para 9). To use an analogy proffered by Temple University psychology professor Laurence Steinberg, teenage brains are like cars with good accelerators and weak brakes: "With powerful impulses under poor control, the likely result is a crash" (as cited in Ritter, 2007, para 1). As they mature into adulthood, however, people tend to gain self-control (Ash, 2012; Oliva, Antolín-Suárez, & Rodríguez-Meirinhos, 2019; Steinberg, 2004; Steinberg, 2007), which is why the data consistently indicate that arrest rates for violent crime peak in the late teens and early 20s and then decline rapidly thereafter (Hirschi & Gottfredson, 1983; Snyder, Cooper, & Mulako-Wangota, 2017; Sweeten, Piquero, & Steinberg, 2013).

For these reasons, it is unconscionable to sentence a child to die in prison, a sentiment with near unanimity across the globe. The United Nations Convention on the Rights of the Child, which has been ratified by every nation in the world except the US, prohibits the use of juvenile LWOP (JLWOP) (Kleinstuber, Joy, & Mansley, 2016; Mehta, 2015; Rothschild, 2017). Yet, while the US Supreme Court has imposed some restrictions on when juveniles can receive a LWOP sentence in a way that it has not limited it for adults and that, in theory, narrows the scope of which juveniles can be sentenced to die in prison to only the most serious offenders, it has not banned the use of JLWOP (*Graham v. Florida*, 2010; *Miller v. Alabama*, 2012; *Montgomery v. Louisiana*, 2016; Rovner, 2021). In fact, in 2021, the Court actually made it *easier* to sentence juveniles to LWOP (*Jones v. Mississippi*, 2021). This leaves the US as the only nation on Earth that sentences children to die in prison (Garrett, 2020; Kleinstuber et al., 2016; Mehta, 2015), and at the most recent count, there were 1,465 individuals serving LWOP in the US for crimes that occurred when they children (Rovner, 2021). Although the Supreme Court's decisions in *Miller* and *Montgomery* contributed to a 38% decline in the number of juveniles serving LWOP between 2016 and 2020 (Rovner, 2021), by reversing many of these precedents and making it far easier to sentence children to die in prison, the Court's ruling in *Jones v. Mississippi* (2021) will likely lead to future increases in the number of juveniles serving LWOP. In *Jones*, the Court determined that a separate sentencing hearing is not required to sentence a juvenile to LWOP, nor must a judge determine that the child is permanently incorrigible. As long as the youth was convicted of first-degree murder and the judge has the *option* to choose a sentence other than LWOP, the Court ruled that it is constitutionally acceptable to sentence children to die in prison.

Lastly, even if the use of LWOP were limited only to the most serious and most aggravated intentional killings, its racially biased usage would still undercut any argument that LWOP serves a retributive function. To align with the core tenets of retribution, a punishment needs to be imposed fairly, based on the culpability and moral blameworthiness of the individual being punished and without regard for extra-legal factors like race or ethnicity. If equally-situated individuals are not being treated equally, then it cannot be argued that those getting punished are truly getting their "just deserts." Instead, they are getting punished for their behavior *and for* their race or ethnicity. Yet, as we demonstrated in Chapter 6, LWOP is more likely to be utilized when the victim is white or when the defendant is Black. While this same objection could probably be leveled against every criminal sanction imposed in the US, racial inequality becomes an even more pressing concern when the punishment involves the permanent exclusion of the person from society. Although it is possible that the racial inequalities discussed in Chapter 6 would be reduced if LWOP was only being imposed for capital crimes or as a replacement for capital punishment, the experience of capital punishment suggests that this is unlikely. Racial bias continues to plague capital charging and sentencing decisions (Grosso, O'Brien, Taylor, & Woodworth, 2014), so it seems reasonable to conclude that limiting the use of LWOP only to cases in which a death sentence would have been imposed will fail to eliminate racial bias in the use of LWOP. This type of arbitrariness violates the core principles of retribution.

Looking at all of these issues, it becomes clear that as currently utilized, LWOP does not align with the basic tenets of retribution. The punishment is not being imposed in a way that is proportional to the seriousness of the offense, the harm caused, or the defendant's culpability and moral blameworthiness. LWOP is being used for crimes other than homicide. It is typically imposed as a mandatory sanction with no opportunity to reduce the sentence due to mitigating factors that might reduce the defendant's culpability. Due to accomplice liability statutes and the felony murder rule, individuals who played a minor role in a crime and had no idea that a killing might take place can be sentenced to die in prison. Perhaps most disconcertingly, children in the US can also be sentenced to die in prison. Under a retributive theory of punishment, none of these individuals should even be eligible for a LWOP sentence; yet, they comprise a large *majority* of those serving LWOP in the US. Even if the scope of LWOP were more limited, ensnaring only those who would have otherwise been sentenced to death, the racial biases that continue to plague the US justice system create a scenario where LWOP would still be imposed in an arbitrary fashion, in contradiction to the requirements of a retributive model of punishment.

Retribution Does Not Benefit Most Victims

A variation on the retribution theme argues that regardless of the proportionality of LWOP to the crime, because victims are often impacted by a crime for the rest of their lives or even killed, LWOP is necessary to bring closure to victims or their families. After all, if victims have to live with the consequences of their victimization for the rest of their lives, then it would seem to make sense that the ones who are responsible for the victims' suffering should also have to suffer for the rest of their lives. However, the existing evidence indicates that victims and their survivors are *not* best served by retributive, punitive sanctions. Rather, they are actually best served by reconciliation (Dreisinger, 2016; Exline, Worthington, Hill, & McCullough, 2003; Umbreit, 2001; Witvliet et al., 2008).

Perhaps counterintuitively, punishing offenders turns out not to help victims too much. When one is victimized, it can create a sense of powerlessness, which can lead to fear and reduce one's productivity and quality of life (Achilles & Zehr, 2001; Daigle & Muftić, 2020; Zehr, 2001). As such, one of the needs of victims following a crime is empowerment (Dreisinger, 2016; Zehr, 2003), but the current practice of trials and harsh sentencing actually disempowers and marginalizes victims because the focus is on punishing the offender, not the needs of the victim (Dreisinger, 2016; Exline et al., 2003). During traditional criminal trials, the victims' needs are rendered irrelevant because when the state punishes someone, it is the state that seizes power over the offender—literally seizing control of his or her body. In this process, however, the victim's needs take a back seat to the state's, which further disempowers victims. They have not regained some sense of control or power over the offender; the state has. Victim-offender reconciliation programs, on the other hand, which promote dialogue between victims and their offenders, help victims to regain a sense of power over their perpetrators. As such, victims who participate in victim-offender dialogue have repeatedly reported experiencing lower levels of fear and greater satisfaction with the justice system than other victims (Umbreit, 2001).

As they help victims receive restitution and restoration of respect, which are two additional needs of crime victims (Dreisinger, 2016; Zehr, 2003), victim-offender reconciliation programs are also superior to punishment in assisting victims with moving on and thus achieving some measure of closure, which is related to improved mental and physical health. Meanwhile, it turns out that vengeance actually tends to forestall closure by causing victims to fixate on their offenders, which tends to lead to aggression and to make it harder to move on (Carlsmith, Wilson, & Gilbert, 2008). Studies have shown that those who do not punish think less about the offender and are thus better able to move on (Carlsmith, Wilson, & Gilbert, 2008) while ruminating about an offender or victimization is linked to posttraumatic stress reactions, interpersonal and psychological distress, anger, and aggressive behavior (Bushman, 2002; McCullough, 2001; Orth, Montada, & Maercker, 2006). Similarly, feelings of revenge, which is what retributive punishment is all about, have been linked to symptoms of posttraumatic stress and hyperarousal, negative affect, anxiety, depression, neuroticism, and lower life satisfaction (McCullough, 2001; Orth et al., 2006). This is even true in cases where someone has been killed: "Among respondents who blamed a third person for the death, those who reported that they 'thought about or sought revenge' reported significantly lower scores on a single-item measure of adjustment than did respondents who blamed a third person for the death but did not report seeking revenge" (McCullough, 2001, p. 102).

As it turns out, forgiveness, not vengeance, is the phenomenon that allows victims to move on and experience closure. As McCullough (2001, p. 101) has summarized, "... forgiving is, in general, linked with better adjustment and well-being, whereas seeking revenge is, in general, associated with worse adjustment and well-being." For example, those with higher tendencies to retaliate tend to have more negative affect and neuroticism (McCullough, 2001) while those who score higher in forgiveness tend to experience reductions in post-traumatic stress disorder (PTSD) symptoms following exposure to interpersonal trauma when compared to those who score lower in forgiveness (Orcutt, Pickett, & Pope, 2005). Additionally, research on forgiveness therapy programs suggests that forgiveness can reduce anxiety, depression, and PTSD symptoms while increasing self-esteem and decision-making abilities (Reed & Enright, 2006), and once again, it is dialogue—not punishment—that helps to foster forgiveness. By causing victims to ruminate about their victimization, punitive punishments, like LWOP, can actually hinder forgiveness. Those who ruminate about an offense have greater difficulty forgiving and thus lower life satisfaction and higher levels of depression (McCullough, 2001).

In contrast, victims who receive apologies or other expressions of remorse are better able to forgive (Exline et al., 2003; McCullough & Witvliet, 2002; Witvliet, Luna, Worthington, & Tsang, 2020). Receiving an apology is also correlated with more positive emotions, less fear, less anger, lower heart rates, reduced cardiac stress, and less muscular tension (Exline et al., 2003; Witvliet et al., 2020). Restitution produces even stronger effects, and receiving both restitution and an apology magnifies the effect of getting just one or the other (Witvliet et al., 2020). Unlike traditional trials, victim-offender reconciliation programs give offenders the opportunity "to hear the victim's perspective, to apologize, to explain their actions, and to offer restitution, all of which can facilitate forgiveness by victims." (Exline et al., 2003, p. 338). Victims are not pressured or required to offer forgiveness in these restorative justice settings, but the existing evidence suggests that "there are features intrinsic to restorative justice that facilitate victim well-being in comparison to retributive justice as well as no justice." (Witvliet et al., 2008, p. 19). Specifically, restorative justice appears to be "more potent than retributive justice in reducing unforgiving motivations and anger" along with fostering prosocial emotions among victims (Witvliet et al., 2008, p. 19). Perhaps most importantly, restorative justice is associated with a higher level of perceived control, which suggests that restorative rather than retributive approaches are better positioned to restore victims' sense of empowerment (Witvliet et al., 2008).

These beneficial effects appear to spill over to offenders as well and may even increase public safety. According to one study, those who receive forgiveness are more likely to comply with a future request while those who receive retribution are the least likely to do so (Kelln & Ellard, 1999). Furthermore, a desire for revenge tends to spread human misery and suffering, not alleviate it. Revenge is often cited as a motivation for many violent and other destructive antisocial behaviors, such as murder, rape, theft, arson, and infidelity (McCullough, 2001), but these retributive impulses can be reduced when an offender apologizes (Exline et al., 2003). In other words, not only does LWOP fail to serve the needs of victims, but by focusing on retribution, it "perpetuates destructive actions—and thus increases crime—by amplifying resentments. Forgiveness promotes social order and peace" (Dreisinger, 2016, p. 84).

Obviously, not *all* victims will be best served through reconciliation and forgiveness (particularly those who are dead), but on the whole, more victims will experience greater satisfaction and less fear by using these mechanisms rather than resorting to vengeance and punishment. This is not to suggest that we should not punish perpetrators of crime. Rather, it is recognition that, in general, doing so, especially with extreme punishments such as LWOP, does not benefit victims—and may very well harm them. Thus, a concern for victims and their wellbeing is not a legitimate rationale for maintaining LWOP.

Conclusion

In addition to the utilitarian arguments that have been made in support of LWOP, some have argued that LWOP is simply a just punishment for some crimes and that this punishment is necessary to provide closure to victims and their survivors. However, the evidence reviewed here suggests that from a retributive standpoint, LWOP is usually disproportionate to the crime committed and that retribution is not normally in the best interest of victims or their survivors. As the functional equivalent of a death sentence, LWOP can only be justified on retributive grounds for offenders who, in the absence of LWOP, would have otherwise been executed—that is, as a replacement for capital punishment. Sentencing someone to death by incarceration when they did not commit a capital murder, without first conducting a capital-like penalty trial in which the sentencer must consider any mitigating circumstances that may have been present, when they only had a minor role in a crime, or when they were only a child at the time of the offense is simply unjust and does not comport with the notions of fundamental fairness that are central to the legitimacy of the criminal justice system. Yet, this reality describes the vast majority of those currently serving LWOP in the US. As such, for most of those serving LWOP, retribution does not demand such a sentence.

Similarly, the needs of victims are not normally met through retributive punishment. If anything, the existing evidence suggests that, contrary to popular belief, harsh sentencing impedes victim recovery. Victims who are able to forgive are better able to move on, regain a sense of empowerment, and experience mental and physical health benefits. Forgiveness is best fostered through victim-offender dialogue and restorative justice rather than retributive justice. Punishment, on the other hand, causes victims to ruminate about their offenders and their victimizations, which impedes their ability to forgive and has negative effects on mental and physical wellbeing. Therefore, there is little evidence that LWOP benefits victims in any way, which means that LWOP cannot be justified as "achieving justice" for either society or for victims.

Notes

1 We supply a range for nonviolent offenders because there were 2,048 persons serving LWOP for "other" crimes (Nellis, personal communication, April 21, 2021). This "other" category includes some violent offenses, but it is unknown how many (Nellis, personal communication, March 1, 2021). Therefore, we calculated how many persons would be serving LWOP for nonviolent offenses if everyone in the "other" category committed a violent offense and if no one in this category committed a violent offense, thus producing the upper and lower bounds of this range.

2 If the number of individuals serving mandatory LWOP sentences for first-degree murder (20,342) stayed the same from 2016 to 2020, then 57% of those serving LWOP for first-degree murder in 2020 (35,844) would have received a mandatory sentence (Nellis, 2017; Nellis, personal communication, April 21, 2021). Of course, due to Court rulings prohibiting mandatory LWOP sentences for juveniles, from 2016 to 2020, the number of individuals serving JLWOP declined by nearly 900—nearly all of whom were initially given a mandatory sentence for first-degree murder (Rovner, 2021). Therefore, it is plausible that the total number of persons serving mandatory LWOP for first-degree murder declined from 2016 to 2020, but since the total LWOP population increased from 2016 to 2020, we think it is highly unlikely that the number serving mandatory sentences for first-degree murder did not grow. Therefore, it is probably a safe assumption that around 60% of those serving LWOP for first-degree murder in 2020 were given mandatory sentences.

References

Achilles, M., & Zehr, H. (2001). Restorative justice for crime victims: The promises, the challenge. In G. Bazemore, & M. Schif (Eds.), *Restorative community justice: Repairing harm and transforming communities* (pp. 87–99). Cincinnati, OH: Anderson.

Acker, J. R., Bohm, R. M., & Lanier, C. S. (Eds.). (2014). *America's experiment with capital punishment: Reflections on the past, present, and future of the ultimate penal sanction* (3rd ed.). Durham, NC: Carolina Academic.

American Law Institute (2017, May 24). *Model penal code: Sentencing: Official statutory text.* Philadelphia, PA: American Law Institute.
Ash, P. (2012). But he knew it was wrong: Evaluating adolescent culpability. *Journal of the American Academy of Psychiatry Law, 40*, 21–32.
Baldus, D. C., Woodworth, G., & Pulaski, C. A. (1990). *Equal justice and the death penalty: A legal and empirical analysis.* Boston, MA: Northeastern University Press.
Birdsong, L. (2006). Felony murder: A historical perspective by which to understand today's modern felony murder rule statutes. *Thurgood Marshall Law Review, 32*, 1–26.
Bushman, B. J. (2002). Does venting anger feed or extinguish the flame? Catharsis, rumination, distraction, anger, and aggressive responding. *Personality and Social Psychology Bulletin, 28*, 724–731.
Callins v. Collins, 510 U.S. 1141 (US Supreme Court 1994).
Carlsmith, K. M., Wilson, T. D., & Gilbert, D. T. (2008). The paradoxical consequences of revenge. *Journal of Personality and Social Psychology, 95*, 1316–1324.
Daigle, L. E., & Muftić, L. R. (2020). *Victimology: A comprehensive approach* (2nd ed.). Thousand Oaks, CA: Sage.
Decker, J. F. (2008). The mental state requirement for accomplice liability in American criminal law. *South Carolina Law Review, 60*, 237–381.
Dreisinger, B. (2016). *Incarceration nations: A journey toward justice in prisons around the world.* New York: Other Press.
Eddings v. Oklahoma, 455 U.S. 104 (US Supreme Court 1982).
Enmund v. Florida, 458 U.S. 782 (US Supreme Court 1982).
Exline, J. J., Worthington, E. L., Hill, P., & McCullough, M. E. (2003). Forgiveness and justice: A research agenda for social and personality psychology. *Personality and Social Psychology Review*, 7, 337–348.
Gardner v. Florida, 430 U.S. 349 (US Supreme Court 1977).
Garrett, B. L. (2020, October 19). *Life without parole for kids is cruelty with no benefit.* Retrieved February 22, 2021, from The Atlantic: https://www.theatlantic.com/ideas/archive/2020/10/life-without-parole-kids-cruelty-no-benefit/616757/
Girgis, S. (2013). The mens rea of accomplice liability: Supporting intentions. *Yale Law Journal, 123*, 460–494.
Graham v. Florida, 560 U.S. 48 (US Supreme Court 2010).
Gregg v. Georgia, 428 U.S. 153 (US Supreme Court 1976).
Grosso, C. M., O'Brien, B., Taylor, A., & Woodworth, G. (2014). Race discrimination and the death penalty: An empirical and legal overview. In J. R. Acker, & C. S. Lanier (Eds.), *America's experiment with capital punishment: Reflections on the past, present, and future of the ultimate penal sanction* (3rd ed., pp. 525–576). Durham, NC: Carolina Academic Press.
Hirschi, T., & Gottfredson, M. (1983). Age and the explanation of crime. *American Journal of Sociology, 89*, 552–584.
Jones v. Mississippi, 593 U.S. ___ (US Supreme Court 2021).
Justia. (2018, April). *Felony Murder.* Retrieved February 22, 2021, from Justia: https://www.justia.com/criminal/offenses/homicide/felony-murder/
Kelln, B. R., & Ellard, J. H. (1999). An equity theory analysis of the impact of forgiveness and retribution on transgressor compliance. *Personality and Social Psychology Bulletin, 25*, 864–872.
Kennedy v. Louisiana, 554 U.S. 407 (US Supreme Court 2008).
Keys, D. P., & Maratea, R. J. (Eds.). (2016). *Race and the death penalty: The legacy of McCleskey v. Kemp.* Boulder, CO: Lynne Rienner.
Kleinstuber, R. (2016). Discrimination and the death penalty. In I. Šimonović (Ed.), *Death penalty and the victims* (pp. 111–127). New York: United Nations Office of the High Commissioner for Human Rights.

Kleinstuber, R., Joy, S., & Mansley, E.A. (2016). Into the abyss: The unintended consequences of death penalty abolition. *University of Pennsylvania Journal of Law and Social Change, 19*, 185–206.

Legal Information Institute. (n.d.). *Accomplice.* Retrieved February 22, 2021, from Legal Information Institute: https://www.law.cornell.edu/wex/accomplice

Lockett v. Ohio, 438 U.S. 586 (US Supreme Court 1978).

Mandery, E. J. (2016, March 30). *It's been 40 years since the Supreme Court tried to fix the death penalty—Here's how it failed.* Retrieved February 22, 2021, from Marshall Project: https://www.themarshallproject.org/2016/03/30/it-s-been-40-years-since-the-supreme-court-tried-to-fix-the-death-penalty-here-s-why-it-failed

McCord, D. (2006). Lightning still strikes: Evidence from the popular press that death sentencing continues to be unconstitutionally arbitrary more than three decades after Furman. *Brooklyn Law Review, 71*, 797–870.

McCullough, M. E. (2001). Forgiving. In C. R. Snyder (Ed.), *Coping with stress: Effective people and processes* (pp. 93–113). New York: Oxford University Press.

McCullough, M. E., & Witvliet, C. (2002). The psychology of forgiveness. In C. R. Snyder, & S. J. Lopez (Eds.), *Handbook of positive psychology* (pp. 446–458). New York: Oxford University Press.

Mehta, S. (2015, November 20). *There's only one country that hasn't ratified the Convention on Children's Rights: US.* Retrieved February 28, 2021, from American Civil Liberties Union: https://www.aclu.org/blog/human-rights/treaty-ratification/theres-only-one-country-hasnt-ratified-convention-childrens

Melamed, S. (2021, February 11). *The nation's oldest juvenile lifer, Joe Ligon, left a Pa. prison after 68 years.* Retrieved February 13, 2021, from Philadelphia Inquirer: https://www.inquirer.com/news/joe-ligon-juvenile-lifer-philadelphia-incarceration-release-lifetime-parole-20210211.html

Miller v. Alabama, 567 U.S. 460 (US Supreme Court 2012).

Monahan, K., Steinberg, L., & Piquero, A. R. (2015). Juvenile justice policy and practice: A developmental perspective. *Crime and Justice, 44*, 577–619.

Montgomery v. Louisiana, 577 U.S. ___ (US Supreme Court 2016).

Nellis, A. (2010). Throwing away the key: The expansion of life without parole sentences in the United States. *Federal Sentencing Reporter, 23*, 27–32.

Nellis, A. (2017). *Still life: America's increasing use of life and long-term sentences.* Washington, DC: The Sentencing Project.

Oliva, A., Antolín-Suárez, L., & Rodríguez-Meirinhos, A. (2019). Uncovering the link between self-control, age, and psychological maladjustment among Spanish adolescents and young adults. *Psychosocial Intervention, 28*, 49–55.

Orcutt, H. K., Pickett, S. M., & Pope, E. B. (2005). Experiential avoidance and forgiveness as mediators in the relation between traumatic interpersonal events and posttraumatic stress disorder symptoms. *Journal of Social and Clinical Psychology, 24*, 1003–1029.

Orth, U., Montada, L., & Maercker, A. (2006). Feelings of revenge, retaliation motive, and posttraumatic stress reactions in crime victims. *Journal of Interpersonal Violence, 21*, 229–243.

Reed, G. L., & Enright, R. D. (2006). The effects of forgiveness therapy on depression, anxiety, and posttraumatic stress for women after spousal emotional abuse. *Journal of Consulting and Clinical Psychology, 74*, 920–929.

Ring v. Arizona, 536 U.S. 584 (US Supreme Court 2002).

Ritter, M. (2007, December 3). *Expert link teen brains' immaturity, juvenile crime.* Retrieved May 17, 2021, from ABC News: https://abcnews.go.com/Technology/story?id=3943187&page=1

Robinson, P. H. (2012). Life without parole under modern theories of punishment. In C. J. Ogletree, & A. Sarat (Eds.), *Life without parole: America's new death penalty?*(pp. 138–166). New York: New York University Press.

Roper v. Simmons, 543 U.S. 551 (US Supreme Court 2005).

Rothschild, A. (2017, May 2). *Is America holding out on protecting children's rights?* Retrieved February 28, 2021, from The Atlantic: https://www.theatlantic.com/education/archive/2017/05/holding-out-on-childrens-rights/524652/

Rovner, J. (2021, May 24). *Juvenile life without parole: An overview*. Retrieved September 3, 2021, from Sentencing Project: https://www.sentencingproject.org/publications/juvenile-life-without-parole/

Snyder, H. N., Cooper, A. D., & Mulako-Wangota, J. (2017, August). *Arrest rates by age for violent crime index offenses*. Retrieved May 17, 2021, from Bureau of Justice Statistics: https://www.bjs.gov/index.cfm?ty=datool&surl=/arrests/index.cfm#

Spear, L. P. (2000). The adolescent brain and age-related behavioral manifestations. *Neuroscience and Biobehavioral Reviews*, *24*, 417–463.

Spear, L. P. (2003). Neurodevelopment during adolescence. In D. Cicchetti, & E. F. Walker (Eds.), *Neurodevelopmental mechanisms in psychopathology* (pp. 62–83). Cambridge, UK: Cambridge University Press.

Steinberg, L. (2004). Risk-taking in adolescence: What changes, and why? *Annals of the New York Academy of Sciences*, *1021*, 51–58.

Steinberg, L. (2007). Risk taking in adolescence: New perspectives from brain and behavioral science. *Current Directions in Psychological Science*, *16*, 55–59.

Steinberg, L., & Scott, E. S. (2003). Less guilty by reason of adolescence: Developmental immaturity, diminished responsibility, and the juvenile death penalty. *American Psychologist*, *58*, 1009–1018.

Sweeten, G., Piquero, A. R., & Steinberg, L. (2013). Age and the explanation of crime, revisited. *Journal of Youth and Adolescence*, *42*, 921–938.

Tison v. Arizona, 481 U.S. 137 (US Supreme Court 1987).

Umbreit, M. S. (2001). *The handbook of victim offender mediation: An essential guide to practice and research*. San Francisco, CA: Jossey-Bass.

Witvliet, C. V., Luna, L. R., Worthington, E. L., & Tsang, J.-A. (2020). Apology and restitution: The psychophysiology of forgiveness after accountable relational repair responses. *Frontiers in Psychology*, *11*, 284.

Witvliet, C. V., Worthington, E. L., Root, L. M., Sato, A. F., Ludwig, T. E., & Exline, J. J. (2008). Retributive justice, restorative justice, and forgiveness: An experimental psychophysiology analysis. *Journal of Experimental Social Psychology*, *44*, 10–25.

Woodson v. North Carolina, 428 U.S. 280 (US Supreme Court 1976).

Young, R. (2016, July 26). *She's still fighting for her brother, sentenced to life at 16 years old*. Retrieved February 27, 2021, from Here & Now: https://www.wbur.org/hereandnow/2016/07/26/juvenile-prison

Zehr, H. (2001). *Transcending: Reflections of crime victims*. Intercourse, PA: Good Books.

Zehr, H. (2003). *Changing lenses: A new focus for crime and justice* (3rd ed.). Harrisonburg, VA: Herald Press.

9

The Power of Second Chances

Stories of Redemption

For some, LWOP is justified as a way to protect society from those "truly incorrigible" offenders who can never be safely released or make a positive contribution to society (van Zyl Smit & Appleton, 2019). It is for this reason that those who are sentenced to LWOP are typically doomed to stay in prison until their deaths. However, due to commutations, clemency, exonerations, or, most recently, the US Supreme Court prohibiting the use of mandatory LWOP sentences against juveniles and thus giving around 2,100 individuals serving juvenile LWOP (JLWOP) access to parole hearings or re-sentencing (Miller v. *Alabama*, 2012; Montgomery v. *Louisiana*, 2016; Rovner, 2021), there are some exceptions to this norm. If it is true that LWOP is targeting such hardened, irredeemable individuals, then we would expect that their releases would be detrimental to society as they would either return to crime or at least fail to be productive, upstanding members of the community. However, by considering the stories of six such individuals who have been released despite having originally been sentenced to LWOP, this chapter finds that this notion is anything but true. On the contrary, each of them have not only been reformed but have also made positive and lasting contributions to their communities that have undoubtedly *benefitted* society. Although at the time of sentencing, they were all considered too dangerous to ever be safely released, each of their stories reveals a journey of redemption that started long before they were released and thus challenges the claim that LWOP is targeting and effectively segregating those who are irredeemable from the rest of society.

The Subjects

The data for this chapter come from first-hand interviews with six individuals who were sentenced to LWOP and then subsequently either had their sentences vacated, received executive clemency, or were released due to the law changes

DOI: 10.4324/9781003161783-12

brought about by *Miller* and *Montgomery*. All six subjects are Black or African American, which is not surprising given the racial imbalance in the composition of those serving LWOP (see Chapter 6). Four are male, all of whom were sentenced to JLWOP for crimes that occurred when they were either 15 or 16 years old. The other two are females. One was 19, and the other was 35 years old when they were arrested and subsequently sentenced to LWOP. Combined, these six individuals spent a total of 178 years behind bars prior to being released. Because all six have been released and their stories are now in the public domain, we refer to each of them by their real names.

Gary Tyler was the first one in this sample to be incarcerated. In 1974, at the age of 16, he was wrongfully accused of killing a white student during a riot that had taken place at his Louisiana high school over the issue of school integration. He was initially sentenced to death and sent to the notorious Angola prison, where at age 17 he became the youngest death row inmate there. Two years later, Gary's sentence was commuted to LWOP when the US Supreme Court declared Louisiana's death penalty unconstitutional. Despite maintaining his innocence, Gary languished behind bars for another 39 years before finally being released in 2016 after agreeing to plead guilty to manslaughter in the case.

Seven years later, in 1981, Mark Clements was arrested in Chicago and charged with committing an arson that killed four people. Like Gary, he was only 16 when he was accused of quadruple murder and, also like Gary, he maintained his innocence throughout his time in prison. Mark falsely confessed after being tortured for many hours by detectives who were under the supervision of police detective Jon Burge. Twenty-eight years later, Mark was released, and his ordeal came to an end when his sentence was vacated after court documents revealing a contradiction between the details of his confession and the facts of the crime were discovered.

In 1986, 35-year-old Shyrl Lamar helped her boyfriend get into the home of a California couple under the guise of selling them some furniture and with the intention of robbing them. Yet, much to her horror, her boyfriend fatally stabbed the couple. Both Shyrl and her boyfriend were sentenced to LWOP. Thirty-four years later, on March 27, 2020, California Governor Gavin Newsom commuted her sentence and the sentences of 20 others in response to concerns over prison overcrowding during the COVID-19 pandemic (Thompson, 2020). The commutation enabled her to seek parole, and she was granted release in December 2020, just months prior to being interviewed for this project. The reason she was able to secure this commutation and eventual release is that she was able to convince Governor Newsom that she had made a significant transformation over the decades that had passed since she was first incarcerated. At the time of their crime, she and her boyfriend had been motivated by their addiction to crack cocaine. High on crack when they broke into the home of the victims, they intended to rob the couple to feed their addiction.

Although they were not addicted to it, crack played just as significant of a role in the lives of the next two interview subjects, Kempis Songster and Robert

Holbrook. Beginning with Kempis, who today goes by Ghani, prior to completing the ninth grade, he and a friend ran away from their homes in Brooklyn in 1987 and rode the train to Philadelphia. By the age of 15, they found themselves in serious trouble. Upon their arrival to Philadelphia, Ghani and his friend quickly got involved with a gang that had locked them in an abandoned house while they prepared crack for distribution. Four months after leaving home, Ghani and his friend were arrested for killing a 17-year-old teenager during an altercation in the abandoned house. They were both charged with first-degree murder and given mandatory LWOP sentences. Thirty years later, following the Supreme Court's *Montgomery* decision, they finally received an opportunity to go before the parole board, and at the age of 45, Ghani was granted parole and released from prison at the end of 2017.

The next person in this sample to receive LWOP was Robert Holbrook, who now prefers to be called Saleem. In 1991, on his 16th birthday, Saleem agreed to serve as the lookout for a drug deal in Philadelphia that went bad, leading to the death of a rival drug dealer's wife. Even though Saleem did not commit the murder or have any knowledge that a murder might take place, he was charged with second-degree murder, which carried a mandatory sentence of LWOP. Unfortunately for both Ghani and Saleem, their crimes occurred in Philadelphia County, which was not only responsible for the majority of JLWOP cases in the state but has also led the nation in the number of juveniles it has sentenced to LWOP (Mauer & Nellis, 2018). As with Ghani, the *Montgomery* decision gave Saleem a second chance at life, and after 27 years of incarceration, he was granted a parole hearing, resentenced to time served, and released back into society in 2018 at the age of 43.

Gladys Scott was the last person in this study to receive a LWOP sentence. On Christmas Eve, 1993, Gladys and her sister Jamie, ages 19 and 21, respectively, were picked up by police from their Mississippi home and were stunned to learn that they were being charged with "accessory to armed robbery" and even more shocked by the supposed details of their part in the alleged crime. They were accused of robbing two men and netting a total of 11 dollars. The "Scott sisters," as they came to be known over the years after they were convicted and sent to prison, were each sentenced to two life sentences, yet they always maintained their innocence. Their mother wrote numerous letters in her daughters' defense to appeal for help from organizations such as the NAACP, the ACLU, and others. It did not take long before a movement was built to free the Scott sisters.

The growing national attention that the movement brought to the case of Gladys and her sister put pressure on Governor Haley Barbour, who eventually offered the sisters a highly unusual deal. Jamie was experiencing kidney failure and had to be placed on dialysis, which was costing the state of Mississippi approximately $200,000 a year. The cost of Jamie's treatment combined with the national media attention being given to the case led Governor Barbour to propose suspending the remainder of the sisters' life sentences if Gladys would agree to donate a kidney to her sister. Although their release appears to have been predicated on a financial decision rather than motivated by a desire to correct an injustice, the sisters were nonetheless elated when they were released in 2011, after nearly 17 years of incarceration.

These six individuals are each remarkable and resilient people who are humble and grateful to have a new lease on life. Most of them have gained national prominence by sharing their stories to audiences far and wide, whether to educate people in their communities or appeal to legislators and criminal justice representatives to assist them in their mission to abolish LWOP. Several years after their release from prison, the Scott sisters published a book to share their story (Scott & Scott, 2015). At a variety of events and in numerous forms of media, the four men interviewed here have each shared their stories of the struggles they endured coming of age within a prison as juveniles serving LWOP. Shyrl Lamar was released less than a year before being interviewed for this project, during the midst of a pandemic, so she has not yet had as many opportunities to publicly share her story.

Regardless of what they may or may not have done in their early lives to cause harm to others within their communities, these six individuals have experienced redemption and are making a significant *positive* difference in the lives of so many people that it is hard to measure their full impact. They each agreed that finding redemption was crucial to their very survival over the decades of their imprisonment. Their mission to reach a place in their lives where they could say that they feel as though they have been redeemed had taken on a personal level of importance that went far beyond simply obtaining their freedom. The primary focus of these interviews, therefore, was to examine their roads to redemption. Obviously, these stories are more intricate and detailed than can be adequately covered in a single chapter, so this chapter only provides a cursory overview of each of their accounts.

Early Days in Prison

As these former lifers sat down to trace the steps they have traveled on their roads to redemption, they each made sure to note that they started down this road long before their release from prison. While it is certainly easiest for those of us in society to take note of all the accomplishments they have achieved since their release from prison, it is also crucial to acknowledge the things they did during their time behind bars. Not only does such an acknowledgment provide a fuller picture of the process of redemption they each experienced, but more importantly, it also encourages us to recognize the countless others who remain behind prison walls and who are traveling a similar road to redemption. If the individuals in this study have each earned a second chance and, in fact, earned that second chance *many years before* they actually received it, then it stands to reason that there are likely many others still behind bars who also deserve a second chance.

Of course, for most of the former lifers in this study, the road to redemption did not begin immediately upon their incarceration. When they were first sent to prison, redemption was typically the last thing on their minds. Half of them maintained their innocence, after all. Thus, these three people felt righteous anger about their wrongful conviction. To the extent that "redemption" entered their minds, the only redemption they saw as needing to occur rested with the corrupt criminal justice system. The other half of the sample admitted that even though they had not acted alone, they were indeed guilty of actions that led to the deaths of their victims. Despite their admissions of guilt, when the two male JLWOPers were sent to prison, they were too focused on their anger, directed both toward themselves and the world, to concentrate on redemption. The only person who indicated that redemption became an immediate focus upon her incarceration, Shyrl, was 35 years old when she entered prison and thus substantially older than the other members of this sample.

In addition to being the oldest person among those in this study, both at the time of arrest and today, Shyrl was the only one who shared that she was battling a drug addiction at the time of her arrest. Just months before she and her boyfriend were accused of murder, they became addicted to crack cocaine. When she found herself involved in the unplanned double homicide, it was a brutal wake up call for her to focus on her sobriety. Shyrl's co-defendant had been her boyfriend for one year, but when he murdered the couple who they were only meant to rob, Shyrl immediately distanced herself from him, stating that "as a matter of fact, as soon as I got arrested I broke all ties" and never had any contact with him or anyone associated with him since then.

As Shyrl sat in a prison awaiting her trial, she knew that she was facing some serious time behind bars. From the moment she sobered up to the gravity of her crime, Shyrl was overwhelmed with remorse for her actions that contributed to the deaths of her victims. While she did not articulate it as such at the time, she reflects back on the early days of her incarceration and realizes today that she had immediately started down the road to her redemption. Shyrl was motivated to seek redemption not only because she felt such a deep sense of regret for the pain that she caused the families of her victims, but also because she was feeling an unprecedented level of regret for the pain that she had brought to her own family, particularly her three teenaged children who would now have to navigate their tumultuous teen years, much less their adulthood, without her in their daily lives.

Most of the others in this study shared that they struggled for quite a few years with the anger and sense of injustice they felt about their incarceration. Regardless of whether they were actually innocent or guilty of the crime they were accused of committing, they knew that they were being treated much too harshly by the court. The righteous anger they each felt upon their incarceration interfered with them getting started down their road to redemption. Gladys shared that she struggled for quite some time to release the anger she felt about her wrongful incarceration. It was not uncommon for her to take her anger out on other incarcerated women and corrections officers, causing her to get in trouble and be placed in solitary confinement.

She stated, "I felt like the system had failed me because of the evidence. The first ten years I was just angry so I stayed locked down because I was fighting a lot afterwards."

Having been wrongfully convicted for a murder that was viewed as racially motivated and subsequently suffering the brunt of racial attacks by white people both inside and outside of the prison, Gary also struggled with the anger he initially felt. Recalling this early period of his incarceration, he was not proud to admit over forty years later, "After my conviction I, of course, grieved and habitually became angry, upset, and started to hate people. I thought that all white folks were bad and I was looking for ways to justify my anger by reading certain material that was labeling white folks as devils."

The way that Saleem dealt with his overwhelming anger when he was initially incarcerated held a grip on him for quite some time until he finally recognized after serving approximately eight years of his sentence that he was dealing with his anger in a self-destructive manner. He had gained an education about the inner workings of the system and had come to realize that it was not designed to intervene in his own self-destruction. Therefore, it was up to him to save himself, and so he transformed his anger into activism:

> I think at first I internalized anger and I internalized an attitude that okay, so they're going to sentence me to life without parole. I said I'm going to do time my way. I was always rebellious and defiant so for me to do that, that was the only way that I knew how to respond. I felt I don't have nothing to really lose except for my life. I'm going to do my time the way that I want to do it. If the guards tell me to go right I'm going to go left. It lasted for maybe eight years until I really started to realize how the system is built. I think the turning point was for me when I was in a special management unit for three years and I realized that they're just taking years from me in solitary confinement too easily and I had to reevaluate and that's when I started to develop more into an activist.

When asked how he dealt with any righteous anger that he felt as a teenager being sent to prison for a life sentence, Mark surprised himself as he reflected back on the early period of his incarceration. He wondered aloud why he didn't struggle with his anger as did others in this study, as well as many of the young men incarcerated with him:

> My resilience came in due to the fact that I knew I did not commit the crime. I realized that placing blame was never going to amount to any good. I didn't go through the anger like most people would. To be honest with you, I don't know how I channeled my emotions at that particular time. I didn't cry. I didn't show any emotions and that is due to the fact that I felt like I did not have to show any emotions because I was not responsible for the offence that took place.

A major factor that seemed to help Mark manage his emotions about his wrongful incarceration seems to be that he was far from alone. Unfortunately, in what came to be known as the Chicago Police Torture Cases, Mark was among more than 110 young boys and men (as well as some young women) who were identified as torture victims under the supervision of Detective Jon Burge (*Chicago Torture Justice Memorials*, n.d.). As a result, Mark was incarcerated with teenage boys and young men, many of whom shared his experience of torture at the hands of the Chicago Police. In the following quote, he describes the support the teens who were incarcerated along with him were able to offer one another:

> Throughout the 1980s and 1990s the prison system was full of young kids. The young kids didn't realize that they did not have anything to look forward to, but they were probably the most happiest people inside of the prison because the totality of their situation had not sunk in. Many of them were 14 years of age when they were arrested and ended up in the prison system. We all looked out for each other and that really made the difference because it allows you to grow.

With these words, Mark identified a protective factor that was also heard in the remarks of the other men in this study who were sentenced as juveniles. When Mark stated that the young age of many of the boys incarcerated with him protected them from realizing the "totality of their situation," he continued by explaining that he was so naïve when he was sent to prison that it "didn't fully sink in" that he was being sent away for the rest of his life. Ghani, who was even younger than Mark when he was arrested, also related to the naïveté of youth preventing him from realizing the gravity of the LWOP sentence that he was facing as he was going to trial:

> I had no thought of life without parole. Even though I heard it and people said that this is what I was facing, it was like Charlie Brown language: wah wah woh wah wah. I really had no concept of what the rest of my life looked like. Not having been on the planet that long, you don't have anything to measure what the rest of your life might be.

Saleem shared similar comments to those of Ghani and Mark as he spoke about the impact of his youth on the difficulty he initially had processing the reality of his LWOP sentence and the moment when it occurred to him that he was sentenced to die in prison:

> When I was sentenced to life without parole I had absolutely no frame of reference. He could have said anything and the reason why is because I hadn't lived. I was 17 years old when that sentence came down. I didn't know what life was like. I had no reference of living, other than living as an adolescent or a child, so when that judge said life without parole,

> I physically remember today going back to the holding cell and walking in the cell and laying on the bed and looking up at the ceiling and saying, "*Life? What the fuck*?" I fell asleep on that bench and two days later I was sent up the state to start serving that sentence. I was in my mid-twenties when I realized that *life is life* and they're going to keep me here until I die because now I have more of a frame of reference. I had 10 years in prison, and I was no closer to going to home than the first day when I walked in, and I'm seeing other people who came in around the same time as me starting to go home, but I'm still stuck and that's when it was like, "This shit is *real*!"

Ghani recalled the bleak moment when the reality of his LWOP sentence fully set in, yet he was also quick to add that in spite of this realization, he maintained hope that he would be freed:

> It wasn't until many, many years later. I was thrown in solitary confinement in a filthy cell with feces and I was in there by myself. I think I was like 20 or 21 at the time and it dawned on me, it was like my brain can process it a little bit better now, that they sentenced me *to die in prison*. That's when it hit me that this here that I'm going through is going to be the rest of my life. But I still believed that *somehow I would be free*.

Ghani's belief that one day he would be freed was echoed by every other person featured in this chapter. Gary stated that, "Due to my upbringing and my belief and knowing that I was innocent, I believed that I would eventually be found innocent and it was just a matter of time." Gladys shared Gary's belief that she too would be freed, declaring "I never accepted the sentence the day that they gave it to me. I never accepted it. I knew then I would get out." Saleem had similar words to share: "I always had hope and did not accept my sentence from the moment I was sentenced. My mindset was about survival day by day in prison, but my objective was to be free. I was always looking for a way out and that was something I *never stopped thinking about*." In spite of her admission of guilt, Shyrl hoped that one day she would be freed, saying "I never gave up hope, but I said to myself, 'Okay, if you're going to be here you better learn to be content with being here.'"

Maturation, the Influence of Their Elders, and the Road to Redemption

Shyrl's words mentioned earlier end with sentiments that were similar to those shared by the others, suggesting that eventually, they all reached a place where they were ready to start down the road to their redemption. For Shyrl, that journey started as soon as she was put behind bars. For the others, it took several years, but at some point, even though they each came to realize that their

LWOP sentence meant that they would not be going home, they managed not to slip into despair by maintaining a hope, if not a strong belief, that they would be released from prison one day. In the meantime, they came to the decision that they would make any time they spent behind prison walls as productive as possible. They need not be happy about their circumstances to find a way to, as Shyrl simply stated, "learn to be content with being [t]here." Over the years, they found numerous ways to be content with their plights, yet the common thread among these methods is that they were heavily focused on service to others. Whether they articulated it as such at the time or not, they were all engaged in the process of redemption.

In order to fully commit to redeeming themselves in the eyes of others, regardless of whether their focus was on prison officials, their families, their victims' families, or the society at large, it was first important for them to feel as though *they were even worthy of redemption.* This proved challenging for most of those in this study, who had survived anything from neglect during their childhood to what amounted to no less than severe child abuse from very young ages. The story that Shyrl shared of her upbringing was particularly horrific. Having been abandoned as a newborn by her mother and raised by her grandmother, who often left Shyrl at home unsupervised in order to go to work, Shyrl had been sexually abused by various family members and the grandfather of a neighborhood friend. She witnessed a great deal of domestic violence as a child, including her grandfather shooting his shotgun in the house, which caused Shyrl and her cousins to scatter and hide. Considering the impact of her traumatic childhood, it is not surprising that she married an abusive man and began using drugs to numb herself to the cumulative trauma of her life.

Perhaps due to her own co-dependency, which is a fairly common adaptive response of young girls raised in dysfunctional families, Shyrl always had a giving nature and enjoyed helping others. As a result, when Shyrl was incarcerated she quickly got involved as a mentor to the younger women with whom she was housed at the prison. Having entered the prison at the age of 35, Shyrl was significantly older than many of the women at the prison, thereby earning the nickname of "Mama Lamar." The altruistic nature that Shyrl possesses took on a redemptive quality once she learned to forgive herself for her actions that had led to the murder of two people. This proved to be challenging, as she had internalized a great deal of shame that stemmed from her childhood trauma. Shyrl said that she realized in one of her classes held at the prison, titled *Beyond Violence*, that society had failed her as a child on numerous occasions. Referring to the abuse she received as a child, she exclaimed "I didn't know anything else. I didn't know any better. To me, this is how life was!" The therapeutic approach of the classes she took at the prison, combined with her renewed faith in God eventually led Shyrl to forgive herself. It occurred to her that "If you are a Christian, you're supposed to be forgiving. If God can forgive us then why can't you be forgiving as well? It doesn't justify anything that we did."

As Shyrl spoke, it was clear that having reached a place of redemption within herself only propelled her more to help others, as if the act of self-forgiveness gave her an unapologetic drive to seek redemption from others through her endless dedication to serving other people. For Shyrl, it was the combination of her religious faith and a new appreciation for the cumulative impact that her childhood trauma, domestic abuse victimization, and drug addiction had on her adult criminal behavior that helped her to finally feel worthy of redemption. For the men in this study, their road to redemption was largely ignited by their good fortune of being housed with "old heads" who saw something special in them when they were still teenagers and decided to "take them under their wings," so to speak, and teach them "how to do time."

When Ghani was incarcerated at the age of 15, he was fortunate enough to have a significant amount of family support. Despite the level of support Ghani's family offered, it was difficult for them to visit him very often. Having run away from his Brooklyn home to Philadelphia in the months prior to the crime, Ghani found himself serving his sentence in Pennsylvania while his family was located in either New York or Trinidad, where he had spent the first seven years of his life. Despite the domestic violence that he witnessed between his mother and stepfather, which was a major factor in his decision to run away from home, Ghani had learned some good old-fashioned manners during his early years in Trinidad. These manners shaped his interactions in the prison with the older prisoners, who had been raised with the same values. Ghani identified these manners he was taught, which were exceedingly rare among most other young men in his generation, much less behind prison walls, as something that attracted the righteous, altruistic old heads to him. Ghani expressed his extreme gratitude for "those seeds that my family had planted in me" because little did he know that it would be "those seeds that were going to sprout behind prison walls and that's what kept me alive." A group of older lifers who carried a great deal of clout in the prison among both the prisoners and the staff saw the potential in Ghani and, in his words, "circled the wagons around me and protected me." When Ghani examined the way that these particular old heads lived their lives he learned what redemption looks like. He credits these old heads, most of whom identified as political prisoners and activists, for helping set him on his own path to redemption because they "gave me books and taught me so much that turned me into a revolutionary."

Four years after Ghani landed in prison, Saleem entered the same Pennsylvania prison. He too was fortunate enough to have been "chosen" by the same group of well-known and respected older prisoners who were helping Ghani work on his redemption. Due to their influence, about eight years into his sentence, Saleem decided to transform his anger into activism. In words reminiscent to those expressed by Ghani, Saleem recalled, "the old heads found me because of the way that I carried myself. You have to carry yourself in a certain way for the old heads to deal with you. I was fortunate when I was in the hole all of those years to link up with political prisoners and other politicized prisoners because they saw my energy and my intelligence." Saleem went on to describe the way the old heads who took an interest in him were able to help him get involved in social justice movements and find redemption in the process:

> Redemption came from political prisoners who were able to change my way of thinking with someone who is caught up in the street neighborhood culture. The political prisoners were actually in prison for defending their neighborhoods from police. They were feeding people in the neighborhood, they were offering services to people in the neighborhood, they were making sure the elders were safe in the neighborhood. I was in the prison for the complete opposite, and also I had to reflect because I'm looking at these men as my example and from them I'm learning about political prisoners and the liberation movement, but I had that one glaring contradiction that I'm not a political prisoner. I'm in prison for harming someone so I had to start reflecting on that the harm that I have caused my community and that was my Road to Redemption.

Gary had almost an identical experience to that of Ghani and Saleem, in that he too was a teenager when he found himself incarcerated amongst a group of prestigious political prisoners. Incarcerated in the notorious Angola prison in Louisiana, it didn't take long for him to encounter the infamous Angola 3, a group of Black Panther Party members who were wrongfully accused of killing a prison guard in 1972. Like Saleem, Gary initially met the political prisoners when he was sent to solitary confinement in the secure housing section of the prison. Referred to as "the dungeon," Gary was sent there for 20 days after he was framed with contraband. What initially seemed to be a setback wound up, quite literally, saving his life. Gary said that Angola was one of the most violent prisons in the nation at that time, with frequent cases of rape and murder between inmates. When a prisoner was killed in the cell next to his, he believed the rumors that there was a contract out on his life. The racial component of his alleged crime had made Gary a target for violent retaliation, but it also sensitized the political prisoners in Angola, as well as many others in the prison population, to his case, which created an unlikely coalition on Gary's behalf.

> When I went to prison, I was a small kid at 17 of small stature. These guys in prison didn't look at me as a threat, but as somebody they've got to keep their eye on because the environment would eat him alive. They saw their younger selves in me and they saw their sons or their neighbor's child. They saw this kid who they thought should not be in prison at all. They saw a typical example of just how cruel the American justice system can be. They knew this was not the place for me. They saw me, after all that they had done in their life, as an opportunity for them to do the right thing, to redeem their humanity. Those guys who were normally at war with each other were like, "We've got this kid here, what are we going to do, man?

> Are we going to feud with each other or are we going to lead by example and help this kid?" So what they did was put their differences aside and everybody wanted to be a part in educating me. Everybody wanted to be my grandfather or my father or my big brother or my uncle, my friend, my mentor, just anything that they could do to help me to prepare myself to make it in prison.

The examples of redemption that Mark was surrounded by as a newly-incarcerated teenager were similar to those identified by the other men in this study. Mark was lucky to have been given a job in the prison library, where he was encouraged to learn to read and write. Having entered prison only able to read at a second-grade level, Mark was very proud of himself when he passed the GED exam on his first attempt. He was motivated to earn his GED so that he could participate in a book club that met in the library, composed of men who were much older than him.

> I saw redemption in the older people because once I learned to read and write they had a book club inside of the prison library and that is something that the younger kids just didn't get involved in, but I found myself getting involved and it was people 40 or 50 years of age. And they enjoyed reading books either about incarceration or books about the history and rebelliousness of the system and how to fight to overturn the situation. Around that time, [Rubin] "Hurricane" Carter's situation came out and all of these stories gave us hope, hope that eventually one day we were going to be freed out of the prison system.

Gladys spoke as highly of the older female lifers with whom she was locked up as the men had about the old heads they befriended. Gladys recalled about the older female lifers, "they would be the best friends that I would have and the best workers because they have learned their lesson and they value their time out here. They are the best returning citizens you can have, all the way." Not only was Gladys inspired by the older lifers to seek her own redemption, but she was also eventually motivated by her religious faith and to be the best mother she could be for her children. When Gladys was sent to prison she had one small child and was pregnant with her second child. Gladys was shackled when she delivered her baby and was made to release her newborn daughter into the custody of her mother. She was so hurt by having to give up her baby that it fueled the anger she had already immersed herself in as she dwelled on the injustice of her wrongful conviction.

Gladys' anger often manifested in self-destructive behaviors, which would practically consume her for the first decade of her incarceration, until her father died suddenly of a heart attack in 2003. The loss of her father was a turning point for her. Gladys stated, "I found redemption when my father passed in 2003, and I started to become the woman that God wanted me to become." She also recalled another moment that crystallized the importance for her to find redemption, which occurred during a visit with her daughter. The following words recall the moment when Gladys' love for her children eventually motivated her to release that anger, essentially propelling her down the road to redemption:

> When my daughter Olivia was 11 or 12 and had come to see me in lockdown, it really made me turn my life around when she said, "*Mama when are you going to come out of this place*?" Olivia was the child who always broke down when it was time to go. She always broke down and never wanted to leave and that made me more stronger and more determined and want to fight.

Finding Redemption and Giving Back

Gladys

Although Gladys appears to have taken longer than anyone else in this sample to get started on her road to redemption, once she got started, she was able to accomplish a great deal through her dedication to serving others, both behind prison walls and after being released. Gladys shared that the 16 years she and her sister had spent behind bars broke them down in many ways, yet she firmly believes that God never left them. Once she was able to shake the stronghold she felt from the anger and injustice she felt not only from their wrongful conviction, but also the numerous abuses she and her sister endured during their incarceration, Gladys and her sister were driven "by an intense compassion to help others."

Gladys had battled her own addiction to crack cocaine as a teenager prior to her incarceration, witnessed years of domestic violence between her parents, ran away from home, dropped out of school, became a teen mother, and was confronted with numerous abusive men in her young life. As a result, there were few problems experienced by the women with whom she was incarcerated that she had not already experienced firsthand. Having survived a decade of fighting with other inmates, who were all too often driven by their own self-serving motives, Gladys eventually began to form connections with other women, whom she would come to consider part of her "prison family." The bonds that she and her sister formed with these women, many of whom are still behind bars, remain strong. The inspiration that they received from their experiences behind bars motivated them to open their own nonprofit organization that provides a variety of services for others reentering society from prison.

Gladys was very proud to earn her GED soon after her release, especially knowing how many women she had met behind bars without a high school diploma or GED. While she and her sister were incarcerated, they offered tutoring for the younger women, "so it just came natural when I got out." Initially, Gladys and Jamie opened their home to women who were reentering society to offer them assistance with finding housing, jobs, education, and counseling services. As they began to receive donations from sponsors who celebrated the work they were doing in their community, they were able to open an office in 2019 for their 501(c) (3) nonprofit that they named Sisters of Hope, which is located in Pensacola, Florida. The primary service offered at Sisters of Hope is GED classes because they discovered many of the women who were seeking their services were functionally illiterate. However, the organization also offers résumé building, job training, and homelessness services. The organization's website notes that they work with probation officers and the Department of Juvenile Justice because they believe that "everyone deserves a second chance" (Sisters of Hope, n.d.).

Shyrl

While Gladys has been home for a decade now, the other woman in this study has been home for less than one year. Having served 35 years of her LWOP sentence, Shyrl was incarcerated twice as long as Gladys, and at 70 years old, she is more than 20 years Gladys' senior. As a result of her time spent inside versus outside of prison, the bulk of Shyrl's redemptive work was done behind bars. Just as a strong faith in God played a key role in the redemption process for Gladys, so too did Shyrl find salvation in her religion. She proudly taught Bible study on Sundays. Throughout the week, she made herself available to the young women in distress who called her "Mama Lamar" to provide them with the words of wisdom they had come to expect from her.

Over the months that have passed since her release, Shyrl has been working on redeeming herself in the eyes of her children, grandchildren, and siblings. In the midst of her reunification with family, Shyrl has been volunteering with the California Coalition for Women Prisoners (CCWP) and has spoken to various audiences as a representative of the organization. She finds that sharing her story is "a way of honoring my victims because I chose never to make anybody else a victim and I want people to know what I did because of my addiction so that maybe somebody won't wind up being in the same place that I am." In addition to speaking on behalf of the CCWP, Shyrl says she is working with others in this organization to get laws passed, including one that will get rid of LWOP.

Gary

While incarcerated in Angola, Gary worked in reentry, helping to prepare people for release back into society. He shared that he knew he was good at this job because "I heard guys tell me that if there was someone like me in the community that most likely they would not be in prison today." This feedback led Gary to believe that he could have a greater impact working in prevention, helping young people *before* they make decisions that could lead to their incarceration. As a result, upon his release, he gravitated toward work helping the homeless.

In the early 1970s, Gary had lived in California with his older sisters, and so after spending more than 40 years in prison, Gary left Louisiana and returned to California, where he now works with homeless youth as an outreach and engagement support worker at the agency A Safe Place for Youth. Confident in the changes he has made in the lives of these youth, Gary proclaimed, "And the person I am? I believe myself to be a trailblazer. I believe in making changes!" As he reflects upon his ability to find redemption, Gary is quick to give credit to the men at Angola who entered his life, stating that "they were the ones who were looking out for my best interest."

Ghani and Saleem

Ghani and Saleem could easily make the same remarks about the influential "old heads" they were fortunate enough to encounter in the Pennsylvania prison system. These older prisoners helped guide both teens (and later men) onto a remarkable journey toward their own redemption. In what follows, we are only able to provide a cursory overview of these men's accomplishments because an exhaustive list of the activities they have facilitated, both during their incarceration and in the years since their release, would be far too long to list here.

Several years before their release, Ghani and Saleem became founding members of Right to Redemption (R2R) along with several other incarcerated men. Their R2R group became one of the groups that founded the Coalition to Abolish Death by Incarceration (CADBI), a grassroots campaign that has grown significantly with the development of several chapters in the struggle to end LWOP sentences in Pennsylvania. While he was still behind prison walls, Ghani also co-founded Ubuntu Philadelphia, a series of community engagements that use open dialogue in an effort to change the city's culture and create safer, more peaceful, and caring communities, which Ghani continues to organize to this day (Amistad Law Project, n.d.). One of the programs that Ghani is most often credited with developing during his incarceration is Fathers and Children Together (FACT), which is a program that was created to build stronger relationships between incarcerated fathers and their children. As he speaks about this program, it is easy to see that he is incredibly proud of its success. In a fortuitous twist of fate, Mural Arts Philadelphia sent an art instructor to the FACT program to help with the children's artwork during their visits with their fathers. Knowing that the *Miller* decision gave him a real shot to be released, Ghani developed a relationship with this art instructor, whom he would later marry and have a son with. Having entered prison at the age of 15, Ghani had been unable to start his own family. Thirty years later, he was finally given a second chance at doing just that. Out of the long list of activities in which Ghani has engaged since his release to show that he has reached redemption, he is most proud of the loving family he has formed with his wife and son. He has gone full circle, now able to apply the lessons he taught so many fathers through the FACT program to his relationship with his own son.

When Ghani is not with his family, he is engaged in a variety of activities in his community, all of which reveal the depths of his redemption. After co-producing a successful radio special for PBS Frontline, titled "Living with Murder," he began his own podcast with the Amistad Law Project, titled "Move it Forward." He joined the staff of Amistad, a public interest law center, shortly after his release from prison, in the role of Healing Justice Organizer to assist them with social justice advocacy work. After three years working with Amistad, Ghani has recently taken on a new role with the Youth Art & Self-Empowerment Project (YASP) as the director of their pilot program called Healing Futures Restorative Justice Diversion Program.

It is not unusual to find Ghani and Saleem at many of the same activist events in Philadelphia, typically organized alongside other CADBI members, as they are both extremely dedicated to the group's mission to abolish LWOP. Like Ghani, Saleem's activism began long before he was released from prison. Twenty years ago, Saleem worked with other prisoners, including political prisoner Russell Maroon Shoatz, who is one of the mentors both Ghani and Saleem credit for their survival from prison both physically and mentally intact, to start the Human Rights Coalition (HRC), which has grown over the last two decades in both size and prominence. Composed of current and former prisoners, as well as their families and supporters, the HRC is dedicated to supporting the families of incarcerated individuals and transforming the correctional system into one that is focused on rehabilitation and reintegration (*Human Rights Coalition*, n.d.). The work that Saleem has done over the years with the HRC is phenomenal on its own, yet like Ghani, it is only the tip of the iceberg when we consider the numerous activities that point to his redemption.

Saleem earned a degree behind bars and helped to build the Abolitionist Law Center when it began in 2012. After being home for less than three years, Saleem was appointed the Executive Director of the Abolitionist Law Center (ALC), after having served as the organization's Director of Community Organizing. In the year that has passed since Saleem took on this role, he has been incredibly successful, so much, in fact, that at the time he was interviewed for this study he had just been invited to join the faculty at Penn Law to teach a class focused on movement lawyering. In the short span of several years, Saleem has literally gone from a forgotten man in a prison cell to standing proudly in front of a classroom of aspiring lawyers as an esteemed colleague in academia.

Mark

Of the six people interviewed for this study, Mark has been home for the longest period, and in the 12 years since his release, he has barely stopped to catch his breath, working just as hard if not harder than any other advocate for social justice. Upon his release from prison, he immediately joined the Campaign to End the Death Penalty (CEDP), which he credits for playing a significant role in his release. The CEDP had taken on the cases of the infamous Chicago Death

Row 10, who had all been victims of the torture campaign that took place under the supervision of Detective Burge. Mark reached out from prison to provide his assistance for his fellow torture victims on Illinois' death row, sharing with CEDP activists that he too was a victim of Burge's police torture tactics. Mark indicated that he cannot overstate the role that the CEDP played in his release, as well as his reintegration back into society and into the activist community, emphatically adding, "I'm not sure how my life would look if it weren't for the CEDP!"

Mark found it easy to join with his comrades in the CEDP because the activists in this anti-death penalty group took a firm position *against life without parole*. From its inception, the CEDP disagreed with those anti-death penalty organizations that see LWOP as an appropriate alternative to capital punishment. Mark appreciates the CEDP for their anti-LWOP position, stating that he could not organize alongside activists who do not oppose *both* capital punishment *and* LWOP, because "everyone deserves a second chance!" In addition to his work with the CEDP, Mark has worked with the Illinois Campaign for the Fair Sentencing of Youth and the Chicago Alliance Against Racist and Political Repression. For the last few years, however, Mark has been working as an organizer with the Chicago Torture Justice Center, which offers clinical healing through trauma-informed services for survivors and also organizes in the community under a restorative justice framework. Mark proudly asserts, "Since being released from the prison system, I have played a role in at least 312 people being released from the prison system, and that is because I believe that restorative justice must give second chance opportunities."

Conclusion

By sentencing each of the individuals profiled in this chapter to LWOP, the American justice system had determined that they were all beyond redemption and would pose a perpetual risk to public safety. Yet, the stories they tell reveal the exact opposite. During their years of incarceration, they all matured and decided to give back to their communities. In their own ways, they found a path that enabled them help others, make a positive impact on society, and potentially, reduce crime. As we noted earlier, the details summarized in this chapter represent just a fraction of the accomplishments of those featured. To do justice to their stories, each person deserves their own book, not just part of a chapter.

Likewise, the stories of these six individuals represent only a fraction of the many stories of redemption that can be found among other LWOP survivors who have found their way home and, more significantly, among the countless others who still languish behind bars. The six people described in this chapter are in an exclusive club. It remains incredibly rare for those sentenced to LWOP to ever be released. The vast majority will, in fact, die in prison, and among them, there are countless stories of redemption that remain untold. Just like the individuals featured in this chapter, the men and women they left behind are capable of redeeming themselves and making a difference in the lives of many people if we are willing to give them second chances, but LWOP denies them this chance. It is crucial that we ask how we want such stories to end for those languishing behind bars. LWOP ends those stories before they even get started.

The point is we do not know what the future holds. Therefore, we cannot know at the time of sentencing who will and will not be reformed, and we do not know what stories of redemption are still to be told. Therefore, LWOP cannot be justified based upon a need to detain supposedly irredeemable, incorrigible offenders because we do not know who those people are *at the time of sentencing*. By sentencing people to LWOP, we foreclose the possibility of change and deny society the opportunity to benefit from the contributions of those who have been reformed. Clearly, many—perhaps most—people who have been sentenced to LWOP are capable of rehabilitation, so we should enact a system that allows us to hear and consider their stories in the years following their initial incarceration: parole.

References

Amistad Law Project. (n.d.). *Ubuntu Philadelphia*. Retrieved from https://amistadlaw.org/ubuntu-philadelphia

Chicago Torture Justice Memorials. (n.d.). Retrieved from http://chicagotorture.org/

Human Rights Coalition. (n.d.). Retrieved from https://www.hrcoalition.org

Mauer, M., & Nellis, A. (2018). *The meaning of life: The case for abolishing life sentences*. New York: New Press.

Miller v. Alabama, 567 U.S. 460 (U.S. Supreme Court 2012).

Montgomery v. Louisiana, 577 U.S. (U.S. Supreme Court 2016).

Rovner, J. (2021, May 24). *Juvenile life without parole: An overview*. Retrieved September 3, 2021, from Sentencing Project: https://www.sentencingproject.org/publications/juvenile-life-without-parole/

Scott, J., & Scott, G. (2015). *The Scott sisters: Revealing the truth, exposing injustice, and trusting God*. Gladys Scott.

Sisters of Hope. (n.d.). *Taking back my life*. Retrieved from Sisters of Hope: https://www.sistersofhopereentry.net/about-us/

Thompson, D. (2020, March 28). *California governor commutes sentences, including for murder*. Retrieved from My News 4: https://mynews4.com/news/local/california-governor-commutes-sentences-including-for-murder

van Zyl Smit, D., & Appleton, C. (2019). *Life imprisonment: A global human rights analysis*. Cambridge, MA: Harvard University Press.

Conclusion and Recommendations

In 1846, the state of Michigan became "the first government in the English-speaking world to abolish capital punishment ..." (Wanger, 2002, p. 38), and ever since then, capital punishment has been the topic of fierce debate. Today, roughly half of American states retain capital punishment—although in practice, only a handful of them actually carry out executions—and the use of capital punishment has been in sharp decline throughout the US for more than two decades (Death Penalty Information Center, 2021). It would not be unreasonable to conclude that the US might soon join the rest of the so-called "western world" and abandon the practice altogether. Yet, this decline has been accompanied by a contemporaneous proliferation in the use of LWOP sentences, or what some refer to as "death by incarceration" (Johnson & McGunigall-Smith, 2008), which are now being dispensed with greater regularity and for a wider variety of offenses than death sentences ever were (Nellis, 2021). Despite resulting in the same outcome as a death sentence (death in prison) and essentially permanently stripping the defendant's life of the most fundamental existential characteristics that make life worth living, such as autonomy, liberty, and a meaningful social existence with friends and family (Miao, 2020; Sheleff, 1987), LWOP has not received the same attention or scrutiny as capital punishment has. In fact, LWOP has received support from both sides of the political spectrum, which has enabled it to flourish under the radar with very little criticism. To address this reality and to fill this gap in our knowledge, we empirically assessed the various justifications that have been offered for LWOP—by both the left and the right. The results of our analyses fail to produce any evidence in support of any of those justifications and thus challenge the claim that LWOP is a justifiable sentencing option.

We began our inquiry by looking at the defenses of LWOP offered by opponents of capital punishment. As we previously discussed, for the past half century, many abolitionists have championed LWOP because they see it as a palatable alternative to capital punishment that is instrumental in winning over public support for abolition and thus critical to the success of the abolitionist movement (*Harvard Law Review*, 2006; Miao, 2020). From this perspective, LWOP may be extremely harsh and overly severe, but it is at least less severe and thus more humane than capital punishment. Therefore, even for those abolitionists who do not like LWOP, it is a bargain most are willing to make in exchange for abolition (Miao, 2020). To paraphrase Voltaire, many abolitionists fear the prospect of the perfect being the enemy of the good and are thus willing to tolerate LWOP if that is what is needed to get rid of capital punishment. In this line of reasoning, the notion that a "life" sentence is inherently better than a "death" sentence is accepted uncritically as an obvious truism despite the clear similarities between the two sentences. So, in Part I, we analyzed whether this belief is true by examining the various ways LWOP is supposedly "better" than death in the eyes of abolitionists, and based upon the evidence available to us, it does not appear that LWOP is superior to capital punishment on any dimension with which abolitionists are concerned—and it may even be *worse*.

First, for the typical abolitionist, the most manifest manner in which LWOP is an improvement over capital punishment is that it does not involve any executions and is thus more humane than capital punishment. This notion has already been challenged on philosophical grounds by numerous other scholars (Berry, 2010; *Harvard Law Review*, 2006; Miao, 2020; Ogletree & Sarat, 2012; Sheleff, 1987; Wright, 1990), but here, we assessed the views of individuals who have *actually experienced* these sentences. The picture that emerges from the interviews with these individuals is that LWOP produces just as much, if not greater, suffering than capital punishment and is therefore just as, if not more, inhumane. This finding is not simply the result of those serving LWOP perceiving the grass to be greener on the other side. Rather, it is a view that was expressed by both those serving LWOP and those on death row (including those who dropped their remaining appeals and volunteered for an execution). This perspective was even shared by the men who were interviewed who had the unique and unfortunate experience of living under *both* sentences, a reality that should give them a greater ability to compare the two sentences than anyone else. In other words, for those most directly impacted by the use of these sentences, no matter which side of the divide they found themselves, the overriding sentiment that emerged from their interviews was the idea that LWOP is no better than a death sentence and may even be worse. If the individuals who have actually experienced these sentences indicate that replacing death sentences with LWOP is not preferable for them, then those who claim to be fighting for them ought to listen. Otherwise, they may just be making their legal situations and their lives *worse*.

While we cannot attest to whether the views of the individuals discussed in this work are representative of the entire population of persons sentenced to die in prison, we are also not the first to discover this sentiment among the condemned (Egelko, 2014; Johnson & McGunigall-Smith, 2008; Wright, 1991), so it seems quite likely that the views expressed by the individuals we discussed are fairly widespread among both those sentenced to LWOP and to death. In line with this perspective, most of Europe and Latin America consider LWOP sentences to be inhuman and degrading, thus violating fundamental human rights. Therefore, as with capital punishment, they have abolished such sentences. When it comes to its tolerance for and use of LWOP, the US is an outlier, housing more persons sentenced to LWOP than the entire rest of the planet combined (van Zyl Smit & Appleton, 2019). When viewing LWOP from these various perspectives, the abolitionists' claim that LWOP is more humane than capital punishment appears dubious at best. On the contrary, it appears to be just another type of death sentence.

Second, many abolitionists have a legitimate and not unreasonable fear that under a capital sentencing regime, innocent people may be executed (something that has, no doubt, already occurred) (American Civil Liberties Union, 2012; Warden, 2012; Wozniak, 2012). LWOP, therefore, protects these innocent individuals from such a horrific demise and should, in theory, provide them with more time to prove their innocence. Yet, this logic overlooks the fact that those who receive capital sentences are given greater access to attorneys and the courts, which may improve their odds of successfully proving their innocence. Therefore, to assess which sentence gives the wrongly convicted a better chance to prove their innocence, we compared the exoneration rate of individuals sentenced to death to several reference groups, and the results indicated that those who are sentenced to death are *more likely* to be exonerated than others sentenced to prison, including those sentenced to LWOP. While we cannot be certain that this reality does not stem from a greater proportion of wrongful convictions among those sentenced to death, the magnitude of the differences identified in our analysis suggest that this factor alone is unlikely to account for the differences. Rather, the greater due process protections afforded to those sentenced to death appears to be a crucial factor in helping to identify and overturn wrongful convictions. Therefore, abolishing capital punishment without extending the due process protections it offers to those facing "death by incarceration" is likely to condemn *more* innocent people to die in prison rather than fewer.

Third, abolitionists often cite the cost of capital punishment as a reason why LWOP is preferable (American Civil Liberties Union, 2012; Dieter, 2014; Warden, 2012), and on the surface, the existing studies unanimously support this argument as death sentences and capital trials invariably cost more than sentencing the same individuals to life. However, upon digging beneath the surface, it becomes clear that there are two major flaws in this logic. The first is that it overlooks the *reason* capital punishment costs more. Put succinctly, these expenditures are not entirely frivolous or wasteful. While some of those expenses are indeed related to the administration of capital punishment and the additional work that goes into the sentencing hearing, capital cases also run a higher price tag because capital defendants and those who are sentenced to death are afforded more due process protections than their counterparts who are not facing a potential execution. In other words, any argument to abolish capital punishment *for the purpose* of saving money is essentially making the perverse suggestion that capital punishment affords defendants *too much* due process and so it should be repealed in order to limit their procedural protections and their ability to challenge the legitimacy of their convictions. Otherwise, repealing capital punishment would not save as much money as abolitionists claim. Regardless of whether those who cite costs as one of their concerns are cognizant of this fact, as has already been seen in the states that have abolished capital punishment, the end result of repealing capital punishment to save money will inevitably be *fewer* procedural protections and less access to the courts for those who would have previously been charged with a capital offense.

The second pitfall of the cost argument is that it simply compares the cost of one capital trial or one death sentence to the cost of one LWOP sentence while overlooking the fact that LWOP has a far greater scale than capital punishment ever did and is being used against individuals who would have never been at risk for a death sentence. Therefore, we sought to determine whether LWOP remains cheaper than capital punishment after accounting for this difference in scale. Our analyses revealed that because of LWOP's greater scale, its total cost almost certainly exceeds the total cost of capital punishment, and that in the best-case scenario, the additional costs LWOP imposes on the system are nearly equivalent to the extra costs imposed by capital punishment. Furthermore, by raising the sentencing ceiling, LWOP has contributed to the aging of the prison population, and the increased cost burden of incarcerating the growing number of elderly persons in prison who could almost certainly be safely released far exceeds the total cost of capital punishment in the US. Therefore, the shift from capital punishment to LWOP is not producing any cost savings—just less due process.

Finally, abolitionists point out that capital punishment is applied in a racially biased manner (American Civil Liberties Union, 2012; Grosso, O'Brien, Taylor, & Woodworth, 2014). Although the Supreme Court ruled that such injustices do not render capital punishment unconstitutional (*McCleskey v. Kemp*, 1987), abolitionists hold out hope that the racial justice argument will be sufficient to convince the public—and by extension legislators—to oppose capital punishment. There is no disputing the volumes of empirical evidence that have been produced showing capital punishment's racial biases. However, there is no evidence to suggest that these same racial injustices do not also infect LWOP. Although the mandatory nature of many LWOP sentences should, in theory, remove the discretion that often contributes to racially biased outcomes, in reality, it simply shifts discretion into the hands of prosecutors, who exercise this discretion in private. The few studies that have been done on this question all demonstrate that LWOP suffers from the same racially biased sentencing patterns as capital punishment, with defendants of color and those who victimize white people having the greatest odds of receiving LWOP (Chen, 2008; Garrett, Seale-Carlisle, Modjadidi, & Renberg, 2021; Johnson, Spohn, & Kimchi, 2021; Mills, Dorn, & Hritz, 2016).

Furthermore, the crimes American society chooses to punish with LWOP reflect the same racial and class biases inherent in capital sentencing. LWOP is typically reserved for "street crimes" rather than corporate crimes, even when the latter cause far more damage to society or are part of a pattern of repeated malfeasance. Being the getaway driver in a robbery that goes bad and results in someone's death is legally regarded as murder and very well may result in someone being incarcerated for the rest of their life. Yet, causing the death of one's employees by repeatedly ignoring safety regulations to save a few dollars is a misdemeanor that is unlikely to lead to any jail time. Similarly, habitual offender laws exclusively target crimes committed by the poor while overlooking repeat white collar offenders. Not surprisingly, given this state of affairs, the population of people serving LWOP is even more racially skewed than both the overall prison population and the death row population are. Black and African American people comprise 33% of those serving prison sentences in the US (Carson, 2021) and 41% of the death row population (Snell, 2021) but 55% of those serving LWOP in the US (Nellis, 2021), 62% of those serving LWOP for crimes that took place when they were *juveniles* (Rovner, 2021), and 65% of those serving LWOP for *nonviolent* crimes (American Civil Liberties Union, 2014). Therefore, from an abolitionist perspective, we were unable to find any evidence that LWOP is an improvement over capital punishment. If anything, it appears to be *worse*.

After scrutinizing the abolitionists' justifications for supporting LWOP, in Part II, we turned our attention to the conservative, tough-on-crime rationales for LWOP. The first of these arguments is the utilitarian one, namely that LWOP is a crucial policy tool for lowering violent crime rates. To assess the veracity of this claim, we ran a series of statistical analyses, and the results of these tests indicate that LWOP is unlikely to be an effective means of reducing violent crime. First, the data indicate that the implementation of a LWOP statute has an inconsistent relationship with violent crime rates. Following the enactment of LWOP, some states saw violent crime rates decrease, but other states saw them increase, and the most common outcome was no change in the violent crime rate. This suggests that if one is seeking to reduce violent crime, then merely enacting a LWOP statute is, in and of itself, insufficient. Therefore, we next sought to determine if increased LWOP utilization—rather than just having a LWOP statute on the books—produces lower violent crime rates. The results of those analyses indicated that increasing the proportion of life-sentenced individuals who are ineligible parole does not result in statistically lower violent crime rates, and if anything, it may result in *increases* in the violent crime rate. In other words, LWOP has no marginal effect on violent crime beyond that which is produced by parole-eligible life sentences, and it may even produce a brutalization effect. Thus, LWOP is not an effective means of controlling violent crime.

The next argument conservative supporters of LWOP make is that such sentences are a necessary form of retribution for the most serious offenders. That is, for some crimes, lifetime incarceration is the only punishment that fits the crime and provides justice (and closure) for the victims. Obviously, there is a great deal of subjectivity in determining what punishment fits what crime, but from a retributive viewpoint, punishments must be scaled to the seriousness of the offense so that the most serious crimes and the most blameworthy individuals receive the harshest punishments (Robinson, 2012). Our examination of LWOP's usage in the US revealed that it fails to live up to this standard. Since LWOP punishes someone for the remainder of their life and permanently deprives them of liberty, it can only be justified on retributive grounds for the most serious offense, intentional and aggravated murder (Robinson, 2012). Yet, in the US, LWOP is being imposed for a whole host of offenses—including *nonviolent* crimes—and on a wide range of offenders without regard for their moral blameworthiness or culpability. As of 2020, more than 20,000 persons—around 36% of the entire LWOP population—were serving LWOP for crimes less serious than first-degree murder, and more than 14,000 of those were not even convicted of a homicide (Nellis, personal communication, April 21, 2021). Even more appallingly, that number includes between 2,340 and 4,388 individuals serving LWOP for *nonviolent* offenses.

From a retributivist perspective, LWOP cannot be justified for any of these lesser crimes, but even among the remainder of the LWOP population, which is serving time for first-degree murder, LWOP does not necessarily fit the crime or the defendant. Recall that we have argued that LWOP is essentially a death sentence in disguise. As such, from a retributivist point of view, LWOP can only really be justified when imposed on someone who would have otherwise been sentenced to death. Before a death sentence can be imposed, the Supreme Court has mandated that a separate sentencing hearing be held in which aggravating and mitigating factors are presented and considered when determining the appropriate sentence (*Eddings v. Oklahoma*, 1982; *Gregg v. Georgia*, 1976; *Lockett v. Ohio*, 1978). The Court has also prohibited the use of capital punishment against "minor" participants in another's crime (*Enmund v. Florida*, 1982). Yet, no such restrictions exist on the use of LWOP. In fact, LWOP is often imposed as a mandatory penalty with no opportunity for the defendant to present or for the judge to consider potentially relevant mitigating circumstances, and due to accomplice liability and felony murder statutes, "minor" participants in an underlying felony that leads to someone's death are routinely sentenced to die in prison regardless of their actual awareness that someone could potentially get killed during the crime (Robinson, 2012). Due to the restrictions on capital punishment, prosecutors only seek death sentences in a tiny fraction of first-degree murder cases, and when they do, they are usually unsuccessful (Collins, Boruchowitz, Hickman, & Larrañaga, 2016; Cook, 2009; Goss, Strain, & Blalock, 2016; Roman, Chalfin, Sundquist, Knight, & Darmenov, 2008). That is, before being sentenced to death, those convicted of first-degree murder go through a winnowing process that dramatically limits the number of death sentences. No similar process exists for LWOP, so *most* of those sentenced to LWOP for first-degree murder received an *automatic* sentence (Nellis, 2017). What's worse, although the Supreme Court has prohibited the execution of individuals who were children at the time of the crimes for which they have been convicted (*Roper v. Simmons,* 2005), LWOP is an available sentencing option for children, and as of 2020, 1,465 people were serving LWOP for crimes that occurred when they were children (Rovner, 2021). Combining these facts reveals that even if LWOP is justified for the most serious offenses, in the vast majority of cases, LWOP is not being imposed for those crimes and is, therefore, unjustly harsh.

A variation on the retribution theme suggests that harsh punishments like LWOP are necessary to achieve justice and closure for victims or their survivors. However, in our review of the literature on this topic, we found that retributive punishments do not typically benefit crime victims. If anything, they cause victims to fixate on the offender and impede their ability to move on, leading to reductions in both mental and physical health and perhaps even contributing to their own anti-social behavior (Bushman, 2002; Carlsmith, Wilson, & Gilbert, 2008; McCullough, 2001; Orth, Montada, & Maercker, 2006). Rather, forgiveness appears to provide victims with the ability to move on, and forgiveness is best accomplished through dialogue, reconciliation, and other forms of restitution rather than retribution (Exline, Worthington, Hill, & McCullough, 2003; McCullough, 2001; McCullough & Witvliet, 2002; Umbreit, 2001; Witvliet et al., 2008; Witvliet, Luna, Worthington, & Tsang, 2020). Victims who receive an apology or other forms of restitution are better able to forgive, and forgiveness has been linked to improvements in victims' mental and physical wellbeing (Orcutt, Pickett, & Pope, 2005; Reed & Enright, 2006; Witvliet et al., 2008). The present court process, which is focused on doling out punishments to defendants, tends to overlook the needs of crime victims, such as empowerment, restitution, and restoration of respect (Dreisinger, 2016; Zehr, 2001). In fact, the sentencing process tends to further disempower victims, making their plight even worse. Therefore, the retributive nature of punishments like LWOP is unlikely to benefit crime victims in any meaningful way. If we truly desire to help victims, we should focus on punishment practices that take their needs into account and provide them the capacity to attain closure rather than reflexively imposing the suffering they have experienced onto someone else.

Lastly, many argue that LWOP is the only means of dealing with incorrigible repeat offenders. As van Zyl Smit and Appleton (2019) have explained, for some, the rationale behind these sentences is that "the truly 'incorrigible' should not be treated but simply detained for the rest of their lives with no prospect of release" (p. 9). This rationale is based on a belief that there are many who cannot be reformed or redeemed and thus must simply be warehoused. However, this logic only works if LWOP is only being imposed on those "truly incorrigible" individuals. Through interviews with several individuals who were sentenced to LWOP and then subsequently released, we found this to be untrue. Each of the individuals profiled had achieved redemption and has made positive contributions to society. There are, no doubt, countless others still behind bars who have been similarly rehabilitated. In other words, LWOP is not simply ensnaring the incorrigible. Many of the people who have received "death by incarceration" sentences are capable of reformation and redemption—and many *have already been* reformed—and so LWOP is not necessary for them. This is not the result of the occasional mistake but rather a fatal flaw in the "incorrigibility" justification for LWOP: namely, there is no way to know *at the time of sentencing* who will and will not change in the future. Therefore, LWOP, which forecloses the possibility of change, cannot be justified since we do not know whether it will be necessary. We do not dispute the possibility that there may be some individuals who are, in fact, incorrigible and irredeemable. We are simply acknowledging that we cannot know in advance who those individuals are and so removing the possibility of release has the potential to *harm* society by denying it the contributions of those who have been reformed while incarcerating a potentially sizeable number of people without achieving any legitimate punishment goal. As such, there needs to be a system in place to evaluate who has and has not been reformed—i.e., parole.

Policy Recommendations

These conclusions lead us to make the following policy recommendations. First, LWOP should be abandoned as a sentencing practice. Rather than promoting LWOP as a viable alternative to capital punishment, the death penalty abolition movement should include abolition of "death by incarceration." Otherwise, we will just end up replacing one type of death sentence with another type—one that is in many aspects worse than the original. We recognize that for many abolitionists, the decision to support LWOP is strategic rather than idealistic. Public opinion polls consistently demonstrate that support for capital punishment declines when LWOP is provided as an alternative option (Banks, 2016; Cochran & Chamlin, 2005; Death Penalty Information Center, 2010; Gallup, n.d.; Miao, 2020), so from an abolitionist perspective, it makes some intuitive sense to promote LWOP as an alternative. However, just because a punishment is convenient does not mean it is good, and getting rid of a terrible punishment does not mean that its replacement should be perceived as any better. Upon analyzing each of the ways LWOP is supposedly "better" than capital punishment from an abolitionist perspective, we were unable to find support for any of these claims, but we did discover several ways in which LWOP might be *worse* than capital punishment. This should not be misconstrued as an endorsement of capital punishment. On the contrary, we agree with abolitionists that capital punishment is barbaric, degrading, inhumane, error-prone, wastefully expensive, and racist. It should have been abolished decades ago, but we also must ensure that its replacement is not as problematic or *worse*. Therefore, from an abolitionist point of view, LWOP should also be abolished.

Even from a conservative, tough-on-crime perspective, LWOP does not appear to serve any penological function. We found no evidence that LWOP is any more effective at preventing crime than life *with* parole or that LWOP is being used in a proper retributive manner. We have further demonstrated that LWOP is not being used exclusively against incorrigible offenders who cannot possibly be reformed or make a positive contribution to society, and the reason for this is that it is impossible to know who will change or how they will change in the future. Thus, even from a conservative perspective, the use of LWOP should either be eliminated or, at the very least, dramatically scaled back so as to only ensnare those individuals who would have otherwise been sentenced to death.

If LWOP is abolished, though, what should replace it? For adults convicted of first-degree murder, we recommend a *maximum* penalty of life with the possibility of parole after no longer than 25 years. We recognize that this proposal is a drastic departure from the current sentencing practice in most states. However, this recommendation would align the US with the general consensus in international law and among most other industrialized nations. As the European Court of Human Rights (ECtHR) has summarized, "[T]he comparative and international law materials before it show clear support for the institution of a dedicated mechanism guaranteeing a review no later than twenty-five years after the imposition of a life sentence, with further periodic reviews thereafter" (*Vinter and Others v. United Kingdom*, 2013, p. 43). The idea behind this practice is that "No human being should be regarded as beyond improvement and therefore should always have the prospect of being released" (van Zyl Smit, 2010, p. 40). We agree with this proposition. Everyone has rehabilitative potential. Not everyone will realize this potential, but we cannot know at the time of sentencing who will and who will not. Therefore, everyone should be given opportunities to improve and then granted a periodic review to determine if their continued incarceration serves any legitimate penological function. If not, they should be granted release.

For all lesser crimes, we propose that eligibility for parole should occur after no more than 20 years. This should be thought of as the maximum possible amount of time one must serve before becoming eligible for parole. Sentences should remain proportional to the crime, so the use of such lengthy sentences should be extremely rare, reserved for the most serious offenses. In line with this suggestion, the use of "virtual life sentences"—i.e., sentences that are so long that no one can reasonably be expected to survive them—should also be abandoned as they are an end-run around prohibitions on LWOP. Furthermore, the "stacking" of multiple sentences for the same criminal incident should either be eliminated or greatly curtailed so that no one is forced to serve more than 20 years for a single criminal incident before becoming eligible for parole. Lastly, when determining an appropriate sentence for these lesser crimes, greater consideration should be given to the age of the defendant—both the cognitive immaturity of youthful defendants that reduces their culpability and the diminishing criminal propensity of older defendants that lowers their probability of reoffending. Due to the way adolescents' brains develop, under no circumstances (including convictions for first-degree murder) should a juvenile be given a sentence length that exceeds his or her age at the time of the offense.

For these reforms to be effective, however, parole boards need to be reimagined in a manner that provides those applying for parole a legitimate opportunity for release and ensures that authorities give full consideration to any changes the applicant may have experienced since the time of the crime. As it currently stands, parole hearings are often a formality that do not provide a meaningful opportunity to earn release. As Robert Gattis, whose death sentence was commuted to LWOP in 2012 once explained to one of the authors, life *with* parole is meaningless if we have a broken system that does not afford people real chances to be released:

> I want to focus on more than just life without parole. The bigger issue is even if we had parole, they have made it so difficult to be released from parole. They are fearful about giving people chances. People should be able to earn their opportunities. This goes to the whole thing of what do they do with people while they are in prison. What good are you after 25 or 30 years have passed by if you've done nothing the whole time you've been in prison? You haven't had a job, so when you get out, you still have no work skills. When you get out there, the only thing that you have is what you left before you came here. If it's really about corrections, why don't you give people opportunities. So, if you don't have life without parole, what do you have? What if that number is 90 years? What is the difference? So, what I'm saying is what about giving people the opportunity to prove themselves? If you have these tools at your disposal, you're not using them.

Gattis' fear that life with parole would really be little different from LWOP seems to be borne out by the evidence; for most of those serving life with parole, the "possibility of parole exists almost entirely on paper" (Slater, 2020, para 4). For example, reports published in 2008 indicated that California's Board of Parole Hearings only recommends parole for lifers from two to five percent of the time, and most of those recommendations are then rejected by the governor (Russell, 2009). In the case of former Governor Gray Davis, he only granted nine of the 371 parole recommendations he received for lifers; his successor, Arnold Schwarzenegger, granted parole to 192 of the first 830 parole recommendations he received for life-sentenced individuals (Russell, 2009). Since then, California has begun to grant parole to lifers more often, with 19% of eligible lifers being granted parole in the first 11 months of 2019 (Slater, 2020), but it remains the norm that life-sentenced individuals who apply for parole are denied release.

As Henry (2012) has explained, "Parole releases for life sentences are increasingly rare because parole decisions have become increasingly politicized. No politician ever lost an election because he or she denied a parole application. The inverse, of course, is not true" (p. 69). This was the case for Mark Singel, whom we described in the Introduction, and it was certainly the case for Michael Dukakis, whose 1988 presidential hopes were sunk by the crimes committed by Willie Horton after he escaped from a weekend-furlough program in Massachusetts while Dukakis was governor (and the ensuing television advertisements prepared by George H.W. Bush's campaign). Therefore, parole boards need to be redesigned so that they are less political. Ideally, these would be apolitical institutions staffed by career experts who enjoy civil service protections rather than by elected officials or political appointees. These experts should be drawn from a variety of disciplines with direct relevance for assessing a defendant's fitness for release, including criminology, psychology or psychiatry, sociology, social work, and other related disciplines. Furthermore, these parole decisions should give less weight to the crime that occurred potentially decades ago and give greater weight to any changes the defendant may have experienced while incarcerated. When making the decision as to whether or not parole should be granted, the scales should be weighted so that release is the presumptive outcome. Denial of parole should only occur upon a showing that continued detention serves a legitimate penological goal, such as the defendant continuing to present a threat to public safety. When someone is denied release, the reasons for denial and the evidence supporting those reasons should be enumerated in a written decision that is both made publicly available *and* provided to the applicant so that they are aware of what they must do to earn release in the future. All decisions to deny someone release should also be appealable in an effort to prevent arbitrary denials. It is our hope that such reforms to existing parole boards will provide those applying for parole, including those sentenced to life terms, a realistically attainable possibility of being released *and*, should they be denied release, detailed instructions on how to achieve release when they next become eligible.

It should be noted that this revised parole procedure does not guarantee that parole will be granted. We fully expect there to be a few individuals who are sentenced to life who will never be rehabilitated and thus will never get out. However, to quote the Council of Europe's Committee of Ministers (2003), "[N] o one can reasonably argue that all lifers will always remain dangerous to society" (p. 12). That is, not everyone will meet the criteria to be released, but most people will, and those individuals should have a chance to win their freedom. Therefore, these reforms are simply designed to provide a realistic probability of release for those who have been rehabilitated and no longer pose a threat to public safety since continuing to confine those persons would no longer serve any legitimate penological function.

Finally, we would like to point out that the recommendations we have made here are only designed to apply to so-called "ordinary" crimes committed by civilians. We take no position on the appropriate punishment for crimes of the state, war crimes, or other crimes against humanity, especially when it comes to the penalties to be applied to the leaders who mastermind and spearhead such atrocities. The gravity of such offenses requires a different type of analysis that is beyond the scope of this book. As such, our analyses should not be considered informative when it comes to determining the proper sentence for those who perpetrate such horrors, and from our perspective, the question of whether the leaders of such crimes as the Sudanese, Rwandan, or Yugoslavian genocides should be afforded an opportunity for release remains an open one.

References

American Civil Liberties Union. (2012). *The case against the death penalty*. Retrieved September 3, 2021, from American Civil Liberties Union: https://www.aclu.org/other/case-against-death-penalty?redirect=capital-punishment/case-against-death-penalty

American Civil Liberties Union. (2014, October 27). *Written submission of the American Civil Liberties Union on racial disparity in sentencing*. Retrieved from American Civil Liberties Union: www.aclu.org/sites/default/files/assets/141027_iachr_racial_disparities_aclu_submission_0.pdf

Banks, C. (2016). *Criminal justice ethics: Theory and practice* (4th ed.). Washington, DC: Sage.

Berry, III, W. W. (2010). More different than life, less different than death: The argument for according life without parole its own category of heightened review under the Eight Amendment after *Graham v. Florida*. *Ohio State Law Journal, 71*, 1109–1147.

Bushman, B. J. (2002). Does venting anger feed or extinguish the flame? Catharsis, rumination, distraction, anger, and aggressive responding. *Personality and Social Psychology Bulletin, 28*, 724–731.

Carlsmith, K. M., Wilson, T. D., & Gilbert, D. T. (2008). The paradoxical consequences of revenge. *Journal of Personality and Social Psychology, 95*, 1316–1324.

Carson, E. A. (2021, December). *Prisoners in 2020—statistical tables*. Retrieved December 21, 2021, from Bureau of Justice Statistics: https://bjs.ojp.gov/content/pub/pdf/p20st.pdf

Chen, E. Y. (2008). The liberation hypothesis and racial and ethnic disparities in the application of California's three strikes law. *Journal of Ethnicity in Criminal Justice, 6*, 83–102.

Cochran, J. K., & Chamlin, M. B. (2005). Can information change public opinion? Another test of the Marshall hypotheses. *Journal of Criminal Justice, 33*, 573–584.

Collins, P. A., Boruchowitz, R. C., Hickman, M. J., & Larrañaga, M. A. (2016). An analysis of the economic CCSTS of seeking the death penalty in Washington state. *Seattle Journal for Social Justice, 14*(3), 727–779.

Committee of Ministers. (2003, September 24). *Explanatory memorandum on Recommendation Rec (2003) 22 on conditional release (parole)*. Retrieved from https://www.legislationline.org/download/id/1468/file/8c6bd0e8e03dae9eb1870651698a.pdf

Cook, P. J. (2009). Potential savings from abolition of the death penalty in North Carolina. *American Law and Economics Review, 11*(2), 498–529.

Death Penalty Information Center. (2010, November 16). *DPIC 2010 public opinion poll*. Retrieved September 10, 2021, from Death Penalty Information Center: https://deathpenaltyinfo.org/stories/dpic-2010-public-opinion-poll

Death Penalty Information Center. (2021, December 16). *The death penalty in 2021: Year end report*. Retrieved December 20, 2021, from Death Penalty Information Center: https://reports.deathpenaltyinfo.org/year-end/YearEndReport2021.pdf

Dieter, R. C. (2014). The issue of costs in the death penalty debate. In J. R. Acker, R. M. Bohm, & C. S. Lanier (Eds.), *America's experiment with capital punishment: Reflections on the past, present, and future of the ultimate penal sanction* (3rd ed., pp. 595–609). Durham, NC: Carolina Academic.

Dreisinger, B. (2016). *Incarceration nations: A journey toward justice in prisons around the world*. New York: Other Press.

Eddings v. Oklahoma, 455 U.S. 104 (US Supreme Court 1982).

Egelko, B. (2014, April 30). *Death row inmates oppose Prop. 34*. Retrieved September 1, 2021, from SF Gate: https://www.sfgate.com/news/article/Death-Row-inmates-oppose-Prop-34-3891122.php

Enmund v. Florida, 458 U.S. 782 (US Supreme Court 1982).

Exline, J. J., Worthington, E. L., Hill, P., & McCullough, M. E. (2003). Forgiveness and justice: A research agenda for social and personality psychology. *Personality and Social Psychology Review, 7*, 337–348.

Gallup. (n.d.). *Death penalty*. Retrieved September 10, 2021, from Gallup: https://news.gallup.com/poll/1606/death-penalty.aspx

Garrett, B. L., Seale-Carlisle, T. M., Modjadidi, K., & Renberg, K. M. (2021). Life without parole sentencing in North Carolina. *North Carolina Law Review*, 279–332.

Goss, E., Strain, S., & Blalock, J. (2016, August 15). *The economic impact of the death penalty on the state of Nebraska: A taxpayer burden?* Retrieved December 22, 2020, from Death Penalty Information Center: https://files.deathpenaltyinfo.org/legacy/files/pdf/The-Economic-Impact-of-the-Death-Penalty-on-the-State-of-Nebraska.pdf

Gregg v. Georgia, 428 U.S. 153 (US Supreme Court 1976).

Grosso, C. M., O'Brien, B., Taylor, A., & Woodworth, G. (2014). Race discrimination and the death penalty: An empirical and legal overview. In J. R. Acker, & C. S. Lanier, *America's experiment with capital punishment: Reflections on the past, present, and future of the ultimate penal sanction* (3rd ed., pp. 525–576). Durham, NC: Carolina Academic Press.

Harvard Law Review. (2006). A matter of life and death: The effect of life-without-parole statutes on capital punishment. *Harvard Law Review, 119*, 1838–1854.

Henry, J. S. (2012). Death-in-prison sentences: Overutilized and underscrutinized. In C. J. Ogletree, & A. Sarat (Eds.), *Life without parole: America's new death penalty?* (pp. 66–95). New York: NYU Press.

Johnson, R., & McGunigall-Smith, S. (2008). Life without parole, America's other death penalty: Notes on life under sentence of death by incarceration. *The Prison Journal, 88*, 328–346.

Johnson, B. D., Spohn, C., & Kimchi, A. (2021). Life lessons: Examining sources of racial and ethnic disparity in federal life without parole sentences. *Criminology, 59*, 704–737.

Lockett v. Ohio, 438 U.S. 586 (US Supreme Court 1978).

McCleskey v. Kemp, 481 U.S. 279 (US Supreme Court 1987).

McCullough, M. E. (2001). Forgiving. In C. R. Snyder (Ed.), *Coping with stress: Effective people and processes* (pp. 93–113). New York: Oxford University Press.

McCullough, M. E., & Witvliet, C. v. (2002). The psychology of forgiveness. In C. R. Snyder, & S. J. Lopez (Eds.), *Handbook of positive psychology* (pp. 446–458). New York: Oxford University Press.

Miao, M. (2020). Replacing death with life? The rise of LWOP in the context of abolitionist campaigns in the United States. *Northwestern Journal of Law & Public Policy, 15*, 173–223.

Mills, J. R., Dorn, A. M., & Hritz, A. C. (2016). Juvenile life without parole in law and practice: Chronicling the rapid change underway. *American University Law Review, 65*, 535–605.

Nellis, A. (2017). *Still life: America's increasing use of life and long-term sentences*. Washington, DC: The Sentencing Project.

Nellis, A. (2021, February 17). *No end in sight: America's enduring reliance on life imprisonment*. Retrieved March 1, 2021, from Sentencing Project: https://www.sentencingproject.org/publications/no-end-in-sight-americas-enduring-reliance-on-life-imprisonment/

Ogletree, C. J., & Sarat, A. (Eds.). (2012). *Life without parole: America's new death penalty?* New York: NYU Press.

Orcutt, H. K., Pickett, S. M., & Pope, E. B. (2005). Experiential avoidance and forgiveness as mediators in the relation between traumatic interpersonal events and posttraumatic stress disorder symptoms. *Journal of Social and Clinical Psychology, 24*, 1003–1029.

Orth, U., Montada, L., & Maercker, A. (2006). Feelings of revenge, retaliation motive, and posttraumatic stress reactions in crime victims. *Journal of Interpersonal Violence, 21*, 229–243.

Reed, G. L., & Enright, R. D. (2006). The effects of forgiveness therapy on depression, anxiety, and posttraumatic stress for women after spousal emotional abuse. *Journal of Consulting and Clinical Psychology, 74*, 920–929.

Robinson, P. H. (2012). Life without parole under modern theories of punishment. In C. J. Ogletree, & A. Sarat (Eds.), *Life without parole: America's new death penalty?* (pp. 138–166). New York: NYU Press.
Roman, J., Chalfin, A., Sundquist, A., Knight, C., & Darmenov, A. (2008, March). *The cost of the death penalty in Maryland*. Retrieved December 23, 2020, from Urban Institute: https://www.urban.org/sites/default/files/publication/31526/411625-The-Cost-of-the-Death-Penalty-in-Maryland.PDF
Roper v. Simmons, 543 U.S. 551 (US Supreme Court 2005).
Rovner, J. (2021, May 24). *Juvenile life without parole: An overview*. Retrieved September 3, 2021, from Sentencing Project: https://www.sentencingproject.org/publications/juvenile-life-without-parole/
Russell, B. (2009). In re *Lawrence* and *Hayward v. Marshall*: Reexamining the due process protections of California lifers seeking parole. *Berkeley Journal of Criminal Law, 14*, 251–276.
Sheleff, L. S. (1987). *Ultimate penalties: Capital punishment, life imprisonment, and physical torture*. Columbus, OH: Ohio State University Press.
Slater, D. (2020, January 1). *Can you talk your way out of a life sentence?* Retrieved September 6, 2021, from New York Times Magazine: https://www.nytimes.com/2020/01/01/magazine/prison-parole-california.html
Snell, T. L. (2021, December). *Capital punishment, 2020 – statistical tables*. Retrieved December 21, 2021, from Bureau of Justice Statistics: https:// bjs.ojp.gov/content/pub/pdf/cp20st.pdf
Umbreit, M. S. (2001). *The handbook of victim offender mediation: An essential guide to practice and research*. San Francisco, CA: Jossey-Bass.
van Zyl Smit, D. (2010). Outlawing irreducible life sentences: Europe on the brink? *Federal Sentencing Reporter, 23*, 39–48.
van Zyl Smit, D., & Appleton, C. (2019). *Life imprisonment: A global human rights analysis*. Cambridge, MA: Harvard University Press.
Vinter and Others v. United Kingdom, 66069/09, 130/10, and 3896/10 (European Court of Human Rights, Grand Chamber July 9, 2013).
Wanger, E. G. (2002). Michigan & capital punishment. *Michigan Bar Journal, 81*(9), 38–41.
Warden, R. (2012). How and why Illinois abolished the death penalty. *Law and Inequality, 30*, 245–286.
Witvliet, C. V., Luna, L. R., Worthington, E. L., & Tsang, J.-A. (2020). Apology and restitution: The psychophysiology of forgiveness after accountable relational repair responses. *Frontiers in Psychology, 11*, 284.
Witvliet, C. V., Worthington, E. L., Root, L. M., Sato, A. F., Ludwig, T. E., & Exline, J. J. (2008). Retributive justice, restorative justice, and forgiveness: An experimental psychophysiology analysis. *Journal of Experimental Social Psychology, 44*, 10–25.
Wozniak, K. H. (2012). Legislative abolition of the death penalty: A qualitative analysis *Studies in Law, Politics, and Society, 57*, 31–70.
Wright, J. H. (1990). Life-without-parole: An alternative to death or not much of a life. *Vanderbilt Law Review, 43*, 529–568.
Wright, J. H. (1991). Life without parole: The view from death row. *Criminal Law Bulletin, 27*, 334–357.
Zehr, H. (2001). *Transcending: Reflections of crime victims*. Intercourse, PA: Good Books.

Index

For Product Safety Concerns and Information please contact our EU representative GPSR@taylorandfrancis.com
Taylor & Francis Verlag GmbH, Kaufingerstraße 24, 80331 München, Germany

www.ingramcontent.com/pod-product-compliance
Ingram Content Group UK Ltd.
Pitfield, Milton Keynes, MK11 3LW, UK
UKHW020147200926
475702UK00016B/2585
* 9 7 8 0 3 6 7 7 5 2 6 9 9 *